TWENTY-FIVE YEARS OF

Dissent

AN AMERICAN TRADITION

TWENTY-FIVE YEARS OF

Dissent

AN AMERICAN TRADITION

Compiled and with an introduction by

IRVING HOWE

Methuen

NEW YORK   LONDON   TORONTO   SYDNEY

Manufactured in the United States of America
First American Edition
Published in the United States of America by
Methuen, Inc.
733 Third Avenue   New York, N.Y. 10017
Designer: Ernst Reichl

Library of Congress Cataloging in Publication Data

Main entry under title:
25 years of Dissent.
  1. Socialism—Addresses, essays, lectures.
  2. United States—Social conditions—1945–
—Addresses, essays, lectures. 1. Howe, Irving.
  2. Dissent.
HX44.T88   1979   335'.008   79-17139
ISBN 0-416-00041-X
ISBN 0-416-00051-7   pbk.

TWENTY-FIVE YEARS OF

Dissent

AN AMERICAN TRADITION

CONTENTS

IRVING HOWE
Introduction

To be a socialist in Europe means to belong to a movement commonly accepted as part of democratic political life, a contender in the
battle of interest and idea. To be a socialist in America means to exist
precariously on the margin of our politics, as critic, gadfly, and
reformer, struggling constantly for a bit of space. Lonely and be-
leaguered as it may be, this position of the American socialist has,
nevertheless, an advantage: it forces one to the discomforts of self-
critical reflection. And that, sometimes fruitfully and sometimes
not, has been a central concern of DISSENT, the democratic socialist
quarterly which, as I write early in 1979, has reached its twenty-fifth
anniversary (notable for any "little magazine," all the more so for one
holding unpopular views). You will find in this book a representative
sample of the best work that has appeared in DISSENT this past
quarter of a century, though not, of course, a systematic exposition of
the democratic socialist point of view. But rather than discuss the
merits or failings of one or another article—the reader can do that
perfectly well, unaided—I would like in this introduction to say a
few words about the historical context in which our work has
occurred.

The story of the left in America is one of high initial hopes,
followed by considerable if not major achievements, and ending
with painful, even disastrous collapse. Why this recurrent rhythm,
enacted now three times in the last seventy-five years?

The first and strongest upsurge of the American left occurred as Debsian socialism, starting before the First World War. Of all the radical movements we've had, this was the most "American." It was the least ideologically "pure," the most inclined to speak in a vocabulary—evangelistic, folksy, shrewd, idealistic—that ordinary Americans might respond to. By 1912 this loosely strung Socialist Party had over 100,000 members; had elected some 1,200 public officials; and was sponsoring 300 periodicals, one of which, the erratic *Appeal to Reason*, had a circulation of three quarters of a million. While not yet a force capable of seriously challenging the major parties, the Socialist Party of that era was genuinely rooted in native experience, blessed in Eugene Victor Debs with a leader of high sincerity and eloquence, able to command a respectable minority of delegates at AFL conventions, and increasingly winning support among intellectuals. This was a real movement, not a petrified sect. Internally, it was extremely heterogeneous, as all American parties tend to be. There were municipal reformers and social democrats on its right; anti-political syndicalists and Marxist theoreticians on its left. There were Midwestern populists, called socialists mainly by courtesy. There were Christian Socialists, for whom socialism meant a latter-day version of Jesus' word. What prompted thousands of ordinary Americans to become socialists was an impulse to moral generosity, a readiness to stake their hopes on some goal other than personal success. It was an impulse that drew its strength from an uncomplicated belief in freedom and fraternity; or to use an almost obsolete word, goodness.

Today, of course, it is hard not to feel that this socialism contained too large a quota of innocence, too great a readiness to let spirit do the work of mind. For the vision of the future which most early American socialists held was remarkably unproblematic—in an odd way, it took over the optimism of the early Emersonian, indeed, the whole American individualist tradition, and transported it to new communal ends. Part of the success experienced by Debsian socialism was probably due to precisely this link to native modes of feeling; its collapse toward the end of the First World War may also, however, have been due to the fact that this native tradition did not prepare it for the toughness that an oppositional party has to cultivate, especially one that, like the Socialists, opposed American participation in the war. The party disintegrated under the blows of government attack and war hysteria; also, because its growing left wing was lured to the nascent Communist movement after the Russian Revolution.

More than a decade would go by before a new resurgence could begin in the early 1930s, smaller in scope than Debsian socialism but with somewhat greater intellectual sophistication. A successor to Debs appeared: Norman Thomas, selfless, energetic, intelligent, a superb speaker. Thousands of young people flocked into the movement, shaken by the Depression, convinced there was no choice for America but fundamental social transformation. The party had a footing in the trade unions, among such gifted figures as the Reuther brothers, Walter and Victor, and it won the allegiance of an influential circle of intellectuals. It was marked by a spirit of liveliness and openness. But again the pressures of historical circumstance undid this burgeoning movement—especially as they presented themselves in the form of difficult new problems American socialists were not yet prepared to solve. These problems have, in fact, been major concerns of all contemporary political thought: first, how to respond to the "welfare state" introduced through Roosevelt's New Deal and, second, what to make of the terrifying new phenomenon of Stalinist totalitarianism.

At the right pole of the Socialist Party in the thirties was clustered a group of old-timers, mostly veterans of the Jewish garment unions, who saw the New Deal as a partial embodiment of their hopes. What mattered for them was immediate social reform, not a shadowy dream of "complete" transformation. But for the party's younger and more militant people, who soon won over Norman Thomas, the New Deal, though some of its particular measures were desirable, represented a patchwork meant to salvage a sick and unjust system. Roosevelt's reforms, they pointed out, had not really ended unemployment or changed the basic situation of the worker in capitalist society. It was a dispute that seemed beyond compromise. The older trade unionists knew that the New Deal had brought crucial improvements: there was now the opportunity to strengthen unions and improve the conditions of millions of people. The left-wing socialists, hardening into a semi-Leninist ideology, were responding not just to American conditions—indeed, to American conditions least of all. They were trying to maintain an international perspective at a time when it seemed that social breakdown

xii   Introduction

cut across national lines. They felt they were living through the apocalypse of international capitalism—had not the Depression, the rise of fascism, the collapse of bourgeois democracy in Europe provided sufficient evidence? Capitalism, they said, could not be reformed nor peaceably changed; social revolution (ill-defined, vaguely invoked) was the way out. Whatever pertinence this outlook may have had in a Europe overcome by fascism, it had precious little in America even during the Depression years, a country in which the democratic tradition remained very strong.

In retrospect (the easiest source of wisdom) one feels there might have been a more flexible socialist stand, acknowledging that the New Deal was indeed a significant step toward desirable reform yet by no means removing the need for a basic socialist critique. But such a nuanced policy was impossible to either side: the problem was still too fresh and stark for compromise, and besides, the classical socialist division between incremental reformers and strict ideologues had already set in.

About the problem of Stalinism, the socialists of the thirties were clearer. A few did begin to flirt with "the Soviet experiment," but most were repelled by its ghastly terrorism, its destruction of working class, indeed, all human rights. Gradually the Socialists began to develop an analysis of Stalinism as a new order of social oppression —but to that we will return a bit later.

Vexed by these problems, the Socialists now destroyed themselves in a round of bitter factional disputes. Meanwhile, the Communist movement, with its mindless loyalty to every turn of Moscow policy and its own deeply authoritarian structure and rigid ideology, was gaining support among a growing number of young American radicals. The tragic outcome of this story is by now well known—a coarse violation of the human spirit, a terrible waste of energy and hope, which left a generation of American radicals broken and demoralized. After the Hitler-Stalin pact, and then the infamous governmental persecutions during the Cold War years, the Communist movement dwindled into an elderly sect; but the damage it had done to American radicalism is beyond calculation.

There was to be one more leftist upsurge in America, that of the New Left in the sixties, passionate, ill-defined, and in the end crashing, like its predecessors, to disaster. In its first phase, the New

Left seemed hopeful to us. This was a phase of populist fraternity, stressing a desire to make real the egalitarian claims of the American tradition, a non- and even anti-ideological approach to politics, and a strategy of going into local communities in order to help oppressed minorities. A major stimulant was the rising protest of American blacks in the early sixties as they began to struggle for their rights as citizens and human beings. The main New Left slogan of this moment, appealing if vague, was "participatory democracy," a hope that democracy could be extended from the forms of representation to the substance of experience.

Things went bad. Perhaps it was due to the desperation engendered among many young people by the Vietnam war, which they rightly saw as a political and moral outrage; perhaps to a romanticism of "revolution" arising from a naïve identification with "charismatic" leaders like Castro and Mao. But by the mid-sixties there had begun a shift from fraternal sentiment to ill-absorbed dogma, from the good-spirited shapelessness of "participatory democracy" to the bitter rigidity of "vanguard" sects, from the spirit of nonviolence to a quasi-Leninist fascination with violence. In this second phase the New Left grew in numbers, yet through the sterile authoritarianism of its now-dominant Maoist and Weathermen wings, made certain that it, too, would end up as no more than a reincarnation of the radical sects of the past.

We had the heart-sickening sense of reliving the disasters of the past (e.g., the way some leaders of Students for a Democratic Society contrived a theory of "liberal fascism"—that the liberalism of American society is "really" fascist—which bore a fatal resemblance to the idiotic Stalinist theory of the thirties called "social fascism"—that social democrats were "really" fascists). What had begun with a bang ended with a whimper: the pathological terrorism of the Weathermen, the brutal factionalism within SDS between the Maoists and other sects, the waste (once more, once more!) of all that splendid hope and energy. Unheeded, we could do little but warn and criticize.

The conclusions, the "lessons," to be drawn from these experiences are obviously far more substantial than can here be put forward. But with a ruthless sort of condensation, let me list—as I see them, some of my friends contributing to this book may not agree—a few points:

• The ideological baggage of Marxism, especially Marxism-Leninism, must largely be dropped if we are to have in America a socialist movement open, alive, and responsive to native feelings. "Vanguard" parties, ideological systems, sneering at "bourgeois democracy"—all this can lead only to the petrifaction of sects. Which is not, of course, to deny the possible uses of a flexible Marxism in political and historical analysis.

• The postures of righteousness that have often marked American radicalism, sometimes deriving more from Emersonian testimony than Marxist theory, can at times stand in the way of a realistic left politics. All three of the radical upsurges of the century suffered from such postures—as, for instance, the notion that working within the Democratic Party is a form of "betrayal." Political conditions in America make increasingly unlikely that we shall have here a mass socialist or labor party on the European model. But that does not mean that socialists cannot exert significant political influence.

• By this point in history, socialism can no longer be seen as a vision of perfection; it cannot be a surrogate for religious yearnings, though all too often, in the left-wing experiences of America, it has become that. We want to build a better world, but even a better world is not heaven on earth. Those with religious needs must try to satisfy them through religious experience.

• Socialism must be committed, without qualification, to democracy—yes, the flawed and inadequate democracy we have today—in order to be able to bring a heightened democratic content to every department of life: political, economic, social, cultural. There can be no socialism without democracy, nor any compromise with apologists for dictatorship or authoritarianism in any shape or form.

II

DISSENT, which started as a quarterly in winter 1954, arose out of the decomposition of the socialist movement of the thirties. Some of us rebelled against the sterility of the sects that still remained from

the thirties, even as we wanted to give new life to the values that had
been petrified in those sects. Others came from different places,
some being independent writers and intellectuals drawn to the idea
of socialism or the need for social criticism.

When intellectuals can do nothing else, they start a magazine.
But starting a magazine is also doing something: at the very least it is
thinking in common. And thinking in common can have unforeseen
results.

The kind of magazine we had in mind was perhaps without
precedent in the history of the American left. Though it would be
devoted to democratic socialism, there would be no "party line" on
political topics. Authors would not be published merely because
they were counted among the faithful. The idea of socialism was
itself to be treated as problematic rather than as a fixed piety. The
socialist movement having reached its nadir in American life, we felt
that our main task was to deal with socialism in the realm of ideas.
This, to be sure, can never be enough. Yet there are moments when
patience is all, and stubbornness too. And then I recall a few lines
from our friend Harold Rosenberg: "The weapon of criticism is
doubtless inadequate. Who on that account would choose to surrender it?"

Even this modest goal was not easy to achieve. The early fifties
were not merely afflicted with McCarthyism and repressions attendant upon the Cold War; they were also the years during which the
"American Celebration," involving a systematic reconciliation between American intellectuals and commercial society, reached its
climax. A good many intellectuals were deluded by the feverish
prosperity of a war-production economy into believing that all, or
almost all, of our socioeconomic problems had been solved and that
poverty had been effectively removed from American life. Susceptible to the genteel chauvinism of the Cold War years, they often
lapsed into a mood of political complacency—sometimes apathy
—in which the traditional symbols and phrases of liberalism did
service for new impulses of conservatism.

Whatever else, we of DISSENT did not succumb to this mood. We
kept insisting that American society, even in its flush of postwar
prosperity, remained open to the most severe and fundamental
criticism: some of which we tried to provide.

For certain of our writers and readers it was this aspect of our magazine, symbolized by its title, that counted most. The idea of socialism, though it might still elicit their approval, seemed to them distant, abstract, and academic; what interested them most was analysis, reportage, polemic about American society today, eventuating in a sustained radical criticism of its claims and pretensions.

For others among us, the idea of socialism as both problem and goal remained central. We suspected that for an indefinite time there would be no major socialist movement in America, but as intellectuals we tried to retain a long-range perspective, to live for more than the immediate moment. And we felt that for a radical criticism of American society to acquire depth and coherence it needed as an ideal norm some vision of the good—or at least of a better—society. This vision was what we meant by socialism.

But as soon as we tried to grapple with the problems of socialist thought; to discover what in the ideology of Marxism remained significant and what had gone dead; to comprehend the failures of socialism as a world movement and to analyze the bewildering complex of moral and political problems that had come with the rise of Communist totalitarianism, the new forms of economy in the West, and the bureaucratization of the labor and socialist movements—as soon as we approached these matters it became clear that any expectation of constructing a new socialist ideology was premature, perhaps a fantasy. We had to learn to work piecemeal, to treat socialist thought as inherently problematic, and to move pragmatically from question to question—with general theories or notions, to be sure, but without a total, world-encompassing ideology.

Socialists, we felt, could make a contribution to intellectual and political life, precisely by projecting an image of a fraternal society in which men planned and controlled their political and economic affairs through democratic participation and in which no small group of owners, managers, or party bosses could dominate the lives of millions. But to do this, socialists had first to question their own assumptions. Necessarily, this led us to place a heavy stress upon the moral component of socialism. We opposed the status quo not merely because it had led, and might again lead, to depressions and human misery, but also because it rested upon a fundamentally unjust arrangement of social relations. It was a society that not only created material hardships for millions of people but gave rise to an ethic of inhumane competitiveness and to a psychic insecurity which in America had reached frightening proportions. And it was for similar reasons that we remained intransigent opponents of Communism.

A second major stress in the DISSENT re-examination of socialism has been upon the indispensability of democracy. Modern society, no matter what form it takes, shows an underlying tendency toward an idolatry of the state, a worship of the bureaucratic machine. All modern societies share in this drive toward transforming man into a passive object manipulable in behalf of abstract slogans, production plans, and other mystifying apparitions. The Western democracies are still far less guilty in this respect than the Communist nations; but the drift toward industrial bureaucratism seems universal. For us, therefore, the idea of socialism could retain value only if a new stress were placed on democratic participation and control. Statified or nationalized economy was not an end in itself; it could be put to desirable or despicable uses. These are the main emphases dominating the essays on socialism that open this anthology.

We had—and have—still other intentions. One of them is to propose intellectual relations with the more independent sections of American liberalism, in order to extend welfare legislation and human rights, further the black and women's movements, and defend civil liberties. It is this perspective which largely motivates Part II of this book and has also been dominant in the pages of DISSENT. For we have been concerned not only with political theory but also with the immediate realities of American society. We have tried, in our modest way, to contribute to the reconstruction of a democratic left in the United States.

III

Two problems of social analysis concerned us with a special intensity during these years, and I think we have made some contribution toward clarifying them—though, of course, other problems pile up, with their predicaments and puzzles. Let me say a few words about these two:

The Problem of Stalinism. A crucial, perhaps *the* crucial, experience of our century has been the appearance of totalitarian systems
yoking terror and ideology and claiming to shape the entirety of
existence: the relentless assault by the party-state upon a defenseless population in the name of a total utopia.

Stalinism seemed a cruel parody, perhaps a self-parody, of the
socialist dream, and it forced thoughtful socialists to reconsider the
terms of their conviction. In Russia a Marxist party had seized
power; it had destroyed private property in the means of production;
it had elicited overwhelming sacrifice and idealism; yet the result
was a brutal and oppressive society, ruled by terror, erasing free
expression, allowing the working class none of the rights it possessed
even under capitalism, and in its essential quality alien to the
socialist vision.

Within this society there sprang up a new social stratum: the
party-state bureaucracy which found its roots in the bureaucratic
intelligentsia, the factory managers, the military officials, and above
all the Communist functionaries. This new social stratum looked
upon the workers as material to be shaped, upon intellectuals as
propagandists to be employed, upon the international Communist
movement as an auxiliary to be exploited, and upon Marxist thought
as a crude process for rationalizing its power and ambitions.

What was the nature of the new society that had arisen in Russia
during the twenties and thirties?

A growing number of socialists concluded that the loss of political
power by the Russian working class meant that it no longer ruled in
any social sense, for, as a propertyless class, it could exercise power
only through direct political means and not in those indirect ways
that the bourgeoisie had sometimes employed in its youthful phase.
Stalinism showed no signs of either producing from within itself a
bourgeois restoration or of gliding into democracy. The bureaucracy
had become a new ruling class, with interests of its own fundamentally opposed to both capitalism and socialism.

This view of communist society—which Djilas popularized
through the phrase, The New Class—held that what is decisive is
not the forms of property ownership (i.e., nationalized economy) but
the realities of property relations (i.e., who controls the state that
owns the property). Can the workers, in whose name power is held,

organize themselves into trade unions to strike against "their" state? Can they form parties to openly challenge the domination of "their" party? As Djilas has remarked: "An unfree people can have no scope in the economic organism."

From such theoretic analyses and speculations enormous consequences followed for socialist thought:

● There is no necessary or inevitable sequence from capitalism to socialism, as many Marxists had believed, nor is there any inherently "progressive" movement within history. New, unforeseen, and retrogressive societies can intervene in the sequence of change.

● The mere abolition of capitalism is not, in and of itself, necessarily a step toward either freedom in general or socialism in particular; it can lead—indeed, in some instances it has led—to societies more repressive than capitalism at its worst.

● Neither working-class rule nor socialism can be defined merely as a society in which private property has been abolished or the means of production nationalized; what is decisive is the nature of the political regime exercised over postcapitalist or nationalized property.

● In the long run the Communist movement may come to seem, not the vanguard of "proletarian revolution," but a movement that could achieve success only in underdeveloped countries, where there was neither a self-confident bourgeoisie nor an advanced working class. The "historic function" of this movement came to be the provision of ideological rationales for a draconian socioeconomic modernization of backward societies.

● The idea of a total transformation of humanity under the guidance of the "vanguard party" is a corrupt fantasy which soon leads to an alternation of terror and apathy.

● Socialism must then be redefined as a society in which the means of production, to an extent that need not be determined rigidly in advance, are collectively owned and in which they are democratically controlled; a society requiring as its absolute prerequisite the preservation and extension of democracy. Without socialism, democracy tends to be limited in social scope, to apply its benefits unequally, and to suffer from coexis-

tence with unjust arrangements of social power; but without democracy, socialism is impossible.

The Problem of the Welfare State. The welfare state preserves the
essential character of capitalist economy, in that the interplay of
private or corporate owners in the free market remains dominant;
but it modifies the workings of that economy, in that the powers of
free disposal by property owners are regulated and controlled by
political organs. (See, for an excellent development of this point,
Henry Pachter, p. 25.) Within limits that need not be rigidly fixed
in advance, the welfare state can be regarded as an algebraic con-
tainer that can be filled with the arithmetic of varying sociopolitical
contents. More important, the welfare state is the outcome, not
necessarily a "final" one, of prolonged social struggle to modulate
and humanize capitalist society. It would be hard to say to what
extent the welfare state is the result of a deliberate intent to stabilize
capitalist society from above, so that it will avoid breakdown and
revolutionary crises; to what extent it is the outcome of relatively
autonomous economic processes; and to what extent it is the partially realized triumph in the struggle of masses of people to satisfy
their needs. At the moment—by contrast to those who feel the
major need for the immediate future to be a kind of benevolent
social engineering and those who see the welfare state as a manipulative device for maintaining traditional forms of economic
coercion—it seems necessary to stress that the welfare state represents a conquest that has been *wrested* by the labor, socialist, and
liberal movements.

For those of us who wish to preserve a stance of criticism without
the sterility of total estrangement, the welfare state has been a
somewhat unsettling experience. Here are some of the characteristic responses of leftist intellectuals in the last few decades:

1. *A feeling that the high drama (actually, the vicarious excitement) of earlier Marxist or "revolutionary" politics has been lost and
that in the relatively trivial struggles for a division of social wealth
and power within a stable order there is neither much room nor need
for political-intellectual activity.* Much of this response strikes us as,
by now, unearned and tiresome. The snobbism of "revolutionary"
nostalgia can easily decline into a snobbism of political abstention.

2. *A belief that the welfare state will, in effect, remain stable and basically unchanged into the indefinite future; that conflict will be contained within the prescribed limits and that problems of technique will supersede the free-wheeling or "irresponsible" tradition of fundamental criticism.* This view accepts the "givenness" not merely of the welfare state but also of its present forms and boundaries. It thereby underestimates the need for and significance of basic moral-political criticism. If I am right in saying this, the traditional responses of the radical intellectual—dismissed though they may be in some quarters as utopian, impractical, etc.—remain quite as necessary as before. Even for making new practical proposals to alleviate social troubles within the present society, a degree of utopian perspective and intellectual distance is required. For essential to such alleviation is a continued redefinition of what, indeed, is practical.

3. *A belief that the welfare state is characteristic of all forms of advanced industrial society; that it offers bread and television, palliatives and opiates, to disarm potential opposition; and that it thereby perpetuates, more subtly but insidiously than in the past, class domination.* Despite its seeming intransigence, this view strikes me as essentially conservative, for it leads to passivity, not action—and inhumane,—for it minimizes the improvements in the life conditions of millions of human beings. Minimizes, above all, the fact that the welfare state has meant that large numbers of working-class people are no longer ill fed, ill clothed, and insecure, certainly not to the extent they were thirty years ago. That automobile workers in Detroit can today earn a modest if still insufficient income; that through union intervention they have some, if not enough, control over their work conditions; that they can expect pensions upon getting old which may be inadequate but are far better than anything they could have expected thirty years ago—all this is *good*: politically, socially, and in the simplest human terms. To dismiss or minimize this enormous achievement on the lordly grounds that such workers remain "alienated" is to allow ideology to destroy human solidarity.

In contrast to these three attitudes, we would propose the following general stance toward the welfare state: The struggles and issues raised within the welfare state are "real," not mere diversionary

shadow plays or trivial squabbles. They matter; they affect the lives
of millions. No matter how mundane the level at which they are
conducted, the struggles for social betterment within the arena of
the welfare state merit our concern and active involvement. That is
why we write and act in relation to poverty, civil rights, education,
urban renewal, Medicare, a host of immediate problems. At the
same time, radical intellectuals seek to connect these problems with
the idea of a qualitative transformation of society. Socialism not
being an immediate option, it is necessary for radicals, while continuing to speak for their views in full, also to try to energize those
forces that are prepared to stretch the limits of the welfare state and
improve the immediate quality of our life. Such a dynamic once set
in motion, there may be possibilities for going still further.

IV

Let your mind go back in time. At a meeting of workers in Berlin
in the 1870s, a social democrat named August Bebel speaks. He
advances a new vision of human possibility. He tells his audience
that men who work with their hands need not be subordinate and
mute, need not assume that the destinies of nations are always to be
decided by superiors in power. He tells his listeners that they, too,
count. They count in their numbers, they count in their capacities to
come together, they count in their crucial role in the productive
process, they count in their readiness to sacrifice. The mute will
speak; the objects of history will become subjects prepared to transform it. This was the socialist message as it began to be heard a little
more than a century ago. It was heard in England in the night
schools, in the labor colleges, sometimes on the edges of the dissident chapels. It was heard in France through the more revolutionary
traditions of that country, in the Paris Commune where organs of
plebeian autonomy were being improvised. And even here in
America, it was heard among immigrants packed into slums or
sweating over railroad beds. It was heard among freewheeling
sailors and lumbermen who preferred a syndicalist version of revolt.
It was heard among Jewish immigrants on the East Side. It was
heard among intellectuals and Christian pastors in New York who
found that the promptings of thought and sympathy drove them to
the socialist vision.

After more than a century, many hopes have been burned out into ashes, whole generations have perished in despair, movements have been drowned in blood, and many people in those movements have lapsed into silence. The socialist idea is no longer young, no longer innocent, and now must compete in a world of sophistication. It cannot hope to grow through mere simple reiteration of simple slogans. Yet anyone looking at the world today must be struck by the power which this idea still holds: the devotion that millions of people, mostly in Europe but elsewhere too, still give to it.

We know the mistakes and the failures of this past century. The notion that as soon as *we* take power, all would be well: this, serious people can no longer believe. Who is that *we*—which self-appointed "vanguard"? The notion that democracy, even in its most corrupted forms, is anything but a precious human conquest, that it's just a façade for the rule of the oppressors: this serious people can surely no longer believe. The notion that social change will come about through the automatic workings of the economy, without human will or intention, just like the opposite notion that history can be forced or raped through the will of a tiny band of chosen intellectuals: this, too, serious people can no longer believe. Intellectuals today, despots tomorrow.

We know that the socialist movement declined at many points into a mere appendage of laborite institutions, and that these institutions could not bring about the changes that we want in society. We know that in some countries the socialist movement degenerated through the Communist heresy into totalitarianism, bringing a kind of "salvation"—the "salvation" of terror and fear. Yet these failures notwithstanding, there remains a living core of socialist belief, commitment, value.

At one point that living core is very close to liberalism: a belief in the widest possible political freedoms, a belief that democracy remains the foundation of all that we want. Without that democracy, nothing is possible, life becomes unbearable. But socialism introduces something new, historically and analytically. It introduces the idea that the plebes, the masses, the ordinary people can rise to articulation, rise to rulership, to power.

We have faith in the capacities of ordinary people, not to become experts in finance, not to understand the mysteries of inflation—though they can hardly do worse than the experts—but to come to sensible, humane conclusions about the major direction of social decisions. If you deny this, you deny not only socialism, you deny the moral basis of democracy as well.

Socialism also introduces a stress on communal life, on the sharing of values, the sharing of responsibility, the sharing of power. We believe the democracy that prevails, more or less, in our political process should also prevail in our economic life, in the ownership and the running of our corporations. The major economic direction of modern society, at least in the advanced nations, is toward an increasing state domination of the economy; the vision of laissez faire has no reality, except in certain magazines. We believe the fundamental issue is this: what will be the relationship between the democratic political process and the increasingly complex economy of modern society? And the control that we want to exert upon the modern economy is not through a vast state bureaucracy, not through some fantasy of total nationalization, but rather through democratic and autonomous agencies which will represent the people who work in a given industry as well as the population at large, so that there can be a balance between particular interests of those in a given industry and the larger interests of the entire society. This commitment to the democratization of economic life is at the heart of the socialist idea today. Democracy here, democracy there, democracy everywhere. The idea is simple, the techniques necessarily complex and difficult.

With this, there goes an emphasis on egalitarianism. That word is not very fashionable these days in American intellectual life, but we will survive that too. Egalitarianism doesn't mean that everyone has to make exactly the same each week. It does mean that the vast disproportions of opportunity and power, which bring with them vast disproportions of the capacity for human fulfillment, should be shaved down a lot.

In the last few years, we've been living through some disappointments with America's quasi-welfare state. People see that partial reforms bring only partial relief, that partial reforms inadequately financed can bring unexpected trouble, that partial reforms occurring in the context of the market and distorted by the priorities of corporate interests and mismanaged by government bureaucracy can lead to anti-social consequences. But the conclusion to be drawn from this is not some churlish desire—impossible in the modern economy, in any case—to return to a laissez-faire or private economy. If, for instance, Medicare as we have it now leads to ripoffs by doctors, the answer isn't to abolish it or to turn down national health insurance; the answer is to deepen the social content and democratic control of health insurance, making certain that such ripoffs don't persist.

A lot of the traditional socialist criticisms of capitalist society— the simplest, most fundamental criticisms—still apply. We read that citrus growers in Florida are delighted by bad weather because it cuts down their crops and will keep up their prices. As long as these people have to function in this economy, I cannot blame them. It makes economic sense. But in terms of any larger social value, it's pure insanity. We should be unhappy at cutbacks in citrus production. There are lots of kids in the United States who could use those oranges. We could all use them at cheaper prices, or we could even—there go those "socialist do-gooders"—ship them at low prices to other places. But that would mean a socially planned economy, a society that, as we used to say and could well say again, is organized for use and not profit.

Just at the time when there are so many troubles, so many social ills, when clearly the system is not working well, we can detect a new wave of neo-conservatism or really reactionary thought. Conservative sages demonstrate that the poor remain poor because they are improvident: you need a Ph.D. for that. Others teach us that there are limits to social policy, more urgently felt as it happens with regard to providing employment for black youth than rescue or bounty for Lockheed and Penn Central. Still other curators of wisdom invoke the fallen nature of mankind—as if once Eve bit into that disastrous apple, it was forever decreed that humanity might rise as high as the peaks of laissez-faire capitalism but not an inch beyond. The assault on the welfare state during the late 1970s is an assault on the deprived, the poor, the blacks. But we believe that this retreat from liberalism, this retreat from the welfare state and social generosity, is not going to take care of the problems that we find all about us. A bit sooner or a bit later, we shall again, as a society, have to confront the inequities of our economic arrangements, the maldistribution of our income and wealth, the undemocratic nature of our corporate structures.

When that happens, the overall perspective suggested in this book ought to have a growing relevance. It is a two-sided view of political and social action within a democratic society. On one side, a constant battle for all those "little" things—better health care, new housing programs, more equitable taxation, the rights of women and blacks—that occupy the attention of liberals. On the other side, a fundamental critique of the society in the name of democratic socialist values. To say both kinds of things, to say them at the same time, to keep a humane balance between the near and the far: that is the view we have tried to advance in the twenty-five years of DISSENT and in the articles to which you now turn.

PART ONE
Visions
of The
Future

MICHAEL HARRINGTON
What Socialists Would Do in America—If They Could
(1978)

Let's pose a far-reaching question, without pretending to answer it fully. What would happen in America if we were able to make socialism come to pass? How would we move beyond the welfare state? What measures would be taken on the far side of liberal reform, yet well short of utopia?

These questions are not academic. In Europe today there are democratic socialist mass parties that are putting them on the political agenda. In America there is, of course, no major socialist movement, yet. But this society is more and more running up against the inherent limits of the welfare state. We can no longer live with the happy assumptions of '60s liberalism—that an endless non-inflationary growth would not only allow us to finance social justice but to profit from it as well. So, for instance, a Democratic president is told by key economic advisers that workers will have to bear the consequences of breathing cotton dust because industry "cannot afford" the cost of protecting their lungs.

In the United States, at present, the dominant reaction to such structural problems is to sound retreat. This may well strike cruelly at the poor, the minorities, women, and all other vulnerable people. But ultimately the forced march to the rear will not work. For there are limits to the ability of the nation to impose the social costs of late-capitalist production upon those least able to defend themselves.

3

So I baldly assert that old-fashioned reaction is not, in the long run, a feasible way of dealing with our problems. There will either be a new-fashioned reaction—sophisticated, modern, planned—or there will be a socialist alternative. It is with this thought in mind that I undertake an attempt to define a socialist policy for the (still unforeseeable) middle distance. First, I will try to outline some of the general problems raised by such an imaginative definition of the future. Then, there will be a brief sketch of that possible socialist future. And finally, I will try to relate these speculations to the immediate present, since I am convinced that projecting what should be must help us, here and now, in devising what can be.

I. SOME GENERAL PROBLEMS

Capitalism is dying. It will not, however, disappear on a given day, or in a given month or even year. Its demise will take place as a historic process that could lead to democratic socialism—or to a new kind of collectivist and authoritarian society. And one of the key problems of locating socialism in this process is that it must emerge in a society that is not capitalist or socialist but something in-between, with elements of both.

Let me now hastily sketch in a few details to support the sweeping statements I have just made.

The way capitalism ends defines the terrain on which socialism becomes possible.* Present-day capitalism is more and more collec-tivist, that is, it increasingly makes its economic decisions politically. This happens because the inherent tendencies of the system subvert the always imperfect "free markets" of an earlier age and because, in any case, those markets could not organize a system of such interde-pendent complexity. Thus far, this process of collectivization within capitalism has been dominated by corporate priorities, even when the collectivizers have been liberals, trade unionists, or socialists.

This last trend is not the result of a conspiracy on the right or of betrayals on the left. It is a consequence of the fact that, as Claus Offe put it, the capitalist state is not itself a capitalist. The economic and political health of the government thus becomes dependent on investment decisions made in private boardrooms. Those decisions

*In what follows, I have summarized the arguments detailed and documented in *The Twilight of Capitalism*. Readers who seek proof for my various assertions will, I hope, find it there.

are critical determinants of the Gross National Product, the level of employment, and indeed of the government's own revenues. The rulers of the welfare state therefore must adapt themselves to corporate priorities—"win business confidence."

Those corporate priorities center on the maximizing of profits. This, obviously, is no longer done in an entrepreneurial or "robber baron" way. The nonowning manager has a much more sophisticated calculus and, corporate collectivist that he is, takes political and even social factors into account. Yet, even in this new guise capitalism remains dangerously and fundamentally antisocial. Capacity is expanded in good times as if there were no tomorrow— or more precisely as if the ability of the society to consume were not limited by the very income structure that capitalist production enforces. In consequence, there are periodic crises. At the same time, the growing social costs of the system are imposed upon those least able to pay—a fact cruelly visible in the devastated cities of the Northeast and industrial Middle West. Markets are rigged with increasing expertise, which is one source of inflation in the midst of recession. Inequality persists because, under capitalism, private wealth, personal and corporate, is the main source of new investment funds.

The welfare state reinforces these trends. Since the health of the entire economy is seen to depend on the will of those who control investment, "trickle down" becomes *the* ideology of late capitalism. Thus the political representatives of the rich are now demanding— in the name of the common good—that further tax privileges should be conferred on the wealthy, while government-spending for everyone else is curtailed.

This corporate collectivism is not, however, a stable system—as anyone who has lived in the '70s can testify. The private, and antisocial, priorities that inform public action are becoming more and more destructive. The anticapitalist measures used to shore up capitalism create a crisis of legitimacy. And eventually, the contradictions of "private socialization" will require basic structural changes. Those could move in the direction of a new class society, a bureaucratic sort of collectivism, or toward a new communitarianism, a democratic socialism.

This summary analysis points to a key assumption of all that follows and helps to define a central problem for socialists seeking to transcend the welfare state. *Socialism will have to define itself in the course of a contradictory transitional period in which elements of both traditional capitalism and corporate collectivism will coexist with, and threaten, socialist innovations.*

It is foolish to imagine a day, a month, or a year when society suddenly "leaps" from capitalism to socialism; the very complexity of modern society precludes that. Where, in some brief period of time, will one suddenly find a socialist cadre capable of taking over from the capitalist managers? How can new psychologies, and new ethics, be created quickly? Moreover, one must have a due respect for socialist ignorance. We know the evils of the old order in great detail, but we do not have all the plans for the new order in our hip pocket. Even if we did, that would be of small help, since a socialist society must be built democratically and cannot be proclaimed from on high.

After all, socialists do not simply propose a new economy. We realize that there must be a transformation of culture, of individual and collective values, if the new structures are to matter. As Antonio Gramsci rightly insisted, socialism is the work of an epoch and it has to do with an entire society, not just with property forms or tax laws.

But that fact creates enormous problems. How, for instance, does one avoid the cooptation of partial measures of socialization in an economy in which corporate collectivism retains considerable power? In a recent book, Serge Christophe Kolm analyzed what this meant in the Chile of *Unidad Popular*. One of the first measures of the Allende government was to increase enormously the wages of the poor while holding down prices. This meant, however, a reduction in the profits of the private sector—profits that had been the traditional source of new investment funds. At first, the problem was not too serious since the wage policy set off a consumer boom. But eventually, there occurred a slowdown and the corporations had to borrow, thereby setting into motion the inflationary spiral. The Nixon Administration, the CIA, the copper companies, the world financial community (including the World Bank), all did what they could to make matters worse.

Still, the relevant point here is that Chile demonstrates the inherent difficulties in introducing socialist measures in an economy still manifesting strong capitalist tendencies. So, alas, does the Tennessee Valley Authority. From its inception under the New Deal until the early '50s, the TVA managed to control floods and generate power in a way that enormously stimulated the region's economy. But from the early '50s on, this public property behaved more and more in a classic private way. It moved from hydropower to coal and in the process was a major initiator of the destructive strip-mining of Appalachia. Indeed, it is possible to make a sad generalization: *most existing nationalized enterprises in the world behave about as badly as private enterprises.* When one adds that those nationalized companies constitute, more often than not, the collectivization of private losses and inefficiencies one gets a sense of the enormous difficulties of a transition toward socialism within the contradictory world of late capitalism. In that setting, the danger of cooptation does not arise, primarily because of the personal corruption of leaders or bureaucrats; it is a structural tendency of the society.

So in imagining socialism as it would emerge just the other side of the welfare state, the imagination must be realistic. How does one begin to create a new society in a world in which there will be capitalist striving for gain, socialist egalitarianism, and "communist" free goods in the libertarian sense of the word as used by Marx in his *Critique of the Gotha Program.* Under such difficult conditions, how is it possible to transfer the control of basic investment decisions from private boardrooms to the democratic process?

In facing up to these issues within the framework of a brief essay, much that is enormously important will be placed in parentheses. I will deal with a single developed society and ignore the international implications of socialism that are, in other contexts, decisive. I will posit the existence of a political movement capable of taking the lead in implementing the proposals I make, and I will focus on economic and social structures and present my illustrations as evocative symbols of a possible future, and not at all as a fully worked-out program.

II. SPECULATIONS AND POSSIBILITIES

First, socialism proposes a national planning process in which all the people would have an *effective* right to participate.

Through a political process, the society would consider its basic options. Put in American terms, the Administration would outline the needs of the next period and the resources available to meet them. Since the latter would not be infinite, there would have to be proposed "trade-offs." A crash program for the improvement of health might limit the growth of education; the decision to take the benefits of increased productivity in the form of more leisure time would mean that the same productivity could not be spent on more consumer goods. This last point is particularly important because one would hope that, as socialist consciousness would rise, so would the tendency toward the decommercialization of life—toward communal, noncommodity forms of consumption, like neighborhood centers or public theaters.

Under such conditions there obviously would be debates over priorities. These would be resolved by a democratic process in which parties would compete with one another over conflicting programs. That, however, would not mean a mere extension of present-day "pluralist" theory, which ignores the way formal democratic rights, precious as they are, can be subverted by economic and social inequalities. In the period of transition, there would not simply be a corporate sector striving to impose its values upon the polity; the government itself would obviously be (and already is) a center of power. For democracy to work in such a context, it would have to be much more profound and real than it is today. Let us imagine two quite unutopian aspects of such a deepening of democracy.

First, if the Administration or even the Administration and the major opposition have an effective monopoly on the machinery and personnel of the planning process, then the formal right to challenge the plan becomes almost empty of content. In French "indicative planning," for instance, the workers are legally guaranteed representation at every level of the system. But they, unlike business and government, do not have the expert staff, the computers, the "knowledge technology" so important in a modern society. Therefore, they normally don't bother to participate in the exercise.

If, then, planning is to be a critical instrument of the assertion of popular control over the investment process, there must be effective provision for democratic participation. Any significant group of people—much larger than a *Kaffeeklatsch*, much smaller than a majority—should be given the means to challenge the official plan(s). This could be done in at least two ways. Such a group could be given the funds to hire its own experts and computers; or it could be given the right to have the official bureaucracy work out the details of its counterplan(s). Within such a framework, when the Administration and the Congress would go to the various regions and ask for popular inputs, there would not be the *pro forma* hearings that so often prevail today. The critics would be technically as well prepared as the establishment.

Second, the political process itself should be democratized. Here, some of the West European countries now are far ahead of the United States. All television time available to candidates for federal office should be allocated according to a democratic formula. And each significant group should either get subsidies for its own press, or else—as is sometimes the case in this country with intraunion oppositions in campaign periods—have legally guaranteed access to the print media.

Let us assume, then, that truly democratic procedures could be established within the planning process, given a little imagination and a mass socialist political movement. What of the content of the plan(s)? How would it (or they) be rationally debated and worked out? How would it (or they) be implemented democratically without an enormous proliferation of bureaucracy?

It would be of utmost importance that everyone in the planning debates know the real costs of all the proposals. It was thus not an accident that, on the few occasions when he explicitly referred to the socialist future, Marx spoke of the need for careful bookkeeping. Like Max Weber, he regarded bookkeeping as one of the great accomplishments of the capitalist era, and then added that it would be even more necessary under socialism precisely because production would be planned. And it is, of course, one of the central themes in a contemporary indictment of late capitalism that this system falsifies prices by imposing its social costs on helpless people and/or the government.

This point raises a technical question that should at least be noted before moving on to a basic issue. In the absence of capitalist-factor markets, can society rationally compute efficient prices? In a famous attack on socialism Ludwig von Mises argued that it would not be possible to do so. He was effectively answered by Oskar Lange, A. P. Lerner, and Joseph Schumpeter (the latter summarizes the debate in *Capitalism, Socialism, and Democracy*). To be sure, I do not accept many of the overly centralist assumptions of their imagined solutions, yet their central point about rational prices under socialism is persuasive. Schumpeter, brilliant Austrian conservative, held that socialist prices would be set by marginal costs; the late Anthony Crosland, a British Fabian, noted that *only* under socialism would such capitalist theories work; and some of the economists grouped around François Mitterand, like Philipe Brachet, have gone into detail as to how this might be done in present-day France. So I will assume that serious debate can take place on the basis of accurate information about "trade-offs."

But does this mean, then, that socialism will operate according to the criterion of profit? And if so, what of the claim that it entails production for use *instead of* profit?

Profit, I would argue on the basis of historical evidence, is the specific form that the surplus from production takes in, and only in, capitalism. Such a surplus exists in all but the most primitive of subsistence societies; it will certainly have to exist under socialism. Under capitalism, the surplus is appropriated by the owners and managers of the means of production, and it is both a title to wealth and to the right to make basic investment decisions about the future of the economy. In precapitalist systems, the surplus was appropriated by political and ideological, not economic, means, i.e., on the basis of "God's will" as backed by the human sword.

Under socialism, there will be a social dividend to provide for those who do not (usually because they cannot) work for depreciation and for expansion (on the last count, it should be remembered that I am speaking of the socialist transition when there will be many urgent needs for new investment, both at home and abroad). But that social dividend will not be a "profit." It will be appropriated by the society and allocated after democratic decision-making; it will not go to individuals in the form of wealth or elite power, as is now the case. Second, although a socialist society will have to create a surplus and will want to measure the return on investments as precisely as possible, the resulting "interest rate" will be an accounting device and not a flow of income to private owners. Third, socialist accounting will compute social cost and social benefit in a way that capitalism, for systemic reasons, does not and cannot do. For instance, mainstream economists today defend the ruin of the Northeastern and Middle Western cities as an inevitable—tolerable if unfortunate—consequence of making a more "efficient" use of resources. But efficiency, it must be understood, is not a mathematical absolute obeyed by technocrats; it is always defined in relation to the interests of different groups and individuals. Under capitalism this is done behind a veil of mystifying rationalization and in the interests of a minority. Under socialism, the term will be democratically defined in public debate in relation to the needs of the majority.

Let us assume, then, that the democratic planning process has determined the basic priorities of the society. How will they be implemented?

There are two existing models, neither of them applicable to democratic socialism. In the Soviet Union and other Communist countries, there is centralized command planning with the bureaucracy setting thousands of prices and production targets. The system is politically totalitarian and economically inefficient—two facts that are closely related to one another. I therefore reject this model because it does not satisfy basic socialist goals. The other model, that of indicative planning, is also not the way to democratic socialism, but it is worth examining more closely for a moment since it highlights one of the critical differences between liberalism (in the American sense of that term) and socialism.

Here is how Stephen S. Cohen described French indicative planning in a 1977 paper for the Joint Economic Committee. There is, he says, an economic "concert" achieved without the participation of the unions, consumers, or small businessmen.

The economic concert is based on a simple political ideology and defines a simple political role for planning. The state needs a high performance economy. This has come to mean a fundamental commitment by the state to the expansion and modernization of the big business sector. Big business needs the active cooperation of the state. It needs the state to maintain a high level of effective demand and to socialize many of its costs. It also needs the aid of the state in managing its own affairs. The overarching organization provided by the state helps industry to regulate competitive forces. In brief, big business finds that it needs a cooperative economy and it needs the state to organize that cooperation. Most modern capitalist nations are doing some

variant of the state–big business partnership model, but
nowhere with such clarity and enthusiasm as in France.

The French planners assume that private corporate priorities are
the pivot upon which all decisions turn and that it is, therefore, the
role of the plan to facilitate, and sometimes humanize, the work of
big business in the name of the common good. This, it will be noted,
is the tacit assumption of much of American liberalism. However, it
should be emphasized that in technocratic, *dirigiste* France, what is
implicit in America has achieved the status of an ideology. I insist
upon this point for a political reason: the American liberals (including labor liberals) who unconsciously accept the corporate premise
are often also hostile to corporations and in the future could become
socialist. This is not true of a principled French technocrat or, rather,
the conversion required in the second case is much more profound.
One of the hopeful aspects of American liberalism is its contradictory
character.

In any case, we have come to a fundamental divide, one that
marks off socialism from all variants of capitalist reform. The latter
believed that liberal goals can be limited to a late-capitalist economic
and social structure, while socialists define that structure as the core
of the problem. What, then, is the socialist alternative? How will
socialists actually implement the lovely choices made in the democratic planning process?

Not by command of the Soviet, or any other, model. However, in
rejecting indicative planning within a late-capitalist society that is
economically and politically dominated by corporate power, one is
not ruling out indicative planning in an utterly different milieu. For
in imagining a socialist transition from capitalism toward the good
society, I hypothesize two different motivations for working to fulfill
the democratic plan and see them as operating within three different
kinds of enterprises.

The first motive is individual gain. The goal of socialism, clearly,
is to transcend greed as far as is possible, and to act upon the basis of
"to each according to his/her need, from each according to his/her
ability." This lies in the distance, although approximations of it
should begin on the first day of socialist transition. But as socialism
emerges from capitalism, there would be differentials in wages
within an enterprise and even differentials between enterprises

within the same industry. At the same time, there would be a progressive, egalitarian tax program to reduce radically the outrageous spread between executive and worker pay in capitalism today. Managers receiving hundreds of thousands a year—and setting their compensation for themselves—are not being paid wages, but if I may speak in an old yet useful language, they are appropriating surplus value in the guise of wages.

The wage structure, then, would be infinitely more progressive than it is within capitalism and would follow the biblical injunction by exalting the lowly and making plain the high ones. Yet, there would be differentials related to skill and output and these would be tolerated, precisely as an incentive for individuals and enterprises to produce more efficiently. Moreover, the differentials between enterprises, even though carefully limited, would be the basis of a certain competition between them. It would obviously be preferable if moral incentives alone would guarantee efficient cooperation with the planned priorities. But in this transitional stage, there is simply no realistic reason to suppose that this would be the case.

The second major motivation would be moral. It would not suffice, in and of itself; but it is absolutely essential as the growing edge of socialist possibility. The point, however, is not self-evident. In the United States moral incentives have played a role during wartime, but only then. Moreover, the American labor movement has been particularly hostile to "work enrichment" schemes, regarding them as artfully designed programs to get more work out of fewer people. More often than not, this judgment has been accurate. Why, then, assume that American workers as they are will be moved to change their attitudes in a socialist transition?

Surely, it must be obvious—not simply the fact, but a fact plain for one and all to see—that the savings of productivity will primarily go to the workers who make them or to the society as a whole. If they go to the workers, then old-fashioned capitalist psychology would explain why this incentive would work. But what does it mean to say that the gains would go to the "society"? Why would that motivate the average worker? The answer to this question is best given in the form of a generalization about the socialist wage in a transition period.

Wage, then, will be composed of three different elements (I borrow some insights from Serge Christophe Kolm). It would be capitalist in the sense that there would be differentials based on performance; it would be socialist in that an egalitarian tax policy would severely limit the differentials and work toward a redistribution of income and wealth; it would be "communist" (in the libertarian sense) in that an increasing part of people's incomes would take the form of "free" goods, i.e., collectively paid goods and services, such as health, education, transportation. So a part of the wage would be received collectively, as a social dividend from heightened productivity.

Farfetched? Not at all. Right now, the socialist parties of Sweden and Holland are moving in the direction of such collective payment, proposing that corporations pay a portion of their tax in stock placed in a worker-controlled mutual fund. And one of the reasons for this development is, precisely, to give workers a communal stake in productivity. This is not, it should be noted, a traditional stock-sharing device where the individual workers get shares in lieu of certain wage increases. In Sweden, this is the conservative alternative. It is a proposal for the *social* sharing of productivity gains.

One last point on wage structure. The capitalist component would be settled by collective bargaining negotiations. That issue, and the more general question of working conditions, would provide one of the bases for the continuing existence of a trade-union movement. The socialist and "communist" components would be determined by a political process in which unions, parties, and other voluntary institutions would be involved. Here again, I am positing the necessity of conflict among organizations that would interpret the common good in terms of the particular good of different strata of the citizenry.

So individuals would be motivated to cooperate in the work of the plan on the basis of capitalist, socialist, and "communist" incentives. What about enterprises? Given the previous analysis, I assume that there will be three main types of economic organization: socially owned; privately owned large enterprises; and cooperatives. There will also be a stratum of privately owned small businesses, but these will function primarily in the area of consumer markets and are not likely to play a decisive role in fulfilling the society's democratic priorities for production.

In all three of the major sectors there will be elected worker representation at every level. This is not merely desirable as a way of dealing with alienation. It is a practical necessity if the sense of communal solidarity—the socialist motive—is to grow. And that, in turn, increases productivity. It is also essential to the antibureaucratic aspect of the socialist program, institutionalizing as many local, face-to-face controls on authority as is possible.

So far, this may sound like the socialist version of apple pie. It is much more problematic—and important—than that. Contemporary capitalist technology, Harry Braverman persuasively argues in *Labor and Monopoly Capital*, did not evolve in a value-free, technical way. It had, and has, social and even ideological functions. Specifically, it is not an accident that this technology worked at every point to expropriate the skills of the workers, to dispossess them of all decision-making, and to try to turn out automatons. Therefore, as a technology incarnating capitalist values is extremely difficult to run on a socialist basis, one of the goals of the transition will be to build different kinds of factories—and offices.

I make the last point about offices for an important purpose. Most socialist language and imagining is focused in terms of plants. But what about the "postindustrial society"? Without going into all the complexities of that question, it should be noted that a major part of the "tertiary sector" is made up of service workers in large, anonymous, factorylike settings, e.g., typing pools, supermarkets, the middling and lower levels of the information industry. Moreover, the skilled and educated reaches of this sector— engineering, universities—often in themselves require collegiality. So I am not projecting workers' control as an exclusively blue-collar proposal.

But then neither can workers' control operate as an absolute. In the socialist transition, as many functions as possible will be located on the most immediate level, where the majority of the people work. But individual enterprises or industries cannot be given the right to veto the democratic plans of the entire nation. It is possible, as the Yugoslav experience shows (and the authoritarian character of that country's political structure is not relevant to this point), for worker-controlled enterprises to develop a collective egotism. The Yugoslavs, for instance, have found it difficult to convince the more affluent collectives to invest their surplus in high-risk underdeveloped areas. So workers' control is not a panacea, and it will require democratic political checks on the part of the society as a whole. It even demands the redesign of technology and economic organization, in the postindustrial as well as in the industrial sectors.

Workers' control will function in all the enterprises of the society—but those enterprises will have different structures.
● First, there is the social property sector. I say social, not nationalized, property for a reason. Any fool or charlatan or dictator can nationalize a plant. In and of itself, nationalization is neither good nor bad. Or rather, to the degree that nationalization suggests centralized state ownership, it is bad. It is not necessary to argue the almost self-evident point that such ownership is politically hostile to democracy and economically inefficient. "Social property" stresses both the direct participation of the actual producers *and* democratic control by society rather than administrative control by bureaucrats.

It is painfully obvious that it is simpler to stitch together such harmonious formulas than to realize them in practice. As John Kenneth Galbraith emphasized in *The New Industrial State*, elected bodies either lack the competence to oversee the managers of public property or, if they acquire that competence, they create a second bureaucracy to regulate the first. Galbraith was thinking of existing nationalizations, which do not involve workers' control, but still his point is a substantial one. As I mentioned earlier, in the very first stages of the transition it will be difficult to impose participatory socialist values upon an antiparticipatory capitalist technology. Therefore, I do not see socialization as an act, a law, or a charter, but as a *process* in which democratic forces will have to struggle during an entire historic period to give real content to their legal rights.

In this same spirit, social property will obviously not be operated as departments of the state run by civil servants. They should be constituted on the model of the TVA, as authorities with relative independence but ultimate responsibility to the elected representatives of the people. Another check upon their power will be economic. There will be a multiplicity of such authorities within each industry. The size of American enterprises, as Robert Lekachman has pointed out, is not determined by the technical requirements of "economies of scale" but is the result of the drive of major corporations to control markets, politics, and consumer taste. Within a framework of democratic planning there would not be an antitrust utopia of Adam Smithian competition among tiny economic units in a perfect market, but there could be a rational policy on corporate size and a consequent decentralization of economic power.

With certain carefully defined exceptions, social enterprises would be required to pay their own way and return a surplus for depreciation, new investment, and the social dividend. Obviously, there would be cases when, in full consciousness of the cost, society would want to continue subsidizing production for "noneconomic" reasons (in the callous, capitalist sense). That, it should be noted, is the case in most nationalized industries today, and although it might also be true under socialism, it would hardly be the dominant model. The point would be to locate social property in surplus-yielding activities. For example, the present private energy industry is completely unwilling to develop alternative sources of energy without huge government subsidies. If it gets that money from Washington it will surely develop a socially inappropriate technology. This, therefore, would be a prime area for society to invest in socially oriented research and development, which it would implement through socially owned enterprises.

Social property would also be a key element in a full-employment policy that would emphasize the growth of all regions rather than a competitive struggle between regions as in the current "beggar thy neighbor" situation in the United States. Instead of providing private corporations with multimillion- (and billion-) dollar bribes to go into the South Bronx or Appalachia—which are always collected and often dishonored—locating new and vital social industries in such areas would do that job much more directly and efficiently.

● The second tier of economic activity would be a profoundly modified private sector.

You cannot, I have stressed, *socialize* an economy overnight. It is possible to nationalize the "commanding heights" at a stroke, but that would have the negative consequences I have already described. So we must anticipate a corporate sector in the socialist transition. But if that is a necessary fact of life it is also a problematic one. A major private company, Oskar Lange argued in one of his classic discussions, is not likely to behave responsibly if it operates within a socialist political environment and feels that it is working, so to speak, on death row. Part of that problem might be met because of developments that postdate Lange's fears: the emergence of a Galbraithian "technostructure" that, except at the very summit, will hire out to anybody as long as the pay is relatively good. But precisely that summit is the controlling factor in today's economic world.

This is why workers' control and public participation in the corporate structure are so important. The private title to corporate wealth and a limited profit have to be recognized; but many of the existing functions of corporate power can be socialized. For example, the worker and public representatives on the board of directors should routinely reveal all company secrets to the public. Secret debate and decision-making with regard to plant location, pricing, new products, hiring and firing policy, etc., are today considered to be "managerial prerogatives." In the private sector during a socialist transition such matters would be made as transparent as possible and would be subjected to social controls within the planning process.

Still, a transitional socialism would have to tolerate private profits from this sector. One of the reasons why people would invest in such undertaking would be in order to make money. (I speak here of investment in new physical assets—real investment—not of the shuffling and dealing of stock certificates in the great gambling house on Wall Street, a parasitic, near functionless waste of resources that could simply be abolished.) The deleterious social consequences of the continuing existence of profit would, however, be moderated by a highly progressive tax policy and, above all, an inheritance law that would effectively end the possibility of transferring large concentrations of wealth from generation unto generation. By now, the Ford family has been more than compensated for cantankerous old Henry's genius.

• Finally, there would be a major cooperative sector, an idea much stressed in nineteenth-century socialism.

In the United States, cooperatives account for less than 1 percent of GNP; in Finland, their share is 10 percent; in Israel, 30 percent. There is, then, enormous room in this country for expansion of the cooperative principle. During the socialist transition we might make great use of one of the Rooseveltian reforms: the Rural Electrification Administration. Under that system, the government has supplied cheap (subsidized) credit to cooperators and thereby accomplished a decentralized, locally controlled electrification of the countryside. (The private sector opposed the program in part on the grounds that farmers did not need electricity!) That strategy could be a major level of socialist policy in the future. It would allow for a proliferation of locally controlled, face-to-face undertakings, including community corporations. In this sector, the capitalist motivation would be most attenuated, the socialist most emphasized as the "associated producers" would actually run most of their own working lives.

The goods and services of these three tiers of production would be distributed in two ways. There would be free goods and services collectively paid for by various levels of government. How would one control waste and overuse in this area? A New York *Daily News* dispatch on the thirteenth anniversary of National Health in Great Britain suggests that the problem itself might be somewhat exaggerated. Not only is British medicine superior in some important indices to its American counterpart, it is also less costly as a percentage of GNP and has a lower rate of patient utilization. Even so, there obviously should be some checks on the provision of free goods and services. An idea that is already partly at work in the United States might be generalized well beyond its present use. Health maintenance organizations now provide lump-sum payments for the care of an entire group. If the providers can maintain set standards but reduce costs, they are able to get some of the savings from their own productivity. This principle might be tried out in other areas, e.g., in transportation.

Second, a transitional socialist society would make full use of the virtues of the market mechanism in the areas where consumers would choose, and pay for, their goods and services. To be sure, there is no point in investing markets with the mystical powers claimed for them by their capitalist advocates—advocates who love to ignore the essential. Thus, after Charles Schultze devotes a lyrical hymn to the power of the "unanimous consent arrangement" within markets, he adds, "if the income distribution is grossly unfair, the concept of voluntary decision and unanimous consent is a charade. . . ." Since this is the prelude to a book that praises markets in the extreme, Schultze never so much as bothers to ask whether the data show that his argument is a charade.

Socialists, however, can do more than probe the question that Schultze side-steps; they can create a new answer to it. That is, if an egalitarian tax policy has enormously reduced the discrepancies in income *and* if public control of the private corporation has severely limited, or even abolished, monopoly pricing—*and* if the engineering of consumer taste is replaced by straightforward information—*then* markets could really function as they are supposed to. They would operate within the broad limit of the democratic plan, and alongside the free sector, in order to communicate the desires of the people and to maximize their choice. The existence of such a market would not determine the basic priorities of the economy, but it would provide more real consumer freedom than capitalist society has ever offered.

Fine, someone might reply. Sitting in a study, socialist writers can conjure up all kinds of glowing dreams. But who will pay for all of these utopian proposals?

The largest single source of corporate investment funds in the United States today is found in retained profits. Within the limits already discussed—relative autonomy of the enterprise, but under the ultimate control of a democratic society—that could well be true under socialism. For, as Marx foresaw before anyone else, capitalism has more and more "socialized" itself within its private framework. Horatio Alger and the individual stockholder long ago ceased to be that important to the investment process. Moreover, as the Meidner Plan of the Swedish trade unionists and similar proposals by the Dutch socialists indicate, a democratic sharing in an essentially social surplus could provide the basis for higher rates of capital formation than are now possible under capitalism.

Second, a useful if somewhat capricious book by a corporate apologist, Peter Drucker's *Unseen Revolution*, helps to focus on a socialist solution to the question of who pays. Private-sector pension funds, Drucker said in 1976, own 25 percent of the equity capital today, and the pension funds of the self-employed, public employees, and teachers account for another 10 percent of the total. By 1985, Drucker calculates, the pensioners will "own" between 50 percent and 60 percent of equity capital, and 40 percent of debt capital. I put "own" in quotation marks for a reason. Most of those funds are employer-controlled and are invested, as required by law, in an utterly capitalist fashion. The workers cannot sell their pension interest during their working life, borrow on it, etc. It is only available upon retirement and since some of those claims are not fully funded, there are even questions about payoffs.

However, the point here is not the inadequacies of the existing pension system; it is to take Drucker's rhetorical fantasy—that "pension-fund socialism" now exists in the United States—and try to turn it into fact. Roughly two-thirds of domestic welfare expenditures today are for people over sixty-five, and there are in addition the private pension claims Drucker cites. Socialists, I suspect, would want to create a single and uniform system, since current practices give government support enormous inequities. But the point here is that societies committed to the decent care of the aging—as all the welfare states, to one degree or another, are—will indeed have to set aside or provide for huge sums of money.

In Sweden some of those funds are already used for investment in housing. Here the AFL-CIO has a program to attract union funds, where possible, into similar undertakings. Why not generalize again? An intelligent and socially motivated investment of pension funds would provide an enormous pool of capital for all three sectors of the economy in a socialist transition.

Third, some individuals might want to save more of their income than others. Within the constraints of a socialist commitment to wealth and income redistribution, that could be accomplished by the revival of an old American institution: the Post Office savings system. And there is still another source of savings: the people would pay for the nonfree goods in the society and the cost would include, as it now does, funds for depreciation and new investment—but not, as now, under the control and to the benefit of wealthy individuals and their hired managers.

Finally, there is another important source of savings in the elimination of some of the outrageous waste inherent in American capitalism. Business today spends about $38 billion (in 1977) on advertising. A little of that money provides the public with useful information about products people truly want and need; a major portion of it is employed in a corporate disinformation program to

gull the supposedly sovereign consumer. Strict standards for private
advertising and public support for a variety of (competing) consumer
services could free much of those outlays, and a fully employed
economy could find useful work for the people now living off them.

I mentioned earlier the parasitic character of a great deal of the
activity on Wall Street and in the financial industry as a whole. A
portion of the American legal profession thrives on the pervasive
venality of the society. A radically progressive income and inheritance tax law, to take but one example, could free the graduates of
many of the elite schools from essentially wasteful and antisocial
lives. There are other activities—antiunion consultants, managerial
psychologists, etc.—which are a cost of capitalist production but not
of production itself. Here again, socialism, even in the confused
period of transition, could offer a more efficient system (always on
the premise of a social, not a corporate, definition of efficiency).

It would thus be possible in a socialist transition to plan democratically, to effectuate that plan realistically, and to finance the
entire process. In making this point, I have not tried to be complete
and detailed in my analysis, only to evoke the direction—and the
problems—of socialist solutions. Moreover, I have been "econo-
mistic" on purpose and not indulged in the poetry of socialism. This
is not to suggest that the culture and personal dimensions of socialism are unimportant. On the contrary, the economic programs
are only means to the noneconomic end of human liberation. But the
cynics impugn those ends by saying that we socialists cannot realistically present a program of means. And that is what I have tried to
do here, in briefest outline.

III. A VISION OF THAT SOCIALIST FUTURE

I am writing this essay during the summer of discontent of 1978.
Proposition 13 has just passed in California and polls in that state
show that the voters want welfare to be cut, first and foremost. There
are many other signs of a growing social meanness. The hope and
good feelings of the first half of the '60s seem to lie a century or so
behind us. Is, then, this description of measures that go far beyond
the welfare state a simple exercise in social fantasy? I think not.

First, there is the reason I have already given. The problems of

American society today are structural and they require deep-going changes. Those, I noted, could be undertaken by sophisticated and modern reactionaries—or by democratic socialists incorporating the best of liberalism in a movement that goes beyond the welfare state. If it is thus necessary to project the middle-distant future in an open-ended way, with both rightist and leftist possibilities, it is certain that incantation, conservatism-as-usual, or political temper tantrums against our complexities will not work. The ideas I have described here are, I believe, more realistic than most of the popular panaceas of the late '70s.

Second, all utopian anticipations of the future are also descriptions of, and prescriptions for, the present. This effort at imagining socialism is rooted in—and, more important, relevant to—the America of the late '70s. In the briefest and sketchiest fashion, let me simply list some urgent and possible contemporary approximations of the more distant hopes whose realization and beginnings I have just imagined.

Here and now the democratic left should:

● Challenge corporate control of the investment process by insisting that public policy concern itself with what is produced, and how it is decided, instead of confining itself to Keynesian "aggregates" and leaving all the details to the private sector. This would include public controls over private investment decisions, such as specifying the conditions under which corporations can leave a locality or oligopolies can raise prices, as well as such public undertakings as a democratically owned and controlled gas and oil company;

● Demand national economic planning for full employment, with the implementation of the Humphrey-Hawkins bill as a first, but only a first, step;

● Suggest public cost-conscious and accurate definitions of economic alternatives in which corporations are charged for their use and destruction of social resources;

● Propose sweeping tax reform aimed at a redistribution of

income and wealth and, in particular, at the unearned income of
rentiers and the untaxed wealth of successive generations of the rich;

• Suggest a rethinking of the entire American pension system,
public and private, with emphasis on using such funds, theoretically
"owned" by the people, for social purposes as determined democratically by the people;

• Urge employee and public representation on the boards of
directors of all major corporations and a radical increase in democratic decision-making by primary workers in factories and offices;

• Propose federal support for a vast expansion of producer and
consumer cooperatives, including funds for community corporations.

Some of these proposals are more difficult to imagine in the near
future than others, yet none of them requires a commitment to
socialism and most have been approved in principle by major institutions of the mass of the democratic left. But why burden such
empirically justifiable ideas by relating them to an ideology called
"socialism"? There are two reasons why I do that. First, time is
running out on the very American creed of utopian pragmatism, i.e.,
the religious conviction that all problems can be solved in the middle
of the road by a process of bumbling along. The ills that afflict our
society—which, to repeat the most obvious and appalling of current
examples, are laying waste entire cities as effectively as a rocket
attack—are systemic. They are the product of a late capitalism that
collectivizes on the basis of antisocial, corporate priorities. Either
the democratic left will find a systemic response to that challenge,
which is fairly called socialism, or the undemocratic right will.

Second, America—Western capitalism, the world—desperately
needs, not simply a legislative shopping list, but a vision. Not a
religion, not a secular salvation; but a new sense of purpose. And so,
in the details sketched out hopefully here there is not only a rational
response to immediate issues but also the intimation of some tentative steps in the direction of a new civilization.

HENRY M. PACHTER
Three Economic Models: Capitalism, The Welfare State, and Socialism
(1964)

In the capitalist economy business decisions are made by the owners of resources; the latter may take the form of money, real estate, machinery and equipment, or of claims and rights to use these resources or to dispose of them, or of power positions in organizations. Since labor also is a resource and a commodity, the ability to buy and to sell it comes under this definition of property.

In the welfare state, these powers of free disposal have been curbed. They are regulated and controlled by political organs, and, in large areas of economic activity, government has substituted its purposes for those of independent agents. These purposes are determined politically: i.e., they may range from establishing a strong defense posture to a concern for the well-being of the majority.

In both systems, income is related to the use an owner makes of his property. Under capitalism, the property itself constitutes a claim on income, to be realized in the market; the welfare state, however, supplements the market by other institutions to create or distribute income. Moreover, the welfare state creates a demand for goods and services which results not from consumer preferences and producer expectations, but from its own political purpose.

Socialism I shall call an economic system which has divorced income from property, and even from the exertion of labor. In contrast to state capitalism, which still recognizes the property of the state as a claim to income, socialism also divorces capital from production decisions.

25

Obviously, I am dealing here with "pure types," disregarding intermediate systems such as monopoly capitalism, syndicalism, corporativism, market socialism, which have in common this basic feature: that the means of production are not owned by individuals but by collective bodies which, however, deal with the property claims as though they were individuals. An especially interesting case is the Cartel General or state capitalism, already mentioned, where this feature has been carried to the extreme: all facilities are owned by one big corporation but the production relations are still governed by the market mechanism.

My purpose is to show what other assumptions must be made to realize each of these models as a working economic system; how each affects the allocation of resources and the general efficiency of production, and, above all, the welfare of its citizens.

However, I deliberately refrain from speculating on possible differences of cultural attitudes or changes of human nature in the three systems. I only assume that humans have a natural aversion to involuntary toil and a natural ambition to excel in self-assigned tasks, but that the degree of their acquisitiveness and cooperativeness is related to the environmental conditions which encourage or stifle their development.

I

Capitalist theory claims that all resources find their most useful employment if each owner tries to maximize his profit in a free market, where labor also finds its price.[1] Fortunately such a pure capitalism has never existed, or else no one would have organized a police, provided courts of justice, built bridges, laid sewers, embellished the public parks, founded hospitals or established universities. It has always seemed to me that the fire brigade refutes the pure theory of free enterprise. What more essential service could one imagine? It ought to command a price and attract the venture capital of an enterprising speculator who wishes to make a profit and therefore allocates resources for this purpose. Yet, nothing of the kind has ever happened; instead of waiting for the free play of the market to prove the usefulness and determine the price of a fire brigade, a committee of the ruling classes on the municipal level went ahead and organized one.

Likewise, the business community felt that private coining privileges led to public losses, and it gave central banks the power to regulate the flow of money, the rate of interest, the value of the currency, and thereby also the direction of foreign trade, the income distribution between various countries and, to some extent at least, the business cycle. Even at its classical freest capitalism is not an entirely "free" economy. To function properly, it polices itself. In public debate, however, the question of controls usually is confused with the question of who should do the controlling. Business prefers the so-called indirect (orthodox or classical) controls: regulation of the rate of interest, reserve requirements, the marketing of Treasury bills—not because they are indirect or because they are not controls but because the controllers of these controls are businessmen.

On the other hand, business expects the state to protect it against foreign competition and, far from leaving the optimum allocation of mineral resources to the competitive spirit of rapacious speculators, it asks the government to enforce conservation practices, to protect patents, and finance research. Even the most ardent theorists of economic liberalism—Professors Mises, Hayek, Roepke—point out that it can function only if a "strong state" enforces the laws of the free market and provides the services which free enterprise does not find profitable. In short, it simply is not true that the free market all by itself results in the optimum allocation of resources.

But quite apart from such empirical observations which under-cut the ideal model of pure capitalism (and we have not spoken yet of the tendency toward concentration and monopoly, of the creation of artificial markets through advertising, of manipulation through government orders or policy, etc.), at least two theoretical grounds militate against the contention of the market theorists. Both are inherent in the model and both have been freely admitted by the better representatives of liberal economics. One is the inequality of incomes and the other is the time limit within which a speculator must expect the return of his capital. It is generally conceded that both are incompatible with the optimum use of resources. I shall explain this problem in greater detail because its analysis does not apply to capitalism alone but also to the two other models, the welfare state and socialism.

Apologists of capitalism often say that a free market permits the consumers to "vote" for the goods which they desire, and that the price mechanism tells producers which goods might give greatest satisfaction to the greatest number. Hence, free enterprise equals democracy, Q.E.D. This analogy limps. The consumers must first buy their "ballots": unless they are equipped with purchasing power, their desires will not become manifest to the producers; or, differently expressed: this "democracy" is based on unequal suffrage. Are those who have no vote incapable of satisfactions? If all votes were equal, the sum total of satisfactions would be substantially greater and the allocation of resources would be much closer to the optimum. Even from the angle of the development of resources, therefore, pure capitalism does not produce the best distribution of efforts. Quite apart from the haphazard method by which the market discovers what is in demand, it does not determine the common good but—at best—the maximum profit for all enterprises.

Paradoxically, this also is the aim of certain types of socialist economy, i.e., the syndicalism practiced in Yugoslavia and preached by Poland's Oscar Lange and his German disciples.[2] In the way these systems function, they hardly differ from capitalism, except that the dividend is shared between the workers and the government, instead of being paid out to the shareholders to be taxed later. The Yugoslavs who first practiced it claim for market socialism two virtues: it establishes that "consumer democracy" which capitalism cannot realize, and the producers' associations tend to acquire the power of true soviets, the best form of political democracy. Someday both claims might be validated, provided the Communist party dictatorship disappears; but today Tito's works councils are far from being soviets, and the consumers can express their preferences only months or years after the central planning board has expressed its views through investment priorities.

In the capitalistic economy, this decision is guided by the profit expectations of investors. But Mises correctly states that profit can be obtained only by meeting "a comparatively urgent demand." If there is no such demand equipped with purchasing power, it may be created artificially, through advertising or by inducing the government to finance it; that way, resources are misappropriated to suit a pressure group. Or—a need may exist, but demand may not become effective and supply may not come forth because the projects are too big or too speculative: only big corporations, monopolists or governments have the means or the foresight to allocate resources for long-term research and development on a large scale. It takes guts, or the assurance that no competitor has the same plan, to construct a bridge, a railway, a power dam at a time when demand is not yet "urgent" and money might be saved by anticipating it long in advance of urgency. If not government initiative, then at least government guarantee of capital and interest is required to bring forth investments in the infrastructure—roads, canals, draining of marshes, harbors and rivers—which rarely yield profits in the foreseeable future. A paper mill may establish a hundred-year cycle of timber exploitation; but this exception proves the rule, for the mill expects to make a profit on the real estate in any event. Even this kind of incidental profit did not prevent the railroads from going broke, and the United States would not have its marvelous rail network, had not some speculators miscalculated! One too often forgets that our industrial empire rose over the bodies of expropriated capitalists and failed investors.

Because of this time factor, classical capitalism does not achieve optimum use of resources. Normally, wherever profit expectations have to be deferred beyond the planners' lifetime, the investment will be undertaken only for a reason of public policy, be it conservation, development, autarchy or strategy. The history of foreign aid shows that private capital will not take the risk of developing the infrastructure in the time interval which is consistent with the rapid population increase and the rising expectations of the laggard countries. If rapid development is desired, colonialists, monopolies or state capitalism seem to be the only alternatives.

II

After a glorious career of continued primitive accumulation, during which capitalism did start, spread, and develop modern industrial production all over the world, it now has reached limitations which can be overcome only by more effective methods of organization—the big trust, the monopoly, the government enterprise, state capitalism. The enterprise has become too big, the time span for the return of profits too long and, on the other hand, the need for political investments too pressing for the free market to remain competitive. If it ever did, it no longer responds to consumer needs in distributing the resources and does not make the most effective use of all factors at the right time. It still is serviceable on the smaller scale of consumer industries or even pioneering in some areas of invention; but big research and big industry now are in the era of imperfect competition, and the claims which continue to be made on behalf of "pure" capitalism are based on a theory which no longer fits the facts. Even Mises admits that under monopoly rule "private profit and social productivity are at variance," hence "however great an evil socialism might be, it would be less harmful than private monopoly."[3]

To make my point clear: what has been said so far does not amount to the old socialist charge that monopolies suppress technological progress. The few instances where a significant invention was temporarily withheld from exploitation are far outnumbered by the inventions which originated in a monopolistic enterprise and could be exploited only by monopolistic practices. On the other hand, a socialist or state capitalist system might find it just as necessary to delay exploitation of a new invention which makes a recent huge investment obsolete. Imagine a new gimmick which would force all of us to buy a new television set: private industry would ruthlessly force the expense down our throat, while government-operated stations might mercifully continue to use the old system. The government also refuses to build all the bomber types the military-industrial complex is trying to sell it.

The point, rather, is that at a certain level of development the equations of exchange become more rigid, the number of independent variables increases, and the number of indeterminate variables decreases. Moreover, the population explosion and government-sponsored research cannot be captured in any system of equilibristic calculations; finally, neither the external nor the internal reserves adjust themselves to the requirements of the equilibrium. Capitalism no longer can incorporate precapitalistic spaces, and the labor force does not obligingly contract as automation makes it obsolete. On the other hand, even the unemployable now refuse to abandon a standard of living which in the most advanced countries has become synonymous with existence. As Marx pointed out, the human factor does not fit into the equations. Hence we must turn the problem around. State capitalism and socialism provide different answers to the question of how to fit the equations for the human situations. We therefore have to say a brief word on the importance of the equations, or what Abba Lerner calls "The Rule."[4]

We said that technological progress now is speeding ahead much faster than old equipment can be written off, while production units are increasing in size and, in the more developed countries, demand is becoming inelastic. Is greater efficiency the answer? In introducing new production methods, capitalism needs to consider only their cost to the enterprise. It will not consider the social cost of firing people—neither the "disutility" of their enforced leisure, nor the money it costs to maintain them in social insecurity, the social losses in crime, disease and illiteracy, etc. The welfare state makes a conscious effort to assume these social costs, or it may even waste more money to fight those undesirable by-products of capitalistic cost-accounting; but it will not effectively force the enterprise to take them into account (it cannot even control smoke and water pollution, preserve scenic views and wildlife, etc). A state capitalistic system has the means to deal with the problem of social cost; it may maintain a railway stop which no longer pays, in order to save the gasoline which the commuters might have to use otherwise. Yet more often, it will leave human beings to fend for themselves. Wherever it is operating today, it tends to suppress the problem rather than to solve it. Only a socialist system, operating under conditions of abundance, can make its investment decisions in full view of all economic, social, and human factors that might be affected. It even may make uneconomic investments which might not save labor and minimize cost, but would spare exertion and misery. But we are anticipating: any economic system that wishes to balance cost and revenue must earn its investments before it introduces new inventions, or the new production methods must produce savings in excess of the capital they make obsolete. That, anyway, is the iron rule for all systems which aim to produce economically, i.e., which fulfill the exchange equations. A free market economy does so by trial and error, through wasteful competition, and at the cost of misallocated resources. It achieves a dynamic equilibrium at the cost of periodic depressions and, even at its best, through violent fluctuations which can be contained only through monopolistic practices, i.e., by destroying the free market.

III

State capitalism—which Rudolf Hilferding called the Cartel General—fulfills the equations by systematizing the monopolistic practices. It avoids the waste of the free market, and it does not permit investments to be misplaced in the stage of development or to become obsolete in the stage of saturation. It can direct investments into ventures which create new demand—Keynes's "pyramids," Tugan-Baranovsky's tower of equipment, a huge defense establishment, or a "new frontier"—and it may even balance inefficient production units against overproductive units. Not for long, though: in the end, state capitalism, too, must balance its budget as well as its other accounts; it must instruct its managers to produce a profit and not to forget that they must earn interest and amortization charges on the equipment which has been placed at each one's disposal. For state capitalism, like private capitalism, is governed by the Rule, and its current production is weighed down by a heavy burden of past investments, some of which no longer may have physical counterparts. (The built-in debt charges in most government budgets are constantly increasing, and the French are still paying for conquests which they have since lost.)

In contrast to private capital, state capitalism must be more prudent in using the resources which already have been developed and can be more daring in developing resources still unexploited. Since both, however, are laboring under the regime of scarcity, commodities and services have prices which constitute costs for the producer. The relations between buyer and seller, employer and employee, debtor and creditor are the same under both systems. Whatever their system of equations, it must be capable of simultaneous resolution: service must be paid; capital must be amortized and must bear interest; even though production may be nationalized, property relations still govern all economic calculations. It may seem that some nationalized enterprises do not show a profit because the government is their only customer and it subsidizes them. Taxes and subsidies are hidden in the price system, which the government seems to fix arbitrarily for reasons of national policy. In the Soviet Union, for example, military hardware is "sold" to the defense establishment at prices below cost. That makes the budget look smaller, but has resulted in such confusion of bookkeeping that the managers are now pressing for an honest price system. Today, Gosplan must keep two different sets of books, one of which shows the real cost of the subsidized articles. These subsidies, however, must be covered by taxes taken from the prosperous enterprises or from the consumers, and if the budget does not balance, inflation threatens to upset all equations. State capitalism, therefore, is striving to increase efficiency and to raise the productivity of labor even more than free capitalism. The whip of hunger has been replaced by the guillotine of control figures: all accounts must resolve themselves, all equations must be fulfilled. While no shareholders expect a dividend, it is as though the managers were merely executing the abstract striving of capital to become remunerative.

Many people confuse socialism with state capitalism, and nationalization with socialization. Oscar Lange is clearly thinking of state capitalism rather than socialism when he writes: "The equations which have to be solved in a socialist economy are exactly the same equations, and they are solved by the same persons, as in a capitalist economy."[5] He does claim three advantages for his system of socialism:

—a greater equality of incomes, conducive to a greater welfare effect of production and to greater overall efficiency in the allocation of resources;

—substitution of social gain for private profit;

—planning, i.e., foresight of needs, avoidance of waste and setting of public goals.

These three improvements are of greatest importance, but they have not yet liberated the economy from the thralldom of value equations. Moreover, they are ambiguous: the "social gain" which is being substituted for private profit does not become available to the consumers or even to the producers. Some profit may be used to build public parks and art galleries; but its bulk must be invested in improvements of the national resources. Lange knows that the workers cannot get "the full proceeds of their labor," as some primitive socialists have demanded. Socialism, we just learned, must follow the market equations, i.e., it must invest its surplus in the same development which would look inviting to capitalists under the profit incentive. These investments are the "social gain" in Poland today.

Recreation facilities and places of learning, however, do not come out of the equations; their cost must be diverted from the profits by governmental decision. Strangely enough, the Polish government has used a large part of the surplus to rebuild destroyed cities in the quaint old style of yore, instead of improving the standard of living. The point is that under state capitalism, which Lange calls socialism, the apportionment of the surplus value among welfare and other national purposes is a matter of arbitrary decision. The government may allot its profits to industrial development, to the creation of a national image, to military power, to welfare institutions and consumer satisfactions, or to a trip to the moon. The equations neither prescribe nor prevent any particular use, and state capitalism therefore is neutral with respect to socialism; it is not incompatible with a distributive economy, but it also is compatible with systems of remuneration according to deserts or to social rank. Under conditions of great scarcity or extreme stress for the sake of rapid development, state capitalism (national socialism) will reproduce the very worst features of early capitalism (or worse, as it did under Stalin); but under conditions of abundance it may develop features of the welfare state or even of socialism.[6]

Which path it follows, however, will depend upon the development of democratic institutions, and in this respect state capitalism is not quite so indifferent. It tends to favor bureaucratic dictatorships; or, better perhaps, state capitalism and dictatorship mutually enhance each other. Particularly if the dictator communicates to the nation a "sense of urgency" for rapid development schemes, he may destroy the germs of pressure groups and of pluralistic bargaining. State capitalism provides necessary economic conditions which tempt the policy-makers toward national greatness. It is the ideal basis for a military, or defense economy. But statism is not socialism.

The arbitrariness of statist production goals has inspired violent protests from partisans of a free economy, and not without reason have they denounced state capitalism as "the road to serfdom." Unfortunately, though, they gave it the name "socialism," and this has created theoretical confusion. The socialists were actually the first to dissociate themselves from all theories of bureaucratic rule. They have insisted, at all times, that the state apparatus should be an instrument, not a taskmaster. In its decadent phase, bourgeois theory no longer has the ability to distinguish between the conceptions of "state" and of "politics." Socialists do not say that the state should organize production and command consumption. They say that demand has come to be politicized.

IV

To explain this distinction, I have to go back to my introductory remarks. Ultimately, the owners of resources do not make one decision but two. They seek profit with those means only which previously they have decided to allot to gainful employment; but they have decided simultaneously what part of their resources and time they wish to retain for themselves. As owner of real estate I might decide to set some of it aside for hunting; as owner of money I might decide to buy jewels or paintings rather than machinery; as owner of labor power I might decide to make myself a monk, thus withdrawing it from the market and raising the price of labor. According to the strict theory as taught by Mises and Hayek, all resources should be competing in the market place for the highest profit and thereby assure the optimum allotment for the greatest satisfaction of the whole, while assuring each worker only the "marginal" wage which will induce him to serve. But in practice this has never been the case. Each owner is a monopolist who may decide to leave his resources idle, to consume them unproductively, or to use them for gain. Thus, workers decided that idleness gives greater satisfaction than work, and by withdrawing labor power from the market they raised its price. They have even conspired to do that, just as landowners have conspired to control the use of land and as bankers have conspired to maintain the value of the currency. These are different kinds of conspiracy, recognized as legal at different stages in the development of modern industrialism; together with the first kind of intervention we mentioned—the care of governmental bodies for health, welfare, security and communications —they are "countervailing powers" which mitigate the arbitrariness, brutality, uncertainty and insecurity of the capitalistic market.

The welfare state is a capitalistic economy which largely depends on the free market but in which the countervailing powers have been politicized and are consciously employed to balance the economy, to develop the national resources or to pursue fixed goals of social policy. Foremost among these goals are economic security, the raising of living standards for the poor, conservation and development of resources. The fully developed welfare state has at its disposal a wide range of economic instruments, classical as well as Keynesian and statist. They include the government's power to regulate, to control, to intervene, to tax and to redistribute the product, to plan and to use its position as a buyer of 10–20 percent of the national product. The welfare state may achieve techniques of industry-wide planning, price-fixing and overall control of development, but though it will nationalize the coal industry in France and England, erect a TVA in the United States and build a government steel mill for India, it stops short of expropriation. On the contrary, its proclaimed aim is to preserve the structure of property and to protect the formation of a free market. Whatever expropriating is to be done must come through the free play of the market, as is being done, for example, in our farm economy despite price supports. The basic relationships of buyer and seller, employer and employee, owner and nonowner are no different from those prevailing under pure capitalism, but they are supplemented by state interference in two important areas: where classical capitalism is indifferent to the distribution of income, the welfare state at least tries to make income differentials less steep; also, whereas under pure capitalism the development of resources is but an accidental by-product of the profit incentive, the welfare state sets itself definite goals of developing public and private facilities, consumer satisfactions, even tastes and standards.

In contrast to pure, classical capitalism, which is totally producer-oriented, the welfare state may plan the deliberate increase of consumer satisfactions, be it in the form of a more equal distribution of income or in the form of raised productivity or in the form of enlarged public services. It does not always do so; it may stop at "full employment" which may be brought about through defense expenditures or pyramid-building without any noticeable increase in the general standard of living and without making more people equal. However, the welfare state must give its citizens more security than pure capitalism, and its planning usually results in higher wage rates, shorter hours, greater opportunities, or, at the very least, in the maintenance of satisfactions which otherwise might be lost. By virtue of both its means and its aims, the welfare state therefore is often dubbed "socialism on installments" or "creeping socialism."

But we should not be misled by its efforts to plan, regulate and control production, to redistribute income and to curb the uninhibited use of private property. At the hub of its mechanics, it is different from socialism. Though some prices and wages are determined politically, on the whole they are determined by the market, and that is true even of the public enterprises;. the regime of property prevails throughout, with the dead weight of past investments burdening the calculation of profit and the decisions on future investments, with at least a theoretical obligation to balance all budgets, and with remuneration still tightly ruled by a man's contribution to the value of the product. Public projects still need to be justified in terms of national policy rather than human needs, and expenditure for defense and similar competitive purposes still exceeds the welfare expenditure.

V

An economy totally controlled by the interests of the ultimate consumers is properly called socialism. We usually distinguish two stages. The ultimate, communism, permits every citizen to draw on the public resources according to his needs. This presupposes a degree of productivity and wealth which probably is not available in any country now, in addition to a development of public morality that may not be achieved in the near future. I therefore confine myself to the penultimate stage, socialism, where distributions may still be proportionate to deserts. Even at this stage, however, a *national dividend* may be distributed among all citizens in two forms: increased public services or the conversion of many essential services (such as higher education, health, theater) from private to public operation;[7] secondly, the distribution of a minimum allowance sufficient to cover the expense of feeding, housing and clothing a family.[8] The minimum allowance would not be generous enough to cover luxury expenses and hence there remains an incentive to earn additional wages to keep up with the Joneses. Wage levels may be governed by demand and supply, through collective bargaining, and there will be wage differentials according to skill. A free market will provide goods and services, allowing demand and supply, to regulate those prices which are not manipulated for purposes of public policy. Both public enterprise and free entrepreneurs or cooperatives may compete for the consumers' favor.

Some prices may be administered to implement public policy. It is easy to imagine, for example, that each citizen is allotted a room of ten by ten feet; but if a man's need exceeds the standard house in his community, he may have to pay progressively increasing rent per additional square foot, window or door. For all these transactions, money will be used as a means of circulation and for purposes of accounting. I can see no reason why a socialist economy should deprive itself of this useful invention—provided the money is not used to form capital and to acquire the control of production facilities.

Capital formation may be prevented by a number of devices, such as steep income and inheritance taxes. This may be important for the period of transition if expropriated owners are to be indemnified. One may also think of Sylvio Gesell money, or a tax on all means of circulation and credit accounts such that money would lose a certain percentage of its value every month. That percentage might even be regulated for purposes of public policy in the same way as we now raise and lower reserve requirements or the rate of interest. The device is not primarily intended to reduce big bank books and it does not even serve that purpose very effectively; its main purpose is to help in divorcing present from past production, a necessity which I shall discuss presently. Here I only wish to insert a remark on private property.

It seems to me that socialists have overestimated the importance of expropriating the expropriators; the symbolic value of this measure far exceeds its economic significance. What matters is not ownership but control. A man like Mattei had a stranglehold not only on the whole Italian economy but on Italian foreign policy, too, though he did not own a single drop of the oil on which he had built his power. Or closer to home: if one has to have a dictator, one might think of better men than Robert Moses; but if any man were to claim as much power merely on the ground that he owns a lot of the state's real estate, he might be harassed by D.A.s in every borough and hounded by tax inspectors in every district. Owners may be parasites, but economically speaking they are mere *faux frais*, or overhead. Their unearned income is not a personal tithe which they exact from the community but a payment for the use of capital. In the capitalist lore, it is indeed the tribute to capital, not to its owner.

VI

A socialist economy does not earn "wages of capital"; in fact it severs the umbilical cord between capital formation and production, or in Marxian language, between past labor and current employment. This may sound utopian, and some readers who so far may have gone along, figuring that the national dividend also is nothing but an extension of welfare state services, may accuse me of economic dilettantism. Indeed, every major economist who has given the matter some thought has emphasized the need for a socialist economy to heed the equations, to follow the Rule, to amortize capital and, if it wishes to invite expansion, to pay itself interest and even ground rent. Schumpeter said that any other notion is "irrational." Abba Lerner worked out schemata showing how the ultimate costs must equal prices, and Mises thought that he had refuted the viability of socialism by showing that under that system "calculation would be impossible." Only Kautsky had an inkling of the importance of "freeing prices from values," but he failed to follow up his idea, and it was an outsider, Peter F. Drucker, who laid his finger on the crucial point:

> The wage rate is the symbol of conflict rather than the issue itself. The basic problem is a conflict between the enterpriser's view of wage as cost, and the employee's view of wage as income. The real issue is not an economic one but one over the nature and function of wage. (*The New Society*, New York: Harper, 1950, p. 48.)

Since we already have severed income from cost in section V, we now have a similar conflict between the state enterprise's view of capital as cost and the consumers' view of capital as expenditure. The issue is not how much capital should earn to remain fair in a socialist society, but what its function can be in such an economy.

The difference between a socialist and any other economy is in the divorce of production from capital or property claims. In the socialist economy capital goods, once created, enter into the consumption funds of the society, to be drawn upon as the need occurs. There is no need to amortize it in any given time or to realize a profit on it. We are using facilities, such as roads, which our fathers built, and we are building facilities, such as airports, which our children may use; strangely enough, such facilities are being paid out of the current municipal, state and federal budgets, but are not carried on the books of these bodies as "assets"; nevertheless, bonds representing the value of these assets are being held and serviced for generations.

Other examples of divorce between real capital value and use challenge the sense of outrage. Daniel M. Friedenberg has shown in DISSENT how tax advantages make it profitable for owners to tear down houses which still might be of service for years, while at the same time rat-infested slums are maintained in service because they still yield a profit. All I suggest is that a socialist society might use this same divorce of past investment from present enjoyment, but for a better purpose. We already have seen that state capitalism is capable of taking losses in one industry while earning profits in another. All that was required to satisfy the Rule was that the profit and loss accounts cancel each other out. But we know that in practice the balance is never achieved in any particular year—for indeed: why must the year be the unit? why not the decade? In practice we draw on present resources to unbalance the budget, or else we could have no development. But then, having established the new facilities, we forbid ourselves their enjoyment and say, in effect: now we must tighten our belts and pay for these goodies. Though we may have created the new investment in order to work less, we now must work more to pay for it. If this is not irrational, words have no meaning.

It is, indeed, a fetishistic way of looking at "value" which makes us demand that capital goods must produce value in all types of economies. They do not affect the prices of goods unless someone claims that they "belong" to him and he must get his reward for letting us use them. It is the same fetishistic view, that man creates "values," which makes us demand that all equations must be resolved simultaneously. They don't have to be; in a distributive economy, we don't have to wait until we find a buyer to turn the merchandise over. On the other hand, such an economy may destroy unserviceable assets or abandon created values—don't we do that to our military hardware anyway?—without suffering the kind of loss that our capitalistic economy finds in its books if that happens; for the loss really has occurred when the goods first were erroneously produced.

I shall admit that this kind of economy encounters certain difficulties. It is rather wasteful; it cannot account for all its transactions in one set of books; its measurements of efficiency are uncertain, and a number of indeterminate variables enter into its cost calculations, not to speak of the numerous political factors which determine its prices. All this is small discomfort, however. A distributive economy is possible only at a fairly advanced stage of development; one cannot distribute poverty, but only wealth. Given this condition and given the enormous possibilities of further increasing productivity, I see no reason why such a society should not make ad hoc decisions whether to use or not to use certain facilities without regard to cost, whether to promote or to retard a certain development without fear of meeting the dividends; indeed, what Mises counts for the refutation of socialism, its indifference to proper cost accounting, I would claim for its virtue.

Nevertheless, no society has unlimited funds, and even the most liberal economist must economize somewhere. The plans must be drawn up with an eye on citizens who might be stingy with their time. Or, certain materials may indeed be scarce, and someone must calculate which of two possible substitutes might be easier to develop. In that case, "easier" means fewer hours of labor, less waste of other materials, cheaper transportation, etc. In other words, a socialist economy may keep a second set of books where all transactions are calculated, either in hours of labor or even in prices (provided the price system has not become too much distorted). But this set of books will have to allow for a kind of wastage unheard of in our present economy: time wasted in experimentation, machines bought not to increase efficency but to make work easier, committee meetings and grievance procedures, special privileges granted to attract workers; on the other hand, the surplus value also will be enormous, as workers demand parks, playgrounds, nurseries and other special distributions. In short, the bookkeepers will be aware that capitalistic enterprise could be much more efficient, and that is the reason why socialist economy must not be managed by the bookkeepers. Indeed, it can survive only as long as it is controlled by organs of democracy on all levels, from the planning boards down to the works council.[9]

Footnotes

1. I do not wish to enter here into a learned discussion of marginal utility and the subjective theory of value. For a detailed analysis see Ben B. Seligman's truly encyclopedic and scholarly work, *Main Currents in Modern Economics* (New York: Free Press of Glencoe, 1963). For theoretical background, I have drawn heavily on this monumental publication, the most complete and the most modern of its kind I know. I am also indebted to Abba P. Lerner, *The Economics of Control* (New York: Macmillan, 1944), and Joseph A. Schumpeter, *Capitalism, Socialism and Democracy* (New York: Harper, 1942).

2. See C. A. Landauer, *European Socialism*, Vol. II (Berkeley, 1959) and B. E. Lippincott, ed. *Economic Theory of Socialism* (Minneapolis, 1938).

3. "Socialism," London, 1924, p. 364 ff.; Schumpeter, however, holds that monopoly is more efficient (op. cit., p. 100).

4. The Rule of marginal utility says that output should be carried to the point where the cost of the last unit matches the price it fetches, or where the marginal social benefit matches the marginal social cost. Since the latter is also measured in prices, the two equations are identical. The assumption here is that "social benefit" and real social cost can be so measured; this I am going to deny.

5. Quoted by Landauer, op. cit.—Jaurès was of the same opinion: "collectivism can be regarded as a special case of capitalism" (ibid., p. 1606).

6. For this reason I speak of only three basic types of economy. State capitalism and monopoly capitalism are derivative forms.

7. In the Soviet Union, these public consumer services now amount to 15 percent of wage income, and are supposed to rise to 50 percent.

8. Anton Menger formulated as one of three basis rights "that each member of society may claim that the goods and services necessary to the maintenance of his existence shall be assigned to him, in keeping with the measure of existing means, before the less urgent needs of others are satisfied." (*Das Recht auf den vollen Arbeitsertrag*, Stuttgart, 1910.) The other two are Louis Blanc's "right to work" and Ferdinand Lassalle's right to a just share of (not the full!) product of one's labor. These "rights" fall short of abolishing inequality and exploitation, but their realization is a condition for a classless society.

9. I have dealt with the philosophical and ethical aspects of socialism in "The Right to Be Lazy," DISSENT, Winter 1956. There I argued that the aim of socialism is not to make production more efficient but to humanize it, and that the so-called "progress" is not the highest of all values.

ROBERT L. HEILBRONER
Roots of the Socialist Dilemma
(1972)

Socialism in our time is undergoing a crisis. It is not a crisis of existence, for our age has seen the arrival of socialism on a scale that surpasses the fondest hopes of socialists of the past generation. Indeed, it is difficult to believe that thirty years ago socialism was to be found in only one country whose very survival appeared to be gravely threatened. Today at least a third, possibly half, of the world's population lives under regimes that, however subject to political change, appear indissolubly wedded to socialism as an economic system. In the retrospective glance of the future, ours will certainly be known as the period in which socialism ceased to be a mere wish, a vague destination of history, and became a major part of current reality.

Nevertheless, when we look not to its outward manifestations of success but to its inward state of mind, there is no doubt that socialism is in crisis. For among those individuals who are, so to speak, the fathers of the socialist faith, there is a visible *crise de foi*. In the hectic atmosphere of the newly founded socialist nations— China, Cuba, Chile, the African socialist states—this crisis is submerged by the struggle to install and manage a new form of society against immense obstacles. But in the calmer setting of the Western world, where that most subversive of all activities—reflection—is still tolerated or even encouraged, one discovers a pervasive unease.

Let me give a few examples of this unease. Less than ten years ago, Paul M. Sweezy, perhaps the leading American Marxian economist, declared that "The *differentia specifica* of socialism as compared with capitalism is public ownership of the means of production."[1] Yet more recently Sweezy has admitted, "I no longer think this goes to the heart of the matter. But I have no neat formulas or definitions to replace it with."[2]

Another critic has spelled out the substance of Sweezy's doubts:

Classical socialism has . . . usually resulted merely in state agencies running state industries in an authoritarian economy, leaving unfulfilled a host of such humanist ideals as freedom, democracy, equality and cooperation. . . . Perhaps most critical in human terms is state-socialism's dynamic tendency toward hierarchy and centralization, for this reduces individual and social responsibility, thereby destroying the basis both for freedom and for a practice and ethic of voluntary cooperation.[3]

Perhaps Irving Howe has expressed the prevailing mood most vividly:

The whole tragic experience of our century, I would submit, demonstrates this to be one of the few unalterable commandments of socialism: the participation of the workers, the masses of human beings, as self-conscious men preparing to enter the arena of history. Without that, or some qualified version of it, socialism is nothing but a mockery, a swindle of bureaucrats and intellectuals reaching out for power.[4]

Thus, starting from many different vantage points, these critics concur that something is missing from the traditional definition of socialism as a society that can be characterized simply in terms of the public ownership of the means of production and the presence of planning. And the reason for the dissatisfaction is not difficult to discover. Our age has encountered with shocking force the problems inherent in two processes of world history—on the one hand, the cumulative addition to our technological capabilities; on the other, the relatively unchanged level of our social and political capabilities. We have faced, to a degree never before experienced in history, a wholly unequal contest between our ability to control the physical environment and thus to alter the setting of society, and our inability to control the political and social repercussions to which these environmental changes give rise.

Before this technological juggernaut, socialism as well as capitalism have found themselves virtually helpless. How to humanize production on a vast scale, how to organize enormous networks of collective effort without equally enormous networks of bureaucratic controls, how to spur incentive without catering to greed, how to adduce political participation without mani-pulation—these are problems that confront every advanced society and that have found solutions in none.

Thus the immediate crisis of socialism appears in a widespread uncertainty as how to manage the societies that socialism will inherit or that it is fast at work building. Not surprisingly, nothing like unanimity marks the present socialist debate as to how to avoid the problems I have mentioned. Everywhere we find a chastened awareness that planning is a word far easier to pronounce than to spell out, but a debate still rages as to whether this requires more efficient centralization or a much greater degree of decentralization. So too there is general agreement that "democracy" is an indispens-able condition for socialism, but nothing like agreement as to the limits of dissent to which a socialist citizen may go. In the same way, alienation is an ailment on which all socialists fasten their gaze, but whose prescribed remedies range from a return to the simplicities of small-scale communal life to the final liberation of labor through total mechanization. And finally, it is surely grounds for rueful commentary that the two socialist nations that have consciously sought to curb the bureaucratic phenomenon—Yugoslavia and China—each regard the approach of the other as a betrayal of socialism.

I do not call attention to the specter of unease that is haunting socialism in a mocking vein. On the contrary, I believe its present intellectual disarray to be a sign of strength, not of weakness. Now that socialism has ceased to be a mere wishful projection of history it must come to grips with the disconcerting realities and paradoxes of life, and the price of this coming-to-grips is inevitably a mood of sobriety. The assurance and clarity that were appropriate for so-cialism at one stage of its career would only be evidence of its dogmatism or barrenness at another. I hope that the present temper of inquiry, self-doubt, and uncertainty does not give way prematurely to a set of intellectual convictions and institutional commitments that socialism (or any other social philosophy) is not in a position to afford.

Hence I shall say nothing more about the substance of the contemporary socialist unease insofar as it concerns the search for institutions. But my reticence is not only an admission that I do not know how socialism should be structured. Rather, it reflects my belief that the roots of the socialist crisis lie deeper than its current confusion before the challenges of technology, bureaucracy, and democracy. For behind the uncertainty with which socialism faces these problems is a much more fundamental uncertainty of which socialists themselves are only gradually becoming aware. It is an uncertainty concerning the nature of the social existence to which socialism aspires. Is the goal of socialism a society that will encourage the freest expression of individuality in art, in sexual and social relations, in political thought and act? But does this not conflict with the vision of socialism as an organic society, one that applies the collective wisdom and judgment of the community in establishing *norms* of behavior, *shared* moral standards, a *unifying* vision of the good life? What are to be the bounds of freedom? What are to be the standards of conduct?

Until socialists know the nature of the society they seek, it will be difficult, perhaps impossible, to determine the institutional means best suited for the future. But that is not the only problem. Behind the hesitation and ambivalence of its social visions are the conflicts in its conceptions of man himself. Is the human being an infinitely plastic creature, capable of "making" himself without any boundaries or constraints other than those he imposes on himself? If so, what boundaries *should* he choose? Or is there an "essence" of man whose primordial and persistent existence can be ignored only at the gravest peril? But if there is such an essence, what is it? What constraints and boundaries does it ordain for men?

Now I cannot hope, in this brief space, to elucidate a problem of such vast dimensions and ancient lineage as the question, What is man? But perhaps I can add some measure of clarification to the present socialist crisis by asking socialists to think about the problem itself in a *radical* way.

What is the "radical" approach to the question of human nature? We get a first definition of the idea if we contrast it to what we usually call the "conservative" view of man. As we ordinarily use both terms, these two words express conflicting judgments regarding the political capabilities of man. Although there are many conservative philosophies, all are marked by an explicit distrust of the motives and capacities of men when they engage in political action. In direct contrast, radicalism rests its faith precisely in the ability of men and women to put their motives and capabilities to effective and morally laudable political use.

We shall return later to the so-called conservative skepticism with regard to political behavior. What I want to examine now is the relevance of the radical faith itself to the crisis of socialism. For unless I am mistaken, much of the unease that underlies the socialist mood stems from the unexamined implications of what it takes to be the radical view of man.

As a declaration of faith in the human capacity for self-direction, radicalism is, as we all know, a very modern idea, scarcely older than the great political revolutions of 1776 and 1789. At its core is the advocacy of an ever-expanding exercise of conscious control by the great masses of men over their individual and collective destinies —here is Irving Howe's entrance of the workers into history.

Although it was originally propounded as a political rather than economic ideal, it is from this declaration of faith in the self-governing potentialities of man that socialism draws its strength. For what is attractive to the radical mind in the conception of socialism is above all the idea that a socialist society is best suited for the active development of the human capacity for self-determination. That is why the radical embraces socialism boldly and eagerly, in contrast to the defensive posture so characteristic of the conservative who chooses those institutions most likely to buffer and dampen the potentially dangerous proclivities of the political animal.

I stress this radical commitment to socialism as a vehicle for human self-direction for a very important purpose. It is here that socialism rests its case for the basic institutional changes it has traditionally sought—the replacement of private by public command over productive property and the disposition of output. However short these traditional aims may fall in bringing about the sufficient conditions for a "humanist" socialism, they are indeed necessary conditions if socialism is to achieve its radical aim of enlarging the area of human self-determination.

The issue is so important in the light of the present self-doubting mood of socialism that I must take a moment to review the argument in its support. Why does socialism insist on the public ownership of productive wealth? Essentially because it maintains that private ownership, under the dynamic conditions of capitalism, constitutes a direct barrier to the widest possible self-direction of man. A society in which less than 2 percent of all family units own some 80 percent of its corporate assets is, from the standpoint of a philosophy that seeks the widest possible individual autonomy, as anachronistic and indefensible as the societies of feudalism or antiquity, where tiny fractions of the population enjoyed the privileges of their social orders.

It may well be, as bitter experience has shown, that socialism will destroy this form of privilege only to replace it with another. In lieu of the aristocracy of wealth, socialism may install an oligarchy of the party elite or of planners. Moreover, as our knowledge of Stalinist Russia makes clear, the gulf between the living conditions of these elites and that of the masses may be as great as that between the capitalist rich and the masses who live under capitalism. Thus I do not maintain that socialism fulfills the radical prescription for self-determination by the mere act of expropriating the expropriators. But I do hold that the abolition of the privileges of wealth associated with capitalism nevertheless constitutes a necessary step for the realization of the socialist ideal.

This is so because noncapitalist forms of privilege, such as those of bureaucratic preferment or naked political or military power, even when they are more crushing than the privileges of wealth, are nonetheless more transparent and self-evident *as* privileges. By contrast, what is so inimical to the cause of autonomy within the structure of privileges peculiar to capitalism is that its prerogatives are veiled and masked by the ideology of the market system. No feudal lord, no Egyptian noble, no slaveowner was unaware of his privileged status, although he may not have felt in any way defensive about it. Neither was any serf, peasant, or slave deceived as to the brute realities of the class structure, although he may have resigned himself to it. But what is unique about capitalist society is that most men are unaware of the very presence of privilege within it. The rich congratulate themselves on the money they have "made." Moreover, much of the rest of society, including many of the poor, agree that the rich have *earned* their favored place because of the contribution "their" capital has made to production. In a word, men who are enthralled by the ideology of capitalism do not see, and cannot understand, the difference between the undeniable contribution made to production by the physical artifacts of capital, and the claims made on that production in the name of the private "ownership" of these artifacts. The socialist institution of public ownership, despite its immense problems of administration and bureaucracy, destroys this deep-seated mystique and thus makes possible an advance toward the radical goal of a society of men who understand and therefore command the conditions of their existence.

Now let me advance a second argument in support of the traditional institutional definition of socialism—an argument that also stems from the radical commitment to individual and collective self-realization. This argument concerns the need to replace the market disposition of resources by a planning mechanism of some sort. Here also harsh experience has taught us that planning, as such, may not succeed in achieving this aim. Especially in its centralized form, planning has proved inimical to self-determination insofar as it has ignored the preferences by which men express their individuality or has manipulated those preferences as shamelessly as corporate capitalism at its worst. Thus, however useful centralized planning may be for forcing economic growth, once beyond the dire needs of an impoverished society, such planning is a dubious instrument of socialism measured by the criteria of radicalism itself.

Indeed, a telling attack can be mounted against the socialist embrace of planning by conservative economists who point out that the much-maligned market is actually a form of "planning" more conducive to individual autonomy than that of any central planning board. I do not quarrel with this contention but only propose to push the idea of "market planning" to its logical conclusion within the framework of a socialist society. It will then be seen that we can use the market as a planning mechanism for the attainment of radical goals, provided that we intervene at one critical juncture of the process, namely, where incomes are set and demand is initially created. Thus planning may well concentrate on the critical determination of income levels, leaving the socialist factory managers thereafter to compete for the purchasing power whose original distribution has received a conscious social approval.

There may be other means of circumventing the bureaucratic incubus of central planning, but that is not my concern here. Rather, I wish only to make the point that the radical aim of systematically expanding the potentialities of all men requires some form of deliberate intervention into the determination and distribution of society's output. Until society has consciously broached and answered the question of what is to be a "fair" allocation of the claims of each individual against the community, the radical goal of individual autonomy cannot be achieved.

These considerations make it clear, I trust, that I believe in the relevance and legitimacy of the now much-questioned institutional definition of socialism as a society in which the ownership of productive resources has been removed from private hands and in which rational planning has replaced the blind play of an unsupervised distribution of individual buying power. This declaration of faith should permit me to return to an examination of the radical philosophy itself. For having declared my belief in the legitimacy of the basic institutions of socialism, I must now declare my futher conviction that radicalism, insofar as it depends on a commitment to the limitless perfectibility of man, is an inadequate guide either for the construction of the society that those institutions must undergird, or for the definition of the nature of the human beings they must serve.

What is deficient in the radical view? Its most vulnerable aspect clearly lies in its initial premise: that man *is* perfectible and capable of moral improvement by conscious design. Essentially this is a premise beyond empirical demonstration. It is a statement of faith—as is also the contrary assertion that man possesses a propensity for evil that will express itself despite all efforts to repress or expunge it.

Yet, however open to question, this is not where I find the radical belief lacking. Whatever man's inherent capacity for evil, I feel reasonably secure in believing that the realized and overt expressions of that evil owe more to nurture than to nature. If one member of every pair of identical twins born in the ghetto and the suburbs could be switched at birth, as in fairy stories, does anyone doubt that the subsequent social histories of those twins would reflect their changed environments at least as much as their unchanged endowments?

It is possibly more difficult to retain a belief in the perfectibility of man if one looks to history, where mass murder has reached a kind of crescendo in the wars of the twentieth century. Yet I cannot even read the historical record in a wholly pessimistic frame of mind. There have been changes in human behavior in the Western world (where the effort to perfect man has been largely concentrated) whose importance we may overlook in our appalled recognition of the extent to which evil still flourishes. Slavery—a condition once taken for granted—has disappeared. Torture, not too long ago publicly offered for the delectation of the spectator, is now conducted in shame and secrecy. Mental illness is no longer the occasion for ridicule and punishment. Even war itself is now the object of a widespread moral revulsion to a far greater extent than ever in the past.

It would be fatuous to claim that the historical evidence is clearly on the side of radicalism. It is quite enough, however, to maintain that it does not contradict the belief in some degree of moral and social plasticity for man. To put it differently, I see no reason, based in history, to doubt that a society that devoted its full efforts to the cultivation of the moral, aesthetic, and intellectual capabilities of its people could elevate the prevailing level of social decency as much above present-day society as the level of Sweden is elevated above that of the Union of South Africa.

What is the weakness of radicalism, then, if we accept its faith in the capacity for human improvement? The answer lies not in the idea of perfectibility as such but in certain human attributes to which the criterion of perfectibility does not apply and to which the radical creed therefore pays no heed. Since I have used the word "radicalism" to describe the idea of humanity that rests on perfectibility, let me, for the moment, use the word "conservative" to indicate these missing aspects of human experience.

I begin a discussion of these aspects by returning again to the wariness with regard to political behavior that I have already singled out as typically "conservative." Now what is it that conservatives are wary about? To the radical it seems to be only a fear that the masses will throw off their habits of subservience and rise against their masters. But this is too easy a reading of the conservative view. For the conservative warnings apply equally to those at the top as well as to those at the bottom. This conservative caution goes beyond the obvious warnings with respect to the behavior of the political leaders of socialism. It is the thought that even men who have "everything" cannot be trusted to act well. Men are dangerous political animals because there is an inner core that remains beyond the reach of reason, deaf to the counsels of morality, indifferent to the best-intentioned policies.

In a word, the conservative sees that man, at the very center of his being, is "free" in the sense of being unpredictable and untamable; and that this freedom is not an attribute that is necessarily congenial with social order. It is thus a view of man at once more hopeful and more skeptical than that of the radical—more hopeful in its denial that men can be totally programmed, more skeptical in its denial that this unexpungeable individuality is an attribute that unfailingly redounds to the higher purposes of society.

This is a view with profound relevance for the radical reconstruction of society. For it locates within man himself an imperative reason for a socialist commitment to the spontaneity and individuality of life. A recognition of an inviolable inner preserve of the personality informs the radical that when he speaks of the "liberation" of the human spirit, he is not merely projecting an ideal of what man could or should be, but also acquiescing in a realization of what man *is*.

Such an acquiescence requires more than a pietistic affirmation for socialism. For the conception of an unreachable core of behavior comes squarely into conflict with the idea of the limitless perfectibility of man. To the extent that radicalism sees in every instance of human misbehavior—in every instance of criminality, laziness,

amorality, political disaffection—a *social* fault, it erects a vision of
man that invites an indefinite degree of social correction. But if the
"conservative" conception is correct in emphasizing elements or
layers of the personality that cannot be managed—or that can be
invaded only at the cost of destroying the person—then socialism
must reconsider its utopian image of what man can be. This involves
the painful admission that perfectibility is not a process that can
proceed indefinitely. More than that, it requires the admission that
perfectibility is a process that socialism does not want to press
indefinitely. In the end a socialist society must reconcile itself to an
indeterminate space within which men and women can express their
wishes and drives, *whether or not these conform to the ideals and
goals of socialism itself.*

But it is not only with regard to freedom that socialism has
something to learn from the "conservative" view of human nature.
Perhaps even more important is the question that this view raises
with respect to the collective morale, the sense of shared well-being
that socialism also aims to achieve. Here the focus of attention turns
away from the problem of individuality and spontaneity to the
opposite question of the norms and values that socialism should
incorporate.

Now it is no more my intention to discuss the specific nature of
these norms than it was to define the boundaries for the expression
of the free human personality. In the present case, as in the former, I
wish only to stress the relevance of the "conservative" view of man in
locating a psychobiological base that may provide a more secure
foundation for socialist thought than that offered by the radical faith
in human perfectibility. For with regard to the problem of norms, as
with that of individuality, it seems conservatism has something to say
that is very different from the standard views of radicalism, and of
the utmost importance.

The difference between the conservative and the radical view of
norms derives from a difference in the perspective with which each
views the drama of life. The radical views life as an epic, a quest, to
be consummated in the future. The conservative views it as a
process of reenactment, of renewal, to be justified in the present.
And from this perspective the conservative again sounds warnings

for the radical. Liberate man? By all means! But liberate him from what? From all that is personal as well as all that is selfish? From all that is ancient as well as all that is archaic? From all that is ritual as well as all that is rote? From everything nonrational as well as everything that is mistaken? From all faith as well as all fetishism?

These questions pose the crucial issue of what *kinds* of norms and values will best sustain a socialist society in the long run. To the radical, intent on perfecting man, norms tend to be hortatory and demanding. For the conservative, intent on reaffirming a persistent elemental nature in man, they tend to be supportive and reassuring. As such, these "conservative" norms have an unrecognized—perhaps a surprising—relevance for socialism. For I do not think it is merely a romantic yearning of our age that makes it discover in primitive cultures a wholeness and psychological security whose absence we feel so keenly in our own. The aim of a socialist society cannot be a return to primitivism, for that would totally conflict with its faith in the capacity of men to understand and order their own lives. But neither can its aim be the relentless pursuit of an ever-receding goal of perfection. In the end, socialism must seek to build a society that is at least as interested in the celebration and preservation of the timeless rules of cherished lifeways as in the continuous pioneering of ever new modes of social existence.

It is with some misgiving that I offer these counsels as being relevant for socialism today. It will be said that the need for social change is so overwhelming, at home as well as abroad, that words such as these can only work harm by instilling doubts where there should be resolve—and that for all the disclaimers one may make, conservatism remains and must always remain a view that favors complacency over indignation and that encourages passivity in the face of social evil.

I am aware of a grain of truth in these charges. I have entirely ignored the practical problems of achieving a socialism that combines the indispensable elements of economic structure we have discussed, along with the political and social essentials of a good society. During the long years in which that effort must be made, considerations such as mine may seem remote, almost diversionary. Yet even—or should I say especially—in the midst of the tactical decisions, uncertainties, and compromises that political struggle must bring, socialism needs some sense of its ultimate objectives, some philosophical counterpart of a magnetic north, past which its compass needle may swing but to which it will return.

The problem, however, is that socialists will not find such a lodestone unless they formulate a surer conception of the human being than the one they now entertain. Thus even in the throes of political turmoil, I ask whether it can be detrimental to the cause of socialism to consider and reconsider the nature of man. More than that, I press the question of whether socialism *must* not reflect on the limitations of the creed of perfectibility, or the elusive core of the individual, or the existential anxieties inextricable from life, as it seeks to build institutions in the name of man.

It is another matter when I turn to the second criticism and consider whether "conservatism" can ever be absorbed within and reconciled to the socialist faith. Here I confess to a certain discomfort. However purified of apologetics,there remains a tincture of regret in conservatism. Perhaps it is for that reason that radicalism and conservatism, like oil and water, can be shaken up together but cannot really blend.

But here too I have an answer that may save the day. For it is not really a conservative *philosophy* that I am recommending for socialism; indeed, that is why I have used quotation marks so often around the word "conservatism." Instead, what I have extracted from conservative thought are assumptions about the nature of man that are in themselves only the constitutive elements of a philosophy, socialist or conservative. And what is such a philosophy to be called if it is to be placed in the service of socialism? I have kept until the very end the proper word to describe a faith that includes a strong belief in the limited perfectibility of man and a recognition that man is more complex, obscure, and defiant than the idea of perfectibility alone suggests. The appropriate word for that faith is, of course, *radical*, in its primary sense of penetrating to the roots.

This is not a mere trick of words. What socialism needs now is a philosophy that searches for elemental moorings along with programmatic change. I do not know any other way to describe such an outlook, at once forward-looking and inward-looking, other than to call it radical. More important, I believe that in such a truly radical view of man—a view that embraces both his potential and his condition, his possibilities and his requirements, his open-ended future and his never-discarded past—socialism may discover the guiding principle that it now lacks.

Footnotes

1. *Monthly Review*, October 1963, cited in Howard Sherman, *Radical Political Economy* (New York: Basic Books, 1972), chap. 15.

2. Ibid.

3. Gar Alperovitz, "Notes Toward a Pluralist Commonwealth" (unpublished manuscript).

4. DISSENT, October 1971, p. 461.

IRVING HOWE
Socialism and Liberalism: Articles of Conciliation?
(1977)

It will surprise none of my readers to learn that after a reasonably diligent search I have not been able to find a serious attempt to bring together systematically the usual socialist criticisms of liberalism. The socialist criticisms of liberalism, though familiar enough in their general features, appear in the literature mainly through occasional passages, unquestioned references, rude dismissals, and, during the last few decades, a few wistful beckonings for reconciliation. What I propose to do here is to construct a synthesis, necessarily open to the charge that it is ahistorical, of the criticisms socialists have traditionally leveled against liberalism, and then to offer some remarks about possible future relations.

Socialists, who are they? and liberalism, what is it? I shall choose here to signify as socialist those thinkers and spokesmen who cannot be faulted as tender toward authoritarian regimes: I shall exclude Communists, Maoists, Castroites, as well as their hybrids, cousins, and reticent wooers. I shall assume that with regard to liberalism there has been some coherence of outlook among the various shades of socialist (and Marxist) opinion. But in talking about liberalism I shall be readier to acknowledge the complexities and confusions of historical actuality.

In the socialist literature, though not there alone, liberalism has taken on at least the following roles and meanings:

1. Especially in Europe, liberalism has signified those move-

ments and currents of opinion that arose toward the end of the eighteenth century, seeking to loosen the constraints traditional societies had imposed on the commercial classes and proposing modes of government in which the political and economic behavior of individuals would be subjected to a minimum of regulation. Social life came to be seen as a field in which an equilibrium of desired goods could be realized if individuals were left free to pursue their interests.[1] This, roughly, is what liberalism has signified in Marxist literature, starting with Marx's articles for the *Rheinische Zeitung* and extending through the polemics of Kautsky, Bernstein, and Luxemburg. In short: "classical" liberalism.

2. Both in Europe and America, liberalism has also been seen as a system of beliefs stressing such political freedoms as those specified in the U.S. Bill of Rights. Rising from the lowlands of interest to the highlands of value, this view of liberalism proposes a commitment to "formal" freedoms—speech, assembly, press, etc.—so that in principle, as sometimes in practice, liberalism need have no necessary connection with, or dependence upon, any particular way of organizing the economy.

3. Especially in twentieth-century America but also in Europe, liberalism has come to signify movements of social reform seeking to "humanize" industrial-capitalist society, usually on the premise that this could be done sufficiently or satisfactorily without having to resort to radical/socialist measures—in current shorthand: the welfare state. At its best, this social liberalism has also viewed itself as strictly committed to the political liberalism of item 2 above.

4. In America, sometimes to the bewilderment of Europeans, liberalism has repeatedly taken on indigenous traits that render it, at one extreme, virtually asocial and anarchic and, at the other extreme, virtually chiliastic and authoritarian. Perhaps because the assumptions of liberal polity were so widely shared in nineteenth-century America (the slaveocracy apart), "liberal" as a term of political designation can hardly be found in its writings. When liberalism as a distinctive modern politics or self-designated ideological current begins to emerge in America—first through the high-minded reforming individualism of Edwin Godkin, editor of the *Nation* during the 1880s and 1890s, and then through the social-nationalist progressivism of Herbert Croly, editor of the *New Republic* when it

was founded in 1914—it becomes clear that it cannot escape a heritage of native individualism, utopianism, and "conscience-politics." Nor can it escape the paradisal vision that is deeply lodged in the American imagination, going back to Emerson and Thoreau, and farther back, perhaps, to the Puritans. Not can it escape a heritage of Protestant self-scrutiny, self-reliance, and self-salvation. Consequently American liberalism has a strand of deep if implicit hostility to politics per se—a powerful kind of moral absolutism, a celebration of conscience above community, which forms both its glory and its curse.

5. Meanwhile, through the decades, liberalism has encompassed a *Weltanschauung*, a distinctive way of regarding the human situation. Despite some recent attempts to render it profound through a gloomy chiaroscuro, liberalism has customarily been an expression of that view of man which stresses rationality, good nature, optimism, and even "perfectibility" (whatever that may mean). Whether or not there is a necessary clash between the Christian and liberal views of man, and despite some strains of continuity that may coexist with the differences, there can hardly be any question that historically, in its effort to gain its own space, liberalism has emerged as a competitor to traditional religious outlooks.

II

That there are other significant usages of the term "liberalism" I do not doubt; but for today these should be quite enough. Let me now schematically note some—by no means all—of the major socialist criticisms of at least some of these variants of liberalism:

• The socialist criticism of "classical" liberalism (joined at points by that of conservative iconoclasts like Carlyle) seems by now to have been largely absorbed in our political culture—with the exception of such ideological eccentrics and utopians as Ayn Rand, Milton Friedman, and President Gerald Ford. That the historical conditions of early capitalist society made a mockery of any notion of free and equal competitors entering into free and equal exchange, with each employing his gifts and taking his risks; that large masses of people were excluded from the very possibility of significant social choice; that even "liberal" governments never quite practiced the noninterventionist principles of "classical" liberalism but in fact were actively engaged in fur thering the growth of burgeois economy; that the notion of "entitle-ment," with its premise of some early point of fair beginnings, is mostly ideological—these have been the kinds of criticisms that socialists, and especially Marxists, have made of early liberalism.[2] The very world we live in—irreversible if inconvenient, and open to almost every mode of criticism except nostalgia for the alleged bliss of pure capitalism—testifies to the cogency of these socialist criticisms.

Yet that is by no means the whole story. One of the strengths of Marxist historiography (I shall come to weaknesses) has been that even while assaulting capitalism it saw the vitality of its early phases, and that even in the course of ridiculing "classical" liberalism as an ideological rationale for bourgeois ascendancy, it honored its liberat-ing role in behalf of humanity at large. The early Marx—he who could write that "laws are positive and lucid universal norms in which freedom has attained an impersonal, theoretical existence independent of any arbitrary individual. A statute book is the people's Bible of freedom"; or who could write that "without parties there is no development, without division, no progress"—this early Marx clearly recognized his ties to, or descent from, the liberalism he subjected to attack and sought to "transcend."

Socialists—let us be honest: some socialists—have recognized that in its heroic phase liberalism constituted one of the two or three greatest revolutionary experiences in human history. The very idea of "the self" or "the individual," quintessential to modern thought and sensibility, simply could not have come into being without the fructifying presence of liberalism. The liberalism that appears in eighteenth-century Europe promises a dimissal of intolerable re-straints; speaks for previously unimagined rights; declares standards of sincerity and candor; offers the vision that each man will have his voice and each voice be heard. It would be making things too easy (at least for me) to say that socialism emerges unambiguously out of this tradition. Obviously, there have been authoritarian alloys in the socialist metals; but when the socialist imagination is at its most serious, it proposes a dialectical relationship to "classical" liberalism:

a refusal, on the one hand, of quasi-Benthamite rationales for laissez-faire economics and a pact in behalf of preserving and enlarging the boundaries of freedom.

• Both in some early efforts at Marxist scholarship and in recent academic revivals, socialists have charged against liberalism that its defenders elevate it to a suprahistorical abstraction, an absolute value presumably untainted by grubby interests or bloodied corruptions, whereas in actuality liberalism, like all other modes of politics, arose as a historically conditioned and thereby contaminated phenomenon, and hence must be regarded as susceptible to historical decay and supersession.

Now, if we see this matter mainly as one of historiography, there is a point to the socialist criticism. No political movement, not even liberalism, likes to have the time of its origins deglamorized, yet there is sufficient reason for subjecting all movements to that chastening procedure. But with regard to a living politics, this criticism is dangerous and has done a share of mischief.

The tendency of some Marxists to regard liberal ideas as mainly or merely epiphenomena of a historical moment always runs the risk of declining into an absolutist relativism, that is, a historicism that acknowledges no fixed point of premise other than its own strategies of deflation. A sophisticated analogue is the "sociology of knowledge"; a vulgar reduction, the habit of speaking about "*mere* bourgeois democracy." This mode of historical analysis ignores the possibility that even movements and currents of thought conditioned by class interest can yield ideas, traditions, methods, customs that will seem of permanent value to future generations. There may not be unimpeded progress in history, but there do seem to be a few permanent conquests. To show that the principles of liberal polity did not descend from Mount Sinai but arose together with social classes whose dominance we would like to see ended or curtailed is not at all to deny that those liberal principles are precious both to newly ascending classes and humanity at large. To show that the Founding Fathers of the United States represented commercial interests or kept slaves or, when in office, violated some of their own precepts is not at all to diminish the value of the Bill of Rights for people who despise commercial interests, abhor slavery, and propose, if in power, never to violate their own precepts. Criticism of

Jefferson's inadequacies is made possible by the adequacy of Jeffersonian principles.

If these remarks seem excessively obvious, we might remember that the history of twentieth-century politics, as also that of the twentieth-century intelligentsia, offers scant ground for resting securely in a common devotion to liberal values. Quite the contrary! We are living through a century of counterrevolution, one in which the liberal conquests of the nineteenth century, inadequate as these might have been, have been systematically destroyed by left-and-right authoritarian dictatorships. "Vulgar Marxism," with its quick reduction of ideas to ideology and its glib ascription of ideology to interest, has become the mental habit of lazy and half-educated people throughout the world.[3] In general, by now we ought to be extremely wary of all statements featuring the word "really"—as in "Mill's ideas really represent the interests of the British, etc., etc." and "Freud's ideas really reflect the condition of the Viennese, etc., etc." Statements of this kind are no doubt unavoidable and sometimes fruitful, but they have too often come to be damaging to both the life of the mind and a polity of freedom.

Insofar, then, as the socialist criticism of liberalism has furthered an element of historical reductionism—unavoidable, I suspect, in the context of a mass movement—it has weakened the otherwise valid insistence that liberalism be treated as part of mundane history and thereby subject to mundane complications.

• A powerful socialist criticism of liberalism has been that it has detached political thought and practice from the soil of shared, material life, cutting politics off from the interplay of interests, needs, and passions that constitutes the collective life of mankind. A linked criticism has been that liberalism lacks an adequate theory of power, failing to see the deep relationships between political phenomena and alignments of social class. (Kenneth Minogue makes the point vividly: "The adjustment of interest conception [intrinsic to contemporary liberalism] . . . omits the crunch of truncheon on skull which always lies just in the background of political life . . .") Still another linked criticism, in the line of Rousseau, proposes that modern man is torn apart by a conflict between the liberal acceptance of bourgeois institutions, which sanction the pursuit of selfish interest without regard to a larger community, and the liberal doctrine of popular sovereignty, which implies that the citizen must set aside private interests and concern himself with the common welfare.

Here, surely, it must be acknowledged that the socialist criticism —in fairness it has also been made by nonsocialists—has all but completely conquered, indeed taken effect so strongly as to become absorbed into the thought even of those who oppose socialism and/or Marxism. Almost every sophisticated (and thereby, soon enough, unsophisticated) analyis of society now takes it for granted that politics must be closely related to, and more or less seen as a reflection of, social interest; that society forms a totality in which the various realms of activity, though separable analytically, are intertwined in reality; that no segment of the population can be assumed any longer to be mute or passive, and that there has appeared a major force, the working class, which must be taken into historical account; and that the rationalism of most liberal theory, though not (one hopes) simply to be dismissed, must be complicated by a recognition of motives and ends in social behavior that are much richer, more complicated, and deeply troubling.[4]

Both in our efforts to understand history and affect politics, there has occurred a "thickening" of our sense of society—indeed, the very idea of society, itself largely a nineteenth-century invention, testifies to that "thickening." We might even say that as a result of Marx there has occurred a recreation of social reality. (The Christian historian Herbert Butterfield praises the Marxist approach to history in a vivid phrase: ". . . it hugs the ground so closely"—which in his judgment does not prevent it from surveying what occurs in the upper reaches.) It is very hard—though some people manage—still to see politics as a mere exercise for elites, or an unfolding of first principles; it is very hard still to see politics apart from its relation to the interaction of classes, levels of productivity, modes of socioeconomic organization, etc. Writing in 1885 about his early work, Engels says:

> While I was in Manchester, it was tangibly brought home to me that the economic facts, which have so far played no role or only a contemptible one in the writing of history, are, at least in the modern world, a decisive historical force; that they form the basis of the origination of the present-day class antagonisms; that

these class antagonisms, in the countries where they have become fully developed, thanks to large-scale industry, hence
especially in England, are in their turn the basis of the formation
of political parties and party struggles, and thus of all political
history.

If the germs of reductionism can be detected in such a passage,
so too can the possibilities for complication and nuance: all depends
on which clause one chooses to stress. These possibilities for complication and nuance were seized only a dozen years later by Émile
Durkheim:

> I consider extremely fruitful the idea that social life should be
> explained, not by the notions of those who participate in it, but
> by more profound causes which are unperceived by conscious-
> ness, and I think also that these causes are to be sought mainly in
> the manner according to which the associated individuals are
> grouped.

Anyone wishing to trace the development of modern thought—
among other things, from socialism to sociology—could do worse
than start with a gloss on these passages from Engels and Durkheim.

The "economism," real or apparent, of the Engels passage was
followed by a vulgarization in popular Marxist writings, but there is
also present in the Marxist tradition another—and for our time
crucial—view of the relation between state and society. In his earlier
and middle years especially, Marx saw that the state could possess or
reach an autonomy of its own, rising "above" classes as a kind of
smothering Leviathan. (The state in Louis Napoleon's France, wrote
Marx, is "an appalling parasitic body, which enmeshes the body of
French society like a net and chokes all its pores.") This perception
could be crucial for a reconciliation between socialists and
liberals—we shall come back to it.

● Yet, from the vantage point of the late twentieth century, it
ought to be possible for socialists to be self-critical enough to admit
that the victory over liberalism with regard to such matters as the
relationship between politics and society, state and economy, has by
no means been an unambiguous one, certainly not a victory to bring
unqualified satisfaction. Apart from reductionism, I would raise a

point that seems to me increasingly important but for which my own tradition offers an inadequate vocabulary. I have in mind what might be called the body of traditional political wisdom, or the reflections of thoughtful men on the "perennial" problems of politics. To speak of "perennial" problems, I want to insist, is to locate them within a historical continuum rather than to elevate them "above" history.

In its historicist relativizing, its absorption with a particular social circumstance, the socialist tradition has given rather short shrift to this body of traditional political reflection. A pity! Marx might have been unsympathetic to Madison's reflections in *The Federalist Papers* regarding the dynamics of faction in a republic; perhaps he would have seen them as excessively abstract or as a rationale for class interest. Yet both of these criticisms could have been cogent without necessarily undermining the value of what Madison said. The socialist movement has sinned and suffered from its impatience with the accumulated insights of the centuries regarding political life. As a result, despite its prolonged attention to politics and its often brilliant analyses of political strategy (from Marx in the *18th Brumaire* to Trotsky on pre-Hitler Germany), the socialist tradition has lacked, or refused, a theory of politics as an autonomous or at least distinct activity. It has had little or nothing to say about such matters as necessary delimitations of power, the problems of representation, the uses or misuses of a division of authority, the relation between branches of government, etc.

Let me cite a fascinating example. In late 1874 and early 1875 Marx read Bakunin's book *Statism and Anarchy*, made extended extracts and attached to these his own sharply polemical comments. Bakunin was anticipating one of the questions endlessly rehearsed by writers of the nonauthoritarian left: how to prevent the bureaucratization of a "workers' state," whether ex-workers raised to power would become corrupted, etc. etc. Bakunin writes that

> universal suffrage—the right of the whole people—to elect its so-called representatives and rulers of the State—this is the last word of the Marxists as well as of the democratic school. And this is a falsehood behind which lurks the despotism of a governing minority. . . . But this minority, say the Marxists, will consist of workers. Yes, indeed, of *ex-workers, who once they become rulers or representatives of the people, cease to be workers.* . . .

At which point Marx interrupts: "No more than does a manufacturer today cease to be a capitalist on becoming a city councilman." Continues Bakunin: "From that time on they [the ex-workers] represent not the people but themselves and their own claims to govern the people. Those who doubt this know precious little about human nature."

One need not acquiesce in Bakunin's hostility to democratic institutions in order to see that, in his own way, he has hit upon one of the "perennial" problems in political thought—the problem of representation, how the elected representative of a group or class can become corrupted or bureaucratized upon acquiring power. Marx's answer seems to me unsatisfactory: the manufacturer representing his class in a city council, though obviously susceptible to corruption, is not expected to help usher in a new, socialist era, he need only defend particularistic interests—while the worker elected to office in a "worker's state" is burdened, according to the Marxist prescription, with great historical and moral responsibilities, thereby rendering the problems of corruption and bureaucratism all the more acute. Surely Marx was able to understand this!—but what made it hard for him to respond to such matters with sufficient seriousness was a historical method, an ideological bent, a political will.

Yet, hidden within the class analyses of the Marxists there have remained—a Marxist analysis of Marxism might suggest that there *must* remain—elements of traditional political thinking. Lenin, the one Marxist writer most impatient with talk about "perennial" problems, seems nevertheless to recognize in *State and Revolution* that a theory focusing upon change must also take into account continuity. He writes:

> Men . . . liberated from capitalist exploitation will gradually become accustomed to abide by the elementary rules of social life which have been known from time immemorial and have been set out for thousands of years in all regulations, and they will follow these rules without force, compulsion, subservience, and the special apparatus of compulsion which is known as the state.

One wants to reply: but if there are "elementary rules of social life . . . known from time immemorial," rules which can be fully realized only in a classless society, then it must follow that in earlier, class-dominated societies those rules became manifest in some way, otherwise we could not recognize their existence. There are, then, "perennial" problems of politics, by no means so "elementary" either—considering the fact that they have never been solved, nor seem likely ever to be entirely solved. And these problems cannot be dismissed by references to class or historical contexts, though obviously class or historical contexts give them varying shape and significance. They are problems, it might be acknowledged, that have been discussed with greater depth, because more genuine interest, by conservatives and liberals than by socialists.

The Marxist/socialist criticism of liberalism regarding the relation of politics to society now seems less cogent, or at least requires greater complication, than it did half a century ago. And this for an additional reason: with the growth of the modern industrial state, in both its Western and Eastern versions, politics takes on a new primacy, indeed, a kind of "independence," vis-à-vis the institutions and mechanisms of the economy. In the Communist countries, what happens to the economy, what is done with one or another segment of the working class, how the peasants are treated in the kolkhoz: all stem from political decision. Far from the ruling party bureaucracy being a mere agency of, or even (as Trotsky believed) a parasite upon, one of the social classes, the party bureaucracy is the decisive sociopolitical force in the country, akin to, even if not quite like, a ruling class. State and society tend to merge in totalitarian countries, so that traditional discriminations between politics and economics come to seem of little use.

In advanced capitalist countries, the state increasingly takes over crucial functions of the market, while still allowing a considerable measure of autonomy to corporations and private business. These developments have been noted frequently and need not be elaborated here; suffice it to say that insofar as they persist, some of the apparently sealed conclusions from the long debate between liberalism and socialism need to be reopened. The traditional liberal notions of politics cannot, of course, be exhumed, but neither can the traditional socialist objections to them be repeated with confidence. What can be said, tentatively, is that the liberal insistence upon politics as a mode of autonomous human action with "laws" and

and "rules" of its own has come to have a new persuasiveness and, not least of all, within socialist thought.

• There is a criticism of liberal politics and thought that runs through the whole of the socialist literature but, by now, can also be heard at many points to the right and left of liberalism: among "organicist" conservatives, followers of the young Marx, Christian socialists, syndicalists, communitarian New Leftists. This criticism is most often expressed as a defense of the values of community— human fellowship, social grouping—against egotism, competition, private property. Necessarily, it raises questions about the quality of life in bourgeois society: the failure of a common culture, the burdens placed upon the family when people lack alternative spheres of cooperative activity, the breakdown of social discipline that follows from laissez faire. This criticism also takes a political form: the argument that democracy requires public life, that it cannot be successfully maintained in a society of privatized persons whose interests are confined to their families and businesses, and that public life depends upon a sharing of political and economic goods. Does it not seem likely that some of the ills of American society follow from the situation described in this attack upon classical liberalism?

The idea of economic man is declared to be a libel upon humanity; the vision of extreme individualism, an impoverishment of social possibility; and the kind of life likely to emerge from a society devoted to such ideas, a terrible drop from traditional humanist and Christian standards.

Most thoughtful liberals have by now acknowledged the force of this criticism. Indeed, there is rather little in it that cannot be found in John Stuart Mill's essays on Bentham and Coleridge. In the long run, then, freedom of criticism does seem to yield some benefits, does seem to prompt spokesmen for major political-intellectual outlooks to complicate and modify their thought. Liberal criticism has made a difference in socialism; socialist criticism, in liberalism.

Still, who does not feel the continued poignancy in the yearning for community, which seems so widespread in our time? Who does not respond, in our society, to the cry that life is poor in shared experiences, vital communities, free brother (sister) hoods?

Yet precisely the pertinence and power of this attack upon traditional liberalism must leave one somewhat uneasy. For we must remember that we continue to live in a time when the yearning for community has been misshaped into a gross denial of personal integrity, when the desire for the warmth of social bonds—marching together, living together, huddling together, complaining in concert—has helped to betray a portion of the world into the shame of the total state.

One hears, these days, celebrations of the fact that in Communist China large masses of people actively "participate" in the affairs of state. They do. And it is not necessary to believe they always do so as a response to terror or force in order to be persuaded that the kind of "participation" to which they yield themselves is a denial of human freedom.

Let us be a little more cautious, then, in pressing the attack upon liberalism that invokes an image of community—a little more cautious if only because this attack is so easy to press. There is indeed an element of the paltry in the more extreme versions of liberal individualism; but the alienation that has so frequently, and rightly, been deplored in recent decades may have its sources not only in the organization of society but in the condition of mankind. Perhaps it is even to be argued that there is something desirable in recognizing that, finally, nothing can fully protect us from the loneliness of our selves.

A social animal, yes; but a solitary creature too. Socialists and liberals have some areas of common interest in balancing these two stresses, the communal and the individual, the shared and the alone. It is a balance that will tilt; men and women must be free to tilt it.

• Functioning for a good many decades as an opposition movement, and one, moreover, that could not quite decide whether it wished to be brought into society or preferred to seek a "total" revolutionary transformation, the socialist movement systematically attacked liberalism for timidity, evasiveness, vacillation, "rotten compromise," etc. It charged that liberalism was weak, that it never dared to challenge the socioeconomic power of the bourgeoisie, that it was mired in what Trotsky called "parliamentary cretinism," etc.

The historical impact of this criticism can hardly be overestimated. A major source of the "welfare state," insofar as we have one, has surely been the pressure that socialist movements have exerted upon a liberalism that has long gone past its early elan. Insofar as the socialist criticism served to force liberalism into awareness of and militancy in coping with social injustice, the results have been for the better.

But also—for the worse. For the socialist criticism (as the rise of bolshevism and its various offshoots make clear) contained at least two strands: one that disdained liberalism for its failure to live up to its claims and one that disdained liberalism for its success in living up to its claims. We touch here upon a great intellectual scandal of the age: the tacit collaboration of right and left in undermining the social and moral foundations of liberalism. In the decades between the Paris Commune and World War II both right- and left-wing intellectuals were gravely mistaken, and morally culpable, in their easy and contemptuous dismissal of liberalism. That the society they saw as the tangible embodiment of bourgeois liberalism required scathing criticism I do not doubt. But they failed utterly to estimate the limits of what was historically possible in their time, as they failed, even more importantly, to consider what the consequences might be of their intemperate attacks upon liberalism. It was all very well to denounce liberalism as what Ezra Pound called—Lenin would have agreed—"a mess of mush"; but to assault the vulnerable foundations of liberal democracy meant to bring into play social forces the intellectuals of both right and left could not foresee. There were, as it turned out, far worse things in the world than "a mess of mush."

Bourgeois Europe was overripe for social change by the time of World War I. But the assumptions that such change required a trampling on liberal values in the name of hierarchical order or proletarian dictatorship and that liberal values were inseparable from cultural decadence and capitalist economy—these assumptions proved a disaster. In the joyful brutality of their verbal violence many intellectuals, at both ends of the political spectrum, did not realize how profound a stake they had in preserving the norms of liberalism. They felt free to sneer at liberalism because, in a sense, they remained within its psychological orbit; they could not really imagine its destruction and took for granted that they would continue to enjoy its shelter. Even the most authoritarian among them could not foresee a situation in which *their* freedom would be destroyed. Dreaming of natural aristocrats or sublime proletarians, they helped pave the way for maniac *lumpen*.

● Still another socialist/radical criticism of liberalism, familiar from polemics of the '30s but urgently revived during the last decade by the New Left, is that the structure of liberties in democratic society rests on a shared acquiescence in the continued power of the bourgeoisie; that these liberties survive on condition they not be put to the crucial test of basic social transformation—and that they might well be destroyed by the bourgeoisie or its military agencies if a serious effort were made by a democratically elected government to introduce socialist economic measures. The overthrow of the Allende regime in Chile has been cited as a telling confirmation.

It is an old problem. Marx and Engels suggested that a socialist transition in such countries as England and Holland, with their deep-rooted democratic traditions, might be peaceful. Most other European countries not yet having completed the "bourgeois revolution" by the mid-nineteenth century, it seemed reasonable to the founders of "scientific socialism" that revolutionary methods might be necessary on the continent—though we also know that later, when the German Social Democracy became a mass party, Engels accepted the parliamentary course. The standard Bolshevik gloss would soon be that since the time Marx and Engels had written, the bourgeois state in England and Holland had grown more powerful, developing a traditional apparatus of repression. Thereby, the expectation of peaceful transition had become obsolete.

I think it would be an error to dismiss the Marxist criticism on this point as outmoded or irrelevant. Changes in class rule have in the past rarely come about without one or another quantity of violence, and as I remember hearing and saying in my youth, ruling classes don't just fold up their tents and slink away. By the same token, I now reply to my younger self, past changes in class rule have rarely, if ever, taken place within established democratic societies, hence could not be said to provide a test of the socioeconomic strains democratic societies can be expected to sustain.

To insist that liberalism and/or liberties must collapse under a serious effort to introduce socialist measures signifies:

(a) an unfortunate concession to those right-wing ideologues who insist that political liberty is inseparable from and could not survive the destruction of private property; or

(b) a vision of socialist transformation so "total" and apocalyptic that the collapse of political liberties in such circumstances could as readily be the work of revolutionary insurgents as of a resistant bourgeoisie. (To concede, after all, that liberalism could not survive a "dictatorship of the proletariat" in the Leninist or Leninist-Stalinist versions is hardly very damaging to the claim that liberalism can coexist with more than one form of economy.)

As for the historical evidence, it seems inconclusive and mixed. A very great deal, perhaps everything, depends on the strength of attachment among a people to democratic values; only a bit less, on the ability of a given society to avoid the kind of economic cataclysms that would put this attachment under excessive strain. If, say, the social democratic governments of Scandinavia and England, ruling with substantial majorities and elected as parties pledged to go considerably beyond welfare-state measures, were to introduce extensive socialist measures, there is not much reason to expect major extralegal efforts to undo their policies.[5] For the tradition of pacific social life and "playing by the rules" seems strong enough in such countries to allow one to envisage a major onslaught against the power of corporations and large business without risking the survival of democracy.

(I referred a few sentences back to governments with substantial majorities. It seems reasonable, after all, that a government that squeaks into office with a narrow margin should exercise restraints in any effort to introduce major social change.)

At least in some "advanced" European countries, the problem would not seem to be the bourgeoisie itself—by now a class without an excess of self-confidence. Socialist anxiety as to the ability of a liberal society to absorb major change might more appropriately be directed toward the middle classes and the army, which can no longer be assumed to act (if ever they did) as mere pliant agents and accomplices of the bourgeoisie. It is by no means clear that the Chilean experiences "prove" that a democratic path to socialism is impossible. What it may prove is:

(a) that a left-wing government trying to maintain democratic norms while introducing major social change must be especially sensitive to the interests and sentiments of the middle class; and that

(b) the army, acting out of its own interests and sentiments, can become an independent political force, establishing a dictatorial regime that it might well be a mistake to see as a mere creature of bourgeois restoration.

The role of armies in contemporary politics is a fascinating problem, beyond discussion here. Except for this: in a variety of circumstances, but especially where a mutual weakening of antagonistic classes has occurred, the army (like the state) can take on an unexpected autonomy. Nor is it clear that this follows the traditional Marxist expectation that the army would be employed by the ruling class to save its endangered interests. Even if that was true in Chile, it was not in Peru. And in sharply different ways, it has not been true in Portugal or Greece. In Asian and African countries, the role of the army is evidently that of a makeshift power compensating for the feebleness of all social classes. There is, then, something new here, not quite anticipated in liberal or socialist thought.

The question whether a liberal democratic regime can peacefully sustain major social or socialist changes remains open. If a categorical negative is unwarranted, so too is an easy reassurance. Given the probable configuration of politics in the Western democracies, there is some reason to conclude that even left-socialist regimes staying within democratic limits would have to proceed more cautiously, with greater respect for the multiplicity of group interests, than the usual leftist expectations have allowed. And the anxiety provoked by a possible effort to combine liberal polity with socialist economy remains a genuine anxiety, shared by both liberals and socialists.

● If we confine ourselves to the "advanced" countries, one criticism socialists have come increasingly to make of liberalism is that it fails to extend sufficiently its democratic concerns from the political to the economic realm.[6] Early in the century the distinguished British liberal writer L.T. Hobhouse put the matter elegantly: " . . . liberty without equality is a name of noble sound and squalid result." I will not linger on this point except to note:

(a) It suggests that the difference between social liberalism and democratic socialism keeps growing smaller, so that at some point it may become no more than incremental. Both traditional liberal thinkers and Marxist theoreticians would deny this; a good many social democrats, in effect, believe it.

(b) It leaves aside what in a fuller consideration could not be left aside: that there remain serious liberal criticisms of socialist proposals, e.g., that efforts to legislate greater equality of wealth, income, and power in economic life will seriously impair political liberty, and that the statist version of socialism (the only realistic one, say some liberal critics) would bring about a fearful concentration of power.

(c) We may be ready to subscribe to the socialist criticism that modern liberalism fails sufficiently to extend its democratic concerns to economic life—e.g., the governance of corporations; we may also share the socialist desire for greater participation of the masses in political and economic decision-making; but, to turn things around, I would largely accept the liberal dislike for schemes involving "mass" or "direct" democracy. Such schemes, insofar as they would brush aside representative institutions (elections, parliaments, etc.) in favor of some sort (but which sort?) of "direct" or "participatory" rule, are likely to end up as hopelessly vague or as prey to demagogic techniques for manipulating those who "participate" in movements, meetings, plebiscites, etc. If the survival of democracy depends on greater popular participation, greater popular participation by no means insures or necessarily entails the survival of democracy. Under modern conditions representative insitutions are indispensable to democratic societies; any proposals for "transcending" them, even if they come through socialist goodwill, should be regarded with suspicion.

• There is, finally, the plenitude of attacks directed against liberalism along a spectrum of positions ranging from the reactionary to the revolutionary, most of them chastising its "deeper" failures as a philosophical outlook. So copious is this literature, there is hardly a need to cite texts or authorities.

Liberalism, we are told, accepts an egalitarianism that a day or two spent with open eyes in our mass society show to be insupportable—while a sage like Professor Leo Strauss makes clear the traditional warrants and esoteric virtues of hierarchy. Liberalism proposes a belief in rational harmony, the "illusion" (to quote Kenneth Minogue) "of ultimate agreement" among men, "and perhaps most central of all, the idea that will and desire can ultimately be sovereign in human affairs"—while a sage like Professor Michael Oakeshott tells us that life is muddle, efforts at rational structuring of our affairs are likely to lead to still greater muddle, even, perhaps, to tyranny. Liberalism congeals into the simplistic notion, as Lionel Trilling has written, "that the life of man can be nicely settled by correct social organization, or short of that, by the election of high moral attitudes." Liberalism, focusing obsessively upon change, distracts us from the essentials of existence largely beyond the grasp of mere reason or public agency. Liberalism has a false view of the human situation, refusing to take into account the irrationalities and aggressions of our nature. (How can a liberal cope with the realities of the Hobbesian jungle? What can a good-hearted liberal make of the Freudian view of the human heart?) Liberalism ignores or dispatches the tragic sense of life, turning people away from that suffering which is unavoidable (perhaps even good?) in our experience. Liberalism replaces the warming cohesion of traditional communities with a rootless anonymity. Liberalism cannot cope with the mysteries of death, as Christianity does through its myth of resurrection, or existentialism tries, through its unblinking gaze into the void.

What is one to say of these criticisms? That often they confuse the historical genesis of liberalism, accompanied as it was by excessive claims, with later and more realistic versions of liberalism; that the alleged rootlessness of liberal man, though clearly surrounded with difficulties, also has brought unprecedented freedoms and opportunities, indeed, entire new visions of the personal self; that the increasing stress of modern liberal thought upon a pluralist society indicates at least some recognition of clashing interests, irreconcilable needs, confrontations of class; that a recognition of the irrational and aggressive components of human conduct can become an argument in favor of limitations upon power favored by liberalism; that we may recognize weaknesses and limitations in liberalism as a *Weltanschauung*—indeed, refuse to see it as a *Weltanschauung*—while still fervently believing that a liberal polity allows for the best realization of human diversity and freedom; that there is no necessary conflict between "dark" views of the human condition and an acceptance of the liberal style in public life.

Let us grant, then, some of the criticisms made of liberal afflatus (usually in the past) and liberal smugness (usually in the present), and admit, as well, the probability that insofar as men need religious myths and rites to get through their time on earth, liberalism is not likely to offer enough satisfaction. What needs to be stressed, all the same, is that a commitment to the liberal style in politics does not necessarily imply a commitment to a total world view claiming to include all experience from private fantasy to public authority. (Perhaps we would all be better off to live, for a time, without total world views.)

Toward these and similar exchanges between liberalism and its critics, socialists have shown a very wide range of responses. The more extreme leftist tendencies, verging on the authoritarian and chiliastic, have been tempted to borrow some of the arguments of the right, especially those releasing contempt for the flaccid moderation of liberalism, its alleged failures to confront painful realities of social life and human nature. But for those socialists who largely accept the premises of a liberal polity, there are other problems, notably the disconcerting fact that the bulk of the philosophical-existential criticism directed against liberalism can be brought to bear with equal cogency against social democracy.

III

Unavoidably, this leads to the question: apart from whatever capacity both liberalism and social democracy show for handling our socioeconomic difficulties, how well can they cope with—I choose deliberately a portentous term—the crisis of civilization that many people feel to be encompassing our lives? The crisis of civilization that besets the twentieth century has to do, in part, with a breakdown in the transmission and common acceptance of values—which may also be a way of saying, with residual but powerful yearnings toward transcendence. Insofar as this occurs, there follows a pervasive uncertainty as to the "meanings" and ends of existence. One sign of this crisis is the resurgence in Western society of a strident contempt for the ethic of liberal discourse and the style of rationality. Partly this arises from the mixed failings and successes of the welfare state, but partly from an upswell of ill-understood religious sentiments that, unable to find a proper religious outlet, become twisted into moral-political absolutism, a hunger for total solutions and apocalyptic visions. Impatience with the sluggish masses, burning convictions of righteousness, the suffocations of technological society, the boredom of overcrowded cities, the yearning for transcendent ends beyond the petty limits of group interest, romantic-sinister illusions about the charismatic virtues of dictatorship in underdeveloped countries—all these tempt intellectuals and semi-intellectuals into apolitical politics registering an amorphous revulsion from civilization itself.

The customary rationalism of earlier generations of socialists (and liberals too) could hardly grasp such a development. Yet, no matter how distant we may be from the religious outlook, we must ask ourselves whether the malaise of our time isn't partly a consequence of that despairing emptiness which has followed the breakup of traditional religious systems in the nineteenth century; whether the nihilism that sensitive people feel to be seeping through their lives may not itself testify to a kind of inverted religious aspiration; whether the sense of moral disorientation that afflicts us isn't due to the difficulties of keeping alive a high civilization without a sustaining structure of belief.

Perhaps, in honesty, there really is no choice but to live with the uncomfortable aftereffects of this disintegration of religious belief, which has brought not only the positive consequences some of us hoped for but also others that leave us discomfited. In any case, nothing seems more dubious than the impulse I detect these days among rightward-moving intellectuals: a willing of faith in behalf of alleged social-moral benefits. Here, finally, liberals and democratic socialists find themselves in the same boat, even if at opposite ends of it. The Fabian course to which some of us are committed seems to me politically good and perhaps even realistic, but we ought to acknowledge that this course fails to stir the passions or speak to the needs of many people. We ought to acknowledge that between the politics we see as necessary and the expressive-emotional needs that break out recurrently in Western society there are likely to be notable gaps. I think, by way of homely instance, of a remark made to me a few years ago by a very decent and intelligent liberal professor: "But the politics of social democracy [he might also have said liberalism] are so boring!" It is a troubling remark, and one that may help explain why cultivated people of liberal training can be drawn to illiberal causes and impulses. We can only worry about this matter, recognizing that it may be one of those instances where virtue entails formidable deficits.

But let me end on a somewhat more hopeful note. Half a century from now, one fact about our time may come to be seen as the most crucial. Whatever the separate or linked failures of liberalism and democratic socialism may be, there have come to us these past twenty or twenty-five years voices from the East superbly reasserting the values of freedom, tolerance, openness of discourse. These men and women have, thus far, "failed"; they have been destroyed, imprisoned, humiliated, isolated. Yet their very appearance signifies an enormous moral triumph for both liberalism and democratic socialism. Beneath the snow, the seed has lived.

Footnotes

1. The philosophical underpinning is provided by Kant: "everyone is entitled to seek happiness in whatever manner seems best to him, provided that he does not interfere with the freedom of others to strive toward the same objective, which can coexist with the freedom of everyone else under a conceivable general law."

2. In *Capital*, 1, Marx applies his powers of sarcasm to such assumptions of "classical" liberalism: "The sphere of circulation and exchange of commodities within which labor is bought and sold was in reality a paradise of innate human rights—governed entirely by freedom, equality, property, and Bentham! Freedom! Because the buyers and sellers of a commodity, such as labor-power, are constrained only according to their own free will. They enter into a contract as free and legally equal free agents. The contract is the final result in which their common free will is given common legal expression. Equality! Because their relationships with one another are purely those of the owners of commodities and they exchange like for like. Property! Because each individual makes use only of what belongs to him. Bentham! Because each of the two thinks only of himself. The only power that holds them together and establishes a relationship between them is their egotism, personal advantage, and private interest. And precisely because each individual thinks of himself and never of anyone else, they all work toward their mutual advantage, the general good and common interest, in accordance with a preestablished harmony of things or under the auspices of a cunning knowing providence."

3. Occasionally, there are counterinstances suggesting that "vulgar Marxism" may meet with correction from within traditions it has debased. A leader of the Spanish Communist party, one Luis, is quoted in the *New York Times* of October 29, 1975, saying: "We do not renounce a single one of the bourgeois liberties. If the bourgeoisie can dominate in freedom we want to provide more profound, more real liberties, not less. Socialism can provide the

economic base for more complete liberty, without restricting a single aspect of bourgeois liberty." How much credence, if any, to give to this man's claim to democratic belief I do not know; but the fact that he speaks as he does must be regarded as significant.

4. A word about the role of the working class in socialist thought, as it contrasts with the frequent claims of liberalism to rise "above" mere class interest. Granted the common criticism that Marxism has overestimated the revolutionary potential of the workers; granted that socialist rhetoric has sometimes romanticized the workers. It nevertheless remains that a major historical and moral conquest of the socialist movement, especially in the nineteenth century, was to enable the masses of the lowly to enter the stage of history and acquire a historical consciousness. Few developments in the last two centuries have so decisively helped the consolidation of democratic institutions; few have so painfully been exploited to violate democratic norms. It would be foolish to say that socialism alone should take credit for the entry of "the masses" into political life; but it was the socialists who gave this entry a distinct moral sanction. At its best, socialism enabled the formation of that impressive human type we know as the self-educated worker in the late nineteenth century. That the rise of the working class to articulation and strength could, nevertheless, be exploited for authoritarian ends is surely a major instance of the tragedy of progress.

5. Harold Laski, in his *Parliamentary Government in England* (1938), questioned whether democracy could survive if a labor government came to power and legislated a socialist program. In 1945 a labor government did come to power and legislated, if not a socialist program, then a huge welfare-state program decidedly akin to, or at least pointing the way toward, socialism. And democracy did not collapse. This does not yet "prove" that Laski was wrong; only that it would be unwise to assume that he was right.

6. A criticism anticipated in general terms by the early Marx: "Political emancipation is indeed a great step forward. It is not, to be sure, the final form of universal human emancipation, but it is the final form *within* the prevailing order of things. . . . Where the political state has achieved its full development, man leads a double life, a heavenly and an earthly life, not only in thought or consciousness but in *actuality*. In the *political community* he regards himself as a *communal being*; but in *civil society* he is active as a *private individual*, treats other men as means, reduces himself to a means, and becomes the plaything of alien powers."

PART TWO
America
in
Turmoil

PAUL GOODMAN
The Devolution of Democracy
(1962)

Democratic power springs from an enlightened electorate. The neglect of this possibility in America—the failure to protect and advance it with new form and content during a century and a half of expanding area and population, of complicating economy and frequently revolutionized technology, and broadening relations with the rest of the world—has resulted in an electorate so demoralized that it is a question if it is possible to govern democratically at all. We tend to take lightly Jefferson's famous remark about the necessity for a revolution every twenty years, every new generation, but it is probably literally true, to renew democracy as he conceived it. (Jefferson was not, in fact, given to ill-considered slogans nor even dogmatism; but in stupider times his Enlightenment daring seems outlandish.) Meantime, during that century and a half, while the democratic power was being corrupted and was dwindling, other kinds of power and inertia have boldly filled up the vacuum, up to our present feudal system of monopolies, military and other bureaucracies, party machines, communications networks, and Established institutions.

The Kennedy Administration came in—one speaks as if it were there a thousand years; will we get out of it alive?—after a marvelously established regime of business as usual. And it was going to "make America move." It would be a rule of things by active personalities instead of a bureaucratic staff; it would be a "disorderly"

Administration, in the sense that ideas and people could leap-frog the chain of command and clash and have it out; it would be rich with ideas, as guaranteed by putting in or near power such notorious thinkers of new thoughts as academics from prestigious colleges. What the activity and thought were to be toward, what the purpose was, was not clear—there were no issues in the campaign, no effort to enlighten the electorate—but it was called the New Frontier. Now in this essay I want to show that this *image* of a government, of active persons with no idea, indeed fits the real situation better than its only rival did, and the voters were aesthetically wise to choose it—by a squeak.

After a year, including a Hundred Days and everything, and having learned that it is powerless and irrelevant except to "lead" in an intensified Cold War (which is itself, of course, powerless and irrelevant to any human good), the boyish *élan* is more sober. A philosopher close to the President now explains to me that the best to be hoped from government is to "mitigate the evils of modern life." This Niebuhrian political theory is not very wise, for if the aim is *merely* to mitigate, and not attack the structure and causes of the evils, one will not *even* mitigate, for the structure aggrandizes itself and produces new evils. It is as with civil liberties: if one merely protects them, without increasing the opportunities of freedom, one loses them. So I demur. I am then lectured to the effect that "if you had lived in the Administration of Jefferson, you would have been dissatisfied in the same way." That is, after a year in "power" under the present conditions, the Administration has begun to rewrite American history and prove that democratic power is a myth.

Since, by this philosophy, man is incurably stupid and his institutions evil, we must not get too hot to reform this or that present evil. And so they think. For instance, when three or four of us ask another Harvard professor to put a little zip into counteracting the nausea of the mass media—we propose to him a couple of excellent libertarian plans and are even ready to write the legislation and outline the campaign to arouse public opinion—we are treated to the popular wisdom that "people get what they want" and "what great art was ever produced by subsidy?" (Needless to say, however, when Cultural Freedom and the Encounter of ideas are instruments of the CIA, means have been readily found to subsidize intellectual groups, even though nothing could be more treasonable to cultural freedom and the encounter of ideas.) But the problem, it seems to me, is an existential one; how does the professor, as an intellectual individual, keep down his nausea in front of the TV screen and not *have* to change? Presumably it is a government of men, and not an automatic machine, or what is the professor doing there?

Finally, on December 10, 1961, we have the answer in the Washington *Post*: scholars in government "are good for ungarbling what thinkers on the outside have written . . . and tabulating the points" (Professor Schlesinger). I am breathless with the thought that Walt Rostow, etc., or even Arthur Schlesinger, imagine they can write more clearly than thinkers on the outside; but I am indignant that such good talents should be misused for writing *précis*; it's like the waste of skills in the Army.

After a year, the conception of a government of active personalities and disorderly clash has crystallized into the doctrine of the "Web of Tensions," the use of internal conflict to generate ideas. This Hegelian notion is psychologically correct. In the present ground rules of the White House, however, it works out as follows: (1) There is a careful preselection of the combatants, so that no too obstreperous voice will disturb the proceedings, or laugh. (2) If anyone *in* the debate does disagree in a way awkward for the Cold War policy—and especially if his predictions prove correct—he is dropped. (3) At best in a megalopolis like the United States government, the Web of Controversy is far removed from even its own staff workers, who nevertheless have to provide relevant materials and know what they are doing when they execute orders. To these workers the effect of the Web of Tensions is confusion, the feeling of purposelessness or divided purpose, of being out of contact and therefore absolutely frustrated when their earnest efforts are disregarded for reasons that cannot be explained to them. They then naturally withdraw into the usual bureaucratic apathy, now not even orderly. (4) Nor is this difficulty helped if the tense thinkers are by disposition in-turned, unfriendly, and unpragmatic. (5) Last but not least, the inventive outgoing moment of the Tension, the reason for it altogether, is horribly inhibited by the fact that the thinkers don't have any power anyway. As one critic has observed, the Web of Tensions simply means that they are getting more tense.

I don't want to be unfair, though it is hard not to be sarcastic. In the centralized power complex that these people are committed to, and with the baroque conception of national sovereignty that they represent in a world that has come to have a different nature, it is probably impossible to govern. Both vested interests and the social-psychology of the people (and the influence of the vested interests in the social-psychology of the people) are fixed on the Cold War. Even the coalition that put Kennedy in office is too variegated to be maintained, and I shall try to show that he is reforming that coalition to be a better Cold War "leader.". The kind of revolutionary attitudes and do-or-die attempts at education that would make for government and tend again toward democratic power, are beyond the talents of these people; nor, of course, do they want them. They did not run, they were not elected, to thwart the "industrial-military complex," as the departing President called it: to make peace and internationalize the world; to diversify and decentralize our economy; really to help backward peoples according to their needs and customs rather than for our own profits and war aims in alliance with their ruling cliques; to revive civil liberties and try to improve the quality of American life. They did not campaign for these purposes, but I am puzzled why, except for the politicians, they did campaign.

II

To get a better view of Washington after a year, let us turn from these Top philosophers to those who are not in the Web of Tensions, though not a thousand miles away. Here is a collection of comments:

"Lot of activism: action for the sake of action." "The way they want to get something moving, you feel that they need to overcome something 'static' that is threatening to engulf them." "They don't know the difference between real power and the juvenile trappings of power." "You say that the Americans in general have a neurotic feeling of powerlessness, but you don't realize that those in power are equally frustrated." "As a matter of fact, there *is* a lot of loose power around, in Congress for instance, but he doesn't wield it." "If some Congressmen had monkey glands—"

"This Administration is peculiarly humorless, like phony actors.

At least Eisenhower was a genuine Rotarian." "'Posture' is the favorite word. The preposterous syntax in the President's speeches: 'Ask not—' 'Let no one think, etc.,' especially when he occasionally mispronounces common words." "The worst was the speech to the Latin Americans, peppered with Spanish quotations but nobody taught him how to pronounce the words. It was embarrassing." "The Roman style is highly esteemed: tough, terse, we play for keeps." "I think they were badly stung by that remark last spring that they were great dribblers but never made a basket. I think that the need to produce at all costs was one reason for the Cuban goof." "Kennedy took full responsibility for it, like a Roman—and made full use of the scapegoat that he had poor Intelligence. But Bobby shut up the ones who apparently had more accurate information."

"They act on schematic preconceptions, with a crazy emphasis on Analysis and Facts; completely unpragmatic." "They have a justified contempt for the 'fuzzy liberals' who spout generalities that have nothing to do with the concrete situations, but they don't understand that to get anywhere, you have to have an ideal, a pragmatic-end-in-view."

"Naturally, being unpragmatic, they are continually projecting and finding scapegoats, rather than having real obstacles to overcome." "They talk about the dilemmas inherited from Eisenhower; but how is their own policy any different?" "They are apprehensive of obstacles that don't even exist, for example, opposition in the Appropriations Committee on issues where there is no opposition. In my opinion, they do the same with the Russians. They never think of clearing up an ambiguity by going and asking; they always figure it out by Analysis and guessing. This isn't helped by an Intelligence that feeds them false facts." "They try to circumvent the preconceived obstacles by tricks. You get a memorandum an hour before the meeting, so there's no time to research it and back up your opposition. Perpetuation of errors."

"He is astoundingly sensitive to criticism in the press. Unlike Roosevelt who got mad and told them off. But Kennedy says, 'Now Jimmy Reston shouldn't have said a thing like that.'" "He calls in *Life* to explain himself to *them!* So it becomes a symbiosis: since he takes them seriously, they are flattered and give him a good press, and he gets sucked in." "Is he still worrying about the close vote? Or maybe

doubtful he should be there at all? By the way, why should he?"
"Kennedy believes that there is a terrific force of reaction, that
mustn't be confronted too fast, and one mustn't go too far."

"Of course, in an enterprise this big there's bound to be confusion and bad communications. But it doesn't help when they play it
cool and by ear. Take the private-shelter story in *Life*: a press officer
gave it out and there was a howl afterwards." "In the Eisenhower
chain-of-command routine, there was at some level a definite decision, also routine and usually lousy. But here one doesn't know *what*
has been decided, if anything." "If he had a policy, why didn't he fire
them all and put in his own people to pursue his policy? How much
obstruction can you put up with? In three years Chile will be
Communist even without Castro." "The difference under Roosevelt
was that the Secretary would draw everybody together and inspire
them with a pep talk; so that in *spite* of the bureaucracy they pulled
together and got going." "Well, in my agency the chief complaint is
that there isn't any contact with the bright young men who have
access to the White House. You ask, what do they talk about in the
White House? Oh, everything."

Finally, "There you are. All this talk around here finally tends to
revolve around what He is like, and that's boring. It is boring
because we're sick of talking about personalities instead of issues, or
is it boring because Kennedy is boring? It comes to the same thing.
Kennedy seems to me to be simple." "Maybe the chief use of this
Administration, especially after the last, is that it shows that livelier,
better-educated, and more likable people are even more boring in
this situation, unless they stand for something."

III

This is not a happy spectacle. Let me point out, however, that it
pretty accurately describes the behavior of a crew of hipsters, as
Mailer called them in 1960, not foreseeing the consequences. It is
the cool and activist role-playing of vitality in a situation of impotence. (The impotence is caused partly by obstacles and partly by
their characters.) Like the artist and live person he is, Mailer responded accurately to the type during the campaign; he missed its
meaning because he is (transiently, I hope) a chump. He is a great

one for the style, the *nuance*, of life; he failed to remember that, as Kant said, a characteristic of art is to be *Zweck ohne Zweck*, purposive without a purpose. More serious has been the error of the liberals who were "realistic" and who, instead of going about their business of dissenting and building a movement that they believed in, supported Kennedy on the theory that, once elected, he would drop the morals and techniques that got him the nomination. But to no reasonable person's surprise, the Administration proves, after the election, to have the same basic character as when the candidate was wresting the nomination and waging an uphill campaign. Being in office, however, is less favorable than campaigning for the display of jumpy vitality well-heeled, morally uncommitted and intellectually shallow. Unfortunately, the end is not yet.

Of course I am judging by a high standard, but otherwise why bother? Why should these people seek office unless they had a useful idea and felt indispensable to execute it? Omit Kennedy and ask about the professors. They have given up citizenly independence and freedom of criticism in order to be servants of the public and friends of the cops. Presumably this is for the utility of power rather than the vanity of power. What? how? The answer is Analysis and Tabulation. In like manner, the scientists make bombs and missiles, but they do not make policy and they do not strike to enforce peace.

IV

The impotence of the Administration is due, I have said, to the past down-slope of our history and its present irrelevance to world history-making. These causes are intrinsically related, for if the United States were not the kind of society it has become, its Administration could work toward a world order. Our emergency is not in Berlin, etc., as the newspapers keep proclaiming, but in the economic, social, and psychological need for the Cold War. (Thus, if I were asked how to save us from Russian bombs, the first step would be to free the TV channels, for real controversy and true reporting on international affairs, for criticism and programming in our municipal and vocational lives, so that people would have to face the things that matter.)

With whatever hopes and purposes the Administration came in (and, as Oscar Gass has pointed out, these were already quite marginal and inoffensive to anybody), it has met the massiveness of the status quo and its established powers, venal, blimpish, police-ridden, prejudiced, and illiberal; officially existing in the Pentagon, the Treasury, the FBI, the Civil Service, the Scientific corporations, a large part of Congress. Eisenhower's Administration, in its personnel and motives and chain-of-command staff work, rather simply expressed these underlying existing forces and inertias; it therefore had—especially in the retrospect of having survived it—a certain solid impressiveness. The picture on the box was the same as the contents. With the best will in the world, the status quo is a rocky mass to move; but of course the son of Joseph Kennedy had no such foolish idea. His first official act was to continue the existing FBI and CIA, and that was already the end of working toward a new America or a new world. The Wall Street stalwarts—Dillon, McCone, Foster, etc.—were brought back as they would have been if Nixon had won. The Pentagon could become only more so. Inevitably the subordinates of the agencies would be unchanged, but in a large number of cases the same types were returned to make policy, or obstruct "policy." (Foreign Aid is a sad example, as if the racketeering governments in the aid-countries were not intractable enough; and although, politically, even the Cold Warriors rightly fear that these countries will be "lost.") Must we not assume that "tragic" bureaucratic mishaps and failures-to-communicate are importantly due to the persistence of forces that want no change?

So we are presented with the embarrassingly *un*impressive spectacle of impotence among men who, by their personality, intelligence, and freer methods have promised to make America move; an irrelevant activism, a "tough" "hard" "posture" (it is necessary to put every word in quotation marks), and an astounding timidity that results from trying to be different from their own class strength and class needs, although they have neither a new idea to give courage nor a revolutionary will to make a change. That, on the domestic scene, there *is* no such new idea nor will to useful change, you can observe by looking out the window or thumbing through *Life*; the scene is, as might be feared, the same, only a year more so. More big money, more unashamed tax dodgers, more cops, and more army.

The war budget is at least 25 percent more than Mr. Eisenhower's last; but otherwise the "public sector," that Ken Galbraith was vocal about, is not further nourished. Some in Washington say that the Education bill was beaten by a "tragic" combination of perplexities —Negro-white, parochial-public, poor states–rich states; others, however, say that Dillon could afford it, that it was legislatively handled precisely in order to lose, and what evidence *is* there that Kennedy cares anything about Education? The *New York Times* has editorially described his interest as "tepid." That is, the program for a better quality of American life was fairly trivial to begin with (the liberals claimed that this moderation was necessary in order to win the election), but the will to achieve even this program has been lacking.

The field of action has been international affairs. It is estimated that three-quarters of the President's calendar is devoted to foreign and military matters, and certainly other matters are considered in this light, as fits the budget. The address to the Manufacturers strongly makes this point: when business is good, we look good in the world. Civil rights for Negroes are never spoken of as social justice but always as enhancing our Image in Africa and Asia. (I asked a young Ethiopian what *was* the image of America in Ethiopia; he said that the vast majority of his people never heard of America.) The pressing problems of Youth are recognized by the Administration either as delinquency to be handled by the Justice Department or in terms of the few thousand, FBI-screened, in the Peace Corps.

Yet here too, because of circumstances, action is impotent— except for the one grim potency of destroying everything. At present the administration of any sovereign state can make world sense only by fitting into and furthering the inevitable development of the world community, and indeed by relaxing its own sovereignty. The interesting and long-range movement of the world has to do with increasing communications, exchange of people, the vanishing of colonialism and the rise of backward peoples from poverty, regional economic cooperation for mutual advantage. These secular movements occur, of course, according to their own laws, independent of Washington. A powerful national government can act in them only by contributing to them, perhaps leading. But an American administration is bedeviled in these things by business as usual and militarism, provincialism, and jingoism. We cannot exchange goods with half the world; we cannot even talk to the Chinese. We cannot feed famine, though we have a surplus; we cannot give help to peoples except through our "friends," their rulers who rob them; and if a region is not a battleground, it is not considered useful to help at all. We put an ex-FBI man in charge of immigration. We cannot educate without propagandizing. We cannot engage in space exploration without competing, nor develop modern technology without polluting the atmosphere. We cannot strengthen the parliament of nations lest it evade our grip. And of course the behavior of all the other sovereignties—including new-fledged cannibals and feudal lordlings as well as tall generals and ideologists even crazier than our own—confounds the frustration.

The sphere of free action diminishes. Even Latin America is increasingly frustrating. The chief current idea seems to be the perfecting of the arrangements begun by Truman and continued by Eisenhower, with the big new power associated with the Common Market. As McGeorge Bundy put it on December 6, "It would be better if Western Europe were one great power . . . with the economic strength, the military self-confidence, the political unity of a true great power"; and on the same day the President plugged for trade arrangements with Europa. (By the way, what will prevent French rights and German skill and money from becoming a third nuclear giant?) Bundy warns that our rapprochement with Europa might amount to a Rich Man's Club against the rest of the world— yes, so it might; but in terms reminiscent of the White Man's burden, Walt Rostow mentions the responsibility of the "North" for developing the "South." In my opinion this allied policy is better than Barry Goldwater's isolated fortress of America, but it will not exactly kindle the enthusiasm of the nations toward the peace and unity of the world.

But the chief outlet for frustrated action is, of course, armaments and threatening postures. Oscar Gass deliciously reports the expression "posture of sacrifice" as a threat. Most often, the style is that of a frustrated juvenile delinquent who fears he might be judged inactive and probably powerless. This is younger than hipster, but it must be remembered that in international affairs statesmen always regress to more adolescent attitudes, whether friendly or hostile.

We play the game of "Chicken." There is gloating that our "tough" "hard" "policy" had "won" in Berlin. Soldiers are mobilized and will perhaps be demobilized. We will have Bomb Shelters and defy them. Walt Rostow is training guerrillas, since Castro did so well with them. (This is puzzling. Into what friendly countryside are the American guerrillas supposed to melt? Surely he means commandos?) The more hip age-level of the same frustration syndrome is Game Theory applied to war. In Game Theory, the Web of Tensions is finally isolated completely from any contact with common reason, biological safety, or even any opponent except one's projections. All members of the Administration are experts in Game Theory.

A necessity for maintaining the Roman or cool posture is to have the situation always under control and not to be embarrassed by a goof or booboo. Unfortunately, this entails many contradictions. Since slant-eyed peasants are not really under one's control, since often one's best-considered efforts, as in Venezuela, work out opposite to what one planned, since from the beginning one is operating by a preconceived scheme, there are bound to be blunders and the threatening posture renders them more disastrous and more embarrassing. It is not possible to relent, atone, make amends, for these postures are "weak." On the other hand, to alibi, to be touchy to criticism, apprehensive of being misunderstood, fearful of future criticism, timid of commitment, forced to be consistent—these postures are also glaringly "weak." (One had the impression that Cuba, etc., was intimidating in this way, as if a gang suddenly realized they were on a tougher block than they had been brought up on.) There is then nothing for it but to strengthen reprisals and enlarge the arsenal. This is called the Cold War, and of course this has become the greatest frustration of all, since the final and only proof of power, to fight and win, entails suicide and losing. That is, the outlet for frustrated activity is a scene where activity is frustrated.

Gordon Christiansen, the chemist, argues that the newer tactics of the Cold War are *solely* for home consumption. Since the bomb shelters are scientifically fraudulent, they will not deceive the Russians; so their purpose, he says, must be a calculated deception of the Americans, to prepare for our making a first strike. This is too shocking to believe; and also, I think, it is too ill-considered as a

political policy for such astute politicians. Given the rising protest of
so many respected scientists and students and even children, and
many mothers, pushing the Civil Defense might result in riots on
the streets. It is simpler to take it as the inevitable accumulation of
frenzied expedients, as with the beast in *The Burrow*. But of course
this comes to the same end result, as Christiansen fears. The breakdown of common sense and morals in the continuing Cold War
makes it more and more indifferent who will be "guilty."

V

As is apparent from all the foregoing, the demography of the
Administration consists of the Status Quo, the Coalition on which it
was elected, and its own characteristic groups, viz.:

(1) Wall Street Republicans, continuing.

(2) The Pentagon, continuing, in which we must include the
aristocrats of military science in Rand and Aerospace. These
latter, since more mentally busy, are more bellicose than professional generals whose aims, on retirement, seem to be intensely
economic and therefore they have an incentive to retire alive.

(3) Bureaucracy and Civil Service in the other agencies, also
mostly continuing.

(4) FBI and CIA, continuing. These are, again, activist-violent
in disposition. The FBI is more lower-class, the CIA more
middle-class. But the aristocrats of the violent-minded are the
new-come professors from the old OSS, trained in the prudence
of Strategic Bombing. About half a dozen members of this Club
have access.

(5) The fuzzy liberals, part of the coalition who don't really
belong. But even Harriman would be called a liberal. (Reuther,
of the UAW, is said to be a useful friend.)

(6) The professors. These are characteristic and fall into various types: for example, Schlesinger, Wofford, or Galbraith more
for thought and speeches; Rostow more for power postures;
Bundy more for administering.

(7) A number of genuine intellectuals, interested in prudent
and ideal action. These are mostly younger men—like the young

instructors or assistant professors at universities, who suggest curriculum changes. This group is also characteristic of the Administration and gives it a livelier tone than its predecessor.

(8) The President's entourage for special assignments, with Irish names that roll on the tongue. We may here include Robert Kennedy. These are called, probably unfairly, the Irish Mafia.

(9) Besides, there is an unofficial night-life circle, generally upper-class and violent-minded. Important is Joseph Alsop who is said to leak hard-to-get data in order to push his activist policies and interests, e.g., the National Estimate of missiles. Alsop's tack is as follows: two years ago he said there was a missile gap, so we had to build fast; now he says that the gap was exaggerated, we are way ahead, so we can take risks. This gets you coming and going.

As might be expected, the glossary and style has strains of (1) Madison Avenue. For example, "hard" and "soft" are applied to research; "hard" research contains numerals. "Shop," as "over in Charley Hitch's shop." "Sanitize" is very good: it means to doctor a report, as to Congress, to take out the virulence. (2) Rand Corporation: "escalate," "hardware," "parameters"—"what are the parameters of the problem?" A horror is "wargasm," meaning all-out retaliation, which I recommend to Mailer for his hipster-theory. (3) Armed services: "tough" and other terms of panic about masculinity. (4) Lionel Trilling–literary, especially "posture."

A curiosity that deserves special mention, however, is "exercise," as "A crude propaganda exercise," referring to a Soviet complaint about a Nazi in NATO. (British? I read in R. H. S. Crossman, "The aim of the exercise is clear," referring to a book he is reviewing.) The denotation is that the activity is only practice, it is not the real thing, it is not for keeps. Addressed to an inferior in a bureaucracy it can be crushingly one-up, for it means that there are grownups who do real things. But when used generally, as it is, it connotes that oneself is not *yet* altogether for real, one is waiting to graduate and get to work. (This is strictly the Cold War situation.) The next meaning—reinforced by the academic metaphor itself—is that *all* activity is merely academic, detached from any serious possibility of life. Since it is necessary to put up an appearance of being alive, one then adopts a posture or stance. *But such persons could commit suicide.*

Finally, I must call attention to words like "discipline" "sacrifice" "responsibility" and "challenge," which in Kennedy's mouth have a special stoical-Catholic tinkle. ("In this grave period, labor must discipline itself . . ." "The press must discipline itself and assume responsibility . . .") This is not the Catholicism that was touchy during the campaign, the prospect of Pope John in the White House (oh, to have had that fat man instead of Kennedy or Nixon!). It is the more moral Catholicism of the little boy who disciplines himself from masturbating and checks off his victorious days on the calendar. Masturbating proves you are weak and makes you weak. In this context, "challenge" is the kind of strenuous excitement possible to persons who, having given up their internal spontaneity, rally to an external demand; and then (as Murray Kempton judges) Kennedy is animated, genuine, physically courageous, and even unself-consciously humorous.

(To my ear, in the rhetoric of Kennedy's big set speeches, there is an incompatibility between the two strains of the stoical-Catholic and the figure-of-history. The sense of duty does not seem to be himself, but his submissive—and evasive—obedience to some grownups; one is not convinced of his moral courage. The call-to-glory is warmer and more personal, but it is juvenile. How can a figure-of-history be spiritually inhibited? He cannot grow his myth but must finally manufacture it. With the best efforts of Madison Avenue and the History Department, such prose will not turn to poetry.)

VI

This brings me to the main theme of these reflections, the possible future of this character of Administration in our present democracy, the formation of what I shall call a New Consensus. We have now had the Cold War for fifteen years and it is about time that it became politically domesticated, with its own ethos and person-nel. In the present Administration we have a remarkable and *or-ganic* amalgam of the heirs and co-workers of America First and McCarthy and the heirs of Democratic Liberalism. This has an historical meaning. I cannot agree with otherwise excellent observers that we can write off the New Frontier as simply another sell for business as usual, for history does not simply repeat. Let me revert to my opening sentence, the failure of democracy by neglecting to improve the electorate. We then have, in scheme, the following devolution:

(1) For Jefferson, the chief use of democracy was to improve the electorate and so itself; people learn by deciding, including making mistakes. He championed decentralization, for people can reasonably decide only what they know about intimately. Madison hit on federalism as a revolutionary device for experimentation, for if the small group made a mistake, it did little harm to the whole; if it found something useful, it could be adopted by others and benefit the whole. One is struck by the pragmatism of such political thought, transforming the town meeting into an experimental, self-improving unit with provision for expanding society. Any basic function could be the principle for the small political unit; e.g., to provide primary education, Jefferson suggested the militia-company or hundred. Applied to industry, the unit is the soviet. The political units select their federal delegates; this is democratic centralism from below.

(2) With the Jacksonian revolution, as de Tocqueville was quick to see, the democratic idea was already abandoned, for the power now resided in the majority of the people *as they were*, with their passions and prejudices uneducated by the responsible give-and-take in a face-to-face meeting that had to make practical decisions and use tax money. Instead, the people would merely vote on issues and party programs. This was an invitation for demagogues and party-leaders to get power, and for lobbying interests, that could deliver votes and cash, to influence the politicians for their own power.

(3) Through the nineteenth century, these nonpublic and non-governmental powers, bankers and industrialists, vastly increased their influence. Attempts to control them, e.g., by silver legislation and trust-busting, themselves centralized and increased the governmental power. But what was tragic was that grass-roots politics, like the agrarian and labor movements, also followed the centralized bureaucratic style. And of course the stresses and dislocations of war

speeded up these processes. It is said that one reason that Woodrow
Wilson hesitated to declare war was that he knew that the industries
vastly expanded and empowered by war could never be displaced
from power after the war.

(4) The imminent breakdown of the system in 1929 brought back
a surge of popular participation in some respects not unlike the age
of Jackson. But this was soon reintegrated into the bureaucratic
central government by the paternalism of Roosevelt and his Agencies. Economic controls, social insurance, and other welfare began
to break down altogether the formal division between government
and the monopolies and other great powers of society. All this was
regularized after the Second World War; by the 1950s there existed
one massive Organized System, inert or expanding by its own law,
immovable by any political public power, and administered, rather
than governed, by the Eisenhower Administration.

(5) The election of 1960 was remarkable in that now there was not
even the semblance of issues or programs for the voters to decide
between. The election was importantly decided by the contrast of
personalities on a TV screen. It was the end of the Jacksonian idea,
since with mass communications and national commodities, people's
passions and prejudices were themselves nationalized. There had
ceased to be a democracy even in form. The Administration would
be, however, the necessary *symbol* of government. (For a rough
analogy, consider the Roman "Republic" and its senators and consuls
during the early Empire.) Now what are the characteristics of such a
symbolic government, and what might be its future development?

VII

Eisenhower was unsatisfactory in many ways. With all his solid
virtues and genuine Rotarian togetherness and Everyman's ignorance, he was often ludicrous as a chief of state. Newsmen had to edit
him, satire had to be suppressed, lest the image of government
break down altogether. Culturally, he was out of place as the head of
a Great Power. But most important, his regime was universally
regarded as dangerously boring. For two reasons: first, the public
will to politics, whether or not it was possible to exert power, had
absolutely no object on which to exercise itself. Discussions of

domestic "policy" fell to an all-time low; and instead, there sprang up a vast literature of criticism of the System en bloc, of the Cars, the Organization, the Suburbs, etc., etc. Most of this was a one-upping cynical product of the system itself, yet it did not express dissent and was disillusioning to the young. The later years of Eisenhower were marked by a resurgence of Youth, acting now in parapolitical movements, Birchite or Beatnik or Pacifist. But secondly, and most important, the adequate administrative inactivism of Eisenhower was symbolically quite inadequate for the affluent rigors of the Cold War. The old-fashioned diplomacy of John Foster Dulles, as brinkmanly as it was, still did not provide sufficient popular identification for so immense and continuing a deadlock. People began to join SANE.

It is essential to consider the social psychology of the Cold War. Robert Engler has recently written a fine study of the cultural effects of the Cold War; but we must ask also what are the moods and paralysis *in* the culture that demand such a sustained, pointless, menacing, and potentially catastrophic enterprise. I have gone into this subject frequently elsewhere—the exacerbation, in modern conditions, of masochistic violence, Enemy-projection, and paralysis—but let me here especially mention the public mood of powerlessness, powerlessness on the job, in the bureaucracy, before the TV screen, in politics, with the police; the sense that "nothing can be done." This powerlessness projects itself in the fantasy of the Big News on the Front Page, the terrific Drama of We and They mutually frowning for absolute stakes. But for this fantasy to thrive, there must be adequate Actors. Nixon plugged as hard as he could his ad hominem clash with Khrushchev, and indeed thereby almost won the election.

In all respects Kennedy's Administration is a find. Kennedy can take care of himself in public and with his peers. His musicale has been praised by Paul Henry Lang who was so brutal to Ike. He is his own Secretary of State. His jaw is commensurate with General MacArthur's.[1] (Russian generals scowl; ours tend to jut the jaw.) He is vigorous and has physical courage. His lack of moral courage is no defect because, with Franco, Chiang Kai-shek, and tommygun-defended bomb shelters, we are far beyond principle anyway; and on the contrary, a slippery idealism, in the style of Luce, makes a good hipster. We have seen that the Administration of active personalities *is* good; unlike with Eisenhower, the Game Theorists now seem at home. Yet the President himself is also a serious man, *sage* in the French sense, commensurate with the need for caution in the Emergency. He does his homework and learns the Facts. He is intelligent—not in the sense that we speak of our friends as intelligent, but in that he can read rapidly through a reasoned memorandum and catch the drift. Though he is high-toned himself, he has a nice family; his brother and sister-in-law have formed a study group in Fairfax County across the Potomac, and Professors Walt and Arthur are going to give weekly lectures.

Most important of all, finally, with the Kennedy Administration there emerges for the first time the possibility of a National Unity to "wage" the Cold War. There is no other figure whose background encompasses McCarthy (and so guarantee that he is not soft on communism) and the Liberal Democrats (and so guarantees that there will be no wage cuts during the war economy). For the remainder of this essay, let us trace the lineaments of the New Consensus as a further devolution of American democracy.

VIII

A new Center is necessary. We saw that it is in the nature of the Cold War, where there is aggressive activism without pragmatic power, that there must be blunders, embarrassing at home and abroad, and even economically injurious and so leading to panic among American businessmen who are notoriously unable to take the long view. Such things jolt public identification. Also, the present Administration came in not only with a tenuous majority but also by a coalition—e.g., of urban Negro preachers and Southern politicians, of leftists and financiers—quite impossible to maintain. Within three months of being in office, Kennedy had lost the more earnest liberals who had supported him anyway only because of their congenital obsession not to leave a blank space on a ballot. He has lost the professors, scientists, etc., who protest the nuclear insanity. Youth has held on a little longer—with the Peace Corps and all—but is pulling away fast in all directions. (A gentleman high in the Administration has said that "Youth is not a class"; he is in error.)

On the other hand, stalwart party liberals like Governor Lehman and Mrs. Roosevelt—and apparently even Bowles and Stevenson —*never* quit when there is the appearance of "influence" (they supported Wagner, and Mrs. Roosevelt is now for bomb shelters if they are community bomb shelters!). So the Center can go this far left. On the other hand, from the beginning Kennedy visited Nixon and Eisenhower and as far as General MacArthur. The plan for the New Consensus, therefore, emerges as follows:

(1) To drop the troublemaking liberals as quietly as possible.

(2) To exclude and ridicule the Extreme Right. The official stamp on this policy was the remarkable statement of J. Edgar Hoover condemning the rabid as unwitting fomenters of communism. He sounded like the anti-anti-Communists of 1953.

(3) By a modest social legislation and a modest advance in Civil Rights, to hold the unions and organized Negro groups, while reassuring business and convincing the Southerners that, in our world position, a progress toward desegregation is inevitable. With the stepped-up production of military hardware, there ought to be no increase in unemployment, even a decrease. Given this much and the continued support of, for example, Senator Humphrey (the Senator is alleged to have said, "When I accepted the leadership, I gave up liberal principles"), the Administration can rely on the ADA milieu of the New York *Post*, without impeding further gains.

(4) The true grandeur and security of the New Consensus come from these further gains: it is beginning to captivate the mass of lower-brow readers of the New York *Daily News* and the educated suburbanites who read Luce magazines and egg on their sons to get good grades and make the prestige colleges. These are the solid centers of Cold War fervor and Cold War mentality. The strengthening of the FBI suits both the righteousness of the stupider and the conformism of the brighter. For the *News* readers, there is an advantage in the friendly ambience of Catholic humanism-plus-discipline, quite oblivious of any notion of civil liberties or social change; for the college-bound, the professors are reassuring of tolerance, and their schools are among the most prestigious. The amalgam of Murrow and Luce in Information has been masterly. To the horror of John Birch, Inc., the TV attitude toward the Communists is often understanding and almost admiring—they are a

powerful enemy, we shall have to confront them for "a generation and maybe two generations" (I quote from a TV documentary called *The Remarkable Comrades*). It is now only the young pacifists who are treated sharply as naïve, misguided, and dangerous idealists. Persons like myself and my friends are gently encouraged as "utopians."

IX

What is the intellectual Idea of the New Consensus? Let us go back to the Professors, who are not now class-objectionable because, in principle, everybody who is not underprivileged goes to college. First, they are not eggheads. An egghead is one who, seduced by intellect and truth, might by chance say something inexpedient or something poetical that illumines the scene. Also, they are not brain-trusters, pragmatists who might come out with future-thinking like the TVA or the uncensored WPA. Rather, as we have seen, the Professors do Analysis and Tabulate Facts. As philosophers, they affirm a broad tolerance of ideas and an absolute pessimism about ideal or "utopian" action. Thus, via Dr. Niebuhr, the sage of *The New Leader*, we get the astoundingly un-Protestant rapprochement of Harvard and the neo-Jesuits!

Washington at present has a pleasantly free atmosphere of discussion. (Naturally I do not know the tone in the middle of the Web of Tensions.) Unlike the previous crew, the Professors know from experience that propositions do not bite, and they do make the best conversation pieces. I myself have been urged, by one who has access, to continue my indispensable "role of dissent." That is, we are the Jester. What is puzzling, however, is that the Administration is continually plaintively asking for ideas; the President asked even the NAM to send him ideas. The implication is, partly, that the carping critics really have no alternatives to suggest. The important fact is that, since the Administration neither can nor is willing to make structural changes, these people would not recognize an idea if they saw it. The openness to ideas, the hunger for ideas, in fact works out as follows:

When a radical reform is proposed—for example, a concrete plan to countervail the technologized FBI or the mass media—at once one hears the most subtle niceties of definition and an amazing purity about constitutionality, possible corruption and abuse, the right of the public to "choose," etc., etc.; and anyway, as the clincher, Congress will never appropriate money for such a purpose. (As a critic has observed, "The wisdom of a policy is measured by the opinion of Mr. Oren Harris of Arkansas.") But if it is a matter of lending a much greater sum to a railroad that every banker has rejected as a bad risk, then there is no difficulty, there is a much looser interpretation of the public interest, and the Administration is willing to push. In the welfare state, there is a nice discrimination between expenditures that subsidize large enterprises and those that are worthless or peanuts. If the Public Sector means roads for General Motors or Urban Renewal for Webb and Knapp, it is attended to; if it means community experiments, work camps for youth, public defenders, or even primary education, it is nicely scrutinized. (But of course this double standard of scrutiny has long been familiar to us in the mysterious law of Economics whereby expenditures in 000,000,000, for armament, are never questioned with regard to nine or ten figures; expenditures for highways, in 00,000,000, are rarely questioned for eight or nine figures. But expenditures for useful domestic purposes, in 000,000 or even 0,000, are most strictly scrutinized; and, as poor people know, expenditures in 00 or even 0.00 require a means test and a quiz on morals.)

"Wagner is a hopeless boob!" exclaimed the Professor. "Then why did you support him?" "It was the chance of getting the Democratic machine away from De Sapio." "But it's *my* city!" I cried, "and you killed a strong reform movement." . . . Yet De Sapio *did* deliver New York City in the nominating convention, after oddly backing Symington, although any honest poll would have given most of the city to Stevenson. There's loyalty! To learn this kind of practical wisdom, you do not need to go to Harvard; you can get it in a poolroom.

Let me illustrate the Higher Science from Aerospace, a wholly government-supported corporation. Attacking Kefauver's anti-drug-monopoly bill, the spokesman of Aerospace explained that it would retard progress in space exploration, for example, in developing medicines for victims of nuclear fallout (Washington *Star*, Dec. 10, 1961). Aren't these people shameless?

Since I am nervous about the self-discipline entailed in the New

Consensus, I ask about Civil Liberties. I am told, "Bobby Kennedy is not *against* civil liberties, he does not have any notion of what civil liberties *are*." I did not have the chance to see Harris Wofford, the adviser on Civil Rights, since he was out of the country. (There is no adviser on Civil Liberties.) Wofford is an excellent and thoughtful man; he has even written for *Liberation* about civil disobedience. But he is a professor from Notre Dame and his view on civil disobedience is that we cannot take away a man's God-given right to rot in jail (he does not go on to Hobbes's dictum that the state breaks the social compact if it jails you, and it's your natural duty to escape). But to my mind the most alarming clue of what the Administration promises on civil liberties was its bland, and entirely innocent, proposal to raise the news rates in order to make the Post Office pay for itself! (This had to be dropped by Congress.) Yet one might have expected it: these people, professors of law and government and history, apparently do not have any notion of what the democratic idea *is*.

X

The New Consensus is an ignoble prospect. It would also be dangerous; for if such a national unity can fully form, we shall drift into a kind of fascism of the majority. If there were then a major reverse—supposing Brazil, Chile, Venezuela would follow Castro —the United States would be a police state.

Robert Engler speaks of the society of the continuing Cold War as a "garrison state." I don't think so; it doesn't look like that. Rather, just the tightening of the existing suburban conformism, grade-seeking education, FBI protection, and mass media, with a little addition of "discipline," "responsibility," and "sacrifice." This would be literally the despotism of the majority that Mill feared, manipulated by a popular Administration to meet a chronic Emergency.

In my opinion, the present Administration is committed to the Cold War (despite some evidence, I cannot believe it plans a first-strike nuclear war). It has no other economic plan than a war economy, no foreign policy outside the CIA, and no domestic idea at all.

If the Cold War is to be relaxed and catastrophe prevented, we must do it by action outside of their politics, by every means and on every relevant issue. There is already agitation for peace throughout the world, sporadically, with increasing frequency, and by increasing numbers.

Footnotes

1. In the East Wing of the White House hangs a picture of the Great Stone Face. Considering the theme of Hawthorne's tale, this is really carrying the profiles of history to the point of juvenile hubris. Like asking Frost to alter his poem at the Inaugural.

BRENDAN SEXTON
"Middle-Class" Workers
and the
New Politics
(1969)

Much of my life has been split between two worlds: blue-collar unions and the intellectual-academic arena—a sort of long-haired working stiff, or at least an uncommon marginal man.

Born in a tough Irish working-class neighborhood and reared on Catholicism, Irish rebellion, and later socialism, I fell into the life of an organizer during the Great Depression and the early days of the CIO. As a reader of everything in reach, I have followed with great regret the growing schism between organized labor and middle-class liberals during the past decade. Like others, I was stunned to see the old liberal coalition finally fragment during the presidential election under the separate discontents of workers (out of sight and mind to most observers, but not, alas, to George Wallace) and the middle-class liberal antagonists of LBJ. What the consequences of the fragmentation will be only Nixon and Agnew may know.

Yet I continue to believe, in my old-fashioned, radical-populist way, that a broad alliance between these two groups at their center remains the best hope for reconstructing our society along democratic-humanist lines.

Many issues need clarifying if we are to halt a national move to the right. I wish to explore only one here: the assumption that blue-collar workers are "middle class" and sitting pretty. I'd also like to suggest some of the political consequences of both the assumption and the reality of workers' lives.

106

In December of 1967 the "average production worker" with three dependents took home $90.89 for a full week's work. Measured against the previous year, his dollar income rose about $2.34 a week. In fact, however, his actual purchasing power *declined by about 6 cents per week*. He was worse off in 1967 than in 1966, and probably even more so in 1968.

Now $90.89 take-home is not "middle-class," especially if you are an "average" family head with three dependents. If such a man puts aside $25 a week for house or rent payments (a modest enough sum), he's left with a little less than $66 a week to pay for food, clothing, medicines, school supplies, etc., for two adults and two children. That comes to roughly $2.37 per day, per person, for a family of four—about the amount a big-city newspaper reporter (or any of us in the real middle class) is likely to spend for lunch.

These figures are distorted a bit by the inclusion of Southern, and largely unorganized, workers. But in 1967, *manufacturing* workers (most of whom are organized) with three dependents averaged only $101.26 in take-home pay. As against the previous year, they also experienced a slight dip in real income and purchasing power.

In New York, the locale of many observers who write so expertly about "middle-class" workers, manufacturing workers averaged a gross income of $114.44. Only in Michigan, among all continental states, where the weekly gross was $145.78, could an average manufacturing worker come close to the national family median (about $8,000) with a full year of work.

At the other end of the scale, retail workers averaged just slightly less than $71 per week during 1967. The retail worker, if he worked a full year, earned a gross income high enough to lift him barely above the "poverty line" of $3,000, but low enough to leave him with less than half the national family median income. This is the extreme example. Still, there are more than eight million workers in retail trade. Even when they wear white collars, they can't, at this rate, be factored into the middle class.

Skilled workers are the aristocrats of labor, yet the median earnings of male craftsmen who were employed full-time in 1966 was only $6,981.[1] Of course, a good many of the elite and highly organized urban craftsmen—electricians, typographers, lithographers, etc.—rise to and above $10,000 a year. For a blue-collar worker, this is really "making it." For the new college professor, fresh out of graduate school, it's just so-so.

Where affluence begins and ends no one knows, but it must be above the levels cited. In late 1966, the U.S. Department of Labor said that an income of $9,191 would enable a city family of four to maintain "a moderate standard of living." Only about one-third of *all* American families reach that now dated standard. Certainly, the typical production worker is much better off than a Mississippi farm tractor driver or a city mother living on welfare, but he hardly lives opulently. He treads water, financially and psychically.

The myth of the "middle-class" worker is kin to the Negro of folklore who "lives in the slums but drives a big new Cadillac." He's there, all right, but his numbers are grossly exaggerated.

Workers with small families and two or more paychecks coming in each week may be able to make it. Among all American families with incomes of $10,000, the multi-incomes are twice as numerous as the single income. Still, millions of families combine two or even three paychecks and yet earn less than $5,000 a year.

The young worker is hardest hit and hence most discontented. He often holds down the lower-paid and more onerous jobs. He is somewhat less likely to work overtime at premium rates and more likely to be caught in temporary layoffs, though in some union contracts he is now protected against loss from the latter.

No less than others of his generation, the young worker expects more. Why not? He belongs to a generation with rapidly rising expectations. As long as he's single, his first paychecks may give him more money than he's ever seen before. He dresses well, owns a new car, and generally lives it up.

But once married, his problems multiply. He furnishes a home, perhaps buys it. He does it "on time." He pays more for furniture and appliances than anyone ever did before. The house that cost his father $12,000, with a mortgage at 5 percent, now may sell for twice that and be financed at 7 percent. The young married worker aged twenty-five or thirty will probably carry twice the burden of debt as the worker aged forty or forty-five. When children come, the wife of the young worker will probably drop out of the labor market leaving him as sole support for perhaps fifteen or twenty years. In these years, his financial needs increase with the size of his family, but his paycheck does not respond to need.

These economic realities confront workers with a long list of harrowing problems. How, for example, do they provide equal opportunity for their children? How do they shelter them against the draft for four years when the cost of sending a son to the state university now averages nearly $2,000 a year? *Perhaps less than a quarter of all high school graduates who are children of factory workers enter college.* (The myth that something like half of all young Americans go to college is very nearly unshatterable. Actually, 46.3 percent of the eighteen- and nineteen-year-olds, but only 19 percent in the age group of twenty–twenty-four are "in school." U.S. Office of Education reports are so unclear here that I suspect the agency of misleading us regarding the accessibility of college opportunities.)

Children of workers are overrepresented in the mass of those excluded from college. Working-class kids make their trips abroad as members of the armed forces, while some middle-class youths, student deferments in hand, spend a junior year at European universities. While the college boy steps on an escalator that moves rapidly upward, the worker's son may step on his father's assembly line and into a job without much promise.

Relatively few colleges, social agencies, schools, or other public institutions mount programs to meet special needs of workers. In many places, even the services provided by "Red Feather" agencies seem more closely geared to middle- than working-class needs.

Inevitably, many workers come to feel they are being dunned and taxed for the benefit of others. Considering the notorious imbalance of our tax structure, they have a point. *In general, the rate of taxation declines as income rises.* This is most obviously true of the state sales taxes. It is almost as true of the federal income tax, under which, in the most extreme cases, some individuals and corporations pay little or no tax at all, though their incomes may exceed $5 million annually. Estimates of total tax loads indicate that 33 percent of the income of those earning $3,000 to $5,000 goes to taxes, and only 28 percent of those earning $15,000 or more.

So we have the case of the "invisible" and aggrieved worker. Many of his breed are even found among Mike Harrington's invisible poor. In fact, about one-third of all heads of impoverished families hold down full-time jobs. They are generally not organized, but they are workers. While millions of workers live in poverty, millions more barely escape it. Most are in income brackets between $3,000 and $10,000 (which includes some 56 percent of all American families), with probably more workers near the bottom than the top.

Reporters often talk about the sweeper who "makes more than a teacher." True, a sweeper in an auto plant in Michigan or New Jersey probably earns more than a teacher in a backwoods school in Mississippi, but his pay is hardly a pot of gold. The sweeper seems to fit a set of hidden assumptions according to which the society is divided, at a magical line, between rich and poor. The premise of this stereotype is that our class structure is a dualism—rich and poor. In this simplified pseudo-Marxian schema, organized workers are seen as part of the richer half, along with bankers, businessmen, professionals. They are, it is assumed, well fed, well cared for, up to their hips in "things," and all-around partners in an open and affluent society.

According to this hidden assumption, all or nearly all the poor are black. They are mostly mothers of large families living on welfare in big-city ghettos. The rest (except for a few Appalachian whites) are young blacks who can't find jobs because they are school dropouts or because they are excluded from unions by corpulent and corrupt union bosses. So goes this version of things, especially popular in some college circles. But in fact about 80 percent of the poor are white, and a startling proportion of them work full-time.

In real life the typical worker has lived on a treadmill, except where union contracts have protected him from rises in the cost of living. Everyone else—including the poor and the militant blacks (at least as their image was cast by the media)—*seemed* to be moving forward, while only *they* stood still, waiting in a twilight zone somewhere between hunger and plenty. Some comforts came to them through expanded consumer credit, but the credit exacted high costs in tension, insecurity, and interest rates. They gave increasing taxes to the government, their sons to the army. They seemed to get little in return: only conflict, and sometimes mortal combat with the emerging black poor over jobs, neighborhoods, and schools.

Here is fertile soil for the growth of resentment. For a time, it grew like a weed under the cultivation of George Wallace. A turning point in the presidential campaign may have come when Hubert Humphrey began to see something Wallace always understood: that while many "experts" said the "old issues" were dead, millions of American workers angrily disagreed and wanted a better life. Many workers were ready, in short, for a campaign resembling Harry Truman's historical effort of 1948, a hell-raising campaign about the "old" economic issues (social justice, more and better jobs, more opportunity, good schools, health care, etc.).

The trap almost sprung by Wallace was set by those "opinion-makers" who dismissed all Wallace supporters as red-necked bigots and opponents of Negro aspirations. Fortunately, they were mistaken. While many workers have no doubt been shook up quite a bit by the black revolt, they have been even more shaken by their own failure to get on in life. Being far wiser than we think, they knew this was not the fault of blacks.

Sadly, some of the Wallaceite resentment was, of course, turned against the poor and the black. Yet it is possible that Wallace's exposed bigotry finally did him in among Northern workers. Industrial workers generally have closer relations with Negroes than any other class, and the big factories in steel, auto, rubber, glass, etc., are probably the most integrated work places in the society. Most workers who were drawn to Wallace because he spoke their economic language must have had problems of conscience about blacks with whom they worked and had friendly relations. As Wallace's campaign became more violent in tone, many of them probably grew uneasy and fell away from his camp.

When "opinion-makers" bothered to talk with workers, they found to their surprise that not all were racists. After talking with Wallace supporters in Flint, Michigan (said to be a hotbed of Wallace sentiment), Mike Hubbard, a student editor of the University of Michigan *Daily*, wrote:

Certainly these Americans do not identify with red-necked racism. . . . No one ever taught them Negro History, but they grew up with blacks. . . . They don't dislike blacks, they just feel black men shouldn't be given a bigger break than anyone else. The white UAW members as a whole do not believe Wallace is a racist. All they know is what he told them, and he never said he hated blacks. Even the most militant Negro workers I talked to didn't feel there was large-scale prejudice in the Union. They dislike Wallace, but not the men who are voting for him.

Others found many Wallace supporters who would have preferred Robert Kennedy, and some even Eugene McCarthy. *Time* found many such in its 150 interviews across the country, and Haynes Johnson of the Washington *Star* reported this comment from a leader of the Wallace movement in Duluth, Minnesota: "The reason I got into this actually was when Robert Kennedy was shot. . . . That assassination—plus that of Martin Luther King—pointed up for me just how sick it was in this country, and I decided to do something for my country."

The "new issues"—the war on poverty and bureaucracy, the struggles for racial justice and world peace—can be lost unless they are paralleled by campaigns on issues that are important to those millions who are often ignored except by demagogues.

The mythology that obscures the realities of working-class life derives in large part from the success story of unions and what various observers have made of that story. Unions have made great gains in wages, working conditions, fringe benefits, politics; but they started from very far back, and they are still very far from the millennium. Since our society has been late and miserly in providing social insurance, unions have had to push hard in collective bargaining for benefits that don't show up in pay checks. Their focus on such goals has had some negative side effects. Fringe benefits mean more to older than to younger workers—and it is the young who are drawn to men like George Wallace.

Unless unions were to act irresponsibly toward the aging (one of the most impoverished and helpless groups among us), pensions had to be won. Pensions cost money, and that money was subtracted from the wage package won at the bargaining table. Also, older workers need and make more use of hospitalization, medical and sickness insurance. These too came out of the total package, leaving less for wages. It was humane to help the older worker, and it helped him retire and make way for younger workers. But it was costly. *In*

*the UAW alone, more then 200,000 members have retired and re-
ceived pension benefits of over $1.5 billion.* Unions sometimes may
have overresponded to the older workers, as in seniority and vacation benefits, etc., but one can hardly look at the life of the aging
worker and say he has too much.

Unions need to make a new beginning, paying more attention to
the needs of the young. An aging and sometimes feeble union
leadership needs to refresh itself with activists and new leadership
recruited among younger generations. Unless the young become
partners in the union movement, they may end up wrecking it. The
dramatic rise in the rate of rank-and-file rejection of union contract
settlements is a clear signal of distress among workers. Usually,
veteran unionists report, the increased rejections result from organized opposition among young workers.

Unions need to do a lot of things, far more than I can mention in
this brief piece. I come from a union that has split from the AFL over
some of these issues, including foreign policy, interest in the poor
and minorities, and general militancy. I have opposed the Vietnam
war, and I think labor should have. I have been involved in the war
on poverty, along with many other unionists—though it is remote
from many others. Still, one observer says, "If the labor movement
in this country moves to the right, it's not least the fault of those, like
Sexton, who will not say a word of criticism of its policies." I leave
nothing to the imagination of readers, for we are all deeply aware of
the shortcomings of unions. I do not dwell on these flaws for another
reason: whatever their blemishes, unions have given workers the
only support and attention they have had—and they needed a lot.

Unions are, however, limited in what they can do for members.
They are limited by their own willingness and that of their members
to go into battle, to strike. They are limited by the public's willingness to accept strikes. The middle-class liberal himself is often
offended, sometimes outraged, by strikers. He may say, "They're
selfish and out for themselves." When the desperately poor hospital
worker strikes, the liberal will see only the patient as victim; but he
will offer no clues as to how else the hospital worker can win a
measure of justice. When subway and sanitation workers in New
York strike for a modest $3.50 or so an hour (to perform some of the
most disagreeable jobs known to man), many middle-class liberals

complain bitterly, without also noting that New York's affluent can afford to pay men decent wages to do hard, often dangerous, always unpleasant work.

Many liberals dismiss as unimportant, if not irrelevant, every claim workers make for their attention and support. In few cases do they distinguish workers from union leaders, for some of whom their contempt may be warranted. It is not surprising, considering their mentors, that so much of the young New Left seems to despise the working class.

Not since the early and dramatic days of the CIO have liberals and intellectuals (with some honorable exceptions) shown much sympathetic interest in workers or unions. Now workers come sharply to their view only when they threaten to make life inconvenient or dangerous. A subway strike, shutdown at *The New York Times*, a large vote for Wallace may do the trick—momentarily.

I believe that liberals and moderate leftists—in whose circle opinion-makers are heavily represented—are out of touch with the reality of American working-class life. Many of them live at rarefied levels where almost everyone's income is at least $15,000 a year. *Less than 10 percent of the nation's families earn that much*; still, they form a mass of between eighteen and twenty million people. Those who live within it can easily come to think that all Americans, except the poor, are living just about as they and their colleagues and neighbors do. Having little contact outside their own circles, and having heard so much about the great gains of unions, they may naturally assume that workers have made it too.

Many of these opinion-makers are men of my generation or near it. Forgetting the ravages of inflation, they may think of $6,000 a year as a fairly substantial income. They may remember maintaining a modest existence on even less. I recall that I was thirty-five years old when I first earned $5,000 a year as president of the nation's second largest local union. Now when I hear that auto workers gross more than $8,000, I too sometimes forget the dollar's decline and assume they've got it made. Relative to most other workers, they have; but they are still far from well off. These opinion-makers greatly influence what appears in periodicals and dailies, and what is said on TV and radio. They often draft political platforms and write candidates' speeches. When they don't, their readers do. They think of themselves as open-minded and sensitive, and sometimes they are. But too often their politics are introspective—concentrated only on issues that touch them, plus a now fashionable interest in the poor.

Their political attitudes are sometimes expressed in the kind of thin-lipped and vinegary liberalism that found its ultimate expression in Senator McCarthy's endorsement of Hubert Humphrey. To the dismay of at least one early supporter—me—McCarthy urged in that endorsement that the rights of honest draft dissenters be protected but said nothing about the draft's discrimination against Negroes, the poor, and the working class, and made no significant comments about other social and economic issues. The Senator's failure to ignite fires outside the middle class can easily be understood in the light of that arid statement. In the primary campaign his speeches (at least in the printed text) were often unexceptionable; but, notoriously, he often left unsaid what decent liberals and radicals on his staff wrote into those speeches. Later in the campaign, and in the Senate leadership fight, the warts on that handsome liberal façade grew larger.

Senator McCarthy, like some who supported him, had to subdue his conscience before endorsing Hubert Humphrey, yet he has always seemed comfortable with Senator William Fulbright, a man whose record on civil rights almost duplicates George Wallace's except for greater gentility of expression.[2] (A friend explained to me that he could support Fulbright because the Senator had "style," a matter of overriding merit to many liberals.) Finally, petulance and spleen seemed to consume this hero of the middle-class liberals when he chose Long over Kennedy.

The chemistry of the Kennedys has been different. The contrast is highlighted in Senator Edward Kennedy's appeal to supporters of his two slain brothers to reject the "dark" and "extremist" movement of George Wallace.

> Most of these people [Kennedy said of Wallace supporters] are not motivated by racial hostility or prejudice. They feel that their needs and their problems have been passed over by the tide of recent events. They bear the burden of the unfair system of

Selective Service. They lose out because higher education costs so much. They are the ones who feel most threatened at the security of their jobs, the safety of their families, the value of their property and the burden of their taxes. They feel the established system has not been sympathetic to them in their problems of everyday life and in a large measure they are right.

If a meaningful New Politics is to work in this country it must be based on the kind of empathy expressed in these words.

Too few liberals realize that millions of workers and voters fit Ted Kennedy's description. Young workers outnumber all college students, and there are perhaps fifteen or twenty of them for every one disaffected youth upon whom various advocates of a New Politics are counting. The big three in auto alone employ about 250,000 workers who are thirty or under. Total UAW membership of that age group may reach 600,000, with perhaps half of these under twenty-five. Among organized workers, possibly five million are young people under thirty.

Young workers seem to be tougher and to have more staying power than students. Their stake in social change may turn out to be greater and more compelling. Most will never experience the softening effects of well-paid, high-status jobs in the professional, academic, artistic, or business worlds—jobs to which most student rebels are on their way. Knowing they're unlikely to escape individually, workers can grow desperate when denied political hope.

One pollster puts many workers in the "no change" coalition. He misunderstands. Workers simply oppose changes that benefit or seem to benefit others while increasing their own burdens.

The auto industry average wage of $3.80 per hour, though the highest in manufacturing, still does not mean affluence. The UAW (like many other unions) has won comprehensive medical protection, including coverage for psychiatric care of a million members. Its contracts now provide tuition remission plans for members who wish to take classes that may help them escape from dead-end factory jobs. In December of 1968, the hourly wage system came close to ending for perhaps a million UAW members; thus, in one industry, workers have almost scaled an important barrier between them and the middle class; they will be salaried rather than hourly workers. UAW contracts have moved toward the guaranteed annual income and retirement with decent security. Gains have been made, yes; but even auto workers still have far to go.

One friend tells me, "Intellectuals still cling to a hopeful and perhaps incorrect view, idealizing the union members as an instrument of class struggle." What members and their unions try to do, at best, is not class struggle in any classic sense. Their conscious antagonists are the employer and the conservative legislator, not the "capitalist system." Yet their efforts have profoundly influenced American life. And unionists have tasted enough of victory so that they generally do not believe in the "final conflict" for which the "prisoners of starvation" must arise.

Those publicists who seek such an apocalypse will not find unionists mounting the barricades with the swiftness and pleasure of student rebels or black militants. Unionists have learned a hard lesson after almost a century of fierce blood-letting on the picket line: *that combat is the last, not the first, resort.* Unionists have possibly been too moderate in this respect, for open conflict sometimes is the only way to rally people and get what you want. But they have learned many other ways to get on with it. They will not be found burning down their own neighborhoods to prove a point, or otherwise sacrificing their own ranks in unproductive, self-destructive conflict. In this respect, interestingly, some black militants seem to be taking a rather active interest in labor studies. Most militants, coming from poor families, are interested in the "old issues" (opportunity, jobs, etc.) and in ways of organizing people for effective action. A similar interest in unions has not come to the campus, thanks to the myth of the middle-class worker and other academic folklore. (My wife and I taught a graduate sociology course at NYU last year in Labor and Society. So far as I know—outside the narrow limits of labor-and-industrial programs—it is the *only* such course taught in the country.)

Workers and their unions have many problems and they need lots of help. On the other side, the middle-class left may find itself isolated if it accepts the standard mythology about workers. If they are to create a New Society, liberals and radicals need to become aware of socially excluded workers and find avenues of communication with them, as well as with Negroes, Latin Americans, and the oppressed poor generally.

Footnotes

1. Gaps of a year or more sometimes occur in government statistics. In all cases, I have used the most recent annual reports available.

2. I don't wish to downgrade Senator Fulbright's obvious courage. We are all in his debt. Some young Americans may owe him their lives. I do wish to point out that liberal and radical intellectuals of principle are also capable of compromise, though their evaluation of issues may differ from the trade unionists or even the black militants.

ALICE S. ROSSI
Women—
Terms of Liberation
(1970)

At least for the moment, Women's Liberation is "in." Its advocates get wide publicity in the mass media, and there is talk, mostly not very serious, about what "those women" want. On campuses, as in professional organizations, there has been mounting pressure to hire and promote more women, to provide child-care facilities for married women students and employees, and to offer courses on the history and the status of women. The voicing of these demands will increase significantly at professional conventions. I predict comparable increases in the political and economic realms, as women organize and demonstrate to change laws and employer practices that discriminate on the grounds of sex. Among activist women there is clearly a new note of optimism.

This optimistic sense does not, however, seem to be shared by many men. The majority of American men appear to be convinced that if they wait out the storm, activism will die down and they can then continue to run government agencies, businesses, and universities. I do not share the view that the women's rights movement is a passing thing. Indeed, I think the movement has not yet reached its crest, though I also believe it faces hard times. What follows is an attempt to sketch both the encouraging and discouraging developments that may mark the women's movement in the next decade.

At the outset I shall draw on my personal experiences in academic and private life, upon participation in several reform

119

movements in recent years, and upon a commitment to fundamental change in American society.

PERSONAL-POLITICAL BACKGROUND

As an undergraduate and graduate student, I had no particular interest in the status of women, sex roles, or occupational choice. I entered college as an English major, pragmatism dictating an occupational choice of high school English teacher, but romanticism prompting a hope I might become a famous writer. I was one of those thousands of bright, eager New York students attending the city colleges, in my case, Brooklyn College. My first sociology instructor was Louis Schneider, and he began his course by reading a Whitman poem and raising the question: who was this man? what does the poem tell about his time, his place on this globe? I found the sociological dimension of literature so fascinating that I fell in love with the field, and began a lifelong affair of the heart and mind that is second only to my own marriage and the three children of that marriage. As a graduate student at Columbia, I was interested in the macroscopic analysis of social institutions; in family and kinship systems rather than the roles of women within family systems; in reference groups, through work with Robert Merton, and in studies of the professions. The occupational role I chose to study in Kingsley Davis's seminar was that of the politician, though not once did I think to look into the sex-linked nature of occupational choice.

No woman in 1970, I hope, could be the total innocent I was in 1950 concerning sex discrimination. I dreamed of being one day the president of the American Sociological Society, and of writing a major opus that would be built on the strengths of my two mentors in theory and research. I discounted as peevish envy the claim of my male peers that I would not get a fellowship "because I was a woman," and then, when I was awarded one, the counterclaim that "someone on the faculty must be trying to make you."

It would have been congenial for me to move from graduate training to an academic position as a teacher and secondarily a researcher. But this is a path difficult for a married woman in academia, particularly if, like myself, she is married to a sociologist. So I spent ten years as a research associate, following not my own interest so much as the availability of funds and openings: intergroup relations at Cornell, generational differences in the Soviet Union at Harvard, kinship in the middle class at the University of Chicago.

Through these research undertakings, I developed a fascination with a problem seldom adequately stated within sociological theory itself: what are the connections, the strains and accommodations between involvement in the family on the one hand, and the occupational system on the other? I was taking a first step away from the predominant theory that the family and occupational systems require "mechanisms of segregation" with only one member of the family participating significantly in the occupational system—a theory I now view as an intellectual put-down providing a rationale for men as the prime movers in work and politics.

The source of this growing interest was not only research and scholarship; it was also my own personal experience as a faculty wife and mother of young children. As a faculty wife, I had ample opportunity to observe that some sociological theorists did a good job of preventing two members of a family from holding significant positions in the occupational system. At Harvard and again at Chicago, I saw numerous instances of women being kept off the academic turf their husbands claimed as their own. I had offended one such theorist by negotiating an appointment at Harvard without first clearing such a horrendous step with him, then my husband's department chairman. I watched women friends leave the university when they became pregnant and being kept out when they tried to return after their children entered school. And during the two years I had my first two children I learned from personal experience the truth of the existential thesis that "one becomes what one does," for I realized with horror that I was resenting my husband's freedom to continue his full-time academic work despite the addition of parental responsibilities, and even more that I was actually trying to prevent his playing an intimate role in the lives of the children, so that I might at least have ascendancy in parenthood to complement his ascendancy in our profession.

But it took a return to academia, involving a traumatic encounter with the discrimination academic women so often suffer, to jar me out of my innocence. I began a long process of reestablishing connections with my earlier life: intellectual exposure to the ideas of Robert Lynd and C. Wright Mills, personal experiences in a variety of working-class and white-collar clerical jobs, and involvement in radical politics (as an undergraduate in the 1930s and early 1940s). I begin to draw together these older layers of the self and to focus the ideas, the personal experience, and the political commitment I now have.

My own trial by fire involved a not untypical story of a bright woman Ph.D. accepting a research associateship to do a study the male principal investigator was not competent to do on his own, and in which he had very little interest. At least initially his interest was low, until I had designed the study, fielded it, and partially analyzed the results. At that point he realized he had a good thing going, and simply announced, despite verbal agreements about co-authorship, that my services were no longer needed. I was a salaried research associate, he a full professor, and as the dean put it bluntly to me, "he is valuable university property; you, unfortunately, are expendable."

My own concern for the status of women, the analysis of sex roles, the study of and active participation in abortion law and divorce law reform, I date to the "slow burn" that began in that first major encounter with sex discrimination in academia. It immediately precipitated the scholarship and writing that led me down the path of immodesty to my first essay on sex equality.

The varied response to that *Daedalus* essay was itself a revealing commentary on American academia. Several male colleagues accused me of troubling their marriages. Young women wrote to say they decided to return to graduate school instead of having another baby. My husband received a sympathetic bereavement card from a West Coast sociologist for having such an upstart wife. A more recent example of this kind was the reaction of male sociologists to the roles my husband and I played at the sociology convention in the fall of 1969. As secretary of the association, my husband was on the platform while I delivered a speech and submitted resolutions for the women's caucus. In the months since then, I have had offers for academic appointments based on the premise that my husband and I are about to be divorced. My husband has been asked how he felt when I delivered that speech, with his male colleagues not knowing how to take his response that he felt pride! During earlier years, my university colleagues criticized me for "not sticking to my last" as research sociologist instead of writing analytic social criticism. Others said it was inappropriate and would "ruin your career" to get involved in the "woman thing," or to be publicly visible as an organizer for abortion law reform, or to write in a woman's magazine that "motherhood was not enough." Nowhere did one hear anything about responsibility for reaching the larger public, nor did one have any sense that there was an obligation for a family sociologist to "do something" about contraception, abortion, or women's rights.

As you may know from reading Eli Ginsberg on life styles of educated women, a supportive husband is an absolute requirement for professional women. Unfortunately, Ginsberg does not understand how a woman gets a supportive husband. It is not a "condition" she is fortunate to have as a base for being something more than homemaker, mother, and husband-relaxer. He is something she looks for, and when she finds him, she marries him. It didn't just happen that my husband is supportive; I chose him in part because he *was*.

From 1964 to the fall of 1969 I enjoyed an unusual status under a research award from the National Institute of Mental Health. This award gave me an academic umbrella to legitimize my status in the university and the independence to undertake my own research. The best education I ever had I acquired on my own during the first year or so of that award: the luxury of getting lost in libraries again, free to acquire that delicious "itch to know," to tackle new fields, turn down any lecture, paper, or course offering that did not interest me. Midway into that five-year award, I undertook a major research study of family and career roles of women college graduates. What time I had beyond this research and family responsibilities was invested in active attempts at social, legal, and political change to benefit women. By early 1969, however, I felt increasingly out of rapport with most of my colleagues in empirical sociology and restless for direct contact with the college-age generation. I had studied these young people; now I wanted to teach them. In the fall of 1969, I therefore shifted from research sociology at Johns Hopkins to undergraduate teaching at Goucher College.

BACKGROUND OF CURRENT WOMEN'S MOVEMENT

It has become fashionable to link the emergence of the women's liberation movement to the participation of younger women in the civil rights movement. These young women, one reads, drew the conclusion their ancestors did from involvement in the abolitionist cause of the nineteenth century: that the arguments developed and the battles waged to free the black American could apply to American women, even though women in the abolitionist as in the civil rights movement all too often found themselves treated as second-class creatures good for cooking, typing, and comforting their male leaders. Without detracting from this point at all, I would only remark that the women's liberation movement is a bit more than two years old, and there were important, though less visible, changes among American women earlier in the 1960s.

In fact, I would argue that it was the changed composition of the female labor force during the period beginning with 1940 but rapidly peaking in the 1950s that provided the momentum leading to the establishment of the Kennedy Commission on the Status of Women and the formation of new women's rights organizations in the mid-1960s. So long as women worked mostly before marriage or after marriage only until a first pregnancy, or lived within city limits where there was a diversity of cultural activities to engage them, there were but feeble grounds for a significant movement among women, since their motivation for working was short-lived. Only among women who are relatively permanent members of the work force could daily experience force an awareness of economic inequities based on sex and a determination to do something about them. It was the women who served on the numerous committees of the Kennedy Commission, followed by the thousands who worked with the state commissions established during the Kennedy and Johnson administrations, who experienced and then stimulated a mood of rising expectations among American women.

These were committed, knowledgeable, largely middle-aged women who had high hopes, as they filed their reports, that American society would finally do something to improve the status of women. Their hopes were dashed by the treatment they experienced at the spring 1966 conference of representatives from the state commissions brought together by the Department of Labor in Washington. From that frustrating experience, a number of women concluded that little significant change could be expected until a strong organization was built that would be completely independent of the political establishment. This was how the National Organization for Women was formed in the fall of 1966. The range of women's problems that NOW is concerned with has broadened greatly since 1966, but the core continues to be equal treatment in hiring and promotion.

NOW includes lively, dedicated women who are pressing hard against the barriers that restrict women in American society. Except for its action in behalf of airline stewardesses, however, it has had relatively little public or media attention outside of New York, at least if compared to the extraordinary press coverage given to the women's liberation groups this past year. Why so? The answer, I think, lies in differences of stress and outlook between these two tendencies within the women's movement.

A fundamental assumption of American society is that men's primary social roles are in work and women's primary social roles in the family. It is conventionally supposed that all men will want to work at a challenging job. Nothing is so threatening to conventional values as a man who does not want to work or does not want to work at a challenging job, and most people are disturbed if a man in a well-paying job indicates ambivalence or dislike toward it. The counterpart for women is any suggestion that they feel ambivalent toward maternity, marriage, or homemaking, probably in that order. In more sociological terms, we might put this as follows: social roles vary in the extent to which it is culturally permissible to express ambivalence or negative feelings toward them. Ambivalence can be admitted most readily toward those roles that are optional, least where they are considered primary. Thus men repress negative feelings toward work and feel freer to express negative feelings toward leisure, sex and marriage, while women are free to express negative feelings toward work but tend to repress them toward family roles.

Applying these hypotheses to the issues that triggered public attention to the women's movement helps explain why reactions are more intense to the women's liberation groups than to women's rights organizations like NOW. There was widespread concern in manpower, government, and university circles when many bright middle-class young men began to depart from an unthinking acceptance of occupational aspirations like those of their fathers, either by shifting away from business, engineering, and science toward teaching, social science, and the humanities, or by indicating that their desire was for a life style with more time spent away from the job.

The movie *The Graduate* symbolized this generational contrast in dramatic form. Universities were concerned when men students expressed resentment to advanced training as a preparation for the adult rat race. But I doubt that anyone would have worried if only women had expressed such resentment. They would simply have been told that if they could not take the academic pressure, they should go home.

Public airing of ambivalence or a shift of values toward the place of work in the lives of men touches a vital nerve in American society. For women, the counterpart is any airing of ambivalence toward what the culture has defined as *their* primary roles, in marriage and maternity. However, once even a minority of women begin to reject their role as sex object, postpone or reject marriage, stop smiling over a shiny waxed floor or, heaven forbid, question the desirability of having children or rearing them themselves as a full-time job, then they touch an equivalent nerve in American society.

Hence, it is when men question work and women question family commitment that we find public responses ranging from a shiver of distaste to a convulsion of hate. It has been the questioning of family roles among women's liberation groups that has triggered the current widespread attention to the "woman issue." NOW's focus on employment issues, dealing with an "optional" role for women, cannot compete for media attention with antimarriage and antisexism campaigns by the women's lib spokesmen.

EMPLOYMENT

What, now, are the immediate problems and possibilities? Let me start with the bread-and-butter issue of women's employment. We must first look at a critical determinant of the changed profile of women's participation in the labor force. A lot of nonsense has been written in the past decade to account for the flow of older married women into the labor force. The emphasis has been on the impact of homemaking simplification via frozen foods and complex gadgetry on the one hand, and the search for self-fulfillment and a solution to the "problem without a name" on the other. This is to look for explanations on the supply side of the economic equation. But in an economy as hard-nosed as ours, such a stress is naïve, for there must be powerful factors on the demand side that prompted employers to open their doors to older women.

A significant factor underlying this willingness lies in the peculiarities of the demographic structure of the American population between 1940 and 1970. Young women were staying in school longer and marrying at an earlier age, thus shrinking the size of the traditional labor pool of young unmarried women. Even more important, the young women of the 1950s were born in the 1930s, when the birth rate was very low, while at the same time there was a vast increase in the number of young children born during the baby boom of those postwar years. As a result of the rippling effect of this low-fertility cohort, employers *had* to seek women workers from other sources than the young unmarried. Consequently, the trigger was in the first place far more a matter of employer demand than of assertive women pressing to enter into the labor force.

These were also years of vast expansion in precisely those segments of the occupational system in which women have traditionally been prominent. Because schools were flooded with the baby-boom children, women college graduates were assured a welcome as teachers despite age, marital and family status. Colleges and universities were expanding at a rapid rate, and married women were taken on as part-time instructors and full-time researchers. Clerical, sales, and service occupations were expanding, and women with high school degrees were able to choose among the available jobs.

This fortunate circumstance is now changing. In the 1970s there will be a reversal in the demographic pattern. The birth rate is now on the decline, the age at marriage creeping upward, and the time interval between marriage and childbearing widening. In the 1970s there will be more young unmarried and childless married women seeking jobs, for they will be the baby-boom females grown to maturity. At the same time, graduate schools will be producing large numbers of young people with advanced degrees, who will face a very different job market from the one that young Ph.D.'s faced during the past twenty years. Up to 1970 the supply of Ph.D.'s was far below the demand in institutions of higher education, but the reverse will hold from 1970 onward: the supply will exceed the demand in universities. This will be especially true for the natural sciences, less so for the social sciences until late in the 1970s. Which is not to say that the society cannot absorb or does not need highly trained people. From one point of view, the excess supply means an opportunity for reducing class size, providing students with better learning experiences, changing graduate curricula to prepare students for nonacademic jobs, etc. On the other hand, higher education is facing a financial crisis due to the cutbacks in government funding, corporations are pruning staffs of "frills," and government agencies are on an internal economy drive.

It is therefore of critical importance that women press hard during the next few years to secure equal protection of the law and to assure adequate representation in all segments of the economy. There is already a first sign that women are withdrawing from the labor force: in the last quarter of 1969 the Bureau of Labor Statistics showed a drop in the unemployment rate, though the drop occurred not because people found jobs, but because unemployed young people and women were ceasing to look for jobs.

What women must do in the next several years does not require new legislation, though passage of an equal rights amendment to the Constitution would cover a wide range of sex inequities in law and practice. Short of such passage, however, it is true that there has been a legal revolution during the 1960s in regard to protection of women's economic rights. Title VII of the Civil Rights Act of 1964 prohibits discrimination based on sex by all employers of twenty-five or more employees, employment agencies and unions with twenty-five or more members, with the exception of educational institutions. The Equal Pay Act of 1963 requires equal wages and salaries for men and women doing equal work. Amended Executive Order 11375 prohibits discrimination based on sex by federal government contractors and subcontractors. The Age Discrimination in Employment Act of 1967 prohibits discrimination based on age between forty and sixty-five. While this act does not prohibit sex discrimination, it could play a significant role in enlarging employment opportunities for women over forty who wish to return to the labor market or change jobs. Municipal and state Fair Employment Practices commissions and agencies administering state equal pay legislation can also be used to protect employment rights. Women in colleges and universities are not covered by the Civil Rights Act, but women lawyers in activist groups are now working through the channels provided by Executive Order 11375 rather than pressing for congressional change in the educational institutions exemption in the 1964 act. WEAL, the Women's Equity Action League, has mounted an important campaign designed to apply pressure on colleges and universities to comply with this executive order or face cancellation and future loss of government contracts—something no institution of higher education would care to risk. Labor Department guidelines were announced in June 1970 to assure equal job opportunities for women on work paid for under federal contract.

The mere existence of such laws does not solve anything unless women press for their implementation, first by concerted efforts to educate their sex, and second by developing test cases that will bring real changes in women's employment status. Though unglamorous and hard work, and rarely making a flashy news story, this is of greater long-range significance than any amount of bra-burning or anti-men speechmaking.

Right now it is not clear how national policies in the coming decade will affect the lives of women. In the post-Sputnik decade, there was a widespread campaign to persuade women to enter the labor force, with the government serving as spokesman for short-handed employers trying to meet personnel needs. The laws serving to strengthen women's economic rights were passed during the '60s. It is only in the past few years that Woman Power has emerged, with younger women questioning conventional women's roles. Even while expectations are rising, a reversal of national policy may lie ahead, as a brake is put on military expenditure, and as conservative political elements come into ascendancy with the new-old cry that women belong in the home instead of taking jobs away from men or making "outrageous" demands for maternity benefits and child-care facilities.

At the same time there will be mounting pressure for a national population policy. We are witnessing the advance wave of this policy with the unprecedented shift in opinion regarding abortion in the United States. Those of us who worked on this issue early in the 1960s are now gratified and disturbed by the ease with which total repeal of abortion laws looms as a reality: gratified because this represents the fruition of long, hard effort, disturbed by the quite mixed motivations behind the passage of such legislation.

Public dialogue on population is increasing significantly, and we begin to hear large families discussed as undesirable for individual couples and for society at large. But the problem is that women are being told to hold back on their fertility in the same era in which there may be a shift away from encouraging them to seek significant work in the economy, and when much volunteer work is being transformed into paid employment for the poor. Two such conflicting policies—low fertility and minimal participation in the labor force—can have serious consequences in undercutting the confidence of young women. It would be like putting them in a revolving door and spinning it: not permitting them easy entry or significant work *outside* the home, yet not permitting them fulfillment in a bountiful maternity *inside* the home. The social price of such a conflict could well be a rise in alienation, escape into drugs, alcoholism, or joyless sex and an even greater tendency to live vicariously through the few children they have.

I would like to think that women would take the lead in calling attention to the human dimensions of national policies that have particular impact on the lives of women. For the organizations directly involved in action concerning women's rights, such a thorough analysis is difficult. It takes time and some distancing from the heat of battle, and hence becomes a special responsibility of women in academia. But their voice will not be heard nor will their analyses be pertinent unless they keep in close contact with the women's rights movement and national policy formation. A good example can be seen in the congressional hearings on the birth-control pill this past spring, at which women's liberation spokesmen engaged in widely publicized protest. Their clamor was, in my judgment, ill-advised. We do not halt smallpox vaccinations because a dozen children die from them each year, or stop using antibiotics because 500 users die a year; by the same token, an element of risk in contraceptive pills is, in and of itself, no basis for calling a halt to their use. In no way is this to say that women should not have completely safe contraceptives, or that more emphasis should not be put on male contraceptives, sterilization, and abortion as acceptable procedures to control unwanted births. What I am urging is that women be more thorough and thoughtful in their analysis of a problem before rushing to the streets and into print with arguments that may appear sound superficially but are actually political posturing.

SEXUALITY

   Research and education in human sexuality, and the implications
of such research for the social roles of the sexes is another matter that
merits increased attention in the 1970s. Fifty years of accepting
Freudian concepts of female sexuality will not be quickly undone by
current research on the human sexual response. Psychoanalytic
theories have penetrated deep into the modern consciousness, and
are reinforced a dozen times a day through commercials that attempt
to sell everything from an Ohrbach dress to detergents. What concerns me equally is to be spared another fifty years of anti-Freudian
polemics from the women's movement.

   Very often such anti-Freudian analyses are couched in Marxist
terms. It may serve unstated political ends, but it is historically false
and analytically simplistic to claim that women's sexual role reflects
the bourgeois notion of man's desire to possess and amass private
property, or to charge that the second-class citizenship of women
merely reflects capitalist society's need to coerce them into domestic
slavery and conspicuous consumption. Marxist analyses of women
and capitalism have an element of truth only if you substitute
industrialization for capitalism. As the Communist nations have
industrialized, the same hard pinch of double jobs is detectable in
the lives of their employed married women, and the same loss of
humane values in the work place. Nor is there much evidence
that the relations between the sexes are particularly different in
Communist nations from those in Western Europe or the United
States. The major difference is merely one of intensity: no country can match the United States for media saturated with exploitative and male-dominant sex, typified so well by the infantile or
cruel acts of physical rape that fill so many pages of Norman Mailer's
books.

   A number of radical-feminist analyses begin with a good critique
of the Freudian fallacies concerning female sexuality. Let us now
assume it to be established that there is no differentiation between a
clitoral and vaginal orgasm; that the myth of women's relative asexu-
ality has been shown to be a biological absurdity; and that women's
sexuality has been suppressed through a socialization of gender roles
that urges passivity and submission to men. Liberation group dis-

cussions of these points can be enormously helpful for the psychological release of the submerged sexual selves of many women. But one must also reckon with the fact that the Masters-Johnson research only illuminates the *physiological* dimension of human sexuality. It tells us nothing about the nonsexual components of human sexual behavior. Critiques of Freud's notions of female sexuality are now commonplace, but I have seen little as yet that suggests an alternative developmental theory, with the exception of recent work by John Gagnon and William Simon. I would suggest that more critical attention should be paid to two factors bearing upon sexual behavior in American society. One is the view that sex is an intense high-pressure drive that constrains the individual to seek sexual gratification either directly or indirectly. This view is apparent not only in psychoanalytic but in sociological literature as well. Kingsley Davis, for example, considers sex a high-intensity, social constant that must be channeled lest it find expression in behavior that threatens the maintenance of collective life. Part of the Freudian legacy, however, is that we have become extremely adept at weeding out the sexual ingredient in many forms of nonsexual behavior and symbolism while rarely engaging in what may be an equally fruitful analysis: an examination of sexual behavior as an agency for expressing nonsexual motives.

For in truth, sexual behavior in American society serves not merely sexual needs, but also power and status needs compensating for a lack of gratification in other areas of life. A further complication is the pressure on American adults to remain pegged at an adolescent stage of development and behavior. A man or woman of forty-five is not the same person as a twenty-year-old, and to perform sexually as if they were is to require that the man overperform sexually and that the woman persist in a girlish style that is equally inappropriate to her stage of sexual and social maturity. In the case of men, overperformance can be stoked by extramarital adventures or self-stimulation via pornographic literature or dramatic productions. Men are good at such detached self-stimulation since they learn sexuality in part through masturbation, which itself paves the way for a greater detachment in the sexual act than women tend to have. It may also be the case that marital satisfaction and happiness decline with duration of marriage in American society largely because adults are expected to perform at forty or fifty as they did at twenty or twenty-five. This is a reflection of what Henry Murray has described as the retarded adolescent stage of development of American society. If, as a culture, we could move in the direction of mature interdependence between individuals, across social classes, religious, racial, and sexual lines, to say nothing of national boundaries, we might come to develop what Kenneth Boulding has described as "reconciling styles" in which we take primary pleasure in life from identifying with the process of change itself: watching and taking pleasure from our own individual growth and change, and the growth and change of our friends, spouses, and children.

What has this to do with the women's movement in the 1970s? I think we should be prepared for intense masculine backlash to the demands women make that are rooted not merely in the specific area of work or home management or parental responsibility, but in displacements from a deeper level. Demands for equality for women are threats to men's self-esteem and sense of sexual turf. Some feminists will say, fine and good: men have been our oppressors long enough, now they must give ground. But most women do not wish to live embattled and manless lives, and my impression is there are far more men in the younger generation than there were in my own who are eager to acquire a new life style, a gentler and more meaningful relationship with women. There is much need for research and sober analysis on the social correlates of varying styles of sexual behavior; following that, a great need for a rather different conception of sex education than anything we have seen in school curricula or gymnastic sex manuals to date.

Some women who have recently been active in women's caucuses in professional associations have begun to compare notes on the responses their demands are eliciting from male colleagues. One of the more interesting hypotheses emerging from these comparisons is that the men most resistant to and in some cases almost hysterical about women's pressure for equal treatment are men known to be sexually exploitative in their relations to women students. One such professor whose feathers were decidedly ruffled when the sociology women's caucus displaced a luncheon meeting he was to speak at, complained prettily, with an expectation that it would flatter rather than anger me: "But Alice, what is all the fuss about? There is always room in graduate departments for an extraordinary woman!" It was beyond his ability or willingness to under-

stand that sex equality in academia would not be achieved until
there was room for as many "average" women as for "average" men.
Some of my caucus colleagues believe that, beneath the surface,
men such as this are not able to relate to a woman colleague at the
same or higher status rank and feel comfortable only in superordi-
nate positions from which they can dispense professorial and sexual
favors.

The male backlash is bound to come, and there are signs of it
already. A male friend of mine recently sent me a xeroxed copy of a
letter of recommendation to the chairman of his department. The
applicant is an unmarried woman who had taught in the writer's
department and taken graduate courses with him. He wrote:

> When Miss X arrived she was somewhat lacking in self-
> confidence, uncertain whether there was a place for her in
> sociology. Now she recognizes that she can, as a female, contrib-
> ute to the field without becoming a spinster or a swinger. I say
> this to emphasize that she is a mature person not swayed by the
> superficial values so evident on campuses today. In short, she is
> not a participant in the women's liberation movement but a
> competent sociologist. . . . She is neither seductive nor emas-
> culating and will be a useful colleague.

I cite such examples to point out that we must have thick skins—at
least as thick as those of our grandmothers in the suffrage, union, and
socialist movements of an earlier day. We shall need every bit of sex
solidarity we can get.

WOMEN'S RIGHTS ORGANIZATIONS

Everyone knows there has already been a good deal of factionalism within the larger women's movement. We have WITCH,
WEAL, Radical Feminists, FEW, NOW, WRAP, and there are undoubtedly more to come. Listening to men, one senses a gleeful
pleasure at seeing such sectarianism; many wishfully view this as a
dissipation of effort in a noisy fizzle. But this need not be true so long
as those who form a new group do not concentrate on fruitless attacks
upon the group they left or on styles of protest directed mainly at
getting attention from the press. Diversity within a movement can
be a strength, for there is no one problem or one solution. Certain

women's liberation groups may be trying to recruit for a political revolutionary movement yet find some of their members graduating from consciousness-raising group sessions in affiliation with a NOW chapter. In turn, many NOW chapters have lost members to the liberation groups. Women lawyers have on occasion separated from the more diffuse organizations, the better to focus on campaigns making greater use of their skills. Other groups may concentrate on demonstrations protesting sex imagery in the media or beauty pageants. There is far more risk in frantically dissipating one's efforts by doing a great variety of things than in organizational splitting.

Let me end with a comment concerning the relationship between the women's rights movement and the movements of black Americans. There is a serious danger that the essentially middle-class and white women's groups will be as guilty of misunderstanding the problems confronting black men and women today as an earlier counterpart in the middle-class suffrage movement of the nineteenth century misunderstood the political efforts of working-class people.

In recent years, many women in the women's rights movement have taken up with great moral righteousness the task of informing black women that they should avoid the trap of moving through the same series of mistakes that middle-class women were subjected to in the past. A conference on women last February at Cornell culminated in a dramatic session on the black woman in America, in which the largely middle-class white audience hissed black women and men on a panel who spoke of the need for black women to give attention to the black man and his position in the community, to be supportive of their men's struggle for greater self-esteem and dignity. Renee Neblett of the Boston Black Panthers defined the black woman as a strong person who can act independently and make decisions but, most important of all, a woman with an ability to relate to men, one who would do anything to help her man retain or regain his manhood and insure the survival of her people.

In reading the transcript of this session, I felt anger and shame that the middle-class women in the audience had not appreciated the difference in the positions of the sexes among whites and blacks. John Dollard's description of caste in a Southern town is as relevant today as three decades ago, when he pointed out that within the white caste the man is in the superior position, and within the black caste the woman is more often in the superior position. If black women, largely poor but still more advantageously placed than black men, have the humanity and dignity to help raise the self-esteem of their men—to realize, as one of my black students put it, that the black female is no better than her man despite a history of educational and economic superiority—then this is a great tribute to black women in America that unfortunately is not matched by a comparable dedication on the part of white men toward their women.

Nor do we sufficiently realize the continuing relevance of class differences in the ways a problem is perceived and experienced. Abraham Maslow's need hierarchy thesis is helpful, for it suggests that middle-class women, whose physical needs for food, clothing, shelter, and sheer security of person are relatively assured, are free to concentrate on a higher level of need. A working-class person or group cannot indulge in such luxury until needs for survival and security are met. I think, therefore, that right now the middle-class women's rights movement can find a collaborative arrangement with black women only on such bread-and-butter issues as protecting and expanding economic and political rights. Beyond this, the white women's movement should try to deepen its understanding of the differences between their relations to men and those of black women. Before giving advice, one must understand. Listen, for example, to a black poet's phrasing of the issue:

> blackwoman
> is an
> in and out
> rightsideup
> action-image
> of her man . . .
> in other
> (blacker) words;
> She's together,
> if
> he
> bes
>   —Don Lee

What white poet has yet said of a man, "He's together if she is."

Despite the optimists in our midst, or the pessimists who anticipate revolution in the streets—after which, of course, a magical
transformation would follow—I think we are in for a long and hard
battle—cultural, legal, and political—before we reach any goal of
sex equality for black or white in this nation. It will be won not by
quickie-action skirmishes but by the persistent beat of the hearts
and work of the minds of at least another generation.

JERVIS ANDERSON
The Agonies of
Black Militancy
(1971)

Although black militancy has been one of the veins of American radicalism at least since the abolitionists, it was only during the early '60s that most people started paying much attention to it or even calling it by that name. More people seem to have been militant in the early '60s than ever before. If that is so, however, it suggests something quite important about that stage of the '60s: that it encouraged more hopes of a breakthrough into freedom, and thus stirred more black activism, than any previous period in the century.

When people started speaking of black militancy, they were not naming the tradition of black militant activity itself, but a mode of activism that seemed to be distinctly part of the style and personality of the '60s. And they were referring to black militancy not in the sense of black nationalism but in the sense of a movement whose controlling impulse was to break down barriers that stood in the way of a full and equal participation in American society, barriers that began to seem quite vulnerable at the turn of the decade. However, the style and personality of the '60s turned out to be more perishable than most of us could have foreseen. And part of what perished as well was that spirit we had come to identify as black militancy. The term is still used, to be sure—however quaint a throwback it may sound, however it may have the forced and somewhat square ring of language no longer quite in fashion. People who still use the term are mostly those who think that nothing much has changed, or those who find it the most convenient catchall for whatever goes on in the precincts of black radicalism.

Whatever happened to the black militancy of the '60s, or the mood that sustained it, is precisely what became of the '60s themselves. Though not everybody sees it that way, the '60s do not seem now to have been the best time to inaugurate new things—except, as it turned out, buildings and highways in memory of dead men and murdered hopes. To a large number of people, and mainly the young, the decade seems now to be littered with the ruins of great expectations: many of its more decent commitments dismantled; its moral language largely discarded; its political sensibility held in contempt; its outlook upon the world withdrawn; its racial promises revoked or betrayed; its moral sense driven up against the wall. Some who do not regard it that way, but mourn it nonetheless, see it as a half-finished house on a deserted road: not a nail has been driven in since the bank canceled its notes; shrubbery has grown up all around it; and vines are climbing over the raw masonry and unpainted woodwork. Some of those who had hoped to find a home in the house have lost faith in banks. Some of them, black militants of the '60s, seem to recall that this sort of thing happened to their forebears several times before. What sense therefore in continuing to believe in promises or in retaining their ties to American idealism?

Anyone who has been raised to respond hysterically to anything with the word black in it—or to find no consoling distinctions between one form of black radicalism and another—may be astonished to hear black militancy associated with the public idealism of the '60s. But such a person should try to remember who were the militants then, what forms their activism took, and what spirit sustained them. They were mostly young people and mostly students. They belonged predominantly to SNCC and CORE, almost the only groups that offered black and white American youth an opportunity to participate constructively in the passions of their time and help set right a society that had long been out of joint. And the tactics they used were sit-ins, freedom rides, disruption of facilities, and a generality of activity described as nonviolent direct action. However irritating most of this may have been to the country, it was somewhat within the American grain. It was certainly what the country seemed to ask of young people then: that they work for change and express their militant energies within the framework of American values. Much of what the young people did then seems rather tame today. But at the time it caused many of their elders in the freedom movement to tear their hair: it was "too provocative" and it could possibly be "counterproductive."

As to the mood that sustained the activism, it was one of optimism—belief that the country was ready and able to respond favorably to demands pressed upon it within the spirit of its own professed ethics. Then came the years between 1963 and 1968 when that belief was shattered by a series of bullets, and the country has not been quite the same since.

Considering whom the bullets struck, they appear to have been aimed directly at the aspirations of the young, the black, and the poor. In any event, most blacks had only one way of seeing it: once again white racism had cast its veto over social and racial progress in America. It does not seem now to be any accident that it was between those years, '63 and '68, that American cities started going up in flames; that young middle-class whites started embracing what have been called un-American heroes and un-American ideologies; that blacks began entertaining—at least expressing—an interest in guns and black power; that the Vietnam war was escalated into a metaphor of contemporary brutality; that this war drove at least half of America out of its skull; that the escape from reality found its most comforting haven in drugs; that almost an entire generation of young people turned to the politics of self-indulgence, self-righteousness, irrationality, violence, and despair.

Today, if there are young blacks who still consider themselves militants, a look at whatever they are "into" will reveal that they are considerably less militant than people who consider themselves something else—people who say that what they are "into" now are things like revolution, liberation, self-determination.

Out of this, where alienated blacks are concerned, two predominant tendencies have taken shape. The first is marked by a set of attitudes which, shared by a variety of individuals and groups, is defined roughly as "nation-building" or cultural nationalism. And the second, a set of political attitudes—roughly described as revolutionary nationalism—is represented most spectacularly by the Panthers.

While it is not the first time that frustration has forced a large number of blacks to withdraw into themselves—and while the black nationalist movement of the '20s was larger than anything that exists today—this is the first time that the withdrawal has appeared so calculated and considered. One cannot recall a time when so many among the educated black young and the lumpen intelligentsia of the streets appeared so utterly at odds with the idea of America, when there appeared to be such a deep and conscious spirit of disaffiliation with the things and processes of the general culture.

Whether it be the movement to salvage and revaluate black history, build up black studies, or talk up the black experience; whether it be the search by young writers and literary intellectuals for a "black aesthetic," different in method, sensibility, spirit, and values from the "white Western aesthetic"; whether it be the claim that black culture is a distinct, independent, and viable element within American society—whether it be any of these, there now seems more intellectual energy and seriousness than ever in the bid to reconsider the blacks' relationship to the society, to define the grounds for dissociating from the culture, and to create "new black men."

Stated simply, perhaps too simply, the black cultural tendency holds a greater feeling for its connection to African cultural forms and roots than for its development within the community of white history and values. Whether such a feeling may have developed in any case—even if blacks had long been accorded what they conceived to be their rightful status in the society—it is hard to say, though it may be worth speculating upon. What seems clear is that the feeling has come about in direct response to a long history of denial in American society.

Much or all of this, however, is in conflict with the ideology of cultural integration held by a more traditional school of black literary and cultural intellectuals. These intellectuals do not so much advocate cultural integration—though the advocacy is clearly implied —as they assert it to be a fact: that there is neither a black nor a white American culture but that the one has been irrevocably shaped and

influenced by the other. There are no more articulate and formidable proponents of this point of view than Ralph Ellison and Albert
Murray, both of whom operate out of a deep sense of the inescapable
interconnections of black and white American life. To them the term
"black American" or "Negro American" is not merely a convenient
political combination but a fine fusion of culture and consciousness
and historical experience.

Ellison's ideas, stated and restated in much of his writings, were
recently quoted in part by James Alan McPherson in an article,
signed by both men, in the *Atlantic Monthly* (December 1970):

> I think that too many of our assertions continue to be in response
> to whites. I think that we're polarized by the very fact that we
> keep talking about "black awareness" when we really should be
> talking about black American awareness, an awareness of where
> we fit into the total American scheme, where our influence is. I
> tell white kids that instead of talking about black men in white
> society, they should ask themselves how black *they* are because
> black men have been influencing the values of the society and
> the art forms of the society. How many of their parents fell in love
> listening to Nat King Cole? We did not develop as a people in
> isolation. We developed within a context of white people. Yes,
> we have a special awareness because our experience has, in
> certain ways, been uniquely different from that of white people;
> but it was not absolutely different. . . . I think . . . that we've
> looked at our relationship to American literature in a negative
> way. That is, we've looked at it in terms of our trying to break into
> it. Well, damn it, *that literature is built off our folklore* to a large
> extent! I ain't conceding that to *nobody!*

In his book *The Omni-Americans* Albert Murray writes:

> White Anglo-Saxon Protestants do in fact dominate the power
> mechanisms of the United States. Nevertheless no American
> whose involvement with the question of identity goes beyond
> the sterile category of race can afford to overlook another fact that
> is no less essential to his fundamental sense of nationality no
> matter how much white folklore is concocted to obscure it:
> Identity is best defined in terms of culture, and the culture of the

nation over which the white Anglo-Saxon power elite exercises such exclusive political, economic, and social control is not all white by any measurement ever devised. American culture, even in its most rigidly segregated precincts, is incontestably mulatto. Indeed for all their traditional antagonisms and obvious differences the so-called black and so-called white people in the United States resemble nobody else in the world so much as they resemble each other. And what is more, even their most extreme and violent polarities represent nothing so much as the natural history of pluralism in an open society.

In pointing out these interconnections within black and white culture Ellison and Murray are absolutely right, of course. That certainly seems to be the cultural reality of the United States. But it is not so much the reality itself which troubles those young people who now want to consider themselves cultural nationalists as it is their experience at the hands of the reality. It may be one thing for them to see that American culture is indeed a composite to which blacks have contributed some of the most vital elements. It is quite another thing for them to realize that those who dominate the cultural composite take no more serious and consequential a view of the blacks' part in it than a white household takes of the traditional black help, or a white audience of black entertainment. What most marks the response of whites in such situations is an enjoyment that rests upon a certain fundamental contempt for those who provide it. The general view of such help or such entertainment is that it is after all what blacks do best, almost the only thing they do well, and of considerably less consequence than the role of whites in the life of the culture. As John Corry up it in a recent article in *Harper's,* "One way or another, white America will try to turn blacks into song and dance men."

Not all blacks will oblige. Were they to oblige, it would be almost like saying that one way or another blacks will acquiesce in America's efforts to keep them second-class citizens. That, of course, is not true. And the same smoldering resentment most blacks feel against the effort to keep them second-class citizens marks their refusal to be considered no more than the song-and-dance men of American culture. Not everybody will want to go in the direction of the cultural nationalists; but the effort they make to cut themselves off

from the general culture, withdraw into a cultural community of
their own, and cultivate the African strains in their historical background, all of this may represent *their* refusal to be seen merely as
the song-and-dance men of the culture.

This feeling of tension with the majority elements in the culture
is connected not only with periods in the past but also with a
tradition of skepticism quite as respectable as the intellectual tradition that supports the idea of cultural integration. As early as the
turn of the century, W. E. B. DuBois was expressing the painful
contradictions of the black American cultural situation in these
words:

> He [the American Negro] would not Africanize America for
> America has too much to teach the world and Africa. He would
> not bleach his Negro soul in a flood of Americanism, for he knows
> that Negro blood has a message for the world. He simply wishes
> to make it possible for a man to be both Negro and American,
> without being cursed and spit upon by his fellows, without
> having the doors of Opportunity closed in his face.

And almost two decades later, during the Harlem Renaissance, Alain
Locke noticed a cultural reaction similar if not identical to that of
today:

> This deep feeling of race is at present the mainspring of Negro
> life. It seems to be the outcome of the reaction to proscription
> and prejudice; an attempt, fairly successful on the whole, to
> convert a defensive into an offensive position, a handicap into an
> incentive.

While neither of these reactions implies or advocates cultural
separation, they have a good deal in common with the reaction of
those who today are in effect crying out as DuBois did against the
agony of being an integral part of a culture that nevertheless spits in
one's face and declares one not yet worthy of being taken seriously.

Why, anyway, is it blacks who are constantly being reminded that
American culture is a composite? Are there not others who appear to
be in greater need of the reminder? Why is it that most whites are
able to get away with forgetting it? Why is it that remembering it
does not seem to make much difference in blacks' experience?

Why—since American culture is so "patently and irrevocably composite"—have the experiences and contributions of blacks been ignored, distorted, or otherwise treated so shabbily in American history books? Why has it been left to blacks to salvage much of their past and their pride from the cutting-room floors of white historians? The answer may well have something to do with power, particularly with those who have it: the power of the majority culture to see as it pleases; to define and impose standards; to promote values and pass judgment; to determine what is of consequence and what is not. Whites "do in fact dominate the power mechanisms of the United States," Murray says. They certainly do. And those mechanisms include culture, which in turn includes the power to dominate and influence the shape of a minority's sense of itself.

The point of all this is not that cultural nationalists are justified in their attempt to withdraw into a cultural enclave of their own or that this is even possible in America. One cannot by sheer fiat or a simple act of will undo the complexities and continuities which have been in process since blacks were transported into the Western experience. The point is, though, that there has been a good deal of anguish felt and a good deal of contempt suffered by blacks while trapped in the cultural crucible of these centuries. The point, too, is that they are entitled to bawl, and deserve to have some attention paid to the cause and nature of their pain.

"There is also," Ellison writes, "an American tradition which teaches one to deflect racial provocation and to master and contain pain." That may be true—though God knows it is hardly a tradition one would choose if he had anything to say about it. But what one knows as well is that experience also teaches us that pain cannot or should not be contained forever, and that a continual deflection of racial provocation may well be achieved at the cost of some awareness of and regard for who and what one is. One can well understand how deep-seated in the white American imagination is the image of silent and noble black endurance—in fact, we know this because it is one of the perceptions forced upon us by the power of the majority culture. But it is simply another fantasy built upon wishfulness and contempt. And, even more important, it is a fantasy that has done its part, a very large part, in helping to maintain the status of race relations in this country and the contradictions in the social and political experience of blacks and whites.

It's time we all stopped believing it. It's time we all realized that humanity may consist more in giving utterance to one's suffering than in containing it, resisting racial provocation than in deflecting it, raging against an unjust status than in accepting it.

If it turns out—and as it appears—that no viable rearrangements are possible within the present reality of American culture, the function of intellectual leadership may well be to speak compassionately to that condition, to provide the rationales by which blacks may confront the stubborn irony of it and make some tragic peace with it.

There is hardly anything to be said about the Panthers that hasn't already been said or that everybody doesn't already know. Whatever insufficiencies the Panthers have been victimized by, they do not include an insufficiency of publicity. Almost everyone has heard about their founding in Oakland; of their claims to be the vanguard of an armed black revolution; their breakfast programs and shoot-outs with the police; their alleged connections with international Communist conspiracies; their trials in and out of court; the fascination they hold for rich ladies in pants suits; and their celebration by the intellectuals of chic, machismo, and cultural fashion. Much of what describes the reaction of the cultural nationalists may be applied politically to the Panthers. Only one aspect of this resemblance will be considered here.

As the latest stage in the continuum of black radicalism, the Panthers are as much in reaction against the society's continued frustration of black hopes as against the failure of the civil rights protest movement to fulfill these hopes. This is of course a hard position to take against the protest movement, since the power of that movement is simply to persuade and not to act. It is also a position that ignores the solid accomplishments of the protest movement, in the early '60s, accomplishments that dramatically widened the frontiers of black freedom. To be a part of the radical spirit of today, however, is to share in the ideology of instant gratification and to hold a contempt for strategies and tactics that may achieve gratification a twinkling later.

Thus—although almost every bit of racial progress this century has been achieved by the civil-rights movement—it is now held to have temporized and compromised too much, to have wasted its time fighting for integration, to have bitten its tongue in the presence of the white establishment, to have asked for what it could get rather than demand what it was entitled to, to have sold out on black manhood. Thus, too, it has come to appear that one of the principal issues around which the Panthers are in motion is the issue of black manhood. An inordinate amount of their rhetoric seems aimed at expressing the essential quality of black manhood which has been denied—a certain mixture of bravery and arrogance. Bravery and arrogance express themselves in a kind of existential revolutionary theater: living dangerously, threatening destruction, cultivating extreme experiences, risking themselves in extreme situations. Since the slave rebels, only a handful of black men have felt the call to live this way—politically. Cleaver: "We shall have our manhood or the earth shall be leveled in our attempts to gain it." Or as someone less prominent said more recently, the only thing young blacks are prepared for in this country is to destroy it.

The last time that black radicalism was so strident in tone—though more intelligent, more thoughtful, and less sanguinary—was in the years between World War I and the middle '20s when the black economic radicals led by A. Philip Randolph attacked American society and the traditional black leadership with a racial militancy and an ideological vehemence that probably still has not been surpassed. And perhaps it was way back there that the possibilities for rational radical action among blacks began to be exhausted, because the black radical movement of the twenties turned out to be pretty much a spectacular failure. If this is so, then, perhaps the country only has itself to blame that the only possibility for the continuation of black radicalism today lies in the areas of irrationality and violence, or—as Joseph Conrad said in a book that has some relevance to our present political experience—madness and despair. Victories in these areas are measured in martyrdom, in suicide, and in how much of the society a rebel takes with him at the moment of his destruction.

As the seventies grow older, this could even get worse. Who's to say what attractions young and embittered black soldiers returning from Vietnam may find in the Panther movement? How many young ex-convicts may be inspired and emboldened by the revolutionary examples of Cleaver and George Thomas? Urban guerrilla warfare led by Panthers, the young black lumpen proletariat, embittered ex-soldiers and ex-convicts may be a nightmare from which it could take a long time to recover—and which many, of course, *many of us* may not survive.

Finally, as periods of black politics have followed periods of intense radical or protest activity, so may the Panther period, as it has been christened by admirers, give way to renewed political activity among many young blacks. Not immediately, of course, for the memory of the more recent frustrations are still too fresh in our minds. The majority of the black population itself represents no more encouragement to the prospect of a revolutionary radical future than America itself does. "The Negro mind," wrote Alain Locke in 1925, "reaches out as yet to nothing but American wants, American ideas."

Ironically, the opportunities for political involvement to which a large number of young blacks may yet turn in the '70s were created by the efforts of the much maligned civil-rights movement. The increase in registered voters, the training of young people as political organizers, the striking down of many of the legal obstacles blocking the way to an open society, the continued if incomplete integration and democratization of the trade-union movement, the election of black candidates to political offices across the nation—all of these have been enabled by the limited but genuine accomplishments of the civil rights movement. They have also created more space in which blacks can maneuver themselves to the levers of American power. One only has to look at LeRoi Jones's political activities in Newark and his new proximity to the levers of power in that city to realize the uses that may increasingly be made of conventional political avenues to power.

One last word, though, about the Panthers. Even those who believe that blacks can at best share equally and democratically in American power, rather than seizing it, are in no position to carp too cheaply at the Panthers. They are paying an enormous human cost in madness and despair. But madness and despair were not embraced voluntarily; they are precisely where the American experience has driven youthful idealism and activism for the foreseeable future. People like the Panthers are witnessing to the madness that all blacks have felt at one time or another—and to the despair that many of us have avoided only by dint of some tragic and incredibly hopeful conception of the world and of our experience.

JESSE PITTS
The
Counterculture:
Tranquilizer or
Revolutionary Ideology?
(1971)

In an essay I wrote a while back, "The Hippies as Contrameritocracy" (DISSENT, July–August 1969), I argued that the movement was essentially a response to meritocratic pressures bearing down not only upon youth but upon the society as a whole, and that it represented a first-line structural response that probably would not endure in its initial form. This argument seems to me still decidedly to the point, but I would now like to go a little further. As of the early 1970s the hippie movement has divided itself into four major cultural streams and organizational patterns; the commune, the drug culture, the music culture, and the political youth movement. While all of these could be found in some form prior to the rise of the hippies, it is the hippies who provided them with momentum, style, and legitimation, so that the hippie look came to serve as their badge of allegiance. Various writers have described this phenomenon under the generic term of "counterculture"; I have described it, with an eye toward its structural origins, as a contrameritocracy.

In some form or other, communes have always existed in the United States. There are some in Europe as well, and a number have lasted for several generations, like the Communauté Boismondeau which, with an 1848 ideology, makes watch cases as a producers' cooperative. Such groups have flourished in the United States, in part because of our abundance of land and space, so that people have been able to "do their thing" without too much popular opposition. Popular historiography presents the Pilgrims as a band of men and women whose religious principles led them to come to the New World and found a commune of their own. *Newsweek* guesses that there now may be 500 communes functioning at any one time, with a total membership of 10,000.

But the significance of this movement goes beyond these small figures. On any campus there are a number of students who experiment with "communal living," which means sharing the money and housework. During the summer and after graduation there are many who try with more or less conviction to live in a communal way in the country and share in the farm labor. The rural commune is where the hippies have retreated in order to escape being swamped by the young "pre-moral" types and exploited by individuals ready to use any kind of violence that will insure them bed, board, drugs, and sex. Communes can select their members and impose some sort of vows upon them. And if the mortality rate of communes and the turnover of members seem rather high, only in the communes do the nonviolent themes of hippie culture retain some vigor.

The hippie communes feature a persistent attempt to organize group life without overt leadership and with a minimum of sex-role differentiation. Yet rural life, because of the premium it places upon physical strength, tends to sharpen the division of labor by sex, especially if there are children around who require close watching. The girls find themselves working in the kitchen, doing the sewing, and caring for the babies—while the men work in the fields, fix the fences, repair the barn, and make expeditions to the square world for canned goods, pot, and spare parts for cars. The urban communes, by contrast, find it easier to reduce, if not abolish, the sexual division of labor.

Leadership is repressed as sex was repressed by the Victorians, and just about as successfully. Commune dwellers avoid words like "directed," "requested," "ordered," as Victorians avoided "thigh" and "belly." Efforts are made to resist the crystallization of leadership, and when they are successful during the season when much hard and monotonous work is necessary, the result is often disastrous for the capacity of the commune to survive on its own. Tools are lost or broken through careless use. Weeding is not done. People disappear at harvest time. Luckily enough, there are checks from home or dividend checks, and people can go away to work for wages and return when they have accumulated enough to buy brown rice and beans for several months.

"Group marriage" also creates problems. Some girls are better-looking than others, and prejudices against homeliness die hard among liberated men and even liberated women. There seems to be an irresistible tendency for the leading "nonleaders" to exercise a powerful attraction upon the more beautiful girls, a tendency that has also been observed in "encounter" and "sensitivity" training groups. Most communes have more men than women and hence some men are always left out. Luckily, commune life does not seem to raise the level of sexual desire among men. Communes frown on "playboy" types, and we know that the threshold of "sexual frustration" is determined more by the norms of the group than by any sort of "biological urge." What seems to work best is some form of monogamy plus some 10–20 percent adultery. In the commune one would speak less of "adultery" than of "experiences" or "switching." Some switching takes place without too much overt pain. In other cases the best way to describe what happens is to say that a top male is replaced in the affections of one of the best-looking females by another male, with the displaced male leaving for another commune or deciding it is time to go to work outside in the flatland for the wages that will replenish the cash pool. Another common way that resolves the shortage of women is for one or two girls to be on a "promiscuous kick." As long as they don't try to seduce the top males away from their women, their constant state of availability will receive gratitude and amused condescension.[1]

Successful farming or even gardening requires a good deal of repetitive and careful work. Urban types tend, after a while, to miss the excitement and variety, or even more the *privacy*, of city life. Indeed, the commune is different from the urban hippie community in that people in the commune are forced to interact and reach some form of harmony. In standard rural life a sharp division of labor, clear-cut lines of authority, and a stress on getting the work done reduces the areas of "problematic intimacy." But in the commune problematic intimacy is the rule rather than the exception. Some are helped by this atmosphere, some put off.

Communes may allow for greater role shifts in their members than do most other forms of small group organization. A personality in search of its identity and strong enough to face the demands of others may find in the commune greater support for the changes he is going through than he can find in his own parents. Communes that are successful in limiting the contacts of their members with the outside world can develop private cultures that are very demanding and also sometimes rather deviant. These, however, are rare. Lack of discipline is so much more frequent that it reduces the capacity of the commune to test systematically new forms of social relations. The mystery, the rich fantasies that surround communes, from the Satanic with Manson, to the humorous as with the Hog Farm, will insure a steady supply of mass-media interest. *Time-Life* waxes sentimental over communes.

The urban-based Hare Krishna, which has an involved set of rules and real discipline, is limited in its impact by its conservatism in regard to sex roles and its Hinduist spiritual and vestimentary transvestism. Since communes have the same appeal for people with sexual hangups as nudist camps used to have—and with the same sedative effects—the Hare Krishna also suffer the public relations consequence of their apparent sexual frugality.

Many communes, even those made up of dropouts from Ivy League and New York universities, attempt a pathetic imitation of Indian life: a search of roots for the rootless; an identification with those too powerless to be guilty; a put-down of the WASP majority for having chased the Red Man from his God-given territory.

Still the communes represent the hubris of the Puritan tradition, the attempt of men and women who feel moved by the spirit to create a perfect community, where the person can meet God face-to-face and be as unique, as true, as giving as God must be: Promethean arrogance that is the dignity and the curse of our Judeo-Puritan civilization, and shall always deserve our respect and our hope that one day we can make it work. The communes remind us that no man is free not to search for God and that in this search resides his honor even if in the end he meets but his fallible self.

II

The second major cultural stream picked up and amplified by the hippie movement is the drug culture. Before the late '50s, marijuana smoking was limited to blacks, Puerto Ricans, and Mexicans, and among whites to jazz musicians who had picked it up from black colleagues. In the Eastern colleges, only the few students who were real jazz aficionados might have some casual contact with marijuana. The radical movement, in its Communist, Trotskyite, or other varieties, was dead-set against all drugs.

In the mid '50s a new phenomenon began: the widespread use of drugs in the treatment of mental disorders. For those not so sick, Miltown became a fashionable remedy against anxiety and tension. In many professional families, where anxiety, hypochondria, and nonconformity describe the social climate, taking tranquilizers became a fashionable exhibit of how many of the world's troubles one had to carry.

The children of these families went to college and there met with at least two currents that would help their conversion to drugs. The first was the poetry-reading fad, often against a background of jazz music, with its heroes the beat poets, Allen Ginsberg, Gregory Corso, Lawrence Ferlinghetti, Gary Snyder, Kenneth Rexroth, and Brother Antoninus, who gave recitals in colleges followed by late-hour gatherings where the "in" crowd would "turn on."

The second current was the civil rights movement, whose undeniable greatness was marred by the transformation of the Negroes into angels with black faces: a form of *ouvrièrisme*, probably inevitable, which led some to imitate the objects of compassion in their speech, their ghetto separation, their music, and even their "vices." Since blacks smoked marijuana it had to be a good thing. Heroin addiction, instead of being horrible, became a sort of secret cult— dangerous, of course, but also a curse of greatness that revealed to the initiates how many jazz musicians were addicted to it.

At the same time, one of the barriers to the diffusion of drugs, the frat culture of football games and beer busts, began to disintegrate. A new elite appeared on Eastern and California campuses; instead of claiming upper-class and old-settler connection, it claimed legitimacy on the basis of political awareness and intellectual activism. Its

name-dropping related more to the *New York Review of Books* than
to the Social Register. The smoking of marijuana became one of its
rituals of solidarity, just as the heavy drinking of alcoholic beverages
had been the ritual of the frats. Many professors who looked with
disdain on the frats looked with approval, if not fondness, on the new
student leaders. Whatever their antics, political or recreational,
these students supported values in tune with high culture even if the
search for the "golden screw" did not allow them to turn in papers on
time. Although they might come from prestigious private schools
and have rich parents, they did not snub their professors. Many
even wanted to join the profession. The period 1957–66 saw the
height of the post-Sputnik meritocratic campus, where professors
attempted to impose upon adolescents from all social classes the
ideals of the intellectual jock.

By 1963–64, however, the ideals of the contrameritocracy—
affirming the right, nay the superiority, of dropping out, and the
claim that drugs gave access to a knowledge superior to rational
knowledge—all became part of the hippie "backlash," which gave
the diffusion of marijuana, soon followed by other drugs, a new
impulse and legitimacy. By 1964 the whole college scene (i.e., the
200 most selective establishments) was permeated with marijuana,
and by 1965 LSD became widely available. In 1967 drugs had begun
to infiltrate the high schools. In 1970 a questionnaire, distributed in
two middle-class high schools located in the suburbs of a large
Midwestern metropolis, showed that only one-third of the students
had never taken any drugs, one-third had had only an occasional
experience with them, and one-third took drugs (overwhelmingly
marijuana or hashish) once a week or more. A tenth of the student
body could be called "serious" users. Heroin users (not necessarily
addicts) were rare, but 1 percent in a student body of 1,500 still
makes fifteen users.

The drug culture gets its organization from "dealers" who in turn
secure their supplies from wholesalers. The dealer is a semibenevo-
lent merchant who barely makes expenses *over the long run*,
wholesalers being the real money-makers. The small-time dealers
"turn on" frequently with their customers. Although sales promotion is not unknown, the dealer prefers to think of himself as servic-
ing a need rather than creating it. Gifts to customers are not un-

common. The small-time dealer becomes a "taste leader" to his clients and this leadership is not necessarily limited to drugs. Clients and dealers meet in an "underground" atmosphere that seems exciting. For many personalities at loose ends the drugs provide a motivational center, a substitute identity, and an occasion to relate meaningfully to others, even if in the process they may kill a certain percentage of those who use them.

Drugs are used, of course, by members of other hippie cultures such as the communes, the music culture, and the political culture. And with time, drugs have lost much of the mystical aura with which the hippie movement had surrounded them. But, especially among some teenagers, drugs have become an end in themselves, a subject of interminable conversations, part tranquilizer, part escape, part dare, a form of Russian roulette with which the middle-class adolescent can demonstrate to himself he has "heart" without engaging in the fights and gang bangs dear to the "grease." It is a juvenile delinquency with low risks, where prosecution does not alienate you from your peers; a means of self-assertion and rebellion, yet a way of imitating older adolescents in the search for maturity. As such, it is already spreading to the junior high schools. The drug culture has its own scale of prestige where the bottom rung belongs to the marijuana experimenter and the top rung to the users of the needle, who inject Methedrine, Seconal, or heroin.

Drugs were publicized heavily by the underground press until 1968. Such youth movies as *Easy Rider* and *Getting Straight* (there is a lame attempt in *Getting Straight* to oppose the heavy use of drugs by showing the "head" to be unreliable), and the rock songs have glamorized marijuana and LSD.[2] At the present time the irony of drug education programs (it is one way of employing excess language teachers) is that they finish the publicity job the rock songs and the movies have begun.

Drugs serve an anti-establishment function through the promise of unconditional pleasure (pleasure without having to "earn" the right to it), and through their relation to an antirationality where astrology and good or bad "vibes" replace the belief that hard work, learning, and persistence will get you where you want to go. They promote "dropping out" of structures that require postponement of gratification (college). Through instant nirvana they lure some of the

young away from the Puritan establishment culture. Drugs also have
an anti-establishment function through the dissonance of illegality.
During Prohibition alcohol rarely had this effect, if only because it
was part of a traditional male culture resonant with the aggressive
toughness of the Puritan ethos and therefore lacking, even in illegality, the tone of subversion.

To evaluate the future of drug consumption in the United States
one might look at the problems of the legalization of marijuana. The
proponents of legalization find themselves caught in several cross
pressures. It is difficult to press for restrictions on tobacco and
pollution while advocating the legalization of a hallucinogen about
which little is known as to long-range effects. One cannot press for
limits to fertilizers, pesticides, and cyclamates, and wish to generalize the unsupervised use of a drug that has a powerful and little-
understood impact upon the brain.

Another cross pressure is that the steady use of marijuana *does*
lead frequently to further experimentation with other drugs. (A
colleague of mine doing research on marijuana effects and using
medical students as his subject population, noted that it was hard to
find cases where marijuana smoking had not been followed by more
or less broad experimentation of other drugs, so that it became
difficult to distinguish between the effects of marijuana smoking and
those of other drugs.) Although the great bulk of drug experimenters
settles down eventually to a "martini-type" consumption of marijuana or hashish, a certain percentage is sucked into a process of
hard-drug addiction, which may last for years before death or remis-
sion occurs. Thirty years ago, seventeen-year-old alcoholics were
practically unknown. Today middle-class drug addicts on pills or
heroin or plain "pot-heads" are not uncommon, and the group most
affected is that of children who participate in the anti-establishment
culture centering around the school's swingy teachers. Many a
potential candidate for an Ivy League college turned on as a high
school junior and found in his senior year his grades slipping to the
point where even graduation is in danger.

In liberal circles which dabble in depth psychology one frequently hears that "if it had not been marijuana or barbiturates it
would have been something else." This sort of fatalism, based on no

data whatsoever, is not very convincing. It comes from the same ideological outlook that sees in the concept of "bad company" an authoritarian or segregationist prejudice, and ignores the insight it contains. The fact is, there are times when, in the necessary process of emotional disengagement from parents, adolescents do become very vulnerable to outside influences, even if their upbringing has given them "good" principles. In most cases there will be a return to these principles, but the experiences that the adolescent may in the process go through can sear his mind and body for life.[3]

Those whose interests in the legalization of marijuana comes mainly from an antagonism to the Puritan ethos must accept the fact that the illegality of drugs reinforces their anti-establishment significance. The legalization of marijuana would destroy the social influence of the benevolent dealer, as well as the dissonance of illegality which tends to promote allegiance to the counterculture. Legalization might also accentuate the pacifier aspect of drug intake and facilitate the co-opting of the drug users into the system. This seems to have been one of the major functions of drugs in relation to the lower strata of India, China, the Arab countries, and the South American Indians.

Yet the legalization of marijuana, like the legalization of pornography (already accomplished *sub rosa* by the courts), could have a strong impact as a symbol of the weakening of the Puritan ethos. But if the Puritan ethos were not mortally wounded in the process, the violent attacks upon it could lead to a fundamentalist reassertion which might crush liberalizing movements and lead to drastic changes in the personnel that mans the gates of the mass media.

Under these conditions the pros and cons of the legalization of marijuana are complex and there is not likely to be a major push in that direction, certainly not while Mr. Nixon is in the White House. Heavy drug use will probably lose its fad appeal as it reaches the junior high schools where it can be controlled more effectively by parents. One frequently meets college freshmen who have already been "heavy" into the drug scene and are ready to leave it, now that drug use is becoming identified with the "freak" part of high school culture, rather than with college sophistication.

Marijuana and hashish will probably remain illegal as prostitution is illegal. Drug use of a heavy and prolonged nature will be the tranquilizer of the stagnant and the defeated, the novocaine of downward mobility. For some middle-class adults who follow the *New York Times Magazine* section in asserting the chicness of marijuana smoking,[4] it will become the equivalent of bathtub gin in the 1920s. For others it may become a middle-class equivalent of what the gin shop in Zola's *L'Assommoir* was to the working class.

III

Now to the third and most creative cultural form in the hippie movement—the music culture. Reaching an apex in the Woodstock festival, it derives its organization from the musicians, the promoters, the disc jockeys, and the record industry.

This movement has its roots in several strands of American popular music. There is the folk singing strand, which had remained an antiquarian interest until it began its slow climb to popularity under the aegis of the Popular Front. Folk singing expressed the wisdom of the American folk and as such deserved the support of the progressive. This was the period when the movement took to square dancing and Pete Seeger was a major troubadour. It continued during the war in "Café Society Downtown" and "Uptown" and eventually developed its own momentum in the 1950s to culminate in the TV Hootenanny (with a little assist from Tennessee Ernie Ford's "Sixteen Tons"). Joan Baez with her voice and Bob Dylan with his poetical talent were to give a new dimension to folk singing in the first half of the 1960s.

Other strands of the music culture were the rock and roll of black popular music and the blues, the latter being one of the great contributions made by the blacks to American and world culture. A synthesis between the two at the end of the 1950s and the beginning of the sixties gave us the particular Detroit sound known as "Motown." Meanwhile Elvis Presley had made a national fad out of his particular fusion of "mountain" music and rock, getting white audiences to accept a much more orgiastic and openly sexual message within the medium.

The Beatles created the new music by synthesizing the rock of Elvis Presley with Motown sound. They brought to the states their "rocker" or young British working-class style, and it caught fire immediately. One might have expected the hippies to look down their nose at the Beatles and return to the records of Ornette Coleman and Leadbelly; but they did not. On the contrary, the Beatles and the Rolling Stones became new culture heroes. Hippie musicians, combining rock, blues, and English sound (the Yard Birds, the Cream) and using Dylan-type lyrics gave young America a music all its own, relegating jazz to the paternal generation. It was partially on the wings of the music created and played by John Mayall, Paul Butterfield, Mike Bloomfield, the Frugs, the Jefferson Airplanes, the Grateful Dead, Jimi Hendricks, the Canned Heat, and many others that the hippie movement became a mass movement, only to explode under the strains of its success, leaving the music culture to develop on its own. The musicians are also close to the drug culture, which they have popularized by their songs and example. Rock musicians (AM rock in working-class districts, FM rock in middle-class districts) have become in the high schools an alternative to the athlete as nonacademic and even anti-academic models.

There is little doubt that the youths who become either players, band followers, or aficionados of the rock culture have a strong antimeritocratic bias. Yet even for them the requirements of professionalization conflict with the cult of spontaneity. Long practice is necessary if one is to obtain proficiency. There is much competition in the music field and the rewards for excellence are enormous, both in prestige and money. The discipline of playing, and the organization of the show that accompanies the playing, stimulate self-control and self-distance. Drugs, however, are a constant temptation for an ego that is put on the block at each performance. But the instability of rock musicians, whether due to their personality types, drugs, life on the road, or the temporary allegiance to music as a career, makes such groups transitory and the quality of their music hard to sustain. Because of their talent, their unusual stability as a group, and the widespread belief that financial success had not spoiled them, the Beatles were the role models. Now that they have disbanded, there seems to be a certain exhaustion of inspiration throughout the rock movement.

Rock music has become a transmission belt for anti-estab-

lishment views, through both the lyrics and the orgiastic color of the
music. It has contributed to the isolation of youth culture from adult
culture by creating a much sharper break between big band music
and rock than there was between ragtime and big band songs—a
process symbolized by the end of the "Hit Parade" program in the
late 1950s.

The music culture does not lead per se to political commitment.
Musicians tend to be "situationists," prompt to underline and act out
the absurd. They find political rhetoric boring, and at the rock
festivals the mood seems hardly conducive to radicalization. How
much lasting alienation from the Puritan ethos the music creates is a
moot point. It may promote a commitment to the "counterculture"
through the prestige it gives to deviant life styles and also has impact
in promoting the counterculture among a segment of working-class
white youth who enjoy the contact and occasional sexual opportunities that rock will give them with college youth.

Drugs and music have made a much bigger impact on youth
society than has the "dropout" message of the hippie movement. Yet
dropping out can take place, even while serving time in high school
or college, simply by the withdrawal of motivation from occupational
and family roles. For most, the moratorium is temporary; for some,
even beneficial.

IV

Perhaps both the drug and music cultures would have developed
without the hippie phenomenon. The connection with the latter's
love and freedom ethos gave the "practitioners" a feeling of group
membership and self-righteousness, which greatly increased their
proselytizing capacity. The same can be said about the political
culture, which was born separately from the hippie movement and
eventually merged into it without losing its identity—just as the
communal movement, the drug and music cultures have done.

It was probably the collapse of the Communist party as a vital
political force after the 1956 Hungarian uprising that provided an
opportunity for the development of a tenderhearted and expressive
oppositional movement, free of the bureaucratic discipline and "rule
or ruin" tactics characteristic of Bolshevik politics. This was the New

Left. It received considerable momentum from the FSM movement at Berkeley (1964), where it first discovered the vulnerability of the university to political protest.

Three social forces were to give unexpected impetus to the New Left. The first was the development of the "technico-professional complex" as a political tendency led by left-wing academics. The civil rights battles were their first experience with mass politics, after which came the peace movement as it found its real start on the campus in the 1965 "teach-in" organized at the University of Michigan.

The second force was the cooperation of the mass media, especially the TV networks and the national news magazines (*Time, Life, Look, Newsweek*), which saw in these movements not only a source of dramatic news happenings but also of an ideology commonly shared by cameramen, reporters, news commentators, and even the vice-presidents in charge of editing the six-thirty news show. The mass media and especially TV will give favorable exposure to the New Left, but with this proviso: it must fit the interests of the technico-professional complex of which they are a part. Their coverage of the Vietnam war in 1967–68 was an extraordinary boost to the peace movement and yet remained "invisible" in its political intent.[5] "The Breaking of the President 1968" was also a major success, although of course they had a major assist from their victim.

The third force was the hippieization of antiwar students and the New Left. From the hippies the New Left took its life style, clothing, hair, language, sex life; and from 1967 onward many hippies renounced nonviolence and political indifference.

The hippieization of the New Left enabled it to attract the drug and the music fans, giving them a political identity of sorts as well as feelings of solidarity. For nonpolitical but disaffected youth, the musicians legitimated the hippie garb. Though it would create difficulties with the world of square adults, the fact that the mass media customarily saw the hippiefied youth as the exemplars of the new style and the new rebellion also helped to push antiwar students toward the New Left. For when the mass media speak of "youth" or "the students," they certainly don't mean the average youth with a vocational orientation toward college, good relations with his parents, coolness toward drugs and promiscuous sex, and a political

outlook slightly to the left of Hubert Humphrey. No Stalinist front
has ever been so successful in endowing the young with its distinctive aura as has the coalition of antiwar students, New Left, hippies,
and the mass media, operating without any formal committees,
secret accomplices, or central apparatus.

V

From this coalition two major currents have emerged as the
standard-bearers of the counterculture. The first is the literary-
sociological assault on the Puritan ethos and the WASP establishment; the second, the Che Guevara type of political activism where
the effectiveness of the action is subordinated to the exaltation of the
participants.

The literary-sociological assault has been carried out by a group
essentially marginal to the academy, but which desires to keep the
aura of the academic commitment to scientific truth. Yet it cannot
accept the uncertainty of scientific truth, its perpetual renewal, its
rejection of the temptation of power. This group, which might be
called the "intellectuoids," searches for a theology in science, a
fighting faith which will help to destroy the country-club set, the
yacht-club set, the deanery, the professorial establishment, Palm
Beach, the military-industrial complex, and install in their place a
brotherhood of freedom.

Inevitably many of these intellectuoids are young instructors and
assistant professors who in their professional fields are ready to
accept the burdens of uncertainty but revert to self-serving
ideologies when it comes to social issues. It is probably too much to
ask that they should approach social science in an intellectual fashion
when many of their own peers in sociology, psychology, and political
science seem to have transformed their disciplines into a sort of
muckraking journalism where the basic "theoretical" orientation is a
new version of *delenda est Carthago* or Voltaire's *Écrasons l'in
fâme*. Too often when opening *Trans-action* and even *Psychology
Today* one can predict the argument of the article from a mere
knowledge of the title, at least if one follows the principle that the
WASP establishment and the Silent Majority are oppressive, de-
humanizing, pig-dominated, exploitative, polluting, inefficient,
sexist, afraid of sex, racist, authoritarian, rigid, frigid, fearful,

paranoid, white-collar criminals, desperate, sick, sadistic, infantile, and ignorant.

Besides *Trans-action*, *Ramparts*, the *New York Review of Books*, the intellectual ammunition of the counterculture on campus is provided by the radical paperbacks dealing with street violence, racism, and the Third World. Marcuse, Fanon, Kenneth Keniston[6] (who sees in the student radicals a breed of moral supermen as, more realistically, Richard Flacks sees in them the new Social Register), and Jerry Rubin's and Abbie Hoffman's nonbooks, Roszak's *Counter Culture* and Charles Reich's *Greening of America* are typical resources of the radical faculty. They have organized courses entitled *Where It's At* and *The Revolution of the Sixties*, the prototype of which is Harvard's full-year course *Social Relations 147–148*, taught to some 600 students rewarded by easy A's. Part of this counterculture is seeping down to the high schools and private schools where, in conjunction with the drug and music culture, it contributes to the development of the "freak" grouping, somewhere between the "frats" and the "grease."

The literary-sociological assault has "radicalized" the culture of "Proper bohemia," to which belong the young college instructors, the civil liberties lawyers, the Unitarian militants, the Quaker work camps, the mass media specialists (especially those below the $40,000 level), the publishing-house readers and editors, movie directors, actors and actresses between jobs, and other professionals and paraprofessionals who gravitate around the university. A few rich businessmen contribute heavily to the financing of the local underground press and often own the FM stations which provide them with tax write-offs and their younger friends with job opportunities.

The counterculture takes from the upper class its casualness about rules, and also its willingness to use four-letter words that show it to be above middle-class constraints. Most exponents of the counterculture are of petty-bourgeois origin, and most petty bourgeois, not having been raised in bourgeois manners, try to bypass them. They imitate the aristocracy's disregard for proper form, believing that they thereby partake of its elegance. They assume the permissiveness of the upper class but not its *noblesse oblige*.

The hippies have provided a pattern of dress which, interpreted by the jet-set boutiques, becomes a badge of being "with it" and a challenge to the status of the traditional Puritan elites. The doctrine of "crystallized establishment violence" has facilitated the transition from the pacifism of the civil rights movement to the legitimation of the violence perpetrated (way downtown) against the establishment and its Irish cops. The worship of the Black Panthers whereby Proper bohemia atones its guilt—sometimes intellectual guilt, sometimes a disguise for ethical vanity, sometimes guilt as to the sources of the parental fortunes—has become another badge of membership and a gambit for claiming moral superiority over the conservative old rich.

In the 1930s Proper bohemia, besides being much smaller, was influenced by the Stalinist version of Marxism and held real power in some publishing houses.[7] At the present time the ideological tenets are more of the hippie variety. Not that hippies invented them (the sophisticates will refer to young Marx and Wilhelm Reich), but they provided the symbolic rejuvenation for some of the old utopian standbys: arts-and-crafts communism, elegant pastoralism, the poor as noble savages (more specifically the black and Indian poor, certainly not the Polack poor). The hippie cultivation of mood has become the emotionalism of sensitivity training; hippie work avoidance, hippie stress on equality of the sexes, the promotion of career aggressiveness in women and of sensualism in men. While the Puritan ethos implied a commitment to abstract values and a suspicion of ascriptive group ties and unearned pleasure, the counterculture promotes a sort of organic groupism in battle against the enemy camp and an existential concern with body pleasures from which active sports are usually excluded.

VI

The meaning of the counterculture is not exhausted by referring to its obvious protection against the pains of possible failure and its utilization as a weapon of class struggle. There are other aspects which might turn out to be effective solutions to major problems of the postindustrial world: the development of an international community of the young; a blurring of the lines between work and play; a considerable decline in status formalism; a greater equality for women.

Everywhere, perhaps even in Soviet Russia, there seems to be an erosion of classical patriotism. By contributing to this erosion the counterculture orients the search for the sacred toward an international community of students. On the other hand, the critique of nationalism too often takes on a shrill quality that denies any obligation of the citizen to the nation. Instead of replacing nationalism by a thoughtful dedication to an entity beyond the nation that requires even more self-sacrifice, there is a tendency toward a premoral affirmation of the primacy of self-interest. The counterculture hatred for the nation is parochial, often too bitter to be the result of a greater love.

Similarly, the counterculture seems to be trying to create the elements whereby the traditional division between work and play can be overcome by a new synthesis. What seems to be wanted is an end to the guilt that attends some of the processes necessary to creative work: the careless as well as the careful experimentation, the trials and errors, the sloth of discovery and the failure to discover anything, the painful fact that most innovations are useless. If we are to solve the problem of work meaninglessness (and I am aware that there is a lot of romantic drivel being peddled under that expression), it is likely that a definition of work less associated with the routine deprivations of discipline must become more generally accepted. Professors know this problem well who feel guilty when they have an enjoyable conversation with their colleagues, a conversation that often leaves a sediment of new ideas, while their superego associates work with the careful reading of Talcott Parsons or the thorough preparation of a lecture which leaves little room for response to the audience.

In the process of this search for a new definition of work the counterculture seems to have been instrumental in the destruction of the post-Sputnik university, whose excesses contributed to the development of the hippie movement and to the spread of drugs. In the present permissive atmosphere of academe most students can accommodate a commitment to the music, drug, and political cultures without any need to drop out from either the university and/or their families. It is possible that the revival of Rousseau's ideas on education, which the counterculture is promoting, may have a positive impact on teaching. So far the older faculty, puzzled and frequently demoralized, laments the passing of the post-Sputnik university, while young faculty want to transform academe into a sanctuary from which to lead students into forays against the Establishment. Meanwhile, little is done about teaching, and the decreased power of the deanery makes it less likely that anything constructive (hence somewhat painful) will be done. It is unlikely that the impulse will come from the students now that they have gained soft grading, Mickey Mouse courses, and mixed dormitories.

A greater rate of discovery and change, even if limited to the expressive spheres of life, will demand a greater solidarity, a willingness to put up with the higher rate of obsolescence and disorder that creativity implies. Thus the counterculture's stress upon the legitimacy of ephemeral art, the poetry of mood, the immediate sensitivity and positive response to others, may just possibly create conditions for a solution to the problem of work, play, and rank in the postindustrial world.

Meanwhile, its search for intimacy often seems like a Hollywood version of the shoe salesman's pseudo-*Gemeinschaft*, a ploy for Portnoy on the make. It mocks work discipline and suspects the poor of "Uncle Tomism" if they take "blind-alley jobs." Since most of its adherents work in bureaucratic organizations where they do not own the means of teaching or administration, contempt for private property may seem to have a revolutionary meaning: the property is that of the pig landlord, the pig stockholders, the pig establishmentarian government. It seeps down to the youth society as indulgence for "ripping off." Solid bases for comparison are lacking, hence we cannot be sure that there is really more stealing in the stores than forty or fifty years ago, or much more cheating in school. On a short-run basis, we all know that cheating and thievery on campuses have reached epidemic proportions. Some of it may be the result of the changing composition of the student body, or of a redefinition of stealing by middle-class students as a matter of taste.

The decline in status formalism may facilitate social mobility and reduce the costs of marginality. Yet the intolerance that the straight upper middle-class reserves for bad manners is more than matched by the intolerance the counterculture shows to those who disagree with its views. In many localities it has created a level of political contentiousness and lawsuit-proneness that did not exist before it gained a substantial following.

One might hope that the positive advantages of destruction and reconstruction created by the counterculture will be gained without disorder and reaction. But this hope seems unrealistic. New solutions for tomorrow may come from a few of the communes, but so far the intellectual caliber of the blueprints for tomorrow proposed by the literary-sociological assault has been disappointingly low. Again the medium has been the message.

The weakness of the counterculture analysis, once it tries to go beyond the exaltation of mood and personal freedom, is partly reflected by the weakness of the political movement it sustains, and which I here describe as the Che Guevara movement. This movement contains the political spectrum that made up the non-Bolshevik section of SDS of 1968–69, and independent groups like the White Panthers, whose leader, John Sinclair, was one of the original Midwest hippies and a good jazz critic. The core of the Guevarist movement is made up of the more romantic and anti-bureaucratic revolutionaries who remind one of the Russian Narodniks (Populists) of the 1860–70s, except that our Narodniks have little desire to convert the white working class and peasantry, and are not often welcomed by the blacks. They meet their best response in the "swinging" and "Proper bohemians" of the middle class, and of course among the college students and/or middle-class dropouts from either high school or college. The Weathermen might well take for their hero Nechaev, who wrote with Bakunin the famous *Revolutionary Catechism* (1869). They have seized the imagination of the revolutionary students by their undeniable courage and flamboyant actions, as well as their luck in avoiding arrest. It will be a while before the police effectively penetrate the organization and corrupt it—which seems to be the fate of all underground movements unable to come quickly above ground and relate directly to the political public.

While the original hippie movement had many aspects of radical Puritanism, this tendency is now found mostly in the rural commune; the Che Guevara tendency is much more overtly anti-Puritan. In contrast with the ascetic patterns of the Bolsheviks, the strength of the American Narodniks resides in their capacity to combine the delights of moral righteousness with the underwriting of sensual release through drugs, sex, music, vandalism, "ripping

off," and violence. They have developed a style of leadership that
permits their roving bands or campus-based groups to have the
benefit of direction without the penalty of felt subordination. To
middle-class youth this seems to have more appeal than the authoritarian "delegate from the Central Committee" typical of the
Bolshevik tradition.

The Guevara movement has had some success (though more
apparent than real) because it was carried along for a time by the
peace movement created by professors of the elite colleges and
universities. Within that movement—which, for instance, in the
mainstream (Michigan) campuses of the University of of Michigan,
and of Oakland, Michigan State, and Wayne State universities receives the support of 70 percent of the liberal arts students[8]—the
Che Guevarists were like fish in water. As a result, until 1969–70 the
revolutionary activists benefited not only from the support of Proper
bohemia, but from the indulgence of some antiwar professors, and
the favorable publicity of the mass media which played down their
provocations but gave maximum publicity to police excesses in
repression. The Guevarists (and the Bolsheviks) thus used the peace
movement as a cover and a resonance box, and in return provided an
energy and drama that academics could not supply. They also benefited from the inexperience of college administrators and police in
coping with the type of disorder created by a group that amounts at
most to 1.5 percent of the student body in the Michigan universities,
and probably to no more than 3–4 percent of the Ivy League under-
graduates.[9]

The present fading of the peace movement has left the Che
Guevara groups stranded. Its activists try to take the leadership of a
new mass of American *bezprizorniki*, the "street people." The latter
are quite different from the hippies and their teeny-boppers, even if
their hair and dress are similar. While the hippies were attached to
nonviolence even when it delivered them to the exactions of hoodlums, the "street people" use knives and guns without much reluctance. Their panhandling is aggressive while the hippies' was
humorous, hiding behind a joke the guilt they experienced. While
heroin was considered uncool by the hippies, its use is not rare
among street people. While hippies would delight in "blowing the
mind" of an ogling tourist, the street people are more ready to roll

him. No doubt hippie centers were not without some of these pathologies, but they were recognized as deviant. The norm of universal love and keeping one's cool worked toward self-control and personal responsibility. "Keeping one's cool" is not an expression one hears very frequently among street people, and this means more than a mere passing of argot.

The street people, roaming, turning on, panhandling, ripping off, raping (i.e., a "gang bang" with a bit of force at the beginning), once in a while getting killed (and killing), hanging around the universities (preferably the prestige ones) from which they secure some crumbs and protection, resemble the sometime students, sometime bums, sometime hoodlums that lived around the medieval universities. The connection to high culture, more and more fictitious, saves the street people from being defined as common juvenile delinquents. The Che Guevarists are trying to dignify the amoral violence that prevails in this group by politicizing it. They hope for rehabilitation through revolutionary uplift and opportunity. Meanwhile the result is more often the spreading of a new set of hip rationalizations for aggressive acting out, which includes bombing and arson, and a ripoff on the new brand of self-appointed social workers.

On the basis of this diagnosis, two scenarios can be constructed. The first is based on the hypothesis that the academic community will not be further influenced by the counterculture and will not attempt to increase its own political power—and that the liberal-left faculty will let the peace movement die on the vine and not allow the Guevarists to use the university as a sanctuary. Then, the faculty would take toward the student movement the same stance it took toward the jock and fraternity cultures which provided much of the contrameritocratic ideology before 1960. Through an interval in the student movement, an irresistible momentum of social assimilation would be imparted to the ethnic and racial minorities that provide its more determined militants. The 1970s would then see a period of university and social adjustments to the strains of the meritocracy, which would motivate a new creative surge at the end of the decade. The counterculture would then be preempted of its useful elements and the rest encapsulated, so as to provide a permanent justification for those whose rewards in the capitalist-bureaucratic society do not seem commensurate with their ambitions. This, paradoxically, would contribute to the long-range stability and productivity of the meritocracy.

Another scenario requires at least two postulates. First, that the faculty—partly because of the threat of downward mobility implicit in the "high-schoolization" of college, partly because of the charisma of science which it generates, and partly because it is the most articulate segment of the technico-professional class—will try to develop the peace movement into a political battering ram, using masses of students and new voters as its army. Second, that the counterculture will reach the white working-class youth.

The politicization of the colleges and universities would lead to the growth of influence of "Proper bohemia" over the "straight" faculty. The disaffection of the intelligentsia and the near-monopoly of the mass media held by groups hostile to the WASP establishment would result in widespread alienation of the youth for whom meritocracy would cease to be meaningful. The result is that economic and military institutions could not be staffed with adequate talent. At the other end of the scale, there would be an accumulation of college diplomates or partial diplomates having to settle for jobs which in the generation of their parents did not even require a high school degree. The experience of downward mobility from the college student status, if not tranquilized sufficiently by the counterculture, would create much resentment and smoldering aggression, especially in a climate where the dignity of labor, the last fortress of pride, had been debunked out of existence.

Meanwhile the WASP establishment, bereft of the symbols of legitimacy, as well as of intellectual advice and support, would lose its nerve and its capacity for social control. The United States would then enter a phase of disorganization, with lesser growth in industrial productivity leading to relative deprivation among the working class. From there one can choose his climax: Berlin, 1930, with a fundamentalist reaction, or St. Petersburg, October 1917, with the assumption of power by a theocracy of politicized intellectuoids, which would bring back order and the comforts of a sacred orthodoxy. Of course, such a disequilibrium of the capitalist order in America might lead to atomic war.

Somehow, the pessimistic scenario does not seem convincing. The mass media have a way of banalizing and sterilizing new cultural forms by giving them instant success. A movement in the United States soon becomes a fad, overwhelmed by the problems of success before it has had time to deepen its insights. Were this Czarist Russia, the disaffection of the mass media gatekeepers (if not of the intellectuals) might herald revolution. But this is multicentered America.

Most of history is dull rather than dramatic, and the 1970s seem more likely to result in the stabilization of a contrameritocratic movement, which would blunt the cutting edges of meritocratic competition. Furthermore, the professional intellectuals have begun a criticism of the counterculture, which should soon result in a decline of its prestige with the mass media.

The professional intellectual has a crucial role to play in the solution of the problems created by the meritocracy if he can find a way to show the society that the true goal of man is the understanding of nature and that the face of God "can be found in the anatomy of the louse." In this contemplation the search for the sacred finds a solution in which achieved rank differences, so emphasized by the meritocracy, are shriveled to insignificance by the cosmic perspective of learning. Within a generation, more than half our population may well be involved in the learning process, as learner, as student, and more often as both. What an opportunity for the professional intellectual to expand his influence if he will only resist the temptation of power! Meanwhile he must put his house in order, dampen his snobbery, strengthen the community of equals and the international community of scholars, take more seriously his teaching responsibilities. He must incorporate the adult community into the universities, and recuperate his legitimacy as the leader in the search for elusive truth. In the disenchanted world of the meritocracy people long for a sense of purpose and meaning. It is the intellectual's urgent task, at this juncture of history, to teach through the word and his example that the passion to know must replace the passion to conquer.

Footnotes

1. Commune dwellers would fiercely deny that they show amused condescension. New value conflicts lead to new areas of repression. Freudianism is not "in" within the commune.

2. The retort by record companies that most listeners cannot tell the meaning of the words and care only about the music neglects the fact that those who understand the words operate as translators. This is certainly one case where the medium is the message.

3. In many suburbs, therapeutic youth centers have sprung up with batteries of phones available to give help to anxious youths whose problems range from boredom to "bad trips" to a need for an abortion. Such centers, heavily steeped in the counterculture, are often directed by a swingy psychologist or psychiatrist aided by mother types out of *Alice's Restaurant*. The bulk of the aid they give is precisely the chance to find a congenial group with a new form of self-righteousness which abates the adolescent's guilt. Here it is not a question of learning to dream in a Freudian manner so as to please the "shrink," but becoming innocent through a put-down of the establishment. It probably does help the youth in getting himself "together."

4. Cf. Sam Blum, "Marijuana Clouds the Generation Gap," *New York Times Magazine*, August 23, 1970.

5. Richard W. Jencks, head of the CBS broadcast group, declared in a recent conference on the problems of broadcasting, where he was being attacked from the Left ("T.V. Neglects Social Needs"): "History will assign television a major role in the black revolution and in the anti-Vietnam war revolution . . ."

6. Kenneth Keniston seems to be having some second thoughts as he discovers the self-serving aspects of moral righteousness in the student radical. Some of the writers used by the counterculture can become quite distressed by their fans.

7. For a good description of this milieu, see Mary McCarthy's *The Company She Keeps* (1942).

8. This is the result of a poll of 1,200 students in these universities in May–June 1970.

9. Figures derived from the Michigan survey mentioned above. There is a higher percentage of revolutionaries among the students at the University of Michigan than at the three other universities.

DAVID M. MUCHNICK
Death Warrant
for the
Cities?
(1976)

Running against New York has emerged as a Ford Administration campaign strategy, symbolizing middle-American contempt for the Eastern Establishment and spendthrift politicians, as well as central cities, blacks, and welfare recipients. The presidential demand for and surveillance of municipal belt-tightening appeal to conservative budget-balancers and corporate borrowers. Federal support for Southern and Southwestern urbanization suits the Republican "Southern strategy" and regional banks. These policies, together, have imposed a heavy share of the burden for the recession, uncertain recovery, and restructuring of American life styles and expectations on Northern and Eastern central-city residents and workers. And now they threaten to sever traditional Democratic party loyalties. The new breed of fiscally conservative Democratic governors and mayors, who are dependent on Washington and private banks for financing, have been forced to levy new taxes, cut popular services, and break the municipal labor unions. New York's unions are expected to make up their city's budget shortage by accepting massive layoffs and a wage freeze, by investing their pension funds in risky bond issues, and by renegotiating their pension benefits. In 1976, there may be sufficient disenchantment with *all* politicians for many traditional and young Democrats to stay home in November and deny their party's presidential candidate many habitual votes. Shades of 1968!

Presidential politics are a necessary but insufficient explanation of the city's plight. As a matter of policy, long before Jerry Ford's presidential fate depended on it, the White House decided that America's immediate future no longer resides in her older central cities in the North and the East.

This policy not only reveals the transparency of the Administration's hardening-softening line on New York's fiscal crisis; it also dispels the major anomaly in current political posturing—the presidential golf partner of U.S. industries and multinational corporations campaigning as prairie populist, defending America's working people against the "large investors and big banks" who "bankrolled New York City's policies for so long."

What this policy is, however, has never been "perfectly clear." Law and order, the new federalism, benign neglect and impoundments have been misinterpreted by liberal critics as the absence of domestic vision. Economic and diplomatic crisis-management has seemed to preoccupy Washington. Nor is there a strong personality with whom to identify a coherent program—there is no domestic Kissinger. Instead, responsibility has rested with dispersed and unglamorous operatives, primarily in the Office of Management and Budget (OMB) and the Domestic Council. Many White House outsiders, special interests, congressional staff, and local officials still doubt the existence of a national urban policy. So far, because of this uncertainty and the narrow, partisan explanations of what happened in New York, the opposition has failed to seriously confront the Administration.

Three programs reveal the contours of executive thinking and the new limits of American democracy: community development, housing assistance, and welfare reform.

These three programs, involving upward of $50 billion annually in federal outlays and income-tax subsidies, embody a centrally determined, not-so-neglectful national urban policy. This policy limits federal investment in metropolitan social needs, shifts development priorities in favor of growing cities and suburbs (especially in the South and Southwest), and hampers the emergence of a political coalition able to challenge these decisions with alternative national goals. The Administration's stand on New York City's financial catastrophe not only follows this policy but strengthens it.

The Community Development Revenue Sharing program is a keystone of the Administration's national urban policy and new federalism. It was introduced by President Nixon in March 1973 and signed into law by President Ford only thirteen days after he assumed office. It provides relatively unrestricted grants for the development of public facilities to states and so-called metropolitan cities—to each central city, each suburban city of more than 50,000 people, and to about 70 urban counties in the country's 243 metropolitan areas. As a result, a city's planning and development process has gained almost complete administrative discretion and nearly total freedom from federal red tape and supervision. Said President Nixon (in a radio message on March 4, 1973), "The time has come to reject the patronizing notion that federal planners, peering over the point of a pencil in Washington, can guide your lives better than you can." Presidential rhetoric is deceptive.

The Office of Management and Budget and the Department of Housing and Urban Development (HUD) never surrendered power to dictate the amount and regional allocation of federal investment in local communities. Their determination of the program's $2.3 billion first-year level ignored not only inflation and the advice of the U.S. Conference of Mayors but also a grass-roots survey of over 200 communities that estimated a national need for $5.5 billion in fiscal 1974 alone. OMB and HUD have shifted federal capital away from the redevelopment of older, Eastern and Northern industrial central cities in favor of the development of growing, prosperous suburbs and cities, especially in the South and the Southwest.

Excepting New York and Chicago (which, because of their sheer size, will fare better financially than they have in the past), the next seventeen biggest central cities in the North and the East eventually will lose an estimated $168 million yearly, compared to their combined average yearly receipts between 1968 and 1972 under previous programs. From a five-year average of $378 million, their funding will be sliced almost in half, to $210 million yearly in fiscal 1980. Philadelphia, Detroit, Baltimore, Washington, D.C., Boston, and Cincinnati will lose over $97 million annually among them. By contrast, Houston, Dallas, Memphis, New Orleans, Phoenix, Jacksonville, Fort Worth, Miami, El Paso, and Birmingham together will gain over $71 million annually. Although ten other large Southern and Southwestern cities will suffer a 32 percent cut by fiscal

1980, these cities will enjoy a 140 percent increase, and the total grants for these twenty cities will rise to $211 million.

To finish the illustration, Massachusetts' fourteen central cities will lose $46 million annually by fiscal 1980, while aid for its suburbs and rural areas will increase by $15 million and $1 million, respectively—a net annual statewide loss of $30 million. Alabama's eighteen central cities will gain $5.4 million annually, while funding for its suburbs and rural areas will increase by $23 million and $6 million, respectively—a net annual statewide increase of $34 million. Nationwide, central cities will lose $276 million annually by 1980, while federal investment in suburbs and rural areas will increase by $757 million and $291 million, respectively.[1]

This regional distribution occurs because all metropolitan cities are "entitled" for the first time to funds as a matter of right. A technical mechanism was needed to provide an automatic basis for dividing the national pie. Population, poverty, and overcrowded housing are three relevant census characteristics of all of these localities and so provide the national data base for the allocation formula. The older central cities dispute the validity of these factors as measures of local needs. They prefer more direct indicators, such as the age or deterioration of an area's physical housing stock or a community's past redevelopment efforts. Local officials of these older central cities argue that the consequences of universal entitlement on the basis of population result in the loss of dollars by cities with declining populations, in the provision of scarce funds to wealthy communities with no poor and no overcrowding, and in the financial, administrative, and political reinforcement of those suburbs that deny residential and occupational opportunities to lower-income workers, poor people, and minorities. Both the Nixon and the Ford administrations have rejected these objections as matters of national development planning, rationalized budget procedure, and local self-determination.

The limit on metropolitan investment and the shift in regional priorities express the fear of a capital shortage and the decision to invest federal money where it will be "profitable" in the future. That is, scarce public capital should subsidize private economic and demographic growth in a mutually supportive way rather than be

wasted in decaying centers already abandoned by business and the
middle class. As early as 1972, former HUD Secretary Romney
warned the annual convention of the nation's Mortgage Bankers
Association that "America faces investment decisions more critical
—more consequential—than at any previous time in our history.
They will have a direct impact on money and credit for housing and
community development." In addition to capital for energy and
environmental needs and economic expansion, he advised

> population migration, despite decreasing population growth, is
> forcing major new investment in housing, retailing, superhigh-
> ways, water and waste disposal systems, hospitals, schools and
> all the rest of the community physical structure—but now in
> more dispersed geographical areas—a dispersal that raises the
> per capita cost of facilities.

Among the trends, Romney noted, were not only the apparent
stabilization of growth, and possible decline, in the New York,
Chicago, and Los Angeles/Long Beach metropolitan areas, but also
interregional migrations from north to south, from east to west; from
hinterland to coastline; from smaller metropolitan areas to those
between one million and two million—the "dynamic growth centers
of the next several decades."

> One thing is clear [he cautioned], these population shifts stimu-
> late and also force major new investment in growing areas—and
> endanger previous investments in declining areas. . . . We must
> avoid at all costs $100 billion public and private investment
> mistakes. For we cannot afford gigantic waste in any area. The
> pressure and demands on our economy in the next decade will
> not permit such a luxury.

At the national level, universal entitlement according to an
objective formula rationalizes previous federal funding practices. It
weakens the power of senior congresspeople to influence commitments to particular localities. It automatically provides funds to
many cities that for political, ideological, or other reasons stayed
away from the earlier grant programs, and it reduces the significance
of "grantsmanship" by enterprising municipalities. The Domestic
Council argues that none of these factors is reasonably related to a

distribution on the basis of need, and that their control is necessary to avoid waste and fiscal irresponsibility. One consequence is the reduction suffered by most northern and eastern central cities.

Another effect is more curious—the increased aid anticipated by New York City under this particular program, from $101 million the first year to $157 million by fiscal year 1978. Previously, the city had been "underfunded" relative to any measure of need because of long-standing congressional and executive hostility to meeting what are thought to be the city's unique problems. New York appears to place unlimited demands on the Treasury, and mid-American congresspeople and executive decision-makers are unwilling to tax their constituents or distort their priorities to pay for the city's troubles. Universal allocation by formula recognizes New York's needs somewhat less arbitrarily and constrains the provincial hostility a bit by providing funds to all localities. The city remains starkly underfunded, however, relative to its own determination of needs—an estimated $240 million for community development in the first year alone. As recent events testify, the antagonism persists whenever the city's needs are made to appear special.

At the metropolitan level, fiscal rationalization has had to be imposed because of the failure of the reform movements for metropolitan government and planning. Metropolitan agencies were to have coordinated community development activities of central cities and suburbs, ending the inflationary pressures·of waste, duplication, and unnecessary spending. But traditions of localism proved too strong, and the Administration's fiscal planners had to act. Their technique is straightforward. After OMB determines the national funding level, the community-development allocation formula makes its first apportionment to each census-defined metropolitan area. Only then are the central city and each suburb allotted their shares from the metropolitan pot to use as they see fit. From a federal budget perspective, the simple step of allocating the first sum to the statistical metropolitan area transcends local boundaries and rationalizes the *aggregate* level of spending in each metropolis.

Because the community development program implements a national development policy and rationalizes the fiscal planning process, the details of local administration are essentially irrelevant to Washington. Therefore, they can be delegated to municipalities under the rhetoric of returning power to local communities. As Ford's Deputy OMB Director Paul O'Neill put it, "[ours is] a national perspective of what the Federal role is, what is happening in the country, what the other levels of government are doing, what the private institutions are doing and where our legislative thrusts should be."[2]

Housing is the second element of the national urban policy. In January 1973, the White House unilaterally suspended the country's four subsidized housing programs. The Washington *Post* subsequently revealed government memos indicating the cut-off was for fiscal, not programmatic reasons. "We had to save a half-billion dollars," said Nixon HUD Secretary and Ford OMB Director James Lynn.[3] Concerned about the federal deficit's inflationary consequences, the budget planners slashed the $500 million programs as part of a $10 billion domestic cut in fiscal year 1974, and, as O'Neill later testified, to avoid being locked into a forty-year obligation for over $17 billion.[4]

Nine months later, President Nixon outlined the Administration's thinking on housing—continued support for private home-ownership, termination of production subsidies for low- and moderate-income housing, and initiation of housing allowances, starting first with the elderly poor. He proposed an interim subsidized construction program (now known as Section 8) to be terminated on December 31, 1975, after which direct-cash assistance would become the nation's *exclusive* assistance policy. (In the 1974 Housing and Community Development Act, Congress refused to ratify the cessation, insisting first on a feasibility report on allowances *early in 1976*. The "interim" program is in effect, and local communities fear to protest the switch to allowances too strongly lest their applications for subsidies be adversely affected.)

The support for homeownership follows the historic thrust of U.S. housing policy—accounting for about $10.2 billion of the almost $15.3 billion in direct expenditures and tax revenues foregone by the federal government for housing in 1972—but now it takes on an additional dimension. This policy will underwrite the residential and industrial development of the rapidly urbanizing South and Southwest. In the '70s, seventeen Southern and Southwestern cities are projected to grow by more than a third, and most smaller southern cities by nearly 20 percent. (Only four Northern and Eastern metropolitan areas are expected to increase by a third).[5] In 1972, two out of every three new private homes in the country were built in the South and West, and the South and Southwest accounted for more than 50 percent of all federally insured mortgages on new dwellings. The Southern and Southwestern real estate industry's contribution to the GNP reached more than $41.6 billion in 1971, providing nearly two million jobs in the nonagricultural sector.[6]

In the North and the East, this policy will continue to provide subsidies for suburban homeowners and secure transfers of ownership in the existing stock of private homes. More than nine out of ten federally insured mortgages in the Northeast in 1972 covered such transactions, compared to 75 percent nationally. In that year, New England, New York, New Jersey and Pennsylvania accounted for only 5 percent of the FHA-insured new homes. Only on the fringes of metropolitan areas are new federally insured units likely to be built. Elsewhere in the metropolis, the higher costs of land, construction, and financing have pushed prices of new single-family dwellings to the limits of federal insurance ceilings, and, more important, beyond the financial reach of more than four out of five American families.

Consequently, access to established communities will be crucial, and competition for reasonably priced housing in better neighborhoods should intensify. Because of higher costs, pressures for new apartment complexes and lower-quality homes on less land should continue. Resistance can be expected not only from homeowners in wealthy suburbs but also from moderate-income groups who, feeling trapped in their present neighborhoods, will seek to protect themselves from encroachment by lower-class and minority people.

In its shift to housing allowances, the Administration provides support for the strategy of residential exclusion. The termination of production subsidies eliminates the most direct method for supplying low- and moderate-income housing in the better parts of the metropolis. It also circumvents the legal requirements that federally subsidized developments be located on sites fostering integration. No longer should residents of exclusively white or wealthy communities have to fear federal housing programs—notwithstanding

HUD claims that allowances will achieve its "first" urban policy goal, "a fairer and more even distribution across the metropolitan area of the central city's basic social and economic problem . . . the artificial concentrations in the city's core of low-income populations."[7]

Allowances represent a significant technical innovation. Instead of subsidizing new production, Washington would add to its system of "invisible" supports for the residential market an income supplement for low-income elderly households, enabling them to pay the costs demanded by the private sector. The change appeals to conservatives because, in the words of HUD Deputy Assistant Secretary William Lilley, III,

> We have accepted Banfield's counsel to let nature take its course. We have accepted the ultimate futility of state-administered allocation decisions . . . in favor of a strategy that emphasizes *free choice* and promises to achieve the goal of a decent home in a suitable living environment for all, not by crashing through the barriers that stand in the way but by subverting them through the *essentially peaceful* bargaining of the marketplace.[8]

This technique receives support from many housing experts who stress the need for the maintenance of existing housing—not for new construction—in older cities with decreasing population and increasing abandonment.

The Administration's version most likely will curtail its residential investment in declining areas, maintain residential segregation, and provide a strategic link with national welfare reform. For fiscal reasons, HUD and OMB apparently are planning a low-cost program that will provide a small allowance payment to a limited class of eligibles, the elderly poor. The Nixon Administration criticized the budgetary impact of the production subsidy programs whose annual costs reached slightly over $2 billion in 1973. By contrast, housing experts estimate costs between $5 and $10 billion for alternative allowance programs covering all families with incomes below $5,000, $7,000, or $10,000. Restricting the plan to the elderly with incomes below $7,500 (not just the elderly poor) would still require an estimated $3.7 billion to $4.8 billion.[9]

Since the White House has little enthusiasm for spending a lot of money, and since most of the country does not need the deep subsidies that New York and a few other big cities do, the eventual program is unlikely to provide payments high enough to increase the supply of low- and moderate-income housing in high-cost metropolitan areas. Rehabilitation and better maintenance are also unlikely because individual allowance recipients will have little bargaining power, especially in tight rental markets. Rather, there will be more dollars chasing existing low-rent units and, therefore, an increase in rents. Whether this rise will at least stem abandonment in the short term is problematic; but collective pressures for tenants' unions, rent control, code enforcement, building maintenance, and the legalization of rent strikes seem necessary to do much more.

The priority on the elderly poor will promote neither residential improvements nor mobility. The elderly poor are probably the least mobile group in the metropolis for numerous reasons unaffected by rent supplements. Many of them live in fear or passivity and may be unable to bargain with their landlords for repairs. Or, in this inflationary period, they may be forced to neglect their desires for home improvements and have to use their increased buying power for food and other essentials. A substantial increase in the number of eligibles and the amount of payments is unlikely. Not only the budget but politics too would work against it.

Were the allowance program extended for all the poor, opposition would come from the approximately eleven million families, above the poverty lines but below the income level necessary to purchase a new home, who would be omitted from the Administration's housing policy. If the extension were large enough to permit all the poor residential mobility, the impact would fall on this group, especially those somewhat above the allowance eligibility level, e.g., with incomes between $5,000 and $10,000.[10] Since the allowance recipients could only afford their housing, since the competition would raise costs, and since they have lost the chance for homeownership to inflation, they will be forced to protect their homes from potential competition by "mobile" allowance recipients. One tack would be to limit the program. The Administration would be sensitive to this pressure—judging from then HUD Secretary (now OMB Director) Lynn's 1974 refusal to reactivate the subsidized homeownership program because middle-income groups would not look favorably on subsidies to modest-income homebuyers when they could not get mortgage money and housing.[11]

Should the political and budgetary constraints fail, there could be a final irony—further metropolitan segregation. Allowances would enable many white recipients to flee the stable, integrated central city neighborhoods in which they are now "trapped" by low incomes. But these allowances would not necessarily foster black migration into white communities. Providing blacks with equal residential purchasing power is itself insufficient to achieve integration.[12] For allowances to do so would require the uncustomarily strict enforcement of open housing laws; and this, as a matter of state and local politics, is improbable.

Since allowances provide neither residential investment nor mobility, what do they offer the elderly poor? The answer is income maintenance. In New York, for example, only 6 percent of the city's more than two million rental units are occupied by potential allowance recipients, and therefore the impact on the housing stock would be marginal. But, in human terms, 132,000 elderly poor households—more than a third of the city's impoverished renters—would receive aid. According to economist George Sternlieb, the city's elderly have "largely been dependent upon the protection of the old rent control law and their relative immobility to keep down housing costs."[13] Yet, in 1970, more than two out of every five of the city's elderly paid over 25 percent of their incomes for rent; fewer than three out of ten paid less than 20 percent. Therefore, the elderly poor will probably not move even with allowances, and the payments should provide some relief for those most oppressed by rising housing costs. Nor is this scenario unique to cities with rent control. In most areas, continued occupancy of their present dwellings may be the elderly poor's best protection against inflation. Adding the social reasons for the elderly's stability suggests that income maintenance will be the human contribution of housing allowances.

It is not surprising, therefore, that the allowance strategy provides an important link to national income maintenance; the coordination of these programs would lessen objections to welfare reform. Conservatives opposed the Nixon-Moynihan Family Assistance Plan (FAP), warning that

a uniform minimum national income guarantee that might do

relatively minor harm in California or the northeast would be so
high compared with prevailing incomes in the deep south as to
tempt a third or more of the population to quit their jobs and
climb aboard the welfare wagon. . . . A uniform minimum welfare handout, in a nation with divergencies of up to 138 percent in
median family incomes among the states, would create far more
serious problems than any it might solve. [14]

One suggested compromise was a federal minimum that took
into account regional variations in the cost of living. Housing
allowances could effect this compromise because, on a regional
basis, the cost of housing varies most of all of life's necessities and
provides an index for differential payments. Tying a variable housing
allowance to a relatively low national minimum income could
provide the necessary device for conciliation.

Overcoming Southern conservative opposition is critical since it
is the legacy of the "old," rural, agricultural South. National income
maintenance, by contrast, represents the future of the "new," urban,
industrial South and Southwest. The federal government and national corporations now have made the decision in favor of urban
industrialism and its ancillary investments in human resources and
welfare supports. As a 1967 report for the Twentieth Century Fund
concluded,

> Large public investments, both from within and from without
> the region, will be needed for some time, if the south is to make
> its full contribution to national progress. Public investments [in
> manpower training, employment counseling, education, hous-
> ing, health care, and income supplements] will yield returns to
> the nation as a whole and to the south much higher than those
> commonly earned in many private endeavors. We can only hope
> that the traditional values and beliefs of southern people have
> changed sufficiently in recent years to permit them and their
> political leaders to join wholeheartedly in such large and con-
> tinuing national efforts to develop the south's full potential. [15]

Accordingly, the Ford administration's Income Supplement
Program (ISP)—as was its predecessor, Nixon's and Moynihan's
FAP—is a critical element of the national urban policy. In October

1974 it commanded wide backing; former HEW Secretary and OMB Director Weinberger, OMB's Lynn and O'Neill, and the Labor and Treasury secretaries had expressed support.[16] (Since then, there has been little public comment on ISP by the Administration. As the election day approaches, they seem to have put it aside lest they offend conservative and middle-American Reagan sympathizers before the convention; if the nomination is secured, they may let sleeping dogs lie, remembering McGovern's ill-fated welfare scheme.)

The income supplement proposal would provide $21.6 billion worth of income supports to 42.2 million Americans.[17] Since it would replace three of the largest welfare programs—Aid to Families with Dependent Children (AFDC), Food Stamps, and Supplementary Security Income—it would add only $3.3 billion in new federal outlays in the first proposed year of operation, 1978. It would give a guaranteed minimum income to every low-income American citizen including, for the first time, working-poor fathers. The basic benefits for a family of four without any income would be $3,600. The amount would decline as a family's earnings increased until, at an earned income of $7,200, the family would receive no supplement. ISP would establish a modern welfare system in the twenty states that pay an AFDC family of four less than its basic benefit; of these, sixteen states are Southern and Southwestern.

ISP—as did FAP for the first time—would provide benefits to rural male laborers who are low-paid but working at the top of their skill levels. According to an Urban Institute paper, more than half of the working-poor fathers eligible for FAP worked full time and full year, and nearly nine out of ten full time for part of the year; over 60 percent lived in rural areas, only 20 percent in central urban areas; 50 percent lived in the South; 72 percent were white; 60 percent had three or more children, and almost 29 percent had five or more; 52 percent had less than a grammar school education. "All of this suggests," the author concluded, "that most of these men are probably working at about as high a productive level as their capabilities and any reasonable amount of manpower investment will allow."[18]

ISP support for male rural laborers is crucial for the orderly development of Southern and Southwestern cities. On the one hand, an influx of low-skilled rural workers that exceeds the employment opportunities available in these centers could threaten political unrest.

National income maintenance could lessen the possibilities of migration. It would reduce the financial pressure on rural labor brought on by continuing mechanization or a major dislocation in the agricultural sector, and it would lessen the pulling power of higher urban wages by subsidizing life in more "comfortable" rural areas. (Consequently, its underwriting of rural wages would stabilize the agricultural labor force for agribusiness.) On the other hand, these rural male migrants would probably lack the qualifications to obtain better jobs since they are working at the peak of their capabilities. Their alternative would be welfare. Without the proposed reforms, this could require a man to desert his family and lead, according to the Moynihan perspective, to family breakdown and the ancillary social problems that would plague the new cities.

In the North and East, the federal assumption of state welfare costs up to the national payment level would relieve some pressure from state and local treasuries. Also, it is argued, the migration of poor people from regions with archaic welfare systems might abate, and reverse migration might even begin. Poor whites and blacks might leave the slums and ghettos of the industrial cities for the more pleasant environment, albeit lesser benefits, of Southern and Southwestern states. This argument, however, is probably rhetoric. Its premise—that the poor migrate in search of welfare—is disputed as a "welfare myth."

Nonetheless, for poor people in the North and the East the reforms are of dubious benefit since state welfare levels usually exceed the proposed federal standard; indeed, many may even have to bear the cost of developing a new system. According to an Institute for Research on Poverty comment on a HEW study paper,

> The Administration is not likely to propose, nor is Congress likely to pass, a program that leaves no beneficiary less well off. What is more likely is that a new universal program would provide more generous benefits to many of the poor, particularly the working poor, than they are now receiving, but less generous benefits than they are now receiving to other poor groups, particularly aid to families with dependent children beneficiaries in the high-benefit states.[19]

A housing allowance tied to the high living costs in these areas would be a useful supplement to limit the political opposition and human suffering induced by an inadequate income maintenance plan.

In sum, reflecting fears of inflation and a capital shortage, the national urban policy underinvests in the country's metropolitan development and redirects its limited investment priorities in favor of suburban, Southern, and Southwestern growth. The President's position on New York's financial dilemma extends this policy.

New York's fiscal crisis has given the White House the opportunity to force a reduction in the spending and capital investment of state and local governments and a curtailment of the "diseased" borrowing practices that sent the nationwide state and local debt over $200 billion in 1975 and threaten to drain off scarce capital in the near future. The President's preference for bankruptcy and a subsequent emergency loan to the city—the "Drop Dead" message to New York and "every other city that follows the tragic example of our largest city"—left the municipal bond market uptight, uncertain, and closed to all but the most prosperous or fiscally conservative cities. Given the federally reinforced strictures on the public fisc, higher interest rates, and marketing difficulties, most cities face hard decisions on critical services and projects—Northern and Eastern Central cities with declining populations and economies, the hardest.

In New York, according to the President, the Administration's "firm" position hastened the state and city action that default and bankruptcy would otherwise have necessitated: raising additional revenues from taxes and pension-fund loans, restructuring the city's short-term debt, refinancing the city's pension plans, and cutting hundreds of millions more from state and city budgets. After these "concrete actions" were taken, the President softened only on the timing of federal aid, offering $2.3 billion in short-term, seasonal loans under "stringent conditions" and Treasury Secretary Simon's continuing surveillance in order to avert default and maintain essential services during the next two and a half years. The basic objectives had been accomplished.

The foundations of the national urban policy and the White House's tightfistedness on New York rest not on a particular presidential incumbency but on an increasingly unquestioned, neocon-

servative vision of America's future and the role its leaders should
play in planning the nation's future. Amid the growing concern
about a "debt economy" and a capital shortage, Treasury Secretary
Simon has emerged, according to *Business Week*, as "Washington's
No. 1 Capital Gap Crusader," and the capital demands of private
economic expansion, independent energy production, and military
modernization have downgraded the priority on metropolitan development and social needs. Moreover, within the new limits on
metropolitan investment, the Administrations' support for urban,
industrial growth in the South and Southwest has wide backing
among economists, corporate interests, Cabinet departments, and
the Presidential Commission on Population Growth. Arguably,
it will alleviate the pressures of migration on Northern ghettos, provide urban and rural Southerners with opportunities for a
decent income in a pleasant environment, and avoid the uncontrolled and wasteful growth characteristic of the Northern metropolis. (Whether it can be achieved is another question.) Therefore,
given the dictates of national economic, political, and social realities, the declining Northern and Eastern Central cities must accept
their fate, reduce their standards of living, lower their "swollen
expectations"—as *Time* labeled New York's —and live within their
newly "shrunken means." They are not to question the national and
international forces that have shrunk their means; they are but to do
and die.

Underlying this new urban realism, furthermore, is a particular
conception of the past decade's urban crisis. Ignoring the widening
inequalities between central city and suburban life, the Nixon and
Ford administrations declared the 1960s urban crisis over because
the explosive features of that period had disappeared. The perspective is Edward Banfield's.[20]

> Most of the "problems" that are generally supposed to constitute
> "the urban crisis" could not conceivably lead to disaster
> [Banfield wrote in 1968]. They are—some of them—important
> in the sense that a bad cold is important, but they are not serious
> in the sense a cancer is serious. They have to do with comfort,
> convenience, amenity and business advantage, all of which are
> important, but they do not affect either the essential welfare of

individuals or what may be called the good health of the society.
. . . One problem that is both serious and unique to the large
cities is the existence of huge enclosures of people (many, but not
all of them, Negro) of low skill, low income, and low status. . . .
[T]he existence of huge enclaves of people who are in some
degree alienated from it constitutes a kind of hazard not only to
the present peace and safety but also to the long-run health of the
society. . . . Unlike those who live on farms and in small towns,
disaffected people who live in huge enclaves may develop a
collective consciousness and sense of identity. . . . In the
shortrun, however, they represent a threat to peace and order.
. . . This political danger in the presence of great concentrations
of people who feel little attachment to the society has long been
regarded by some as *the* serious problem of the cities—the one
problem that might conceivably produce a disaster that would
destroy the quality of the society.[21]

If it contains this political danger, the national urban policy need not
pay the price for *all* cities to be comfortable, convenient, amenable,
and economically advantageous. If it arrests the cancer, it need not
treat the fatal complications of pneumonia.

Finally, the national urban policy enacts the administrative
structure that enables the White House to fulfill its world role and
frees the President for the personal triumphs of international diplomacy. As Melvin Laird and Daniel Patrick Moynihan once argued,

The biggest problem of running the nation from Washington is
that the real business of Washington in our age is pretty much to
run the world. An American national government in this age will
always give priority to foreign affairs. A system has to be developed, therefore, under which domestic programs go forward
regardless of what international crisis is preoccupying Washington at the moment.[22]

Within the budget priorities of this global mission, new
federalism's techniques of revenue sharing and income supplements
delegate administrative discretion and market choices to state and
local governments and individuals, freeing the federal executive
from the time, cost, and political conflicts of domestic details. They

do not resolve the social, economic, and political conflicts of metropolitan development; but they seek to insulate Washington from direct involvement. Following new federalism's decentralist rationale, therefore, President Ford and Secretary Simon repeatedly labeled New York's and any city's financial distress a local responsibility, avoiding any direct national accountability until, interestingly enough, a short time after West European leaders expressed their fears of the international effects of default.

Whether or not new federalism's administrative delegation will revive democratic participation in local development conflicts remains to be seen in most cities. But its response to the fiscal crisis has hastened the death of political democracy in New York, and, nationwide, it has not increased the public's right to participate in national decision-making. For, cloaked in the ideology of restoring power to local communities and freedom of choice to individuals, new federalism rationalizes and legitimizes the centralized political power and economic planning that produced the national urban policy and the fiscal quarantine on New York City. New federalism is Tenth Amendment federalism turned upside down: all effective power not specifically delegated to states and localities is reserved by Washington.

What then is necessary for change? Once upon a time, municipal default and bankruptcy appeared to be the ultimate mayoral weapon to force Washington to provide more aid to the cities, assuming major banks and private investors pressed for protection of their holdings. But the White House's reaction to New York indicates otherwise, using default to extend the national urban policy. As vital as its predefault loans and the liberals' predefault loan guarantees are for the uninterrupted provision of essential services and the ongoing administration of New York city and state governments, their enactment would not change it. Even the loan guarantees were conditioned on state tax increases, local budget cuts, restructuring of the city's debt, and renegotiation of municipal employees' wages and pensions—all under the monitoring of a nonelected board of federal officials. No proposal challenged federal disinvestment from the central cities. No proposal would soothe the municipal bond market sufficiently to empower political democracy in New

York and other troubled cities to challenge the national political and economic forces of decline.

Central city riots may break out again, but, as with bankruptcy, the White House can accommodate them. Rioting would not only generate coercive measures but could also push enactment of national income maintenance (albeit after the election). Nevertheless, although nationalization of welfare would anger old-line political conservatives and ease an estimated $700 million annual burden on New York City, it is a part and not a reversal of the national urban policy. Following the Administration's view of the urban cancer, national income maintenance is more than humanitarian. Its political objective is civil order in the cities. Not only would it defuse the rural poor's migration to the hard-pressed cities; it also maintains a monetary pacifier for the "critical mass" of poor people already there. It would directly attack the locus and political danger of the urban cancer—the hearts and minds of the city poor.

At a minimum, all Americans, regardless of race, class, region, urban, suburban, or rural residence, share a common interest in a stronger federal investment in the quality of domestic social life, public and private. To realize this requires a united national polity able to press Washington for the curtailment of unnecessary military spending, an end to favoritism for irresponsible private capital accumulation, and the elimination of budget ceilings dictated by the economy's inflationary potential and the government's inequitable tax structure rather than by human needs and public choices.

Nonetheless, the national urban policy divides the country. It not only channels capital into the South and Southwest where recently attained urban affluence and lingering conservatism make demand for reform least likely, but Washington's paramount concern for strong armed forces supports the South's military heritage and its economy's continuing reliance on defense installations. It must seem too good to be true that all this can be accomplished under a new governmental structure that appears consistent with states' rights and eliminates the Great Society's links between Washington and local black, poor, and liberal activists.

In Northern and Eastern states, this policy reinforces metropolitan segregation and political divisions. It accepts racial and economic inequalities as natural, inevitable, and just, and it gives local governments, with whose boundaries these differences often coincide, a principal role in their defense. It provides financial support, administrative discretion, and political legitimacy to present municipal structure and practice, enabling many localities to continue their denials of equal residential, educational, and occupational opportunities by invoking the heretofore neutral value of localism. In the process, the American democratic ideal of an integrated national community of equally participant individuals is abandoned.

Struggling among themselves to protect their communities, to obtain better homes, or to slice meager local and household pies, middle-class, working-class, and poor families continue to define each other as enemies. Suburbanites fear integrationists. Middle- and working-class taxpayers fear the poor's economic and residential threat. The poor feel the others as the albatross upon their necks. And the President's condemnation of New York's local politicians as solely responsible for the city's fiscal catastrophe polarizes these suspicions and divides communities from one another. Thus the power of a potential domestic coalition is turned inward upon itself.

The national urban policy not only sets priorities for urban development and *dis*development; it also restricts unified, effective public participation in national choice-making. Ironically, perhaps, two conservative Republican presidents have brought the United States to the point where national planning is an emergent institutional reality. Their concern for world affairs is intimately connected with the structure of domestic planning. Regardless of its local consequences, new federalism has turned American democracy into a national technocracy free to plan and manage its domestic and foreign objectives from a global perspective without effective popular participation. Or—to draw on President Nixon's characterization of the American people as children in need of a strong father—under the new federalism, Washington's technocratic patriarch retains the power over critical national choices and leaves America's children to play, more or less democratically, with an allowance of local toys. If the patriarch decides that any city has overspent its allowance, its spanking will be severe, its democratic privileges will be suspended and its allowance will be "seasonally administered" and terminable at will. As Secretary Simon told the Senate Banking Committee, he should be put in charge of any New York aid "to determine that the city was irrevocably and unalterably on the path to fiscal responsibility. Such aid should be so punitive in its terms and so painful that no other city not facing absolute disaster would think of applying for help."

Footnotes

1. Fiscal 1980 estimates use the $3 billion appropriation projected by the U. S. House of Representatives, Committee on Banking and Currency, *Directory of Recipients: Housing and Community Development Act of 1974*, 93rd Congress, 2nd session (Washington, D.C.: Government Printing Office, September 1974).

2. Quoted in John Herbers, "The Other Presidency," *New York Times Magazine*, March 3, 1974, p. 36.

3. Susanna McBee, "Subsidized Housing Frozen Before Justification by H.U.D.," Washington *Post*, December 3, 1973, p. 1.

4. U.S. Senate, Committee on Government Operations, *Hearings on the Nomination of Paul O'Neill*, November 20, 1974, p. 66.

5. Joint Center for Urban Studies of the Massachusetts Institute of Technology and Harvard University, *America's Housing Needs: 1970 to 1980*, pp. 3–6 ff. and Exhibit 3–1.

6. Norman B. Ture, Inc., *Real Estate in the U. S. Economy*, report for the National Realty Committee, Inc., tables XVII, XX, XXV, XXVIII.

7. William Lilley III, H.U.D. Deputy Assistant Secretary for Policy Development, "Toward a Rational Housing Policy," speech delivered at the 1973 Congress of Cities, San Juan, Puerto Rico, December 3, 1973.

8. Ibid. (italics in original).

9. See, e.g., General Accounting Office, *Observations on Housing Allowances and the Experimental Allowances Program* (Document B-171630, March 28, 1974, Washington, D.C.); Henry Aaron, *Shelter and Subsidies* (Washington, D.C.: Brookings Institution, 1972), pp. 168–70.

10. See Ira Lowry, "Housing Assistance for Low-Income Families: A Fresh Approach," in U.S. House of Representatives, Committee on Banking and Currency, *Papers Submitted to Subcommittee on Housing Panels on Housing Production, Housing Demand, and Developing a Suitable Living Environment*, 92nd Congress, First Session (Washington, D.C.: Government Printing Office, 1971).

11. Housing Affairs Letter, May 17, 1974, p. 2.

12. See, e.g., U.S. Commission on Civil Rights, *Homeownership for Lower Income Families* (Washington: Government Printing Office, 1971).

13. George Sternlieb, *Housing and People in New York City* (City of New York Housing and Development Administration, Department of Rent and Housing Maintenance, January, 1973), pp. 209–10.

14. Henry Hazlitt, "Compounding the Welfare Mess," *National Review,* February 24, 1970, p. 205.

15. E. Maddox, et al., *The Advancing South: Manpower Prospects and Problems* (New York: Twentieth Century Fund, 1967), pp. 216–17.

16. J. K. Iglehart, "Welfare Report/H.E.W. Wants Welfare Programs Replaced by Negative Income Tax," *National Journal,* October 19, 1974, pp. 1559ff.

17. Ibid.

18. J. T. Allen, "A Funny Thing Happened on the Way to Welfare Reform," Urban Institute paper, January 1972; reprinted in U.S. Senate, "What should be the role of the federal government in extending public assistance to all Americans living in poverty?" U.S. Senate Doc. No. 93–12, 93rd Congress, First Session (Washington, D.C.: Government Printing Office, 1973), p. 23.

19. I. Garfinkel, "Toward an Effective Income Support System: An Overview Paper," in Barth, et al., *Toward an Effective Income Support System: Problems, Prospects and Choices,* H. E. W. staff paper (Madison, Wis.: Institute for Research on Poverty, 1974), p. 162.

20. In his 1973 speech, Lilley named Banfield, Moynihan, and Jay Forrester as setting the "intellectual framework which, necessarily, must define the present discussion of future policy options."

21. E. Banfield, *The Unheavenly City* (Boston: Little, Brown, 1968), pp. 6, 12–13.

22. M. Laird, "The Case for Revenue Sharing," in Laird, *Republican Papers,* pp. 63, 73; quoted in D. P. Moynihan, *The Politics of a Guaranteed Income,* p. 207.

CHANDLER DAVIDSON
On "the Culture of Shiftlessness"
(1976)

Since its formulation almost twenty years ago by Oscar Lewis, the concept of "the culture of poverty" has been at the vortex of controversy.[1] For some writers, it provides a key to the mystery of poverty. For others, it is merely an obfuscation that diverts us from the true causes of economic deprivation.

In its strongest version, the culture-of-poverty hypothesis states that a value system, or culture, which denigrates hard work, discipline, ambition, and the sacrifice of immediate gratification to future satisfaction, results in laziness. In turn, laziness causes poverty. Passed from parent to child, this culture is perpetuated from generation to generation. If the hypothesis is correct, one would expect to find that the culture of poverty is more widespread among the poor than the nonpoor, and that it accounts for the smaller amount of work performed by the poor, relative to other classes.

Critics have usually tried to show either that the behavior of poor people is not a manifestation of a genuine culture or that their tendency to work less is a function of some aspect of the larger socioeconomic structure: racial discrimination, for example, or job scarcity. While there is merit in these arguments, they tacitly concede two crucial assumptions: first, that the values of this culture are more likely to be found among the poor; second, that the poor do indeed work less than the nonpoor. An examination of these two assumptions is my subject.

Is the culture of poverty peculiar to the poor? Curiously, a terminological fact has discouraged the issue from being raised. The term "culture of poverty" is inherently biased, for it presumes to answer, more or less by definition, the empirical question I am posing. It is a marriage of two distinct concepts: culture, referring to a set of values, and poverty, referring to a lack of monetary or material means. Once these two concepts are joined together in unholy matrimony, it is difficult to appreciate that the culture and the economic reality of poverty can vary independently of each other. It sounds odd, in other words, to ask if the poor are more likely to belong to the culture of poverty than the rich. It sounds rather like asking if French culture is more likely to be found among the French than the Chinese.

Lewis exacerbated the problem by confusing poverty with cultural traits he believed were associated with it—although he sometimes distinguished between them, as when he estimated that no more than one-third of the American poor belonged to the culture of poverty. Linking a cultural syndrome and poverty in a single descriptive term invites this confusion. And it virtually precludes asking whether the DuPont family in Delaware shares some of its values with the Martinez family in a San Juan slum.

The same objection applies to Edward Banfield's "lower-class culture," which refers to some of the same values. Like Lewis, Banfield is able at times to see that lower-class culture is distinct from the lower class. At one point in his book, *The Unheavenly City*, he writes: ". . . one who is rich and a member of 'the 400' may be lower-class . . . ," meaning that a rich person may belong to the lower-class culture.[2] But his unhappy choice of terms, just like Lewis's, makes it sound absurd to ask what proportion of the rich belong to the lower class.

A new term is required that leaves open the question whether the cultural values under consideration are more widespread among the poor. First, however, Lewis's definition of the culture must be narrowed sufficiently to render it plausible as an explanation of poverty. His famous list of sixty-two traits, which comprise the culture,[3] has rightly been criticized for its everything-including-the-kitchen-sink comprehensiveness—one that brings together a welter of disparate qualities having no inherent relation to one another. Banfield's concept is an improvement, in that it salvages

from Lewis's cultural smorgasbord those elements that hang together and plausibly explain why people who belong to the lower-
class culture are in fact poor. In Banfield's words:

> The lower-class individual lives from moment to moment . . .
> Impulse governs his behavior, either because he cannot disci-
> pline himself to sacrifice a present for a future satisfaction or
> because he has no sense of the future. He is therefore radically
> improvident: whatever he cannot consume immediately he con-
> siders valueless. His bodily needs (especially for sex) and his
> taste for "action" take precedence over everything else—and
> certainly over any work routine. He works only as he must to stay
> alive, and drifts from one unskilled job to another, taking no
> interest in his work.

Ignoring the obvious fact that no one who was this "present-time
oriented" could live more than a few days, one can agree with
Banfield that impulsiveness, or radical improvidence, is a more
plausible explanation of poverty than such of Lewis's traits as
machismo, early initiation into sex, an impoverished sense of history, or hatred of the police. Surely one can bully his wife, flaunt the
law, confuse Andrew with Henry Jackson, have sexual intercourse
before the age of ten, and still possess the virtues that enable one to
become wealthy, if not healthy, respectable or wise.

I propose a term that not only does justice to the essence of the
concept but is more pleasantly colloquial. For "culture of poverty"
and "lower-class culture" I shall substitute "the culture of shiftlessness." Webster's *Third New International* defines shiftlessness as
follows:

> 1. a. Lacking in ability or resourcefulness. . . . b. Lacking in
> ambition or incentive: IDLE, LAZY. 2. Marked by lack of ambi-
> tion, energy or purpose.

Shiftlessness, of course, has a derogatory connotation, just like the
term it is meant to supplant. The difference is that it wears its bias on
its sleeve instead of hiding it behind jargon. Even more important, it
leaves open the question whether the attitudes it describes are
peculiar to the poor. It does not sound odd (just impertinent) to
inquire if the rich are shiftless.

The earlier question is now reformulated: Is the culture of

shiftlessness more likely to be found among the poor than the nonpoor? Among students of poverty the answer would likely be yes. True, hardly anyone now argues that all the poor belong to it. Even Banfield, who sees the shiftless poor as a major source of America's urban problems, estimates that only 10 to 20 percent of families with incomes below the government-established poverty line are shiftless. Moreover, most poverty scholars would probably accept the contention of Hyman Rodman or Elliot Liebow that shiftlessness is a value system that some of the poor adopt *faute de mieux;* they do not subscribe to it wholeheartedly.[4] But few social scientists have seen fit to ask whether the culture actually is concentrated among the poor.

In a recent secondary analysis of sample survey data collected by the Texas Research Institute of Mental Sciences with the assistance of the National Opinion Research Center, Charles Gaitz and I tried to discover whether the attitudes toward work expressed by the poor, as classified by government standards, varied from those expressed by the nonpoor.[5] The data were drawn from a Houston sample. We limited our analysis to the twenty- to sixty-four-year-old age group, and controlled for the effects of both sex and ethnicity (black, Anglo, and Mexican American). Subjects were asked questions about intrinsic work motivation, commitment to "work and achievement" rewards, and "time orientation." No statistically significant differences were observed between the poor and nonpoor in any ethnic category. The ethnic minorities, on the average, expressed more support for work-oriented values than the Anglo majority. Our evidence, in other words, casts doubt on the view that the cultural *values* of shiftlessness are more common among poor people.

It was only in the course of our analysis of values, however, that the even more interesting question arose: Do the poor actually *work* less than the nonpoor, quite apart from their attitudes toward work? The phenomenon we were trying to explain by calling it the culture of shiftlessness, namely, the work differential between the poor and nonpoor, was itself suddenly in doubt. Yet the assumption that the poor work less is so ingrained in the sociology of poverty that it had not previously occurred to me to ask if there were any evidence to support it.

Historically, the idea of the shiftless poor has vied in the popular mind with that of the shiftless rich. In the work of Thorstein Veblen, for example, it was the rich who stood indicted as nonproducers. *The Theory of the Leisure Class* was an academic reflection of the widespread turn-of-the-century outrage at the socially subsidized shiftlessness of the wealthy of that day, symbolized by the extravagant potlatches of the Astors, the Vanderbilts, and the Harrimans. Today the rich are treated more gently. We are told that they are not leisured—that ours is a generation of the "busy rich," the hard-driving Nelson Rockefeller rich; and that right beneath them, nipping at their heels, are the ambitious middle classes who are equally ensnared in the toils of the Protestant ethic, fully deserving of every tax loophole, emolument, or "perq" that comes their way.

The most influential academic version of the busy rich was advanced by C. Wright Mills, who was as stern a critic of the American upper class as Veblen, although for different reasons. "Veblen's theory," wrote Mills in 1953, "is not 'The Theory of the Leisure Class.' It is *a* theory of a particular element of the upper classes in one period of the history of one nation." To the extent that Veblen's view still applies, Mills believed, it is to "the *nouveau riche* of the new corporate privileges. . . and of course among recent crops of 'Texas millionaires.' "

> The supposed shamefulness of labor on which many of Veblen's conceptions rest, does not square very well with the Puritan work ethic so characteristic of much of American life, including many upper-class elements. . . . But of course, there is and there has been a *working* upper class—in fact, a class of prodigiously active people.[6]

At the time this assertion was first made, Mills offered no evidence, nor, in a sense, was there a need for it. Obviously many of the rich and near rich do work hard. But this is just as true for those at the foot of the social ladder. It is not whether they do or don't, but what percentage of the various classes work, and how much—questions requiring *comparisons* of the work habits of the classes.

Like the notion of the culture of poverty, however, the notion of work is loaded with class ideology. Mills correctly criticized Veblen for dismissing the business activity of the rich as nonwork because it was not socially productive labor. But now that the pendulum of blame has swung in the opposite direction, the bias operates against the poor: their labor is dismissed as nonwork on the same grounds, i.e., that it is less socially useful or less "functionally important." Such an argument is no more plausible than Veblen's.

Instead of measuring work in terms of social usefulness one might measure it in terms of energy expenditure . . . in which case there is the very real question of whether an hour spent in the boardroom or on the company jet entertaining clients is equal to an hour spent pouring concrete or roughnecking on a drilling rig.

Consider the following case. Lehman Brothers, the investment banking house, was instrumental last year in persuading Standard Oil of California to buy up some $300 million worth of new shares offered by Amax, Inc., to raise equity capital. To clinch the deal, executives from all three firms flew to San Francisco. In the words of a *Business Week* reporter:

> Glanville and MacGregor flew out in Amax's plane. Ball—who was in Vancouver—came down, and on the night of Memorial Day, over a six-hour dinner with Haynes and Bell in a private room of the Carnelian Room restaurant, on the 52nd floor of the Bank of America building, they put the deal together.

The problem is how to classify the activities of these busy executives, culminating in a six-hour repast in the Carnelian Room. Was it work? Or was it something else? The same problem is posed in the *New York Times* obituary of Charles Revson of Revlon: "Despite his interest in the social whirl, and the amount of time he spent aboard the *Ultima II*, the 257-foot, 1,200-ton yacht he bought from Daniel K. Ludwig, the multimillionaire shipbuilder, Mr. Revson never lost contact with his office."

For a sizable number of the affluent, the rather nebulous activity of "keeping in contact with the office" seems to be all that distinguishes their daily routine from leisure.

Compare the activities of the executive and professional classes with those of Walter Brown:

> Walter Brown, aged 40, is a coke oven worker at the Clairton, Pennsylvania, plant of the U.S. Steel Corporation. Mr. Brown

wears wooden pallets under his shoes and a rubber mask for protection. He works all day on top of a battery of hot brick ovens, pulling off the heavy steel oven lids with a long iron bar and dumping in coal. As *The Wall Street Journal* has reported, his job "is hot, filthy, monotonous and dangerous . . . surrounded by thick acrid smoke. The bricks he walks range in temperature up to 180 degrees, and the steel lids up to 480 degrees. Walls of flame from surrounding ovens shoot over his head. There is no roof; when it rains or snows, it rains or snows on Walter Brown." Mr. Brown has worked at the mill for 18 years, seven on this same job. He inhales tar, methane, benzine, hydrogen sulfide, carbon monoxide, coal dust, coke dust, and particles of pure carbon. He has headaches. And he is ten times more likely to die of lung cancer than the average steelworker.[7]

The point is that work performed by the manual occupations—the "working class," after all—comes closer to the intuitive notion of work as a strenuous, exhausting, burdensome task than that performed by their social betters. It is an "energy intensive" activity; and if one measures work by the energy spent, then the laborer may outwork his boss even when putting in fewer hours.

Even so, the number of hours worked is the best single measure of work we have. (This is so because time units are easy to apply to any activity, and are more "objective" than, say, energy expenditure or productivity.) By this criterion, who works more? The evidence is skimpy. Government employment statistics indicate that the poor are more likely to be unemployed. But unemployment rates are calculated as a percentage of the labor force—those working or looking for work—and labor-force participation may vary by class. Fortunately, our above-mentioned Houston survey data contained information about the respondents' work habits, and enabled us to compare the poor and nonpoor irrespective of labor-force participation.

Our findings were that among men, the black and Anglo poor were less likely to be employed than the nonpoor (68 percent vs. 86 percent for blacks; 53 percent vs. 83 percent for Anglos), a matter of 18 and 30 points difference, respectively. Among Mexican American men, 86 percent of the poor vs. 91 percent of the nonpoor were employed: no statistically significant difference. Nor was there an appreciable difference, among employed men of all three groups, in the number of hours worked by the poor and the nonpoor. Among women, there was no significant difference by poverty status in hours of housework performed by either Mexican Americans or Anglos. Poverty-status black women put in more hours of housework than other black women—and more hours than nonpoor Anglo women. Moreover, when various kinds of activities besides employment in the narrow sense of full-time paid labor were lumped together—such as looking for work, and going to school—there was no significant difference between the poor and the nonpoor in any ethnic or sex category. Our findings therefore raise questions, not only about the allegedly unequal distribution of the culture of shiftlessness, but about the poor's tendency to work less. I am unaware of other studies with similar controls that compare the poor and nonpoor in this manner.

Comparisons between the rich and the nonrich are also sparse. Our Houston sample did not contain any rich people, as distinguished from middle-class respondents. Mills presented data on the "very rich" in *The Power Elite*, published in 1956. His sample consisted of three generations of the ninety or so reputedly richest people in the country in 1900, 1925, and 1950. Although Mills interpreted his findings as supporting his earlier contention that "the very rich in America are not an idle rich and never have been," it turns out that 26 percent of his 1950 group were, in his words, "rentiers and not much else." Moreover, the percentage of idle rich had increased from 14 percent in 1900 to 17 percent in 1925 and to 26 percent in 1950. Projecting the trend to 32 percent in 1975, we discover that the percentage of idle rich is the same as that of the idle black impoverished men in the Houston sample, and greater than the idle Mexican American impoverished men. But the comparison is shaky, not only because of the small sample size but because 70 percent of Mills's 1950 sample of the very rich were women. Nor did he tell us how many were of retirement age.

On the basis of this information, we can tentatively conclude that the poor have been unfairly singled out as the shiftless class. If the poor differ from the nonpoor, it would seem to be primarily in the amount of compensation those who work receive for their efforts, and in the amount of subsidies those who do not work—the disabled, the lazy, the very young and old and, of course, those who cannot find work—receive from society.

I am not denying that shiftlessness exists in some small but significant measure among the poor. My suggestion is simply that shiftlessness is fairly equally distributed among social classes, and hence cannot be used to explain income differences. But if this is true, what accounts for the continuing influence of the culture-of-poverty hypothesis? The answer is that it serves the ideological function of rationalizing the inequitable distribution of income in America. And, as is true with all genuine ideologies—deeply held world views that serve a group's interest—it influences the perception of the facts upon which the acceptance or rejection of the hypothesis depends.

This can be illustrated in no better fashion than to recount a brief history of a woman whose life is enmeshed in the culture of shiftlessness. The subject is a female, age forty-seven, who has been intensively studied over a period of years. I shall call her Willie Mae Smith, although that is a pseudonym.

Willie Mae comes from a highly disorganized family milieu. Her father, Buck, was pathologically unstable. He drank too much, and was a skirt-chaser and gambler. When he went broke during the Depression, his father-in-law had to bail him out, paying Buck's rent on condition that he straighten up. Unable to do so, Buck began fighting with Mary Ann, Willie Mae's mother. The couple separated, and then began to compete for the affections of their children, Willie Mae and her younger sister, Laura. Buck initially won out. He visited his daughters often, spoiled them shamelessly, and taught them his philosophy of playing "hard to get" to attract men.

Mary Ann's remarriage was a blow to him. The originally extroverted Buck became "tuned out." He drank heavily. Willie Mae, in the words of one observer, "was emotionally scarred by the events in her family situation."

As a young woman she held a job briefly, and then married Roosevelt, a man much like her father, with a reputation for sexual promiscuity. He, too, came from a family prone to violence and tragedy. Three siblings died violently, one was divorced, one was mentally retarded, and another's wife had psychiatric problems. A married brother had been implicated in the drowning death of a girl friend, but the police were never able to pin anything on him.

More than twenty years passed before Willie Mae got another job. "The first one had been fun," she said much later, "but toward the end I got tired. It taught me not to expect too much and not to take things for granted."

The marriage lasted ten years—much longer than one might have expected, given Roosevelt's sexual adventures, Willie Mae's compulsive spending on clothes and baubles for herself, and the fights that resulted. It was a decade punctuated by family crises. Her father, a pathetic drunk, finally died. Her sister Laura divorced and remarried, after having had a relationship with Jimmy, an older man whom Willie Mae was later to marry herself. Willie Mae conceived five children by Roosevelt, only two of whom are alive today. They were largely reared by others. Willie Mae's marriage ended abruptly when Roosevelt was shot to death on the street by a man who was thought to be deranged. She remained single for a while, but because of her looks and her image as a "man's woman," she had no lack of male attention. One person described her as "attracting men like honey does bees."

Her second husband was Jimmy, a divorced man whose scrapes with the law seemed to contribute to his sex appeal. Willie Mae had known him before Roosevelt's death. Rumor had it that her sister Laura had slept with Jimmy before Laura's first marriage broke up, and then again after she remarried. Jimmy had seen Willie Mae soon after Roosevelt was killed, and their relationship continued until their marriage, which was said to have infuriated Jimmy's favorite long-time girl friend, as well as a number of his more casual ones.

As Jimmy's wife, Willie Mae continued her life as a "party girl." Sometimes with Jimmy, sometimes without, she stayed up till dawn "painting the town." As this case history was being written in early 1974, there were signs that their marriage was on the rocks. They fought often. Jimmy's daughter by a previous marriage was said to hate Willie Mae, and this seemed to be dampening Jimmy's ardor for his wife.

To sum up, Willie Mae's life style exemplifies many of the characteristics of the "culture of poverty." She has an aversion to work, even though she could get a job. She hates housework and child

care. Her life has a random quality to it, as Willie Mae has no
disciplined commitment to a life goal. She is the paradigm of the
"present-time oriented" individual, sometimes justifying this by the
pain and suffering she has endured. She compulsively spends money
on clothes and adornments. Her kin networks are remarkable for
their pathology—the involvement of their members in violence,
drugs, divorce, illicit sex. The families tend to be large, and internal
tensions often lead to deviance. Add to this a penchant for high
living, the "dog" which is exhibited in the men, the pursuit of sex
and alcohol and late-night adventure, and you have precisely that
admixture of impulsiveness and irresponsibility that epitomizes a
"lower-class culture."

It would hardly be surprising, therefore, if denizens of this
culture were likely to be poor and to contribute more than their
share to the social and economic problems that plague urban
America. Yet the thumbnail sketch I have presented is relatively
abstract, and if various other details are filled in, problems of interpretation arise. Most important is the fact that Willie Mae is not
poor. She was born into a family of established wealth. Both of her
husbands were even wealthier than her own family.

Willie Mae is the fictitious name of a well-known person. But
aside from having altered her name and those of the other principals,
I have taken no liberties, in the above "case history," with any of the
known facts or published rumors about the life of Jacqueline Kennedy Onassis.[8] That is, I have taken no liberties except the one most
commonly taken in sociological accounts of the poor: I have selected
the facts to suit a predetermined interpretation of an individual, and
I have used some loaded words to describe them. Students of
poverty, going a step further, have built a one-sided case against an
entire social class—the poor. The ideology of poverty influences the
way sociologists see and describe the poor, even though the researcher is often unaware of it. But whether he is aware or not, his
description serves the interest of the affluent, by justifying the
present inequitable distribution of wealth and income. If the poor
can be saddled with the responsibility for their poverty, and the
public convinced that the poor are the sole carriers of the "disease"
of shiftlessness, the goals of a full-employment economy and a
guaranteed decent standard of living become pointless.

The political use that is made of the image of the shiftless poor is illustrated in an incident that occurred during a vice-presidential visit to Houston in December of 1975. Nelson Rockefeller arrived propitiously on a day that enabled him to address the 26th annual dinner of the Houston Business and Professional Men's Club, an organization of black businessmen. The theme of his address that night was the virtue of hard work.

"I understand what it means to try to seek to achieve and produce through hard work and that's what builds America," Mr. Rockefeller told the black audience. "Basically," he went on, "those who really care, really want to do it, are going to do it through hard work." The Vice-President admitted that there were many, including himself, who did not have to work. "But when they find out the joys and satisfaction that comes through work," he said, "they do so and that's what built this country."

It is possible that Mr. Rockefeller simply seized upon the occasion of addressing a group of blacks to lecture them on the virtues of the industrious life, as any apostle of self-improvement would have done. More likely, his message was not really addressed to the black business leaders, but to the largely white middle-class readers of the next day's newspapers. In either case the implication of his message was the same. One does not lecture on virtue unless vice is suspected. His speech might have been entitled, "Lecturing the Colored and the Poor—or Their Ostensible Leaders—on the Virtues of Work, or How to Imply, without Actually Saying so, that They Wouldn't Take a Job if It Were Handed Them on a Silver Platter."

Hylan Lewis, an anthropologist and longtime student of poverty (not to be confused with the late Oscar Lewis), early on recognized the significance of social science's concentration on the so-called culture of poverty. "My own view," he wrote, "is that the most important research in this area now should focus not on the culture of poverty but on the culture of affluence—this is the culture that matters more and that is far more dangerous than the culture of poverty." He was right, I believe, but we have yet to see very many social scientists act on his suggestion and begin to make forays into the ghettos of affluence.

The reasons are obvious. The government and the private foundations are not about to fund academic probes into the bedrooms of Park Avenue, the boardrooms of Wall Street, or the cloakrooms of

Congress, when the intent of the research is to study time orientation, ability to defer gratification, or machismo among the upper
classes. Nor will the rich open up their lives as graciously or gullibly
as the poor have done.

One can hope, however, that at least a few intrepid researchers
will not be deterred by the funding problem. We are badly in need of
a fresh, imaginative, and objective look at the patterns of work and
leisure among the nonpoor, and especially the rich. When the
evidence is in, I suspect that the poor will come off better than either
the popular stereotype or the academic "poverty literature" has
portrayed them.

Footnotes

1. Oscar Lewis, *Five Families: Mexican Case Studies in the Culture of Poverty* (New York:
Basic Books, 1959).

2. Edward C. Banfield, *The Unheavenly City* (Boston: Little, Brown, 1968), p. 48.

3. Oscar Lewis, "A Puerto Rican Boy," in Joseph C. Finney, ed., *Culture Change, Mental
Health, and Poverty* (Lexington: University of Kentucky Press, 1969; reprinted in paper, New
York: Simon and Schuster, 1970), pp. 149–54.

4. Elliot Liebow, *Tally's Corner: A Study of Streetcorner Men* (Boston: Little, Brown,
1967); Hyman Rodman, "The Lower-class Value Stretch," *Social Forces* 17 (December 1963),
pp. 205–15.

5. Chandler Davidson and Charles M. Gaitz, "Are the Poor Different?: A comparison of
work behavior and attitudes among the urban poor and nonpoor," *Social Problems* 22 (December 1974), pp. 229–45.

6. C. Wright Mills, "Introduction," in Thorstein Veblen, *The Theory of the Leisure Class*
(New York: New American Library, 1953), pp. xiv–xv.

7. Fred Harris, *The New Populism* (Berkeley, Cal.: Thorp Springs Press, 1973), pp. 30–31.

8. I relied primarily upon Freda Kramer's *Jackie: A Truly Intimate Biography* (New York:
Award Books, 1975).

THEODORE DRAPER
Ghosts of
Vietnam
(1979)

The Vietnam war was beyond doubt the most demanding test of American foreign policy and its makers since the Second World War. The war in Vietnam was not just another crisis in thirty years of successive crises; it was by far the most costly and most stultifying. It lasted longer than any other war and ended in the most humiliating failure in American history. It resulted in over 210,000 American casualties, including almost 57,000 dead and more than 150,000 wounded. The monetary cost has been officially estimated at from $180 billion to $210 billion. This bill for the war ignores all the indirect costs, such as the corrosive economic inflation it stimulated and the feverish social turmoil it provoked. As for the havoc inflicted on North and South Vietnam, it belongs to a different order of magnitude. No wonder that the memory of Vietnam is so oppressive that Americans seem to want to stuff it away in their collective unconscious.

One might well assume that the present custodians of American foreign policy had been chosen because they were proven right in their judgment of the war. It could come as a surprise that, in order to rise to the top of the post-Vietnam American political system, it was almost necessary to be wrong, hopelessly and certifiably wrong. Yet, in some odd way, this is what happened. The false counselors were rewarded with more power than they had had before they made their ghastly mistakes about the war.

President Jimmy Carter consistently supported the war and

208

was saved from making his support too conspicuous only by his relative obscurity in national politics. Secretary of State Cyrus Vance was another proponent of the war, also sheltered from too much public notice by his inability or unwillingness to speak out very forcefully about anything. Both of them seem to think that it was enough for them to say, "Sorry, folks, we were wrong about the war," to gain political absolution. They were more fortunate than Professor Zbigniew Brzezinski and his predecessor as national security adviser, Dr. Henry Kissinger. Kissinger managed to find bad reasons to support what he knew was a bad war; Brzezinski hit on essentially the same reasons for what he thought was a good war. And now, as the most influential member of his staff and his closest confidant, Brzezinski has with him Professor Samuel P. Huntington, one of the hardest of prowar hard-liners and the least repentant.

In one respect, the problem of the Vietnam war resembled that of the Korean war. Since American interests in both Korea and Vietnam were minimal, other reasons had to justify American intervention. In the case of Korea, American policy-makers considered North Korea to be nothing but a Soviet puppet ordered by Moscow to attack South Korea as the opening move in a larger strategy to "probe for the weakness in our armor," as former President Truman put it, in order to start a process of disintegration in the entire American structure of allies and dependents throughout Europe and Asia.

Fighting Russia in Korea was what made the war seem necessary and worthwhile. According to this reasoning, the Soviets should have taken advantage of their success in bogging down the bulk of American armed forces in Korea for three years, particularly at the time of the crushing defeat of General MacArthur's forces by Chinese armies across the Yalu River at the end of 1950, which was presumably what the wire-pullers in the Kremlin had been waiting for. Instead, the Korean war increasingly lived a life of its own. The original rationale for getting into it became dimmer and dimmer, and all that remained was to get out of it as gracefully and cheaply as possible. The Korean war turned out essentially to be a *Korean* war, which ultimately made it tangential to America's larger interests and preposterously expensive for what we could get out of it. Whatever the Russian role might have been, as we still know little for sure about it, the Korean war was far more a feint than the real thing.

The Vietnam war followed the same general course. In the beginning, the Truman Administration injected itself into the French imbroglio in Indochina with vast amounts of financial assistance and military equipment, ostensibly to bolster French pride and stability and to gain French support for American defense plans in Europe. After the outbreak of the Korean war, the struggle in Indochina took on a wider connotation as part of a worldwide Communist "conspiracy." With the defeat of France in 1954, the Eisenhower Administration took over responsibility for South Vietnam, now split off from North Vietnam by the Geneva accords, on the ground that loss of all of Vietnam would inevitably bring about the loss of all the other "dominoes" in Southeast Asia, including Thailand, Malaya, Burma, and Indonesia. In the stage of massive, direct American intervention during the Johnson Administration, the real enemy in Vietnam became China, a point of view put forward most extravagantly by then former Vice-President Richard M. Nixon in 1965 and with monumental obtuseness by Secretary of State Dean Rusk in 1966 and afterward. Without superimposing a larger framework on the Korean and Vietnam wars, American policy-makers would have been forced to acknowledge that essentially they were civil wars—civil wars with outside backing but still primarily localized civil wars—and not the opening shot of the Final Conflict. We might still have been drawn into them, but at least we would have known what we were doing and what they were worth to us.

II

How difficult it was to justify American intervention in Vietnam intellectually is strikingly shown by the travail of two outstanding foreign-affairs intellectuals—Henry Kissinger and Zbigniew Brzezinski. If they could not think up better reasons for supporting the war, no one could.

Kissinger's position on the war made its first public appearance in *Look* magazine of August 9, 1966, in the second year of massive American intervention. In an article written after he had made two trips to Vietnam at the invitation of then Ambassador Henry Cabot Lodge, Kissinger set forth two principal propositions. One was that the war could not be won by military means. The other was that it had to be settled by negotiation. In effect, he succeeded in establishing some distance between himself and both the extreme hawks and extreme doves. Kissinger had clearly learned enough during his two tours of Vietnam and from his Pentagon sources to make him extremely cautious about committing himself to anything that might be called "victory."

After outlining this equivocal approach, Kissinger fell silent on the issue of Vietnam for almost two years, an uncharacteristic reticence that his friendly memorialists have had great difficulty explaining.[1]

Kissinger broke his silence on Vietnam in the summer of 1968, by which time even the inner circles of the Johnson Administration had given up the war as a lost cause. At a conference on Vietnam in Chicago in June of that year, sponsored by the Adlai Stevenson Institute of International Affairs, Kissinger savagely criticized American policy, especially its "concepts"—military concepts, traditional liberal concepts, balance-of-power concepts, indeed the entire "American philosophy of international relations." If American policy was that bankrupt, one might imagine that the best thing to do would be to get out of the war as soon as possible at the least possible cost. But Kissinger did not offer any new concepts or policies himself; he merely called for a "prayerful assessment" of the procedures and concepts that had landed us in such a mess.[2]

Kissinger saved his own conceptual prescription for the speeches that he composed for Governor Nelson Rockefeller in the presidential campaign that summer and for an article in *Foreign Affairs* written in his own name in the same period. The basic idea—or, to use Kissinger's favorite term, "concept"—was that of a negotiated settlement, hardly a novel one at the time. More important were the conditions that Kissinger attached to such a settlement. It had to be arrived at in such a way that it did not shake "confidence in American promises" or compromise American "credibility," "prestige," or "steadiness." The key word was "honorably"—the war had to be ended "honorably." He conceived of doing so by means of a U.S.-Soviet-China "subtle triangle," whereby the United States would improve its relations with the two leading Communist powers and thereby achieve or at least advance an honorable settlement in Vietnam through them.[3]

By this time, the United States in essence had no other stake in

Vietnam than its "honor." Here again, the hard questions were evaded. What if the United States could not end the war "honorably" without paying an exorbitant price for the attempt, and then not succeed anyway? What if the road to peace in Vietnam did not run through Russia and China? What if Russia and China themselves were to work at cross purposes in Vietnam and elsewhere? Kissinger's honorable settlement in Vietnam was fitted into his rickety new "global, conceptual approach," which presupposed that Russia and China could restrain North Vietnam and that the Thieu regime in South Vietnam could be made capable of defending itself without American armed forces. Without these presuppositions, it would have made no sense for the Nixon-Kissinger policy to drag the American people through four more years of a war emptied of all meaning but that of getting out of a trap into which the United States should never have fallen.

When did Kissinger awake to the realities of the war? His friend Professor John G. Stoessinger tells us that it took Kissinger until the fall of 1971, all of three long, bloodstained Nixonian years, to realize that "Hanoi would not compromise." In 1972 Kissinger thought that he could get a Soviet "linkage" to a Vietnam settlement through the grain deal, which gave hundreds of millions of dollars' worth of American wheat to Russia at bargain prices at the expense of the American consumer, a price that, Kissinger argued, "was well worth a Vietnam settlement." Again he was disappointed. Finally, on the day that Saigon fell in the spring of 1975, Kissinger told Stoessinger: "Vietnam is a Greek tragedy. We should never have been there at all. But now it's history."[4] As an epitaph on this war, "We should never have been there at all" may never be excelled.

Unlike Kissinger, Brzezinski was at first much less circumspect. He was one of the first of the most militant defenders of the prowar faith; he supported the war aggressively in a notable television debate in which his opposite intellectual number was Professor Hans Morgenthau, who was never taken in by the war. Brzezinski's service in behalf of the war helped to get him an appointment in 1966 to the State Department's Policy Planning Council. *Newsweek* hailed him as "one of the fastest-rising stars in the Johnson Administration" and "one of the architects of U.S. foreign policy" after only four months on the job. As for "his hawkish position on Vietnam," the magazine's piece entitled "Diplomacy: The Thinker," went on, "he is apt to act as though he had a monopoly of the truth." The cheering was premature; Brzezinski returned to Columbia University after two years in Washington, apparently sorely disillusioned with the exercise of planning without power.

In this period, Brzezinski had little sympathy with antiwar demonstrators. In an article in *Foreign Affairs* of July 1966, he put them down as "a manifestation of a psychological crisis inherent in modern society." Vietnam, he wrote scornfully, was merely "an outlet for basic cravings and fears, and if that issue did not exist, some other one would provide an excuse for the expression of personal and political alienation." This was one way of exonerating the Vietnam war of blame for the widespread popular unrest and widespread opposition to the war.

By 1968, Brzezinski's attitude toward the war showed signs of unbearable strain. On the one hand, he gave up a clear-cut victory in Vietnam; he was now satisfied with denying victory to the enemy, though he never explained how the no-victory-no-defeat for either side was going to be calibrated. On the other hand, he told the *U.S. News & World Report* of February 26, 1968, that he wanted the United States to make it clear that it was willing to continue to fight in Vietnam for thirty years in order to prove to the enemy that "we have the staying power" and "happen to be richer and more powerful." He gave as his reason for such a long-range projection that the United States could not "commit itself to the extent it has, and 'chicken out.' "

By now, there was little or nothing in Vietnam that made thirty years of war advisable or necessary, even to a hitherto fervent supporter of the war; it was the American "commitment" itself that condemned us to an almost unimaginably interminable bloodletting. Thirty years of war was so breathtakingly long that Brzezinski might as well have said "forever." And all this for not even victory. Rereading this interview, one cannot take it seriously. What it suggests is that even as sharp and knowledgeable a specialist in foreign affairs as Brzezinski had completely lost his way and no longer made sense when he talked about the Vietnam war.

By 1969, Brzezinski himself must have realized that he had to find his way back to some kind of sanity about the war. Richard Nixon was now President and vast demonstrations all over the country for a

Vietnam "moratorium" had just taken place. In these circumstances, Brzezinski advised Nixon to pledge the removal of American forces from Vietnam "by a particular date (say, two years)." In this statement to the *New York Times* of October 17, 1969, Brzezinski forgot about the thirty-years war and neglected to make clear why it was better to "chicken out" in two years rather than immediately.

After this, Brzezinski apparently decided that it was the better part of valor to leave the Vietnam war alone. While the country was in an uproar over it during the first Nixon Administration, he turned his attention to other matters—the "technetronic era," Japan and Africa. This intellectual flying-trapeze act took him out of the line of fire and broadened his horizon in preparation for bigger things to come. It was also an admission that the war had become too much for even its most ardent and hardened supporters. It had become intellectually insupportable and even unmentionable.

Brzezinski's advice against "chickening out" and Kissinger's emphasis on ending the war "honorably" were essentially similar in motivation. We were supposed to go on fighting to prove something to ourselves or to the world at large, not to achieve anything of material or political interest in Vietnam. Brzezinski's temporary aberration of fighting on for thirty years was the logical outcome of this line of reasoning. If we could not end the war "honorably" and could not "chicken out," it had to go on and on indefinitely. Brzezinski's bravado was thus the *reductio ad absurdum* of the Vietnam war. Even he seems to have realized it in time.

In the end, Kissinger blamed Watergate and a failure of nerve for the debacle in Vietnam. The American people, Congress, South Vietnam, North Vietnam and the Soviet Union had all conspired to let down Henry Kissinger. The implication that his own people had failed him suggests that Kissinger's understanding of warfare left something to be desired. A good general—and even a good lieutenant—assesses his own strength as objectively as that of the enemy; he does not go into battle without taking into account what his own forces are capable of accomplishing and, in the particular case of the American people, what they are willing to fight for and at what cost. It was violation of this cardinal rule of warfare, not failure of nerve, that brought about the dishonorable end of the Vietnam war. It was the very nature of the war—a hopeless war in a land where we should never have been at all—that made its continuation so intolerable and its end so ignominious. There was no good way of getting out of the Vietnam war, but the worst way was to pay the price of getting out later rather than sooner.[5]

In effect, Kissinger and Brzezinski, two celebrated intellectuals who lent their considerable talents to a prolongation of the war, gave up the job of justification when they fell back on ending it "honorably" and not "chickening out." If they could do no better than that, the job was hopeless. Or so it seemed until now.

III

For we have just been offered a book that promises to relieve the American people of a sense of guilt for the Vietnam war and to absolve the United States of "*officially condoned* illegal and immoral conduct." The book is *America in Vietnam*, by Professor Guenter Lewy of the University of Massachusetts at Amherst. The work comes recommended by Charles B. MacDonald, a military historian, as "a sober, objective answer to polemicists on all sides" that "should enable the Vietnam veteran at last to hold his head high." Has Lewy succeeded where Kissinger and Brzezinski failed?

It should be said at once that those who read this book in order to assuage their guilt over the war are doomed to disappointment. The idea that it will enable a Vietnam veteran to hold his head high is utter rubbish. It does not attempt to answer "polemicists on all sides"; it polemicizes almost exclusively against the antiwar "polemicists." The author, his admirers, and his publishers may have made a mistake in presenting the book as if it were a wholesale apology for the war. This presentation may be enough to arouse curiosity but it does an injustice to the book as a whole.

It is a schizophrenic book. In large part, it made me writhe all over again at the willful stupidity and obdurate delusions with which the war was prosecuted. An almost unrelieved recital of mistakes and misdeeds fills pages and pages of the book. There are two Lewys in this work—one makes an admirable effort to get the facts straight; the other wants to give the United States a clean bill of health or at least the benefit of the doubt. Thus the book lends itself to different conclusions or interpretations depending on what chapter and even what paragraph one chooses to cite. The scholar and the advocate struggle for supremacy; sometimes one wins, sometimes the other.

It would be a mistake, therefore, for critics of the Vietnam war to reject Lewy's work *in toto* because he betrays a special animus against them, sometimes unfairly, or for hard-core supporters of the war to accept it with glee because he seems to favor them from time to time. Much of the book is the result of serious and painstaking research. If I had to draw up a list of a half-dozen books worth reading on the war, I would put this one among them, despite its flaws.

But does the author make good his claim that "the sense of guilt created by the Vietnam war in the minds of many Americans is not warranted"? That is what the argument over this book is likely to be about.

The answer partly depends on the answer to another question —guilt about what? There may be justifiable guilt about some things and not about others. Lewy never makes the distinction clear. He himself contributes the most damaging evidence that American officialdom was disastrously guilty of misconceiving and mishandling the war; he also attempts to clear it of some specific varieties of guilt on a most selective basis. Yet his generalizations would make it appear that the United States has no need to feel guilty at all about anything. Here and elsewhere, Lewy undermines his own book by overreaching and overstating.

For example, the American forces in Vietnam deliberately pursued a policy of "the encouragement and creation of refugees." This meant that combat operations, crop destruction, and "specified strike zones" were utilized to drive Vietnamese peasants from their homes in the hundreds of thousands. The most cruel and senseless practice for "generating" refugees, or as it was also called euphemistically, "relocating populations," took the form of "free-fire zones." An American commander would simply decide to designate an area, often a huge one, as such a zone so that anyone who remained in it was arbitrarily considered an enemy and thereby subject to annihilating artillery or air bombardment. This policy was pursued on a large scale for at least five years. Only in 1968, after over two years of this practice, were commanders in the field advised that they should not generate refugees "needlessly and heedlessly," with little effect on the actual tactics employed; and only in February 1969 were commanders officially instructed to give at least seventy-two hours notice to civilians in the areas, as if Vietnamese peasants in

far-flung areas were likely to receive and understand such notices or
do more than save their disrupted lives if they did.

Lewy knows what was wrong with this horror. He lists seven
"inherent weaknesses," including the fact that it was militarily useless and even played into the hands of the enemy. The vast majority
of those driven from their homes were old people, women and
children; few refugees were males of military age. Even so, the
battlefield was not cleared, because refugees persisted in returning
to their hamlets. The political madness of the policy comes out in his
words: "Not surprisingly, attitude surveys showed a high degree of
correlation between forcible evacuation and pro-Communist attitudes." He acknowledges that the crop-destruction program made
the local people, not the Vietcong, suffer. He reveals that the American crop-destruction missions were disguised as South Vietnamese
activity because the damage obviously could not be limited to the
enemy forces to conform with the Army's own manual of land
warfare.

Lewy documents more of the same. The fatuous policy of "body
counts" encouraged the indiscriminate lumping of combatants and
noncombatants, with the result that the killing of villagers could give
as much credit as the killing of enemy soldiers, and the only ones
really deceived were the Americans themselves. The strategy of
attrition was an abject failure. The villagers turned against the
United States because American military doctrine called for
methods that were insensitive to political and human costs; the
South Vietnamese and Korean allies trained in that doctrine behaved even more abominably. American commanders often gave
only "token compliance" to orders from above to restrain their
excessive use of fire power, so that "the worst features of the traditional mode of operation persisted." Corruption in the South
Vietnamese army was so extensive that it enabled the enemy to purchase supplies in South Vietnamese cities, obtain war materiel and
food from South Vietnamese officials and officers, and buy positions as hamlet and village chiefs. The once highly touted South
Vietnamese land reform was no more than an "empty gesture."
American brigade and division commanders falsified reports to hide
their persistent utilization of an unauthorized herbicide agent.
Lewy also retells the story of the secret bombing of North Vietnam,

based on fictitious enemy-action reports, which brought about the demotion and retirement of General John D. Lavelle, commanding officer of the Seventh Air Force. He has an entire chapter on American "atrocities" in Vietnam, one of which was the My-Lai "massacre," using these very terms—"atrocity" and "massacre." He also describes the leniency of court-martials that dealt with these "war crimes"—again in this context his term.

The single American who comes off worst in Lewy's book is no ordinary officer or soldier. He is General William C. Westmoreland, chief of U.S. forces in Vietnam from 1964 to 1968, when he was recalled to become Army Chief of Staff. Lewy seems to hold Westmoreland most responsible for keeping to the disastrous strategy of "the big-unit war of attrition" long after it had been proven futile and self-defeating. In his most scathing indictment of Westmoreland, Lewy goes so far as to doubt that the general could defend himself against the charge that he was guilty of "dereliction of duty," because he should have known that American "violations of the law of war" were bound to take place in the circumstances of Vietnam and should have taken the necessary measures to prevent them.

If one sought to make a devastating condemnation of the Vietnam war, one could do so out of Lewy's book, as I have just done. But such an exercise would reflect only one side of the work. In another, the author seeks almost desperately to muffle his blows on the war and even to lead the unwary reader into believing that he is rushing to its defense.

IV

One way Lewy tries to make a bad war look better is the soft reproach.

For example, President Johnson told reporters after the decision was made to use American troops in Vietnam that he knew of "no far-reaching strategy that is being suggested or promulgated." Lewy's comment is: "Needless to say, Johnson here was being less than candid." Needless to say, Lewy is being less than candid; Johnson knew that a far-reaching strategic change had been initiated and had deliberately misled the reporters and the American people. Or Lewy demonstrates that the so-called Rules of Engagement, ostensibly designed to minimize the destruction of civilian life and

Draper

property, were extensively and sometimes wantonly disregarded in
practice. Lewy's comment is that "this level of familiarity was obviously less than satisfactory." He might have said more satisfactorily
that the level of familiarity was grossly unsatisfactory and even
culpably negligent.

Sometimes Lewy likes to have it both ways. He raises the
question whether South Vietnam could have survived if U.S. aid had
not been cut off in 1975. His first answer tends to be highly
pessimistic—"there is reason to believe that, everything else being
equal, internal weaknesses on the part of the South Vietnamese
armed forces alone might have been sufficient to cause defeat in
1975." A few pages later, however, he seems to backtrack. The odds
were still against the South Vietnamese but their defeat was not a
"foregone conclusion." If President Nixon had been able to dissociate himself from the Watergate burglars and had been able to
reintroduce American military power in Vietnam as he had promised; if Congress had been persuaded to provide South Vietnam with
adequate military supplies; if the OPEC nations had suffered an
early breakup and oil had continued to be cheap; if the North
Vietnamese had made a few major mistakes; if South Vietnamese
nationalists and anti-Communist sects had been able to overthrow
the Thieu regime. . . . After this long string of "ifs," Lewy concludes: "None of these events was impossible, and if their occurrence in combination was unlikely, this was no more so than the
combination of opposite events which did in fact take place." In this
way, Lewy cuts the ground from under his own work. He has spent
most of his book making quite credible the combination of events
that in fact took place, with particular emphasis on the internal
weaknesses of the South Vietnamese armed forces. Then he turns
around, belies his own work, and makes the historical record no
more likely to have happened than the conveniently early breakup
of OPEC. This is not the only instance where he seems to flinch from
the implications of his own findings.

What, above all, gives Lewy the air of being a defender of the
prowar faith is his criticism of the Vietnam war's critics. He always
refers to them with a particularly wrathful peevishness. Sometimes,
his tantrum gets in the way of elementary fairness.

I will offer myself as a case in point.

My book *Abuse of Power* was published in 1967. It was based on work done in the previous year and a half or so. Since Lewy's book has come out in 1978, eleven years later, it would be odd if he had not consulted material not available to me or to other critics a decade ago. In any case, Lewy decided to teach me a lesson about a major turning point in the war—President Johnson's decision in February 1965 to initiate large-scale bombing of North Vietnam.

To justify this momentous step, the State Department issued later that month a White Paper entitled *Aggression from the North: The Record of North Viet-Nam's Campaign to Conquer South Viet-Nam.* The thesis of the White Paper was: North Vietnamese forces had invaded South Vietnam in such numbers that the previously officially regarded civil war had turned into a foreign "aggression." The question naturally arose whether the incursion of North Vietnamese forces was large enough to justify the massive intervention of American ground forces. The White Paper was a propaganda flop because it failed to sustain the claim of a large-scale invasion from the North. Lewy admits the "weakness" of the White Paper. But then he goes on:

> Theodore Draper alleges that at the time the bombing of North Vietnam started, Hanoi had only 400 regular soldiers in the South. The U.S. converted this into an "invasion" in order to have a justification for its own escalation.[122]

The footnote ("122") goes even further and changes the "allegation" into a "canard." An allegation implies a statement without supporting evidence; a canard means an unfounded and especially a false report. Could my treatment of the issue fairly be described as either a mere allegation or an outright canard?

I devoted almost eight pages to the question of the North Vietnamese infiltration southward. I related that Secretary of State Rusk had claimed that the entire 325th Division had been moved into South Vietnam by January 1965. But I noted that the White Paper the following month had not even mentioned the 325th, as it might have been expected to do. I also pointed out that Secretary of Defense McNamara, who should have known best, had in April 1965 confirmed the presence of only one battalion, estimated by him at 400 to 500 men, of the 325th in the South. Over a year later, in June 1966, Senator Mike Mansfield, the Democratic majority leader, had publicly repeated the number of "only about 400 North Vietnamese soldiers" in the South at the time of "the sharp increase in the American military effort" in early 1965. An inquiring reporter had subsequently learned that Senator Mansfield had obtained his figure from the Pentagon. Other evidence pointed in the same direction.

After laying out all the available information, I commented:

> Clearly we cannot be sure whether a battalion or a regiment or all of the 325th Division crossed into South Vietnam by January 1965 or at any other time. We could not be sure even if Secretaries Rusk and McNamara agreed, and their disagreement adds a dash of farce to what was otherwise one of the most grievous moments of the war. The most we can conclude from the available evidence is that it was extraordinarily necessary for the Secretary of State to have an "invasion" of South Vietnam by a North Vietnamese organized unit at least as large as a division before the United States began its systematic bombing of the North in February 1965.

Thus I did not even foreclose the question of the number of North Vietnamese regular soldiers in the South in February 1965. I rather emphasized the official disparities, which at that time would have led any fair-minded observer not to know what to believe. My final word was: "We may still not know much about the elusive 325th, but we can know a great deal about how it was bandied to and fro by high American officials who could not even convince each other." Nor did I say that the United States had converted the smaller number of North Vietnamese regulars into an "invasion"; I said that Secretary Rusk, the only one who then vouched for the presence of an entire North Vietnamese division in the South, had shown an extraordinary need for at least a division to justify the U.S. bombing campaign in the North. My very point was that leading officials of the United States were divided in their pronouncements on the subject.

Can my treatment be fairly described as an "allegation," as if I had picked out a number without reason, or as a "canard," as if I had spread a demonstrably false, unfounded rumor? The real authors of the report about the 400 North Vietnamese regular soldiers in the South were Secretary McNamara and Senator Mansfield, no inconsequential authorities on such a matter, and their information had clearly come from the Pentagon. The most that could be said at the time was that Secretary Rusk and the State Department claimed to know better.

Lewy, however, has triumphantly brought forth a new source of intelligence on what I called "the elusive 325th." It comes from a "Working Paper of the U.S. State Department on the North Vietnamese Role in the War in South Vietnam," issued in May 1968. According to this "working paper," which did not appear in print in the United States until 1969, 4,000 North Vietnamese regulars went south by February 1965 and another 1,800 by March 1965.[6] If the ultimate source was South Vietnamese, Lewy himself, in other connections, tells us how unreliable this source was; and if the data were provided two or three years after the event, it would be even more suspect.

Lewy's use of this "working paper" is so uncritical that it betrays his anxiety to defend the U.S. bombing at all costs.

• First, it appeared in 1968, almost three and a half years after the event and a year after I had shown what unholy confusion had attended the whole matter. Obviously, I could not have known of a 1968 "working paper" in 1967. Neither could Secretary Rusk have based himself on it in 1965.

• Second, the 1968 paper originated in the Department of State, not in the Department of Defense. There was nothing new about the State Department claims. I had already made known similar claims by Secretary of State Rusk in 1965. The problem arose because Secretary Rusk was controverted by Secretary of Defense McNamara and Senator Mansfield. A fair treatment would not have taken something put out by the State Department years later and subsequently generally ignored as if it were the last word on the subject; the discrepancy between the State Department and the Pentagon was the real question worth looking into, but Lewy chooses to ignore it.

• Third, the reason I was struck by the remarkably dissimilar versions of North Vietnamese infiltration by February 1965 was the inordinate importance attached to it as the justification for America's massive intervention. Whatever the number of North Vietnamese regular troops in the South in 1965, the U.S. combat force in South

Vietnam was already far greater. The U.S. force increased from 23,000 at the end of 1964 to about 125,000 in the summer of 1965. Even if the 1968 "working paper" is taken at face value, the number of North Vietnamese troops in the South increased from 2,000 at the end of 1964 to 7,000 by September 1965. The "working paper" itself alluded to the "relatively slow pace of the [North Vietnamese] buildup" in all of 1965. It was already clear to me in 1967 that the American decision to intervene on a large scale was based "on South Vietnamese weakness rather than North Vietnamese strength." After all his pious protests against my "allegation" and "canard," Lewy ends by agreeing with me on this point. Somehow, a mere "allegation" and an outright "canard" had enabled me to reach the right conclusion.

I have gone into this example of Lewy's polemics against the "polemicists" because it shows how lacking in sobriety and objectivity he can be. It was necessary to go into it in some detail because the present reader could not be expected to have Lewy's book and mine at hand to refresh his memory regarding the background and significance of the question at issue. In effect, Lewy's book sometimes suffers from an excess of zeal, especially in his frequently intemperate dismissal of premature critics of the Vietnam war.

V

The heart of the matter is the peculiar strategy that Lewy employs to relieve Americans of a sense of guilt created by the Vietnam war and to dismiss from their consciences "charges of *officially condoned* illegal and grossly immoral conduct." He convinced me that this form of apologia is as doomed as the American war effort in Vietnam.

It is important to be clear about what Lewy defends. He does not defend the American way of war in Vietnam. He condemns its "obtuseness and mistakes in judgment." All that he affirms is that these were not the result of "culpable negligence." If the negligence was not "culpable," no war crimes were committed. He is operating here on a very narrow defensive front. The only sense of guilt he seeks to relieve is that for very legally circumscribed, intentional "war crimes."

The word "intentionally" plays a crucial role in his brief for the defense. He is willing to admit that "the rather free use of napalm and attacks upon fortified hamlets with artillery and air strikes can be criticized on humanitarian grounds"—to put it mildly in view of his own account of the ruthless, senseless devastation wrought by the "free-fire zones." Yet he can still find it "morally significant" that the tactics employed "did not intentionally aim at inflicting casualties upon the civilian population." Nevertheless, he had previously shown that, year after year, almost all the casualties brought about by these tactics were inflicted on the civilian population. He had previously shown that these casualties had been remorselessly inflicted on the civilian population because Vietnamese civilians and enemy soldiers or agents had been stupidly, arbitrarily, and indiscriminately lumped together. What in these circumstances is the meaning of "not intentionally"? What makes it so remarkably different for our sense of guilt from "intentionally"?

On one page, Lewy's apologia reveals its essential hollowness and heartlessness. His conclusion to a chapter on "American Military Tactics and the Law of War" begins with a general absolution:

> The American record in Vietnam with regard to observance of the law of war is not a succession of war crimes and does not support charges of a systematic and willful violation of existing agreements for standards of human decency in time of war, as many critics of the American involvement have alleged.

But the first sentence of the very next paragraph goes this way:

> If the American record is not one of gross illegality, neither has it been a model of observance of the law of war.

Here we have Lewy trying to have it both ways again. The second time around he merely absolves us of "gross illegality." How gross is "gross"? We can now see why Lewy italicized two words in his formulation of unwarranted charges of *"officially condoned* illegal and grossly immoral conduct." The conduct may be illegal but it is not all that bad unless it is *officially condoned*; it may be immoral but not anything to feel guilty about unless it is *grossly* immoral. How far up in the military hierarchy did illegal conduct have to go in order to be officially condoned? The "free-fire zone" horror was not merely officially condoned; it was officially conceived and carried out at the very top. It was persisted in by the American military command despite what Lewy calls its lamentable "cost-benefit equation." Lewy's tricky formulas do not white-wash illegal or immoral conduct; they defend it only from the most extreme accusations of such conduct.

In fact, Lewy betrays a guilty conscience of his own. In the very last paragraph of the same chapter, he draws back from making his entire case depend on the "law of war":

> In the final analysis, of course, law alone, no matter how comprehensive and carefully phrased, cannot assure protection of basic human values. Back in the seventeenth century, Hugo Grotius, the father of modern international law, quoted with approval the advice which Euripides in *The Trojan Women* put into the mouth of Agamemnon addressing Pyrrhus: "What the law does not forbid, then let shame forbid." This counsel retains its moral worth. While the law of war is an extremely important means of mitigating the ravages of war, it cannot be considered an adequate and sufficient measure of human decency.

The implication is clear: Americans who read *Americans in Vietnam* should not feel guilty; they should feel ashamed. This substitution of terms is really the core of Lewy's case; it may make some readers feel better. It is a continuing shame, however, that the shamefulness of this war should be incidentally mentioned in a book designed to cover up the shame by taking refuge in narrow and dubious legalisms. I said at the outset that this was a schizophrenic book; it is never more schizophrenic than in a chapter that starts by seeking to acquit us of violating the "law of war" and ends by implicitly condemning us to shame.

I have thought it necessary to deal at some length with *America in Vietnam* because it is the most ambitious effort to decontaminate the American role in Vietnam. It is a vain, self-defeating effort. It will serve a useful purpose only if it makes us more acutely aware how stupid, miserable, and costly that war was.

VI

The main reason for the predicament of Kissinger and Brzezinski in the past and Lewy in the present is that they had difficulty fitting the Vietnam war into a larger framework. The war was never worth

fighting for Vietnam alone; it always had to be made subsidiary to a
larger purpose. The trouble was that it did not quite fit any of those
imposed on it.

Kissinger's reason for going on with the war made the entire
American position in world affairs and even world peace depend on
an "honorable" ending. "What is involved now is confidence in
American promises," he wrote in 1968, and "ending the war honorably is essential for the peace of the world." In the end, an
"honorable" settlement came to mean the preservation of the South
Vietnam regime or the frustration of a North Vietnamese victory,
which amounted to the same thing. Thus the survival of a regime
that almost all Americans in positions of authority regarded as hopelessly corrupt and hopelessly weak was endowed with a value and
importance out of all proportion to what it could bear. The tangibles
of national strength and stability were sacrificed to intangibles such
as American "prestige" and "honor." Estimable as the latter may be,
they were not worth the price that had to be paid for them in real
assets. Even worse, honor went when power failed.

Kissinger's rationale for continuing the war betrayed a basic
misunderstanding of both the world and the American people. It
was darkly said that America's allies in Europe would lose all faith in
American commitments if the United States let down South Vietnam. In fact, America's allies were increasingly alarmed at the
frittering away of American resources in Vietnam and the social
turmoil in the United States that threatened to escalate out of
control. Ominous fears were also expressed as to what the American
people might do if and when they woke up to the reality of a lost war,
as if Nixonian America were Weimar Germany. When the war ended
as badly as a war could possibly end, at least for the South Vietnamese, the popular American reaction was one of relief and fatigue.
If it had been otherwise, former President Nixon would have been
driven out for the sins of Vietnam instead of for the crimes of
Watergate. The American people were not interested in an "honorable" end, whatever that might have been; they were interested in
the end.

In his fighting-on-for-thirty-years period, Brzezinski made a
similar miscalculation. He thought it was necessary to prove to the
enemy "that we have the staying power" and "happen to be richer

and more powerful." It was wrong for the United States to "chicken out," he said, because "the consequences of getting out would be far more costly than the expense of staying in." By 1968, when this rationalization was made, it was already abundantly clear that the riches and power that we had were not the right kind for a war in Vietnam and that we would be much less rich and far less powerful the longer we stayed. It was ludicrously wrong to have made the consequences of getting out far worse than the expense of staying in. These terrible consequences were supposed to have beset the United States in the world at large, not in Vietnam, and all the world did when we got out was to heave a sigh of relief.

Ten years later, Lewy knows better than to bewail our loss of "honor" or "prestige." His problem is to explain the American failure in Vietnam, not to prevent it. He hints at an explanation without reflecting on what its implications might be.

Lewy twice uses the same phrase—that the United States and its allies in Vietnam failed "to understand the real stakes in a revolutionary war." He never explains what he understands by an American "revolutionary war" in Vietnam or how we could possibly have waged it. But the suggestion is dropped, and it is worth considering.

To have waged a revolutionary war in Vietnam, we would have needed a revolutionary South Vietnamese regime. Lewy has no illusions about the corruption and unpopularity of the Thieu regime. He even quotes a statement, with which he says many agreed, that "if Thieu wants to eliminate corruption in the army he must fire himself." Lewy also recognizes: "The war not only had to be won in South Vietnam, but it had to be won by the South Vietnamese." In effect, the United States could not have made it a revolutionary war even if it had wanted to do so. The politics of this war, which was decisive, was essentially decided by the Vietnamese themselves. The dilemma that this situation presented was: the war could not be won if it was not revolutionary, and it could not be revolutionary if it was up to the South Vietnamese.

Lewy also makes clear why the American armed forces were incapable of fighting a revolutionary war in Vietnam. He reports "the growing disdain for the Vietnamese people among U.S. military personnel in Vietnam." So many American soldiers were killed or wounded by mines and booby traps in or near hamlets that "it became the prudent thing to doubt the loyalty of every villager." The result was: "Some soldiers began to adopt the so-called mere-gook rule, the attitude that the killing of Vietnamese, regardless of sex, age, or combatant status, was of little importance for they were, after all, only gooks." Elsewhere, Lewy changes "some" to "many" soldiers who lived by this "rule," which helps to explain the high civilian casualties, civilian inclusion in the inflated body counts, and the deliberate "generation" of a vast horde of refugees. A survey of marines in 1966 in one province revealed that 40 percent disliked the Vietnamese; small-unit leaders ranked highest in their "negative attitudes." Fewer than 20 percent of noncommissioned officers had "a positive attitude" toward the South Vietnamese armed forces.

A "revolutionary war," then, was and is a political pipe dream. The Vietnam war could not be put into a revolutionary any more than it could comfortably be put into a larger international framework. When Kissinger at long last saw the light and told his friend Professor Stoessinger that "we should never have been there at all," he was saying only part of the depressing truth. The rest that needed to be said was that we should have decided to get out of the war as soon as possible, to cut our losses as soon as possible, to stop killing Vietnamese and Americans and wasting our national substance as soon as possible.

Of course, if the Carters and Vances and Kissingers and Brzezinskis had said all this prematurely, that is, when it needed to be said, they might not be where they are today. All they might have is the dismal satisfaction of knowing that they were right.

Footnotes

1. In his *Kissinger: Portrait of a Mind* (New York: Norton, 1973), Stephen R. Graubard claimed that Kissinger "had nothing to say" because he still "did not know enough about the issues" until 1968 (pp. 279–80). Graubard gives no evidence of knowing about Kissinger's article in *Look*—it is not listed in his bibliography—in which Kissinger had quite a lot to say before 1968. And if two anything-and-anyone-you-want-to-see-and-hear personal tours of Vietnam, lasting altogether a month, and top-level briefings in the Pentagon, let alone mere reading of the newspapers, were not enough to give one something to say about Vietnam, very few Americans would have felt obliged to summon up the moral courage to take a stand against the war. John G. Stoessinger in his *Henry Kissinger: The Anguish of Power* (New York: Norton, 1976) gave two different reasons—that Kissinger did not speak up until 1968 because he was interested "in a global conceptual approach" and because he was looking for an opportunity to

test it in action (p. 43). Stoessinger also seems to have been ignorant of the *Look* article, which would have spoiled his time scheme, and which, in essence, already contained the Kissingerian conceptual approach, albeit not with its "global" trappings.

2. *No More Vietnams?* Richard M. Pfeffer, ed. (New York: Harper & Row, 1968), pp. 11–13.

3. The article on "The Vietnam Negotiations" in *Foreign Affairs* of January 1969, written in the late summer and early autumn of 1968, was reprinted in *American Foreign Policy* (New York: Norton, 1969). The idea of the "subtle triangle" appeared in one of Rockefeller's speeches (Graubard, op. cit., p. 252).

4. Stoessinger, op. cit., pp. 60, 65, 76–77.

5. Lest the reader think that this is hindsight on my part, I may be permitted to recall that I also attended the Chicago conference on Vietnam of the Adlai Stevenson Institute of Foreign Affairs in June 1968. In view of the coming presidential election, I said: "Do we have a presidential candidate in sight who can say to the American people, 'We have suffered a failure in Vietnam; it is costly to get out; it is more costly to persist.' I fear that unless this is said now and clearly, we will not get out of this morass" (*No More Vietnams?*, op. cit., pp. 97–98).

6. Lewy says that only a part of the "working paper" was published in *Viet-Nam Documents and Research Notes*, issued by the U.S. Embassy in Saigon in June 1968. It appeared in its entirety in the United States as an appendix to *The Vietnam War and International Law*, Richard A. Falk, ed. (Princeton, N.J.: Princeton University Press, 1969), Vol. II, pp. 1183–1206. All the paper gives is the number of prisoners and captured documents on which the data is based, but not their provenance or anything else about them. The paper is said to be based on a "compilation" of material, which, however, is not given. One cannot tell from the paper itself how "carefully researched and documented" it is, despite Lewy's touching assurance.

ROSE L. COSER AND LEWIS COSER
The Commune as Perverse Utopia
(1979)

For twenty days, until December 8, 1978, the Jonestown horror story made front-page news in the *New York Times*. In the course of five hours, 911 adults and children were killed or killed themselves. There had been no threat on their lives from the outside, nor was there any strong transcendental cause that leader or followers meant to serve. The leader had claimed he wanted "socialism" and "Marxism," and had mixed his missionary zeal with religion because he allegedly believed the followers "needed it." So for years he gave them "opium for the people," and in the end cyanide.

The usual questions being asked as the result of the wide news coverage are: What kind of people were these commune members? Were they without roots? Were they the rejects of society—the drug addicts, the convicts, the prostitutes, those not embedded in the social fabric of their society? And who was the leader? What manner of man commanded such obedience? How did he grow up in the small town where he was born? Had he given signs of such wickedness earlier in his life?

It turns out that the followers were of all kinds. There were the poor, the rich, and those who were neither one nor the other. There were convicts and there were lawyers; there were the elderly; there were young prostitutes; there were physicians and nurses; blacks and whites. There were those with weak moral beliefs and those with a strong social conscience. The answers defining the characteristics of the members are not satisfactory. At best they tell us who was attracted to Jim Jones, but they cannot tell us why they obeyed him even unto death.

Nor do the characteristics of the leader tell us much. It is interesting to hear that as a child he killed animals and said mass after their death, and that his mother had predicted her son would be a messiah. But surely, the Jekyll-Hyde personality occurs frequently, and many people have fantasies of omnipotence. Some even become murderers, and occasionally there is one who manages to kill as many as a dozen people. But they do not kill, or are not capable of killing, almost a thousand people in one sweep. This is hard work. While psychological predispositions in the leader and his followers explain some of their mutual attraction, they cannot fully explain this horrible success story.

Let us turn from personal to structural characteristics. Perverse as it was, Jonestown was a species of the genus *Utopian commune.* Ever since the Industrial Revolution and earlier, even in antiquity, blueprints for a more satisfying social organization—from *The Republic* to *Utopia* (which coined the generic name) to *Looking Backward*—were drawn up in response to widespread discontent with the prevailing quality of life. These Utopias transcended the here-and-now, served as guidelines for social criticism and as foci for human strivings. Yet, as Lewis Coser and Henry Jacoby wrote years ago, "We are appalled to discover that many of the rationalistic fantasies of the world improvers contain a large admixture of what we now recognize as totalitarianism."

Not only blueprints but actual experiments in utopian living over the years attracted the socially committed and the morally courageous, the physically and psychologically deprived, and those yearning for a new morality. Yet, in most communes morals and social relations tended to be regulated from above; personal and public allegiances were monopolized by a central authority; and what had started out as an experiment in liberation usually ended as an experiment in the total absorption of personality. Communes have an innate tendency to become, as one of the authors wrote, "greedy institutions."

Communes did not usually end in the destruction of their members, and some of those inspired by vigorous religious beliefs even managed to survive for several generations. But most of them ended in splits, fights between rival factions, bitter disputes, mutual recriminations, and sordid intrigues among rival leaders. Their isolation from other social institutions, their inward orientation, the absorption of the members' total personality often led to a disintegration of the commune, even as it deprived members of the ability to sustain personal relations both within and without.

Jonestown was a community isolated by design. In a sense, if not literally, it was an incestuous community. To survive for even the short period it did, it operated in secrecy, erected strong barriers around itself. Rank-and-file members had to break all ties with the outside. This prevented interference from nonbelievers, but it primarily prevented reality testing. Any personal or social values members brought with them from their previous lives were destroyed. Personal relations, whether sexual or otherwise affective, were broken up, thus assuring the absence of interpersonal allegiances and creating complete dependency, similar to the dependency of a newborn child, on one person and one person only.

THE ISOLATED SOCIETY: "WE HAD NOWHERE TO GO."

Anthropologists and sociologists are generally agreed on the proposition that society is possible because libidinal energies and affective orientations, within or between generations, are directed outward, so that self-sufficiency is prevented. This is the basis for the incest taboo. A certain amount of what Philip Slater has called "libidinal diffusion" is necessary for social survival, since it facilitates exchange among various units of a society. Groups that monopolize affective energies within themselves tend to be subject to inner decay and to have low survival value. As a case in point Jonestown's members were isolated from any but the minimum contact with the outside world and had no place to go: no place to go to test reality, no place to go with libidinal energy except to one man, no place to go to obtain or receive support except from him.

Jonestown seems to have been incestuous in more than the figurative sense. The leader, who was called "Dad," had sexual relations with the commune's members, that is, his "children," men or women, sometimes as many as sixteen a day, as he bragged to

Charles Gary. He explained that he did this "to assure their loyalty to him." By working to monopolize the affect of the community's members, and making them withdraw their libidinal energy not only from outside relationships but inside as well, Jones reduced his followers to a narcissistic stage of infantile dependency that Bruno Bettelheim had shown to develop among inmates of concentration camps.

Rank-and-file members had little contact with the outside, and no one could leave the premises except some trusted aides who could go as far as the Georgetown headquarters, where control of movement was as tight as it could possibly be. Ron Javers describes the physical isolation from the plane that took him to Port Kaituma—a six-hour jeep ride from Jonestown.

> At some points the trees were so thick we couldn't see the ground. . . . Elsewhere there were large stretches of flat, deep, red mud. There were no roads. It was startling to realize how isolated people could be only 150 miles from the capital. There was no way to get to Jonestown except by air or by a long boat trip along the Atlantic coast and up the Kaituma River.[1]

The isolation of the site was a criterion for selection when Jones first conceived of the settlement. From its early days, the People's Temple tried to erect boundaries or break relations with the rest of society (even as Jones tried to influence, cajole, or threaten politicians and the press). Several times he had picked up and moved when outside intrusions threatened. Around 1965 in Redwood City, it became known that there were guards around the Temple church and dogs along the fences.

There was isolation from the media as well. Jones controlled the news and the members' access to it. When *New West* magazine was to appear with disclosures about the doings at the Temple, and he departed for Guyana, he instructed his aides to buy out the magazine from newsstands in Oakland, San Francisco, and Los Angeles, where a copy might fall into the hands of Temple members or their relatives. He also instructed his aides to forbid followers to read newspapers or watch television. Later, in Jonestown, members were asked to listen to news broadcasts selectively, and they had to write out their reactions and send them to "Dad."

Without newspapers and with only occasional news that had to be "understood" in a prescribed manner, barricaded by the jungle, how would it ever be possible for any rank-and-file member to test reality? How could anyone have looked for evidence of the alleged fact that mercenaries were waiting in the woods to invade the settlement and torture its members? The only place to go with one's assessments was into the jungle—even if, as is doubtful, the need for such assessment were perceived by the members who anyhow "knew" that they must depend on "Dad."

Isolation could not be maintained without secrecy. In the mid-'60s in Redwood Valley, the Temple members' children were said to lie, and to be evasive at school about what they did at the Temple. Isolation and secrecy, if they are to be organizational requirements, must be enjoined upon and upheld by all individual members. Many Temple members had to forgo bidding their relatives good-bye when they left for Guyana, and others were called in the morning and told they would leave for Guyana the same night. Parents called their children to tell them they were leaving on a trip immediately, and refused to tell them where they were going or how long they would be gone. Relatives of those who had gone to Jonestown without leaving word were met with silence when they made inquiries at the San Francisco Temple.

While isolation and secrecy were organizational requirements for Jones's designs, they served social and psychological purposes as well. Group members who break off all relationships on the outside will become totally dependent on the group. Not only will it be difficult for them to return home if they so desire, but their whole cognitive and affective orientation will be inward-directed so that the outside world fades from view—much as it does with those involuntarily confined in concentration camps, or subjected to long-term imprisonment or hospitalization.

Temple members who made the trip signed away their cars, homes, and other possessions to the church as many had before them. When they arrived at Jonestown, whatever money they had left was confiscated along with their passports. In San Francisco church members had been talked into cashing their life-insurance policies and turning the money over to the Temple, or into signing over power of attorney, and, back in Indiana, couples had been persuaded to sell their houses, turning the money over to the

church. The well-to-do had been made to give up their means of
survival on the outside. The poor were required to hand over an
ever-larger percentage of their meager earnings.

All this money made the People's Temple a viable financial
operation. But it served another purpose as well: it deprived the
members of all independence. Jones did not want the money simply
for selfish or organizational purposes: it became a problem merely to
dispose of the wealth that piled up. "Jim was giving the stuff away
just to get rid of it," one former member said. But, most important,
people deprived of their money would have no options but to stay
with the Temple. "The Temple ended up with everything I had,"
said Jeannie Mills. "That's what made it so hard to leave. We *had
nowhere to go* and nothing to fall back on."

The stage was now set for the total institution that was to be
Jonestown, but to assure its survival, two more things had to be
accomplished: the remaking of personal values, and the prevention
of solidarity within the settlement. These, paradoxically, led to its
destruction.

THE INVERTEBRATE: "I KNOW I'M LIKE A BANANA."

Having no place to go was not enough. Not *wanting* to go would
be better. And so we read in one of those required letters of confession: "I'm an elitist and anarchist. . . . I've come a little way. . . .
Here I don't have any intention of becoming a traitor or going back to
the United States" (Avis G., quoted in the *New York Times*,
November 29).

People's behavior as well as their personal attitudes and moral
values had to come under the scrutiny of all. Individuals had to
submit to physical and mental humiliations, and more: they had to
humiliate themselves. Former Temple members report that men
and women would be forced to strip off their clothes at the public
meetings and admit to being homosexuals or lesbians.

Already in San Francisco Jones spent much of his time presiding
over such "catharsis" sessions, which were grueling, drawn-out
spells of emotional dissection by the followers.

Why did she wear such new clothes when there are millions of
people starving? Wasn't it true that he wanted to make love to

another man's wife? Admit it! How could anyone complain about working until dawn after getting off work when Father is in such pain for us all.

Beatings, tortures, mutual accusations and confessions— techniques that had started back in San Francisco—remind us of the social-psychological processes in the concentration camps as described by Bruno Bettelheim. At Jonestown, those who, like Bettelheim's camp inmates,

> did not develop a childlike dependency were accused of threatening the security of the group. . . . The regression into childlike behavior was inescapable. . . . [They] lived, like children, only in the immediate present; they lost their feeling for the sequence of time; they became unable to plan for the future. . . . They were unable to establish durable object relations. Friendships developed as quickly as they broke off. [*Journal of Abnormal and Social Psychology*, 1943.]

For the acceptance of this new life, everything that had to do with the personal life of the past or of the present—relatives, friends; social, personal, and intimate values—had to be defiled. "When your name was called, people would scream, 'Get down there,' and swear. It was hostile," said a former member. "Everyone related to you was required to run up and accuse you." Any loyalties, any solidarity, any relatedness between the members of the Temple had to be broken up, and mutual accusations, hostilities, and mandatory denunciations were used to bring this about. Nobody could trust anybody. Not being permitted to establish relationships with one another, they soon became incapable of doing so, like Don F., who wrote in one of his mandatory letters of confession: "Now I know I'm like a banana, just one of the bunch. I have come a long way" (*New York Times*, November 29).

"SEX WAS ONE OF JIM'S SPECIALTIES FOR PULLING PEOPLE APART"

Children were removed from their parents, spouses separated, matches made and broken up. Family ties within the church were always kept under Jones's direct control. Jones knew that the

most effective way to control personal relationships is to control
libidinal attractions. When he bragged to his lawyer, Charles Gary,
about having "fucked fourteen women and two men" on that one
day, he explained that this was to assure their loyalty to him.

Jones ordered marriages ended and rearranged. Many of his
marathon six-hour sermons dwelled on sex, including directives to
members to abstain from sexual relations. He had established a kind
of spy group in the church that regulated everything including hand
holding, forced divorces and shotgun marriages. A high school boy
seen talking to a girl who did not belong to the Temple would be
called before the assembly to talk at length about his sex life.

"Sex was one of Jim's specialties for pulling people apart," said a
former member. Married couples were forced apart and told to
refrain from sexual intercourse because it was evil.

Lewis Coser has argued elsewhere that such manifestly opposite
sexual patterns as abstinence and sexual promiscuity serve the same
purposes (*Greedy Institutions*, New York: Free Press, 1974). Both
promiscuity and celibacy help prevent stable dyadic bonds, for such
bonds detract from emotional attachment to the community and its
leaders. Whether members refrain from all sexual relations, as did
the Shakers, or whether there is a controlled form of promiscuity, as
in Oneida, it is sociologically unimportant. What these communities
share is a deliberate attempt to prevent dyadic personal relationships so that emotional energies will be purposely channeled. A
similar pattern prevails in other totalistic communes, for example, at
Synanon. A *New York Times* report (December 10, 1978) describes
the policies introduced by its leader, Chuck Dederich. They include
forced vasectomies for male members, mandatory abortions for
women, and orders from Mr. Dederich for more than 230 married
couples to divorce and switch to other partners within the group.

"I'M DEAD INSIDE"

The problem, it seems to us, is that emotional energies cannot
simply be "channeled" for the common or not so uncommon good.
Arbitrary and unpredictable interference with them leads to their
being damaged at best and destroyed at worst. The latter happened
in Jonestown. When people are cut off from emotional bonds with
their fellows they have no psychic energies left that can

be mobilized, even in situations of extreme peril. How many among the hundreds of adults standing in line for cyanide asked themselves, like Odell Rhodes, "How can I get out of here?" Could he not at least have made eye contact with someone who had similar feelings? It seems that at the high point of the ceremony of self-immolation everyone was but an atom unto him- or herself, unable to relate even in imagination to others who might share some doubts. They must all have felt, as Odell Rhodes later stated about himself, "dead inside" (*New York Times*, November 29).

Jonestown was more "greedy" an institution than has probably ever existed. It successfully "devoured" its members by making total claims on them and by encompassing their whole personality. By claiming—and receiving—undivided loyalty, and by reducing the claims of competing roles and allegiances, it succeeded not merely in totally absorbing members within its boundaries but in reducing them to human pulp as well. Not only did it erect insurmountable boundaries between the inside and the outside, between the "re-born" collective present of the members and their "disreputable" private past; it also succeeded in maiming them by breaking up any mutual attachments, sexual or otherwise. The stable relationship, *voilà l'ennemi*.

Even as we recoil in horror at the unfolding of the Jonestown story it behooves us not to look at it in isolation. It did, after all, unfold at this time and in this place. While it would be fatuous to blame what happened on "American society," we must keep in mind that the damned and the lost and the hopeful who flocked to Jones and the People's Temple did so because the society in which they lived had failed to provide satisfactory bonds, meaningful community, and fraternal solidarities. To them their society felt like a desert devoid of love, and this is why they turned to the People's Temple as they would to an oasis. Although their quest turned out to be a delusion, we cannot deny that their need was acute.

Footnote

1. Marshall Kilduff and Ron Javers, *Suicide Cult* (New York: Bantam, 1978). The reader will note several further quotations from this book.

PART THREE
Ideas
on Politics and
Culture

HAROLD ROSENBERG
Marxism: Criticism
and/or
Action
(1956)

We have to go back to the witch doctors or the Shakespeare of *Hamlet* or *Macbeth* to reach a world in which specters, abstract beings, names come to life, "objective powers" play so large a part as they do in that of Marx—from that "mysterious thing," the commodity, which floats in the shadow of the physical products of modern industry, to those "personifications of economic relations," the social classes, which, according to *Capital*, are the protagonists of the political-economic drama. Each of these entities, in one of Marx's most characteristic phrases, "takes on an independent existence over against the individuals" and dominates human behavior. It is they who supply both the actors and the props for the stage of history; living men and women, magically bound to their service as Caliban by the wand of Prospero, act but to effect *their* ends. Even the hero, Marx takes pains to demonstrate, while imagining that he follows his own will, actually sustains in his thought and feeling the mode of life, the limits and half-conscious purposes of a collective person, the class which has chosen him; and he is lifted or cast down according to its condition.

With Marx, of course, these incorporeal figures and powers have not migrated into the human sphere from nature or the supernatural; they are offspring of men's own activities, and precisely of the most practical. They are concretions of behavior as it has been given its shape within the social whole; phantom as they are, they

241

are inseparable from human reality. For instance, a social class for
Marx is an "illusory community," but it arises from and embodies the
most basic relations, the "materialist connection of men with one
another." A class is composed entirely of alter egos, since individuals
"belong to it only as average individuals" and not as unique persons;
yet this community of doubles is the individual's exclusive ground of
self-realization. For Marx the ruling principle˜of civilized life is
metamorphosis, in which nothing is real except in its transfictional
state.

We hesitate to call "myth" this system of constructs which are not
merely mental but the specific forms of the human world. "The
difference," says Marx, "between the individual as person and what
is accidental to him is not a conceptual difference but an historical
fact. This distinction has a different significance at different times."
Nevertheless, we cannot avoid speaking of these changing creations
in metaphors of the imaginary. In history, as in the dream, past
actions become incarnated and continue to incarnate themselves in
effigies of living events. The present is displaced by these residues;
and this deprivation of immediate, waking time is the common
anguish. Our acts as soldiers, as mechanics, as radical critics, encase
us as if they molded themselves in clay or metal upon our bodies.
The tyranny of the done causes our very skills to betray us, like that
knife thrower of De Maupassant's so expert he could not miss his
target by a hair's breadth even when he wanted to. Man makes
himself against himself. "*Le mort saisit le vif*," Marx quotes in the
Preface to *Capital*. But it is not only the survival of anachronisms
that he wishes to combat.

Marx is not slow to celebrate the tremendous physical onslaught
of capitalism against all traditional forms and institutions, as well as
the scientific criticism it has applied to ancient superstitions. "Constant revolutionizing of production, uninterrupted disturbance of all
social conditions, everlasting uncertainty and agitation, distinguish
the bourgeois epoch from all earlier ones. All fixed, fast-frozen
relations, with their train of ancient and venerable prejudices and
opinions, are swept away, all new-formed ones become antiquated
before they can ossify." The single individual has emerged and has
declared his independence, claiming his association with others to
be the result of a free contract.

Capitalism, however, has not broken the siege of the past upon the present. It has banished religious fetishes only to succumb to *a process of fetish-making* of its own. Bourgeois society was itself born out of myth, explains *The Eighteenth Brumaire;* the revolutions that brought it into being summoned up personages, costumes and rhetoric out of long-vanished states. Most important, it has established as its essential activity the conversion of living human energy into spectral force—for to Marx that is just what *capital* is, a quasi-thing incorporating the past actions of men and women and able to control what they do now. "In bourgeois society, living labor is but a means to increase accumulated labor . . . in bourgeois society therefore the past dominates the present." Folded in the center of capitalist dynamics Marx detected a stasis in which completed being embodied itself continually.

It is toward this motionless center from which emanate like steam from a crack the Delphic wraiths of capitalism that *Capital* directs its tremendously detailed, systematic analysis. Assuming in the form of capital a fierce mechanical vitality, the dead labor of men extends in every direction a web of abstract entities that change the world as if in obedience to a will of their own. Marx's major work sets itself the task to translate these magical excrescences back into their human matter. Behind the system of "independent existents"—the commodity, money, the market—it exposes the processes by which expended labor is converted into the economic plasma which is the source of capitalist vigor and the drama of class coercion, spiritual poverty and revolt that accompanies that conversion. The bias for this exposure is Marx's unlimited hostility to mystification and his stubborn belief in the immediate possibility of a society in which, as in the communism described in *The German Ideology*, it will be "impossible that anything shall exist independently of individuals, in so far as things are only a product of the preceding intercourse of the individuals themselves."

Since the effigies of the unalive rule both inside the mind and in the physical organization of society, they can be expelled only if their independent existence, and with it their superhuman power, is destroyed in both. All criticism, Marx had written early, is criticism of religion, and criticism and revolution complement each other. By demonstrating how capital, the commodity, property, are actually frozen human acts and relations, criticism dissolves these deities in the consciousness and makes them contingent on the history of classes. In turn, by demonstrating how social classes are actually compounded out of changing modes of producing subsistence, criticism destroys the illusion of the independence of these collective egos and makes them contingent on economic behavior and the material world. The evolution of class struggles, Marx wrote to Wedemeyer in 1852, had been described by others before him, as well as the economic physiology of classes: his own contribution, he said, rested on three propositions, the first of which was: "that the existence of classes was tied up with certain phases of material production." If inside the economic system operated the human drama of class compulsion and resistance, inside the bodies of the classes circulated the routines by which real men kept themselves alive. This double unmasking, peeling abstraction from abstraction in order to reach the facts from which all abstractions have grown, is the innovation of materialist criticism. In everything "the root is man."

For Marx's dialectics, history itself is an unmasking; the uncovering of reality takes place not in the mind alone but through an actual corporeal stripping of the social and historical "integument"— another characteristic expression—which makes the human fact what it is. History is like the tragedy of the Greeks: behind the present fact on the stage there exists the hidden fact, which is coming out and will be recognized through its inevitable enactment. Without the tragic enactment, criticism is only an opinion. By itself, without change in the situation, it can never win lasting conviction, for the "unreal" fact stands forth to deny it. Since the source of social myth is the real relations of society, the mere critic of existing forms is doomed to be the hero of a fable of frustration. Every image the exasperated modern Tiresias laboriously scrapes from the brain of his auditors is restored without delay by the factories and streets. If criticism is not to be an end in itself, it must be a means to put an end to those material conditions from which the mirage is bred—"those conditions whose life-principle has already been refuted" but which survive nevertheless as a fetter upon life. "In themselves," Marx complains with a note of the boredom of the philosopher with the lag of existence, "they are not sufficiently worthy of attention but are a state of fact both despicable and despised." The aim of materialist analysis is not to continue an endless practice of unveiling particular examples of animated death but to help eliminate all of them by laying bare their common social cause to a stroke of force.

Criticism, then, for Marx is an action. More exactly, it is the beginning of an action; one that demands completion by social transformation. It is in regard to the latter phase of attack upon the myth-content of civilized life, the part that has to be carried out by others than the critic, that the great practical problems of Marx's thought arise, including those of its strategy and its ethics—and with these the related questions of the revolutionary roles of the individual, the political party and the social class.

For Marx the assault of criticism upon the "objective powers" is to be made effective by the revolution of a class, the proletariat. If, as has been maintained, Christian philosophy differs from the pagan in that it centers upon a unique event of the past, the Crucifixion, Marx's historical materialism distinguishes itself equally from all other philosophies in centering on the future victory of the working class. In his letter to Wedemeyer cited above, Marx enumerates two further innovations of his thought, in addition to his explanation of classes: the idea of the *necessary* conquest of power by the proletariat, and that of the function of that power in ending the class struggle by bringing to life a society of free individuals. At the heart of Marxism is its contention that its criticism and the revolutionary action of the working class have the identical objective, revolution by the second being the material equivalent of the first and supplying its positive social content. This daring concept, whatever be its scientific validity, is a precondition for thinking as a Marxist.

Was the correspondence between materialist analysis and working class ingression into power to be the result of the adoption by a decisive quantity of individual workingmen of Marx's theories? The answer is, definitely, No. Apart from his contempt for ideologists and utopians, including "Marxists," who see in ideas the cause of historical happenings, Marx's entire perspective excludes the notion that an historical effect can originate with an individual or an association

of individuals. The conqueror of classes and of class struggle must
itself be one of history's collective pseudo-organisms, a class. The
action of the proletariat paralleling materialist criticism was to be
self-motivated as a necessary result both of the nature of the proletariat and of the objective stimuli of its revolt.

To qualify the working class for its meta-critical role, Marx
evoked the negative process of capitalism which, in denuding the
proletariat of illusory being must cause their revolutionary action to
come forth as an accurate expression of their situation and to guide
them with ever-deepening clarity. Primarily, the unique competence of this class to attain to the real arises from the utter futility of
the daily acts of the factory laborers in conferring individuality upon
themselves. They exist as an incorporation of generality. If all men
belong to their respective classes only as "average individuals," with
the proletarian, "average" is the whole of what he is. His time is a
wage rate, his product not a self but an interchangeable commodity.

Thus in the modern worker the difference between the individual person and his class has been suppressed, and with it the illusory
nature of both. Members of all other historical classes, split by the
division of labor, have achieved their real existence in the mas-
querade of types compounded by society out of their activities of
yesterday. In the proletariat capitalism has created the very personification of self-loss through social behavior, those "newfangled
men," as Marx called them, who, like the machine, are "an invention
of modern times" and are multiplied automatically with the accumulation of capital. With the worker the social process of appropriating
the individual's past and using it to dominate his present has been
carried to its extreme. Since his work assumes the form of capital
which is taken away from him, he is constantly drained of his "life
content"; his acts produce no accretion of individuality, not even an
illusory one. On the contrary, the products which are the substance
of his being are in their transmuted form applied only to extract
more labor from him.[1] Wrung dry on this wheel of both his past time
and his living time, of both memory, and imagination, the worker
exists as an "abstract individual."

But by the very fact that the workingmen are through their
activities constantly rendered into human nothings, Marx sees them
as "put into a position to enter into relations with another as *individ-*

uals" (his emphasis) and to act together in the daylight of genuine self-interest. No past, personal or class, no socially constructed self, stands between the factory worker and his fellows, nor between his sense of community and the reality on which it is based. If he begins to act for himself, his act will be a genuine self-expression, at the same time that it will be an act for all. "Only the proletariat of the present day, who are completely shut off from all self-activity, are in position to achieve a complete and no longer restricted self-activity."

But the workers cannot act for themselves without breaking the social mechanism which transforms their acts and siphons them off as capital, that is, without a revolution against the ultimate source of modern hallucination. Hence the choice stated by Marx—"The working class is either revolutionary or it is nothing"—is at the same time the formula both for his own critique of capitalism as a specific epoch in the history of human alienation, and for the impulse of the workers to revolution as a revulsion against the void within them. Whenever a crisis of capitalism reproduces the vacuity of the proletariat as physical hunger and the direct threat of death, the *final* revolution is on the order of the day.

By his revolutionary action the worker starts a psychic increment that makes him an individual; he arrives, as Rosa Luxemburg emphasized, at ethical existence. The appearance of this class upon the stage of history brings new persons into the world (not molecules of a mass), whose characters are derived from the single social activity that cannot harden into a thing, from revolution. The restoration of alienated labor would destroy these persons, in destroying their freedom; hence the condition of their survival is the "revolution in permanence." The new existence itself of the working men depends on their day-by-day triumph over surplus value as a social force against each; and this victorious existence, constantly augmenting individuality, is itself socialism and the "transition to the abolition of all classes."

For Marx, therefore, the socialist revolution is immanent in the nature of the proletarian class and the need of its components to achieve individuality. On the other hand, individuals, *apart from their intellectual struggle against mystification*, have no deciding role in the historical drama; their free action as such can begin only *at the end of* history and with the vanishing of class.

Materialist criticism is the revolutionary action of the individual; revolutionary activity is the materialist criticism of the working class. Marx's conviction of the interrelation and the inevitable synchronization of these two processes constitutes the key to his politics and assigns to individuals and the class their different roles in it. The Communists, whether consisting exclusively of Marx and Engels, or of an association that multiplies the Marxian voice, were not, according to *The Communist Manifesto*, to form a separate group competing with other working-class parties for control of proletarian action. Their revolutionary function was to carry on the double unmasking of materialist criticism: "in all political movements they bring to the front as the leading question in each the property question, no matter what its degree of development at the time," showing changes in the relations of production to be at once the means and the end of the transformation of society. Conversely, in all social and economic questions they expose the content of class coercion and struggle. Taking for granted the growing organization, cohesion and will to combat of the proletariat, spontaneously brought about by the processes of capitalist production, Marxian criticism would act upon the proletarian revolution in two ways: 1) as the "head of passion" it would help change instinctive action into conscious action by bringing before the workingmen the formulation of their position and of their experience as a class; 2) as the irreconcilable challenge of the mind to mystification, it would provide a model of suspicion and hostility toward bourgeois society, a sentry for the class of workingmen against delusions through which they might be made a tool to defeat their own interests. (See Marx's letter to Bolte.)

So long as it assumes that it is operating in the presence of rising proletarian revolt, Marxian criticism is an action that remains criticism. Where, however, its intellectual attack against society no longer takes for granted the parallel movement of the victim class, a terrifying confusion besets Marxism, particularly with regard to historical roles of individuals and classes. Its political concepts and social values become ambiguous, or even reappear in reverse. Personalities, parties, ideas, become all at once prodigies of history-making and responsible day by day for the destiny of man.

In theory unwavering as to the revolutionary capacity of the proletariat, Marx was not tempted to put criticism into a position inferior to action. For him the plot of history was given, including its denouement. The process by which labor is converted into capital also holds the secret of capitalism's future wreck: using its transportable energy, capital, it continually augments both the class of wageworkers and the productive power of labor by creating a constantly widening interplay of men and tools, at the same time that, through the accumulation and centralization of wealth, it narrows the slit through which this growing force must pass in order to be changed into capital. An ever-mounting pressure, ever more closely confined—and which is reflected in the tensions of the classes, their preparations, their strategies. In the explosion which is inevitable, unless truly popular forces create the means for bringing about socialization by stages, the cave of illusions vanishes and labor is left in the open air of the free cooperation of individuals.

This prediction, that capitalism must automatically develop the elements of the society that will supersede it, presents, of course, the famous "contradiction" in Marx between the inevitability of socialism and the call to revolution. It is pragmatism, however, not Marx that sees the historical protagonists as free individuals needing the stimulation of an undetermined end in order to strive for a social form which they have chosen. In Marx's own terms, which allow for no point of individual contemplation and decision outside the drama of history, the so-called contradiction is meaningless. If the "higher powers" that combat each other existed entirely separate from us, we could passively await their self-destruction. If, on the other hand, they were mere images, analysis could dissolve them like the superstitions left over from dead societies. Since, however, classes and their phantom by-products both control our behavior as external powers and live in us as ourselves, our lives *are* the actions we take with regard to them. We need no desired outcome to induce us to fight the class struggle—the struggle fights us. And if the Marxist critic wills the victory of the proletariat, it is not for the sake of the future of others but from the necessity of his own present thought. His intellectual effort is a resistance to the shapes of nightmare, a resistance which the conviction that waking is near does not weaken. History is the action of mass—"I" 's and the command being always present, passivity is equally characteristic of the action of individuals as of their abstention from action. Even hesitation is an action, as in *Hamlet*, for Marx the typical action of the lower bourgeoisie, as the class pressed between classes, and productive of its destiny. In a profound sense Marx's view dissolves the aura of grandeur and irrationality around historical performance responsible for revolutionary conceit.

Concentrating on the mass actors of the historical drama, Marx was not interested in the political choices of individuals but only in the accuracy with which their views and their acts mirrored the hidden movements of the social process—for instance, his well-known admiration of the royalist Balzac in contrast to his scorn for socialist litterateurs. The moral issue of individual adherence (and betrayal) which has taken on so much importance in conspiratorial Marxism is irrelevant to Marx's conception of historical change; one looks in vain in his writings for reflections on the logos of individual, party and class identification. When he himself takes part in organizational activities, it is exclusively as the promoter of his own conclusions. Nor in the absence of such activities does his work pause: the proletarian mass hero must wait for favorable conditions, including his own inner development; the critic need not wait: his exposures are the intellectual equivalent of the situation as it happens to be and as the crisis will define it. Nowhere is there any hint in Marx of a wish to change himself nor to add ethical density to his existence through revolutionary commitment. Since a man's intellectual products, like any others, stand against him as an alien force, Marx does not seek in his ideas a clarification of himself and, as noted above, "Marxist" is to him a derogatory term. Communism could not be for him a school of self-effacement nor of self-definition, and the meditation, to be or not to be a Communist, is never addressed by him either to himself or to others.

With the loss of its metaphysical assurance, with the admission of doubt regarding the capacity of the proletariat and its destiny—a doubt upon which were founded both the absent-minded revisionist socialism of Bernstein and the elite-activism of Lenin—Marxism has seen its functions as criticism and as action split apart and enter into conflict with each other. For Marx, as we have seen, the disclosure of the material realities cloaked in political concepts, mass movements, etc., is futile if no social force is being born to change them. But no sooner does Marxism itself turn into an ideology uniting the actions of individuals, than it abandons its critical position and with it its dialectical relation to social transformation. The Party as the association of Marxian professionals stands as an independent power over and against both the class of laborers and its own individual members. The discontinuity of the proletariat, its rise from and relapse into nothingness, which is the pathetic basis of its experience of itself, as well as the impetus of its future freedom, is attacked by the whip of the Party leaders, for whom revolutionary politics exist as a thing. In place of resistance to deprivation converting itself into political action through an expansion in self-consciousness, inter-communication and comprehensiveness of program, acceptance of the Party leaders' decisions by individual workers becomes the basis of working class unity. With the lifeless discipline of the machine and the appropriation of his action extended into the political realm, the worker remains set fast in his abstractness, a personification of nullity with Marxist slogans as his ideal content. At the same time, working class revolt, since it is no longer a reflex of the worker's situation, ceases to serve as a revelation of the internal processes of society, so that revolutionary criticism is deprived of the data by which to correct itself. The Party as idea and as past becomes fixed in the revolutionist as his illusory character. From being a repulse of the unreal, revolution becomes a surrender to a fetishism of the act—an equivalent to those other forms of vertigo in which products of the human brain and previous human relations appear as endowed with vitality and engaged in transactions with the human race. The Party (and its foes) now takes on the appearance of being infinitely active, while the individual communist and the working class are found repeatedly collapsing into apathy. Needless to add, the critical activities of individuals, the only historical initiative possible to them as such, are put to sleep. For all their claims to manipulating the gears of history, and despite their tactics of ubiquitous "activation," modern revolutionary parties actually promote an enormous passivity.

Marxism is unthinkable apart from its premise of proletarian victory and its all-liberating effects. It is a philosophy suspended upon an event, a monologue in the drama of history which only the action of its mass hero can save from being a soliloquy. Its human content, the future that it desires, is to be found not in its own formulas but in the liveliness of the huge shadow by its side: "The great social measure of the Commune," said Marx in *The Civil War in France*, "was its own working existence."

No one is a Marxist who does not anticipate the proletarian transformation of society and strive to bring it about as the means for putting the demons to flight. Contrariwise, no one is a Marxist who, in the presumed interest of working class liberation, consents to serve the powers of a new otherworld. If Marx's proletarian solution to alienation turns out to be a mirage, if this promise in his thought must be canceled, Marxism is dead, however possible it may still be to discover in his conception clues for novel strategies of power resting upon an apathetic proletariat (e.g., neo-Bolshevism). But Marxism or no, what remains valid in Marx's analysis is the negative force of its example in persistent social unmasking, precisely the force of which hallucinatory Communism deprives it. Moreover, the systematic indication in Marx's writings, though from the point of view of Marx himself they cannot surmount the impotence of mere criticism, have by no means lost their pertinence so long as the processes that produce a proletariat continue to operate; under these circumstances, they may even be indispensable for an understanding of the situation presented by proletarian *nonaction*. The consequence of the failure of the proletariat in the face of the advancing socialization of production could, for Marx, be nothing else than "barbarism," the proliferation of a modern Darkest Africa of unreal beings, sacred apparitions, secular cults, illusory unions. Will anyone deny that the bad dream and farce have become commonplaces of the public life, to say nothing of the private? Or is it necessary to prove that these phenomena have something to do with that process of depersonalization through one's calling described as "proletarianization"? With the expanding social appropriation of work in all fields, with private accumulation increasingly more rare particularly in the more dynamic industrial nations, with the growing dependence of the individual and with it his inner isolation, the condition of the factory worker has, regardless of occupational statistics, become more and more the rule throughout society. Abstract man multiplies; a progressive flattening of personality takes place, irrespective of salary categories, standards of living, bureaucratic rank. Demoralized by their strangeness to themselves and by their lack of control over their relations with others, members of every class yield themselves to artificially constructed mass egos that promise to restore their link with the past and the future. Instead of the self-creating revolt of nothings at the base of society, history appears to hold out a horror-utopia of universal de-individualization headed by leaders who are their masks. Within this half-formed world of real specters, Marx's criticism of modern industrial society as centered on the proletarian void offers at least a conceptual foothold. The weapon of criticism is undoubtedly inadequate. Who on that account would choose to surrender it?

Footnote

1. *Capital* in describing this process resorts to melodramatic language: "Capital is dead labor, that vampire-like only lives by sucking living labor, and lives the more labor it sucks."

DENNIS H. WRONG
The Idea of
"Community":
a Critique
(1966)

The "loss of community" in modern society has become a major theme in contemporary social criticism. One could even say that the discipline of sociology begins with a concern over the decline of such traditional forms of association as small towns, neighborhoods, religious congregations and social classes, following upon that "creative destruction" we call the Industrial Revolution. Books with titles such as "The Quest for Community" or "The Eclipse of Community" have a contemporary resonance extending far beyond the circle of social scientists or even the educated public.[1] Used as a counterconcept to "mass society," "anomie," "rootlessness," and similar terms, "community" replaces the more politically focused labels of the past. Emphasis on the erosion of traditional ties that once bound men together becomes central to most sociological thinking that goes beyond the technicism of fact-finding and/or abstract theory-building.

The intellectual prestige of sociology since World War II is largely a result of a decline in political faith among Western intellectuals. One of the most influential sociological interpretations of extremist political movements defines them as efforts to create a new "community of ideology" to supplant traditional group allegiances that have been destroyed by rapid social change. Students of totalitarianism have shown how the psychic dependence of militant supporters frees its leaders from bondage to the manifest ideology that is the movement's ostensible *raison d'être*. Totalitarian leaders possess, therefore, a flexibility of political maneuver that is unavailable to power-seeking groups demanding a less than total commitment from their supporters. The paradox of totalitarian movements is that they are able to combine a fanatical following of "true believers" with a political strategy that is almost entirely opportunistic and in no way constrained by an official creed. Totalitarian movements are "orthodoxies without doctrines," as Raymond Aron once said, because their unity is founded on the community of ideology they create rather than on any definitive political goals affirmed by their ideology.

European writers who have described modern industrial society as a "mass society" in which men are lost and rootless, have seen it as inherently prone to produce destructive, ideologically fanaticized mass movements. This alleged political consequence of mass society, however, has never had such plausibility when applied to America. Impressed by the stability of the American political order, an influential group of political sociologists in this country has denied that the United States is a mass society and characterized it instead as "pluralist." But these writers slur over the fact that America remains the classic land of "mass culture," impersonal large-scale bureaucracy and population mobility. As Hannah Arendt remarks, the American body politic "has at least endured to the present day, in spite of the fact that the specifically modern character of the modern world has nowhere else produced such extreme expressions in all nonpolitical spheres of life as it has in the United States."[2]

To recognize the search for community as a major force in American life need not commit us to apocalyptic theories of mass society that see totalitarianism as the inevitable outcome. Tendencies that have elsewhere found expression in organized mass movements may be contained by the American political system; but still they do exist and manifest themselves in nonpolitical forms. Commitment to an "ideology of community," rather than the attempt to create a "community of ideology," has been a characteristic American response to mass society, although it is, of course, by no means peculiarly American. Even the recent political activism of young people has

combined political goals like civil rights and world peace with heavy
rhetorical emphasis on such nonpolitical concerns as the overcoming of alienation, sexual freedom, and the need for generational
solidarity.

Since awareness of loss of community in modern society is over a
century old, we need to recognize that responses to this awareness
have become part of the very social reality we seek to understand.
The increasing popularity of sociological accounts of our plight has
created an ideology of community that shapes our social relations, or
at least our consciousness of them, in much the same way that
popular Freudianism shapes our psychological self-awareness.

We need go back only as far as the 1930s to find a change in the
conditions and institutions alleged to be responsible for our "lack of
community." In that decade leading social critics complained of the
competitiveness of men under capitalism, their ruthless pursuit of
wealth and success, and their preference for "making good" over
"being good," to use a phrase of Margaret Mead's. The goal of
success was held to be demoralizing when all are urged to pursue it
under circumstances where opportunities are highly unequal. These
indictments of American society were clearly influenced by socialism in its various forms and by the New Deal. Changes in the
structure of the economy achieved by political means were looked to
for the creation of a community that would substitute fraternal
cooperation for divisive competition. With varying emphases, these
themes are central to the writing of the 1930s of such social scientists
as Margaret Mead, the Lynds, Ruth Benedict, Abram Kardiner,
Robert K. Merton, Lawrence Frank and others.

Today, at least on the surface, the complaints seem to be just the
opposite. There is too much "community," not enough individualism; too much conformity to others and sensitivity to their feelings
rather than indifference; too great a readiness to participate in
collective tasks as opposed to sturdy independence. David Riesman
has argued that middle-class Americans today are more like the Zuñi
Indians, described and idealized by Ruth Benedict in her *Patterns of
Culture*, than like the status-proud Kwakiutl, whom she, like Thorstein Veblen before her, saw as caricaturing American competitive
values. Business organizations are criticized—by William H. Whyte,
for example—not for ruthless exploitation, but for being big happy

families eager to transform their employees into self-satisfied "organization men." If the critics of the 1930s were futuristic in outlook, hopeful for a new social order, the critics of the 1950s were nostalgic, looking back to a more individualistic past.

The contrast between these two styles of criticism is bewildering. Is it just that the fashionable values of intellectuals have changed? Or have Americans taken to heart the earlier criticisms and overdone it in trying to rectify them? Daniel Bell has argued for the latter:

> The early theorists of mass society condemned it because in the vast metropolitan honeycombs people were isolated, transient, anonymous to each other. Americans, sensitive as they are to the criticisms of others, took the charge to heart and, in building the postwar suburbs, sought to create fraternity, communality, togetherness, only to find themselves accused of conformity.[3]

Although Bell is correct in maintaining that the American middle class has responded anxiously to its critics, he too readily dismisses their complaints as stemming merely from the ideological bias of "European sociology." The very receptivity of the audience indicates that an exposed nerve has been touched. Very often the critics combine in apparently contradictory ways the older themes attributing the absence of community to competitive and hostile men, with the new-style complaints about the smothering conformism of life in suburbia. However, as Bell acknowledges, the various targets of criticism are dialectically related. An ethic of conformism, the search for suburban oases and the loyalties of organization men are responses to the conditions described by the *earlier* critics: urban anonymity, social and geographical mobility, and the values of competitive individualism, which have for so long been characteristic of America and have by no means disappeared.

There are a number of different emphases in recent social criticism centering on the themes of loss of community and conformity.

Writers who are not professional social scientists frequently confine themselves, in the name of individualism, to a straightforward attack on all contemporary forms of group life, from suburban togetherness to the "engineered consent" of the mass media and the imposed uniformity of authoritarian political movements. Present-

day targets are simply latter-day versions of *Babbitt* and *Main Street*
and the critics remain in the tradition of the revolt against village,
church and provincial bourgeoisie that initiated a new trend in
American writing some decades ago. This critical perspective is not
based on an ideology of community. It merely asserts with refreshing
directness the need for protecting individuality from *any* social
pressures. It is often essentially aesthetic in outlook, defending the
antinomianism of the creative artist as an ultimate value. Frequently
it tends to become nostalgic in tone, idealizing the small-town and
nineteenth-century past, overlooking the tyrannies of Main Street,
and picturing our grandfathers as firm, principled "characters" in
contrast to the flabby herd men of today. It thus contributes to an
indigenous American nostalgia which, in the absence of any systematic conservative ideology, is exploited by promoters of right-
wing causes.

This brand of social criticism, while blunt, often zestful in its
assaults on institutions and fashions, and always needed, has limitations from the point of view of both the professional sociologist and
the social critic who has learned from the sociologists. For the
sociologist, the relation between individual and society is always a
crucial problem. Sociology itself began with the sense of a disturbance in the relation between individuals and society created by the
modern political and technological revolutions. The sociologist's
very definition of man asserts that he is profoundly shaped by the
group, by the dominant values of society; in consequence the
sociological critic cannot, without violating his professional conscience, confine himself to affirming the values of individualism and
personal autonomy while failing to consider the social context in
which these values might be realized. To see the community merely
as something to be resisted, as the source of false identities which
stifle an essentially private self, is to deny that men live in communities as naturally as fish in water and that their private selves are
necessarily closely intertwined with a self shaped by public pressures.

Accordingly, critics influenced by sociology locate the source of
individual malaise in the fragmentation and disorder of modern
society rather than in society's demands for conformity as such. At its
most simplistic, such an approach stands in direct opposition to the

moral and aesthetic defense of the individual against the claims of society, to which I have previously referred.[4] Though the more perceptive sociological critics, such as David Riesman, Erich Fromm and W. H. Whyte, have assigned part of the blame for contemporary conformism to the popularity of vulgarized versions of social science, these writers are nevertheless themselves sociologically sophisticated and are not content merely to reassert the values of individualism in face of the imperatives of modern social organization. By singling out "status-seeking" as a major target of criticism, they often manage to combine the anticapitalist attack on competitiveness of the 1930s, the moral-aesthetic defense of individuality against pressures towards conformity, and the more recent indictments of suburban and organizational groupism. The compulsive quest for status weakens community by pitting people against one another as competitors while at the same time encouraging frantic conformity to the shifting group fashions that set the terms on which status is granted. Unlike the material acquisitiveness condemned by the critics of the thirties, competition for status both unites and divides people, creating what Riesman (borrowing a term from William Graham Sumner) has labeled "antagonistic cooperation." Hence the prevalence of judgments such as the following:

> In the desert of the suburb, community life has lost whatever vestiges of meaning it ever had for Americans; if any community life exists at all, it exists frantically at the synthetic level of the club and church; it has a tinny quality betraying a lack of conviction on the part of all concerned. Nowhere is there more consciousness of the need for community; nowhere does this consciousness of need reveal more clearly its hopelessness.[5]

The diagnosis of our discontents put forward by these sociological critics is often a convincing and powerful one. Their sociological realism saves them from the kind of purely romantic protests against modern life which refuse to recognize social necessities as distinct from the demands of the individual psyche. But because they no longer believe in the political solutions favored by their predecessors of the thirties the specificity of their diagnosis stands in marked contrast to the vagueness and virtual absence of any prescribed remedy.

In general terms, the restoration of a "true" or "organic" community is seen as the ultimate remedy. The goal is a community which will both bind men together in intimate, fraternal relations and at the same time allow individuality to flourish. "It almost seems as if community in the anthropological sense is necessary before human maturity or individuation can be achieved, while this same maturity is, in turn, a prerequisite for community," as Maurice Stein puts it.[6] The call for the re-creation of community maintains a link between contemporary sociology and the conservative critique of modernity first formulated in the aftermath of the French Revolution.[7] For, "if there is one thing certain about the 'organic community,' it is that it has always gone," as Raymond Williams remarks.[8] Some convince themselves, like George Orwell, that it was there in their childhoods, others locate its last incarnation in the vanished rural village or small town, in nineteenth-century bourgeois society, in the medieval commune or in the *polis* of the ancient world. Others, like Stein, go all the way back to primitive societies to discover models of community "in the anthropological sense."

These nostalgic excursions into history end in remarkably similar exhortations. Bewailing the disappearance of organic community, the literary critic F. R. Leavis, writing in 1932, concludes: "We must beware of simple solutions . . . there can be no mere going back . . . the memory of the old order must be the chief incitement towards a new."[9] Nearly thirty years later, Maurice Stein, a sociologist, strikes the identical note: "There is little to be gained by sentimentalizing about primitive life or advocating a return to it in any form. We are far too deeply committed to urban-industrial civilization even to think of abandoning it now."[10] The problem is seen as that of realizing community under the new conditions of urban-industrial mass civilization.

The trouble, however, is that this insistence on community as a value apart from its concrete manifestations produces precisely the aborted forms of striving for group adjustment that the social critics themselves condemn. The anxious audience reads the critics and, made self-conscious about community, strives to sink roots in the suburbs, to define occupational groups as devoted brotherhoods, and to stress the importance of belongingness in child-rearing. Made aware of the loss of community, the audience tries to create out of whole cloth a social ethic and a true community. The effort is

analogous to that of those Americans who have made popular psy-
chiatry the basis of a personal ethic, becoming self-conscious, even
hypochondriacal, about their "mental health," which comes to be
seen as the goal of life instead of as the by-product of a life with
meaningful goals. The error lies in conceiving of community as a
kind of end-in-itself, apart from the particular activities and
functions that actually bind people together, and apart from those
values that constitute a truly shared vision of life. As Ortega y Gasset
once pointed out, "People do not live together merely to be together. They live together to do something together."

Thus the social critics who deplore status-seeking and the
mechanical kind of community of our Park Forests, paradoxically
perpetuate the conditions they complain of when they re-assert the
values of *true* community and *stable* identity. They end up providing
their audience with a new and updated ideology of community,
reminding one of books on child-rearing that tell parents not to rely
on books on child-rearing but to be "spontaneous." The very
willingness to follow the prescribed antidote to the disease is a
symptom of the disease and indeed aggravates it. Even status-
seeking—the target of attack most closely linking the older social
criticism directed against ruthless individualism to the newer
charges of overconformity—receives a kind of sociological warrant
(as in Vance Packard's book, which has been aptly described as a
pornography of social class in America). For status requires valida-
tion by others and implies shared values in a way that money or
power as goals do not. But the emphasis is on the sharing of values
rather than on their content.

The ideology of community thus provides the basis for a popular
social criticism that influences its audience in ways providing new
material for the critics to assault. Just as psychoanalytic therapy,
which originally presupposed a stable social world with relatively
fixed moral standards incorporated into the patient's superego, is
now itself often expected to provide the values and meaningful
life-goals the individual feels he lacks; so sociology is looked to in the
hope that it will itself remedy the loss of community. The result is
that clichés about group "integration," "role-playing," "identity,"
"belongingness" and "we-feelings" fill the vacuum.

Consequently, instead of a genuine conformity based on shared values, we find *conformism*—the belief, rarely articulated as such, that one should act, think and feel as others do for its own sake. Instead of a status system in which individuals are rated according to stable dominant values, we find *status-seeking* in which status itself becomes a value no matter what the terms on which it is awarded. Instead of loyalty to families, churches, local communities, occupational associations and other established groups with multiple purposes and often possessing deep roots in the past, loyalty attaches itself to functional organizations, thus making a specialized collective instrumentality into an end-in-itself. Erich Kahler's distinction between a *community* and a *collective* is relevant here: "Collectives develop through the joining of pre-established individuals for some specific purpose. Collectives are established by common *ends*, communities derive from common *origins*."[11] To Max Weber, the modern mood of "disenchantment of the world" was the result of the spread of bureaucracy, of the proliferation of functional organizations organized to pursue limited goals and lacking the aura of sacredness traditionally associated with family, church and nation. But Weber did not anticipate the "organization man" who strives to invest bureaucracy with the intrinsic value and loyalty usually given to these older forms of association.

The achievement of community, like the achievement of mental health (or, for that matter, of happiness, as John Stuart Mill argued a century ago), cannot come from pursuing it directly as a goal but only as a by-product of the shared pursuit of more tangible goals and activities. Community may result from the concrete forms of political, economic, familial and cultural association among men, but it cannot be willed into existence by exhorting people to immerse themselves in group activity and to find greater significance in their social identities. The inevitable failure of the ideology of community to deliver the elusive good it promises then gives rise to a social criticism that at its worst simply becomes a counter-ideology making a shibboleth of "nonconformity" or exploiting a romanticized version of an allegedly more individualistic American past.

The failures and inconsistencies of recent social criticism suggest that there are limits to what we are entitled to expect from social science in general and sociology in particular as a source of remedies for our deeper discontents. Sociology can analyze the events and processes that have destroyed older values and forms of community; it cannot create new ones. Only moral, religious and political inspiration can do that.

Footnotes

1. See, for example, Robert Nisbet, *The Quest for Community*, New York: Oxford University Press, 1953; Maurice R. Stein, *The Eclipse of Community*, Princeton, N.J.: Princeton University Press, 1960.

2. Hannah Arendt, *Between Past and Future*, New York: The Viking Press, p. 140.

3. Daniel Bell, *The End of Ideology*, New York: Collier Books, 1961, p. 36.

4. See, for example, Everett K. Wilson, "Conformity Revisited," *Trans-Action* 2 (Nov.–Dec. 1964), pp. 28–32, and the rebuttals to Wilson by Dennis H. Wrong and Ernest van den Haag, pp. 33–36.

5. William J. Newman, *The Futilitarian Society*, New York: George Braziller, 1961, p. 355.

6. Stein, op. cit., p. 248.

7. A recent account of sociology's conservative intellectual pedigree is Nisbet, op. cit.

8. Raymond Williams, *Culture and Society*, New York: Doubleday-Anchor, 1960, p. 277.

9. Quoted by Williams, ibid., p. 279.

10. Stein, op. cit., p. 248.

11. Erich Kahler, *The Tower and the Abyss*, New York: George Braziller, 1957, p. 87.

DAVID SPITZ
Pure
Tolerance
(1966)

Ever since men climbed down from the trees and found it necessary
to establish ground rules, they have fought over what those rules
shall be. They have fought longest, and perhaps most bitterly, over
the most fundamental rule of all—the rule by which the ground
rules themselves shall be determined. For he who controls the
ground rules is in a position to control the game.

That the rule of tolerance is this fundamental rule is revealed by
the fact that dictatorships exclude it and democratic states make it
central to their enterprise. Only in democratic states are governments established and changed in response to the free play of
conflicting opinions.

This—the securing of responsible government—is not of course
the only reason for supporting tolerance. Those who defend it also
contend that tolerance makes for diversity, which is essential to
progress and the development of individuality, and thus to the
common good. They also believe that tolerance, at least in a pluralist
society, is the only principle under which diverse groups can live
together without resorting either to mutual slaughter or to an authoritarian regime that will impose one group's creed on others.

The argument for intolerance, in contrast, is generally put forward by men who mean to have their way but fear that free discussion will "mislead" other men—either because those others are less
wise or virtuous than they or because conditions are such as to favor
the false doctrine.

I

Now, the classic case for tolerance has been set forth in John Stuart Mill's celebrated essay *On Liberty*. Ever since Mill published that essay in 1859, the critics of tolerance have been diligently at work refuting him. It needs to be said, if unkindly, that one obvious reason for this is that later critics have recognized the difficulties that earlier critics have had with him. It is a mark of no mean significance that this process still continues; indeed, it has become the foundation of a flourishing industry.

As a part-time member of this guild (though one essentially in sympathy with Mill), I can do no other than commend it to the newcomers. I ask only that they first familiarize themselves with already existing products. Then they might spare their readers, if not themselves, the labor of re-encountering ancient formulations under the guise of a new suit of phrases; and in doing so they might also learn to distinguish reputable from shoddy merchandise. For it needs also to be said that much of what is produced by this industry today is neither novel nor imaginative nor important. That is the judgment I propose in regard to a new book, *A Critique of Pure Tolerance*, co-authored by Herbert Marcuse, Barrington Moore, and Robert Wolff.[1]

What distinguishes the three essays that constitute this book is *not* an awareness, and hence transcendence, of these elementary considerations. It is rather the marshaling and occasionally the revision of old arguments to attack Mill from what might (for the moment) be called radical perspectives. Traditionally, Mill has been identified with the Left and his critics with the Right. This ideological cleavage by no means accounts for all of Mill's critics; some of them—Dorothy Fosdick, J. C. Rees, and Isaiah Berlin, for example—have dealt with Mill and his arguments in terms divorced from such partisanship. But it accounts for a good many of them, including, I venture to think, the three critics who here attack Mill's plea for complete freedom of thought and expression on the ground, so they say, that it prevents, or at the very least militates against, the supremacy of "correct" ideas, that is, "their" ideas. And because they profess to be of the radical left, Mill stands condemned (in their eyes) as a protagonist of the "wrong" ideas, as a purveyor of a political philosophy that safeguards the status quo.

The keynote of their argument—on which, despite other differences, they are agreed—is contained in this introductory sentence: "For each of us the prevailing theory and practice of tolerance turned out on examination to be in varying degrees hypocritical masks to cover appalling political realities." And here I must begin with a confession of inadequacy: I have tried, but I am unable to make sense of this statement. What, apart from its strident terminology, does it mean? Is the theory referred to one that accounts for the practice or one that articulates an ideal to which that practice should conform? If it accounts for the practice, then the theory is not a mask but a revelation of the realities. If it articulates an ideal, then the theory stands not as a description of what is but as a prescriptive norm, and hence as a criterion of judgment by which those realities are to be judged. If it is replied that theory here means what people say, then we are simply confronted by the usual dichotomy between rhetoric and performance, between espoused or intended conduct and actual behavior. But a theory is never this; it is always an attempt to describe the true reality—our function, Klee somewhere said, is "not to reveal the visible but to make visible the real"—or to prescribe the proper conduct. Then, if we omit the word "theory" and look only at the word "practice," all that the statement seems to mean is that people do not behave very nicely, which is hardly a piercing insight.

In what sense, then, can the theory or practice of tolerance be termed hypocritical? Presumably in the sense that the theory is at odds with, and a rationalization of, the practice. But this means only that the theory (as explanation rather than as prescription) is deficient, that in fact it is not a theory at all but an ideology.

What, finally, is meant by the phrase "prevailing theory"? Is it Mill's theory of liberty, or what the writers call the doctrine of "pure tolerance"? If so, there is obviously a considerable gap not only between Mill's teaching and current (e.g., American) practice, but also, I think, between that teaching and whatever may be said to be the dominant legal and political view (or views) of liberty. Is it some other theory, a doctrine more in keeping with what our three writers are pleased to call the realities of an industrial democracy? If so, this is not identified. What they attack, then, is not *the* prevailing doctrine of liberty, and not always, as will become clear, Mill's doctrine, but doctrines and conditions imputed to Mill and which, in their view, constitute the hallmark of a sorry liberalism.

Let us consider the contentions of our three critics.

II

Take, first, the argument of Robert Paul Wolff. I am not altogether sure whether he misunderstands Mill or intends his readers to misunderstand Mill, but to the extent that I may read him correctly he depicts Mill at one point as an exponent of psychological egoism and at another as an advocate of individual liberty free of all social restraints. Neither of these characterizations accurately describes Mill. He also asserts that Mill defended the freedoms of thought and of action so long as these did not harm others. But Mill clearly and explicitly distinguished his defense of freedom of thought, which he made an absolute, from freedom of action, which was conditioned by its consequences. Wolff makes the important point that tolerance should not be confused with neutrality or condescension but should be recognized as a positive good; however, though Wolff does not mention it, this is also central to Mill's thought.

What is of interest, then, is not Wolff's critique of Mill—which is, strictly speaking, essentially irrelevant—but the fact that his essay, though it is entitled "Beyond Tolerance," deals less with tolerance than with the conditions that make it ineffective. Wolff believes that tolerance is a doctrine that has emerged from and is only appropriate to a particular stage of historical development, namely, the stage of democratic pluralism. But—and this is what he is most concerned to show—democratic pluralism is no longer adequate to the so-called stage of modernity in which we now find ourselves, and for two reason primarily: it discriminates against certain disadvantaged social groups or interests—those that are outside the Establishment, that lack "legitimate representation," and that are not consequently given a place or a voice in society— and it discriminates against certain social policies, most directly those that look to the promotion of the common good rather than to the satisfaction of diverse particular interests or claims. As a result, democratic pluralism in its concrete application—though not, Wolff adds, in its theory—supports inequality, maintains the status quo, blocks social change. What is required, Wolff concludes, is a new philosophy of community, of the common good, one that goes "beyond pluralism and beyond tolerance."

Now it is curious that one who, like Wolff, relates ideas in near-deterministic fashion to particular stages of historical development—and I must bypass here the familiar and age-old controversy over this asserted but still unproved thesis—should ignore the fact that earlier theories of tolerance, those of Locke and Milton, for example, and perhaps even of Socrates in the *Apology* before them, were not merely arguments for a *qualified* tolerance, but were in a very real sense also arguments consistent with a kind of homogeneous, or largely homogeneous, society. To go beyond pluralism is presumably to plead for a new type of homogeneity, and hence for a new kind of orthodoxy; for from what individuals or groups, and for what purpose, will new and diverse ideas then emerge?

What makes Mill distinctive, and vitally important, is that while he recognized and even pleaded for a sense of national cohesion and for the pursuit of the public interest, he insisted along with this that it was necessary to respect and to build upon a certain heterogeneity, that progress required *both* the promotion of the common good and the furtherance of individual and group differences. Consequently, in line with his utilitarian philosophy, he argued for the absolute toleration of ideas and for the maximum toleration of variety in practices. He sought a unity that would contain rather than eliminate diversity. In these terms, to argue against pluralism and for the idea of a common good, as if these were opposing and mutually exclusive principles, is to argue for a self-defeating proposition; for it may well be—and I am convinced it is—that democratic pluralism, properly understood and properly institutionalized, is precisely what defines or constitutes the core of the common good.

It is noteworthy that Wolff nowhere defines or articulates the nature of his common good; nor does he set out a program for its realization. Were he to attempt to do so, he might find, as many another writer has found, that in a multigroup society the common good requires not the rejection of pluralism but the determination of the appropriate kinds and degrees of pluralism compatible with a political goal. Otherwise there can emerge only a deadening, even if new, conformity. However this may be, if it is true, as Wolff admits, that the fault is not in the theory of pluralism, or of tolerance, but in the shortcomings of its practice, why does he attack the theory of pure tolerance? Why does he not focus instead on the conditions—whether of structure, institutions, attitudes, or all of these combined—that hinder its attainment and impair or delimit its free exercise, and on measures calculated to redress those deficiencies? For it is not Mill and his theory of liberty but the arrangements and practices of modern industrial society that are clearly the issues at stake.

III

Barrington Moore's essay, "Tolerance and the Scientific Outlook," is a more sophisticated and relevant effort. In part, this is because Moore is aware of many of the foregoing considerations and avoids certain elementary confusions. In part, it is because Moore restates and builds upon a number of Mill's arguments—though he does not, curiously, acknowledge this indebtedness. In part, finally, it is because Moore advances an interesting argument of his own.

With respect to Mill, the most important of Moore's restatements is the proposition that the intellectual's task is not to agitate or fight for a particular doctrine or ideal "but to find and speak the truth, whatever the political consequences may be." The latter part of this proposition is, of course, standard Millian doctrine, as may be evidenced by Mill's familiar plea (in his essay "On Civilization") that the very cornerstone and object of education "is to call forth the greatest possible quantity of intellectual *power*, and to inspire the intense *love of truth*; and this without a particle of regard to the results to which the exercise of that power may lead . . ." But the first part of Moore's statement does not, alas, confront the obvious question: What if one's discovery of the truth is at the same time the discovery of a correct doctrine or ideal? Does his commitment to the truth not require him then to advocate, even agitate for, that doctrine? Does the intellectual not then become a partisan *malgré lui?* If

I am to infer Moore's answer from the content of this essay, it is clearly positive. But Moore does not explicitly say so; nor does he pursue the implications of that conclusion. Mill, of course, essayed both roles, precisely because he saw no necessary incompatibility between them.

Moore properly maintains that historical disputes can often be settled by an appeal to the evidence. But does it follow that "tolerance for different 'interpretations' based on different *Weltanschauungen* merely befuddles the issue"? Or that "a scientific attitude toward human society [does not] necessarily induce a conservative tolerance of the existing order"? Clearly, what constitutes relevant evidence is itself a matter of interpretation; and the issue is not whether tolerance or a scientific attitude implies acceptance (or, for that matter, rejection) of a particular interpretation or social order—it does not—but whether it implies acceptance of one's right to entertain and advance *ideas* that defend (or reject) a particular interpretation or social order. When Moore says, as he does, that tolerance of conflicting interpretations befuddles the issue, does he mean to suggest that the natural consequences of a serious examination of alternative doctrines will always, or mostly, lead to the adoption of the wrong doctrine? This, I think, can only be affirmed by repudiating the value of reason itself, which Moore does not and of course will not do. But if reason itself is not at fault, the rational examination of alternatives cannot lead to befuddlement. What makes for confusion, instead, is the intrusion of unreason, of prejudices or interests or the operation of weighted conditions that militate against the free play of intellect. But then Moore's indictment should turn not on the principle of tolerance but (as with Wolff) on the social conditions in which tolerance is practiced—conditions that deny reason its day in court or that perpetuate the deficiencies of reasoners. All of which would seem to be confirmed by Moore himself when he says that "every idea, including the most dangerous and apparently absurd ones, deserves to have its credentials examined."

This, however, is not the message that Moore is most anxious to communicate. He is concerned rather to argue three things: (a) that the secular and rational (i.e., scientific) outlook, by which he means neither "technicist science" nor "academic humanism" but a conception of science that embraces "whatever is established by sound reasoning and evidence," is adequate both for understanding and evaluating human affairs; (b) that this outlook is able, in principle, to yield clear-cut answers to important questions, including the question of "when to be tolerant and when tolerance becomes intellectual cowardice and evasion"; and (c) finally, most importantly, that in the present historical moment it may well behoove us to abandon the "nauseating hypocrisy" of "liberal rhetoric," to refuse to work under the prevailing system, and to consider "the conditions under which the resort to violence is justified in the name of freedom."

This is a hard teaching, but not for that reason to be avoided. We must first ask, however, whether it is also true. And here, it seems to me, the answer is by no means as simple as Moore takes it to be.

Consider Moore's claim—(a) and (b)—that objective knowledge and objective evaluation of human institutions are possible, thereby yielding correct and unambiguous answers, independent of individual whims and preferences. If Moore really admires Morris R. Cohen, whom he cites approvingly, he should have borne in mind Cohen's important distinction between the meaning of what is asserted in verified scientific theory and the degree of certainty of its verification. This certainty is always a matter of degree; it is never absolute; for what is verified is the theorems, not the postulates, of the theory. This is why Cohen, like Mill, believed that scientific *method* encourages toleration even as it enables us to differentiate beliefs and opinions which have been confirmed from those which have not.

Now Moore avows his commitment to scientific method. He recognizes that as a method it is a procedure for the testing of ideas, from which it follows that no conclusion, including the contents and very conception of science itself, is permanently above and beyond criticism and, possibly, fundamental change. How, then, can he confuse the principle of tolerance, which at one point he explicitly equates with this scientific procedure, with the acceptance of a particular doctrine or system of order, or assert the possibility not merely of objective knowledge but of objective evaluation, of correct answers to human problems? This is not to deny the relevance and utility of scientific method in the evaluation and solution of such problems; it is only to suggest that the most scientific evaluation, along with its alleged clear-cut answers, is still but tentative rather than absolute, relative to our assumptions and values, and always subject to revision.

Moore, however, confident of his "truths," seems prepared to reject the prevailing system and to adopt a revolutionary attitude. So long as three conditions are met—that the prevailing regime is unnecessarily repressive, that a revolutionary situation is in fact ripening, and that through a rough calculus of revolutionary violence one can reasonably believe that the costs in human suffering inherent in the continuation of the status quo outweigh those to be incurred in the revolution and its aftermath—the resort to violence, Moore holds, is justified in the name of freedom.

It is not easy for one who views the prevailing regime (or regimes) with considerable unhappiness, and who would consequently welcome certain fundamental changes in the social order, to cavil at Moore's revolutionary posture. Clearly, unless one is prepared to say that under no circumstances may men rebel, that men must remain always at the base of even the most burdensome pyramids of unjust power, there are moments in history when the resort to violence is fully warranted. That many contemporary nations, including the United States, celebrate their own past revolutions is only the more obvious of many instances in point. Thus, as an abstract statement of conditions that require and justify violence to overturn an indecent social order, Moore's argument merits respect. (Though it should not go unnoted that he here goes counter to his own earlier contention that the intellectual is not to be a partisan in the cause of this, or any other, ideal.)

Nevertheless, if we apply his (very far from precise) conditions to the modern industrial societies of the Western world, his argument becomes less than conclusive. For one thing, it is not at all clear that Western industrial societies are so oppressive that violent overthrow of the entire system is justified. For another, it is questionable that the cultural and human drabness to which Moore presumably objects is, in fact, amenable to correction through political action. For still another, the applicability of his second and third conditions is more than problematical. Nor do his conditions take into account certain useful and perhaps necessary distinctions: those, for example, between a class and a national revolution, or between a revolution initiated to seize power and a revolution, like the National Socialist Revolution, imposed after power has been effectively seized. Finally, his argument either neglects or gives insufficient weight to certain risks attendant upon all revolutionary efforts. Of these inconvenient but ever-present risks, I have space here to note only two.

One is the corrupting effects of the revolution itself, which often degrade and alter the characters and principles of the revolutionaries themselves, so that men who emerge at the top after a successful revolution are rarely the same men (even if they retain the same names and carry the same bodies) as those who made the revolution, with all that this implies in the way of altered ends, new hatreds and antagonisms, and new repressions. To be sure, some consequences of a successful revolution may be praiseworthy, e.g., the institution of certain reforms designed to eliminate or abate injustices and discontents. But other consequences are more than likely to be catastrophic. Of these the most immediately probable is the suppression of freedom of speech and political opposition. For it is not uncommon that governmentswhich have survived revolutionary attempts, or which have come to power through revolution, seek with grim determination to eliminate the possibility of further revolutionary efforts. This, certainly, would seem to be one of the more evident lessons of revolutionary movements that have come to power since, say, the Second World War. Thus the appeal to revolution often invites the destruction of the very principle that makes the revolution possible—the principle of tolerance.

The second dangerous risk is the high improbability of success. Paul Kecskemeti has called attention to the striking fact that, despite all the revolutionary talk of the past century, if we except the Iberian peninsula, there have been no serious attempts at internal revolution in peacetime Europe since 1848–49; and if we consider the abortive Hungarian revolution of 1956 (which took place after Kecskemeti wrote), the point is underscored that in the modern industrial state, with its specialized technology and advanced systems of weaponry, and with the support of powerful external armies and governments, civil revolt is in the ordinary course of events most unlikely to succeed. In fact, the normal complement of apathy, contentment, and especially fear—not of sporadic outbreaks but of wholesale violence and disorder—makes it more than unlikely that the masses will venture to disrupt the prevailing system of order by revolutionary means. It is, then, one thing to call for a revolutionary attitude, quite another to call for and expect revolutionary action. (I speak, let it be emphasized again, not of primitive or developing societies, but only of modern industrial societies; for it is only to such states that our authors apply their arguments.)

Once again, therefore, we are back to the central confusion inherent in this criticism: that which equates the principle of tolerance with the restrictive practices of states avowedly committed to that principle. The criticism actually testifies only to the limitations of those practices, and thus leaves untouched—at least at this level of argument—Mill's plea for freedom of thought and expression.

IV

We come now to the most extreme and convoluted, yet in some ways the most intriguing, of our three indictments of pure tolerance: Herbert Marcuse's essay "Repressive Tolerance." It may seem outrageous to suggest that this very title is a contradiction in terms, as are also other phrases employed by Marcuse, for example "totalitarian democracy" and "the democratic educational dictatorship of free men"; but I shall make this suggestion nonetheless. I am aware that Marcuse, as a neo-Hegelian (also a neo-Marxist and neo-Freudian), prides himself on his dialectical thinking. But the dialectic—or, as Marcuse likes to say, the negation of the negation—aims to produce not a conjunction of two opposites but a synthesis which is different from either of them. And expressions like "repressive tolerance," "totalitarian democracy," and "democratic dictatorship," because they mismate rather than synthesize opposites, are self-contradictory and therefore meaningless. They should be banished from the literature. It is necessary to say this at the outset because Marcuse has dwelt harshly and at length on the inadequacies, even the Orwellian evils, of ordinary language, yet has also condemned philosophers who employ linguistic analysis in an effort to avoid the pitfalls of meaninglessness. Why, then, does he himself foster rather than transcend obscurity?

I will have occasion to return to this problem. Let me first, however, try to state the essentials of Marcuse's argument. Briefly, for it is a reiteration and extension of his argument in *One-Dimensional Man*, it comes to this: We—and by "we " Marcuse means the peoples of *all* modern industrial societies, whether "democratic" or otherwise—live today in a totalitarian system. It is totalitarian because, with the concentration of economic and political power and the use of technology as an instrument of domination, and under the rule of monopolistic media, "a mentality is created for which right and wrong, true and false are predefined wherever they affect the vital interests of the society." Rational persuasion is thus all but precluded. In such a situation tolerance "is administered to manipulated and indoctrinated individuals who parrot, as their own, the opinion of their masters." It is a tolerance abstractly "pure" but concretely "partisan," for "it actually protects the already established machinery of discrimination." It is thus repressive rather than true tolerance. For tolerance to be real, it must discriminate instead against falsehood and evil; it must cancel the liberal creed of free and equal discussion; it must preclude harmful ideas and harmful behavior. It must in fact encourage subversion of the existing order, even if this requires "apparently undemocratic means."

Marcuse articulates these "apparently undemocratic means" as follows:

> They would include the withdrawal of toleration of speech and assembly from groups and movements which promote aggressive policies, armament, chauvinism, discrimination on the grounds of race and religion, or which oppose the extension of public services, social security, medical care, etc. Moreover, the restoration of freedom of thought may necessitate new and rigid restrictions on teachings and practices in the educational institutions which, by their very methods and concepts, serve to enclose the mind within the established universe of discourse and behavior—thereby precluding a priori a rational evaluation of the alternatives.

All this, Marcuse admits, is censorship, "even precensorship," but warranted because the distinction between liberating and repressive teachings and practices "is not a matter of value-preference but of rational criteria"; and these, Marcuse insists, are empirical in nature, turning on the real possibilities of attaining human freedom in a particular stage of civilization. To the question: Who is to draw these distinctions and make these decisions?—the answer (and here Marcuse mistakenly believes he is following Mill) is: Everyone in the maturity of his faculties as a human being, that is, "everyone who has learned to think rationally and autonomously." To be sure, such men will constitute a minority, but since all systems—even "democratic democracies"—are in fact controlled by a few, the only questions are whether they are the correct few and whether they act in the interests of the many, in short, whether they are qualified to exercise Marcuse's "democratic educational dictatorship of free men." Such free men are not to be identified with any social class; they are rather "fighting minorities and isolated groups . . . hopelessly dispersed throughout the society." To liberate these few, and through them the society as a whole, it is necessary "officially" to practice intolerance —both in speech and in action—against movements from the Right and to be tolerant only of movements from the Left. Through such "repressive tolerance" alone, Marcuse concludes, we can hope to realize the objective of "true tolerance."

Of the many things that might be said by way of analysis of or in reply to this argument, I shall limit myself here to three points: (1) Marcuse confuses the meaning of freedom with its conditions and consequences and hence misunderstands tolerance. (2) Marcuse's argument is essentially, though in reverse, the argument of Dostoevsky's Grand Inquisitor, of the Right. (3) Marcuse's solution is contradicted and rendered impossible of attainment by his own analysis.

(1) Freedom is not, as Marcuse variously affirms it to be, "self-determination, autonomy" or "a specific historical process." It is rather, as Hobbes properly said, the absence of chains. Since in the real world men who are unrestrained come into collision with one another, societies have always and everywhere confronted—and each in its own way resolved—the problem of determining which liberties are worth protecting, for whom, under what conditions, and to what degree, and, as a necessary consequence, which restraints must be imposed. Freedom then becomes an ordered system of liberties and restraints. Men may differ as to the right order of priorities with respect to such liberties, but some order of priorities there must be. Thus, in democratic states a high value is given to freedom of political opposition; in dictatorships it is not. But to assure and protect this freedom, restraints must be imposed on

those men (and practices) who would interfere with it. This is one,
though not the only, function of law; but it is not, of course, merely a
matter of law, for it involves a complex set of attitudes and appropriate behavior in other realms of social life as well.

Now Marcuse may deplore the particular freedoms granted in a
specific society. He may properly object that a formal or legal
freedom is in fact negated by informal or social pressures. But
freedom as a principle is always a matter of specific liberties and
concomitant restraints. It is not self-determination, though a measure of self-determination may be achieved through a particular
combination of liberties and restraints. Nor is it a specific historical
process, though the specific combination of liberties and restraints
may be conditioned by and reflect the values of a particular historical
period. Nor, again, is freedom limited to rational and autonomous
men. While Mill clearly preferred a society made up of such men, he
was realistic enough to recognize that this could not be a necessary
condition of freedom. Thus, while he would not apply his principle
of liberty to children and immature peoples, i.e., those not capable
of improvement by free and equal discussion, he would and did
apply it to all mature (not necessarily "autonomous") men, and not
simply to Marcuse's elites. Nor, finally, is freedom vindicated only
by "good" results, or rightfully "confined by truth." Freedom is in
part a value in itself, in part an instrument of individual development, in part a necessary means of social change. That men and
societies might make the "wrong" or "false" choices is clearly possible, but this too is an essential aspect of freedom. Otherwise a select
group of allegedly wise men will make these choices for them, and
this, by whatever name it may be called, is not freedom.

From all of which it follows that tolerance is not the freedom to
express only the right ideas, but the freedom to express even stupid
or loathsome ideas. The results may improve or depress the lot of
men or societies, but the results are distinct from the principle of
tolerance itself. And those who argue for tolerance, even absolute
tolerance of ideas, do so because they believe that reason and
experience are not calculated to lead men to the wrong decisions.
Marcuse's rejection of pure tolerance is in these terms either a
distrust of reason itself or a belief that the conditions under which
reason operates today are such as to vitiate the process of reason, and
probably both. But to the extent that it is the second, his attack is

properly directed to those conditions and not to the principle of tolerance. Clearly, the "tolerance" he espouses is intolerance, and so it should be called, lest we abandon all semblance of meaning in our ordinary use of terms.

(2) Those who believe not merely that there is an objective truth but that, by some mystery of incarnation, it has been given to them to know it, have rarely been willing to respect the claim to such knowledge by others. For such True Believers, allowing others to disseminate what is believed to be true but what in fact is false, is to make possible the adoption of error. For error, seductively presented, may prevail over truth even in free and equal discussion. How much more likely is it to prevail when the conditions are not free and equal, when those who propound the error (because it gratifies their passions or promotes their conceived interests) also control the sources of information and media of communication, and where the objects of the debate are neither rational nor autonomous but "conditioned" men! In such circumstances to trust to an abstract but spurious toleration is to yield the cause. For truth to prevail, the "right" men must impose it—either by altering the conditions or directing otherwise irrational men, and generally both. In this way men will be governed by truth, and thus, even though forced, they will also be free.

This, it is clear, is the argument of Socrates in the *Republic*. It is the argument of Rousseau in the *Social Contract*. It is the argument of the Grand Inquisitor, both of the Roman Catholic Church and of Stalin's Russia. It is the traditional argument of the Right, of all who would usurp the gates of heaven and in the name of a higher morality insist, as with Gerhart Niemeyer, upon "a firm official stand for what is known as right, true, and good." And it is, in all essentials, the argument of Marcuse. But it is not the argument of John Stuart Mill.

For Mill, as for all democrats committed to the liberal idea of freedom, to believe in Man is not to dispel one's doubts about men. Men are fallible and cannot presume to know the whole truth. Room must therefore be left for the rectification of error and the discovery of additional knowledge. This requires tolerance, the free exploration and articulation of ideas. It may well be that there are deficiencies in the intellectual marketplace, but the remedy is not to mistake Marcuse's authority for truth; it is rather to correct those deficiencies. To substitute one allegedly right authority for another, to compel or manipulate men to do what Marcuse (or anyone else) is convinced it is proper for them to do, is not to force them to be free. It is simply to subject them to Marcuse's (or another's) will. This, by any name, is coercion. It ill accords with the purposes of one who professes to respect humanity.

(3) Finally, and briefly, Marcuse's argument collapses because the reality he portrays renders unattainable, and is in turn contradicted by, the proposals he recommends. If it is true that we live "in a democracy with totalitarian organization" and that this "coordinated society" rests on "firm foundations," how is it humanly possible to change it? Surely not by election, for the "conditioned" masses will simply acquiesce in the opinions of their masters. Surely not by education, for the rulers control both the educators and their media of communication. Surely not by revolution, for who will revolt but "hopelessly dispersed" minorities? It may well be, as Marcuse thinks, that in such a situation the alienated man is the "essential" rather than the sick man, and that rebellious men merit applause rather than condemnation. But such men, however viewed, cannot overturn a firmly established order. Then to whom, and for what purpose, does Marcuse speak? Is his message really more than a tocsin of futility, a summons to surrender?

If, on the other hand, we are to take seriously his plea for fundamental social and political change, for the establishment of "real" tolerance (or, as he says, "official" intolerance), it can only mean that the society is less than totalitarian, that its foundations are not altogether firm, that there are chinks in the monopolistic concentration of power.

Marcuse cannot have it both ways: either his analysis is correct and his recommendations are unrealizable, or his recommendations are meaningful and appropriate, in which case his analysis cannot stand.

V

It would be less than just to conclude these remarks without noting the deep anguish and high moral commitment that animate all three of our critics. They are disturbed, and properly so, by the injustices that disfigure modern societies. They are distressed by the realization that these injustices are maintained by an indifferent, because unseeing, or acquiescent public opinion. Consequently they probe to the roots in an effort to uncover the sources and the interests that mold that opinion. And they have found, as every sensitive observer of human societies has always found, that within our cities there are still two cities—the city of the rich and the city of the poor, with all that this implies in inequalities of power, of access to privileges, and of opportunities. One need not accept everything that A. J. Liebling has written in *The Press*, or that C. Wright Mills has written in *The Power Elite*, to recognize that freedom of speech, for example, has a different meaning for those wealthy enough to buy a newspaper or to purchase time on radio or television, than it has for the masses of individuals who may wish to express their thoughts but have no effective access to the various media of communication. Nor does it require undue imagination to note that men cannot choose what they do not know exists, or will not choose what they have been taught to believe is evil. For these and other reasons, it is less than convincing to argue that the principle of equality accurately characterizes the world of public opinion, or that the free play of ideas does in fact afford people a full range of alternatives.

In underscoring these objectionable features of contemporary life and in urging their correction, our three critics manifest a concern for Man rather than for rich or powerful or prestigious men. Further, in their readiness to foster even revolutionary social and political change in an effort to elevate Man from what he presently is to what he ought to be, to what he *can* be, they identify themselves with an abiding radical tradition. They are legitimately of the Left.

But a wise radicalism seeks to overturn not all things, only unjust and harmful things; and not everything that men have thought and done in the course of human history demands repudiation. There have been achievements, too, and of these not the least noble has been the slow and painful liberation of the human mind. Whatever the merits or demerits of liberalism as a political and economic doctrine, in the realm of the intellect it should command our supreme allegiance: for it has freed reason from the chains of dogma and superstition; it has broken the back of orthodoxy; it has given us a method by which we may continue to correct our errors and improve our understanding. And whatever the merits or demerits of a particular social system in observing, or failing to observe, the principle of liberalism in the intellectual sphere, it is necessary— and I believe that even under circumstances that most humanly approximate the ideal, it will remain necessary—always to distinguish the fact of public opinion, what may be called the will of the people, from the motives and influences that elicit it. Democracies rest on the volume, not on the quality, of that will; and though no one would contend that it is better to have a stupid or misguided will, what distinguishes democratic from nondemocratic governments is that the former rest upon that will even though oligarchic or plutocratic influences may have been powerful in creating it; while the latter reject that will, or at most seek to mold it in support of their policies; it is not, as in democratic states, an initiating and controlling will. To render that will a purer or wiser will is surely a proper concern of democratic (whether liberal or radical) theorists, but this means that they must look not to the removal of that will, or of the process that alone gives it the opportunity to be formed after a consideration of alternatives, but to the correction of those conditions that limit or block the introduction of new and conflicting ideas. In any case, the fact of will and not its purity or disinterestedness remains the foundation of the democratic state.

Those who, therefore, in the name of a social revolution, would destroy not merely the conditions that still constrain reason but the principle of tolerance that alone gives reason its chance to prevail, defy the grim lessons of history. What, then, can one say of those who, like Marcuse, seek to reverse history by substituting for even the imperfect democracies of our day an intellectual and political authoritarianism that would allegedly act *for* the people, on the ground that a government that really acts in the interests of the people is better (and more democratic) than a government *by* the people that may, through ignorance or irrationality, act contrary to those best interests? Such men are neither radical nor liberal but, let us use the cruel word, reactionary. This is why, despite all the legitimate criticisms that might be (and in the course of the past century have been) made of Mill's philosophy, or of his political and economic teachings, or even of the subsidiary doctrines and incidental observations in his essay *On Liberty*, the central argument of that essay remains fundamentally unimpaired.

Not Mill's theory of pure tolerance but the repressive intolerance of our critics is, then, to be condemned.

Footnote

1. *A Critique of Pure Tolerance*, by Robert Paul Wolff, Barrington Moore, Jr., and Herbert Marcuse. Boston: Beacon Press, 1965.

ERAZIM V. KOHÁK

Requiem for Utopia
Socialist Reflections on Czechoslovakia
(1969)

Two days before the Soviet army entered Czechoslovakia, I received a letter from a student friend in Prague. The writer is an intelligent young man who received his entire formal education under the Communist regime. He had participated vigorously in the Czechoslovak reform in the spring of 1968, and had spent his vacation the following summer visiting first Nanterre, then Berlin. He speaks German and French fluently, reads English, and has made extensive contacts with his Western colleagues. His reflections on socialism East and West are worth quoting:

> Western socialism, especially in its radical form, took me completely by surprise. It seemed so completely unreal, something from a different planet or a different era. You have completely dissociated theory and practice. The men I met are all properly repelled by the realities of authoritarian rule, but they keep on preaching the same weary Utopian ideologies that can lead to nothing else. They live in a romantic dreamworld in which their dear radical rhetoric is perfectly consistent with their apparently sincere faith in freedom and justice. But do they really think they could apply their radical Utopia in a real world and still respect their libertarian commitments? Do they really think their Utopias could be benign if their revolutions were not comic-opera coups on indulgent campuses but real ventures in the exercise of power?

I met a few hard-headed colleagues, but most of the men who clamored for attention were three-semester intellectuals, pampered children of your permissive, affluent society, throwing tantrums because Father gave them only education, security, and freedom—but not Utopia. They bitterly resent society because it does not treat them as the fulcrum of the universe: though from what they told me about themselves it seemed that their families did treat them that way. I can't take them seriously. They seem to have no idea of the cost or the value of the privileges they receive abundantly and *gratis*. They dismiss them as "bourgeois"—in Czechoslovakia we are struggling for just a fraction of what they dismiss. I suppose their histrionics do have some individual cathartic value, like the old duelling fraternities, but socially they seem infinitely irrelevant. Can you imagine one of them in Czechoslovakia?

What surprises me most is not that they take themselves seriously—students always do, and we are no exception—but that their elders take them seriously. In the West it seems possible to grow quite old without having to grow up—you have so much slack, so much room, so much padding between yourselves and reality. You can afford a great deal: we can't. For instance, can you imagine reading Sartre's *Les communistes et la paix* here in 1952? That was just at the time of the Slansky trials. Or reading Marcuse on repressive tolerance, in Prague at the time of the Writers' Union Congress? It was not until I started visiting the West that I began to understand that a Sartre or a Marcuse can simply afford a great deal of illusion. You all live in a different era—you still believe in Utopia. You simply haven't faced up to the fact that you can't build a Utopia without terror, and that before long, terror is all that's left. You have little stomach for terror—after twenty years, we have even less. But you like your radical illusions too well.

We've had our fill of Utopia. No more. Now we are building piecemeal, building a democratic society that will be as imperfect as the people who live in it. It will be socialist because it is an industrial and a democratic society—it just doesn't work the other way around. It won't be a Utopia, but it will be a human kind of society, fit for people to live in.

I read this letter while listening to the Soviet Ambassador explain that the armed might of his country had descended upon the Czechoslovak Socialist Republic in order to protect socialism.

II

Not that I think my friend right in everything—there is much he does not know and understand. Still, his grasp of the dynamics of socialism is uncomfortably accurate.

The strength of socialism has always been its steady effort to build the prerequisites of democracy and social justice in an industrial society. But the appeal of socialism has been something different, something much less tangible—the promise of the millennium. Social-democratic parties in the nineteenth century were transforming society through a persistent, unspectacular effort to build a place in the social structure for the underprivileged, and to assure them the means and ability to assume that place. But what drew workers and still moves intellectuals to the party had little to do with concrete social progress. It was the ageless vision of a millennium, a fairytale kingdom in which men would still live together, but all the frictions of social existence—and, by implication, all the frustrations of individual life—would disappear. For the tedious, frustrating work of social progress the party needed a vision and the myth of apocalyptic revolution or, later, of the *Massenstreik*, the apocalyptic General Strike which would usher in the millennium, filled that need.

The millennial rhetoric was always grossly inconsistent with the evolutionary, progressive practice of socialism. On the one hand, the party worked to give the workers the wherewithal of social progress, to help them gain self-respect, economic and social security, education, legal protection, and to transform social structures in depth, "radically," making them responsive to the needs of all men. On the other hand, its orators dismissed all such effort as irrelevant and proclaimed the coming of a Hegelian cataclysm from which a perfect society would arise as if by magic, in which depraved workers would suddenly become capable of establishing and administering a perfectly humane society, and in which new, just institutions would spontaneously spring up precisely from the depth of deprivation.

The pattern here is that of the familiar romantic myth in which the very handicaps of the underprivileged become an asset. Touched by the magic wand, the princess loves the peasant lad precisely because he is crude (unaffected) and boorish (spontaneous). In revolutionary mythology, the magic wand was Hegelian dialectic. While in practice imperfect progress was won in patient, tedious, determined work, in millennial rhetoric the law of negation of negation was to produce Utopia in an exhilarating cataclysm, with the necessity of a law of nature. In his "Critique of Hegel's *Philosophy of Right*" in the *Deutsch-Französische Jahrbücher*, Marx announced that precisely because the German working class was completely depraved, precisely because its condition was beneath critique, it would establish a genuinely humane society.

There is nothing particularly socialistic about this apocalyptic utopianism. Quite the contrary. Socialism is first of all realistic, tackling the concrete problems of making human existence possible in an industrial age. Marx himself damned utopianism in his controversy with Schapper-Willich, citing the undeveloped condition of the German workers as reason for fifty years of preparation required for political power (Mehring, *Die Geschichte der deutschen Sozialdemokratie*, vol. I, p. 430).

But, as Marx himself noted, men can stand only limited doses of reality. They need their illusions, and as long as actual power with its limitations and responsibilities was not a real consideration, the revolutionary mythology could seem harmless enough.

With the upheaval of World War I and the collapse of the Russian empire, the situation changed radically. Russia in 1917 was a society virtually devoid of overt structure, radically open to experiment. At the same time, it was hopelessly backward. The problems it faced were not those of an industrial society, and Western socialist programs were wildly inapplicable to it. Its urgent need was pre-socialist, practical—the need to build a modern society. Socialists might have been able to contribute to the process, but the only way some of them knew to profit from it was to emphasize the Hegelian ideological superstructure of socialism, the revolutionary fairytale of the peasant lad becoming a shining prince at the touch of a magic cataclysm.

The men who carried out the Communist revolution finally did just that. They were not practical men. In temper, they were intellectual aristocrats interested in changing the ideological façade but having little patience for the unspectacular, ambiguous work of concrete, deep-reaching ("radical") change. A truly basic change requires work, the detailed, tedious, patient, persistent work of rebuilding basic attitudes and relations. A revolution is necessarily a poor instrument for such basic change. No matter how spectacular and exhilarating it may be, it leaves basic attitudes, habits, and relations among men unchanged; the social structures that emerge from it, though their ideology reflects the revolution, still articulate the old social orientation. Not surprisingly, Russian society, its paternalism, its stratification, its police apparatus, its provincialism, its primitivism—even the foreign policy of its government, in both goals and techniques—remained relatively constant in spite of the revolutionary change of façade. T. G. Masaryk's sociological study *The Spirit of Russia* published in 1913 (English trans. 1919), may have appeared momentarily out of date in 1920, but it is quite accurate in 1968. Ideological labeling has changed—for "Orthodox Church" read "Communist party," for "Czar" read "First Secretary," for *"Okhranka"* read "MVD"; but basic attitudes and relations, those which socialists recognize as the real fabric of society, have remained unchanged.

Unfortunately socialists, long accustomed to their revolutionary mythology, are easily dazzled by ideological trappings. Hammer and sickle on the flag of a sovereign state, the whispered names in an official hagiography, red stars on soldiers' caps, all the trappings of power and success easily outshone both the sordid realities of Russian life and the tangible social progress of unspectacular Western socialism. With the Russian Revolution, the Hegelian ideological myth became respectable. Worse, it became "socialism."

To be sure, even the dazzling façade of Russian *Parteistaatssozialismus* could not quite conceal the persistent Czarist mentality. It was Lenin who characterized Czarist Russia as "a state which is a cross between Asiatic despotism and European absolutism . . . not an organ of any class of Russian society but a military-administrative machinery whose task is to resist the pressure of a higher Western civilization" (*Iskra*, March 5, 1904). That description fitted the new Communist regime all too well. But men

who desperately wanted to believe could always find excuses as to
why the magic failed to work. Russia was backward, it was encircled
by hostile states, etc., etc., and of course all of that was true. For fifty
years the energies of socialists have been drawn away from the
urgent tasks of social progress to a cataclysmic utopian fantasy. In
Czechoslovakia in 1920, the socialists lost their considerable parliamentary majority and the chance to build a social democracy
because the ideological, Communist-led wing of the party chose to
withdraw from Parliament and wait for an apocalyptic revolution.
Ever since, the pattern they set has been repeated throughout the
West, down to the young ideologues of today whose conception of
becoming involved is to abstain from elections.

III

The significance of the Czechoslovak experience is that with us
the millennium did come, under conditions as ideal as an imperfect
world can offer. Czechoslovakia was an advanced industrial country,
far more so than the England or Germany of Marx's time. Culturally
it was part of the West, with a mature democratic tradition; yet it was
surrounded by friendly "socialist" countries. Its industries had been
socialized several years earlier, and there was no hard-core political
opposition. The Communist party had won, in 1946, some 38 percent of the vote in a reasonably free election, yet had subsequently
seized power in an armed coup, and so was unhindered by any
constitutional guarantees of personal or social freedom. The Hegelian myth that had lured socialists for half a century was finally being
acted out exactly as three generations of visionaries had imagined.

The men who guided the experiment were true believers. From
the beginning, they applied the theory of a radical break in all
aspects of personal and social life. Tight internal and external censorship sealed off the country from the outside world and from its own
past. History was rewritten and rebuilt. Organizations and men,
whether Communist or non-Communist, who had any pretensions
to autonomy disappeared. Not that the Czechoslovak Communists
were any more crude or repressive than their rhetorical colleagues
in the West—they weren't. But they were engaged in rule, not
rhetoric—and in practice. A theoretical revolutionary can speak of

"protecting the freedom of the people to develop along a socialist path unhampered by reactionary propaganda"—the ruling revolutionary has to censor the press and liquidate offending writers, and that is what the Czech Communists did. The human, social, and economic cost was tremendous, but the break was complete— everything and everyone even vaguely associated with the past was wiped out. The new Czechoslovakia was a completely "liberated" country, free of anything that might have repressed its development.

According to utopian rhetoric from Lenin on, new institutions, social relations, and new men, free, unalienated, should have sprung from socialist praxis. Life had been liberated from all impediments, it should have blossomed, free and abundant. But nothing of the sort happened. The new institutions expressed nothing but the new masters' conception of Utopia. Creatures of theory, they remained theoretical—alien, lifeless, apathetic. The people proved apathetic rather than zealous, preferring their lost freedom, even their folly, to perfection. They were willing to be socialists, and they were willing to be enthusiastic, but they were not willing to be enthusiastic about socialism. At the height of the Stalin period, a Czech friend told me, "At home they expect us to have sex orgies with socialism." The story, in a nutshell, of Czechoslovakia's utopian experiment is that Czechs and Slovaks continued to prefer women.

It was at this point that the hidden logic of all social messianism came to the fore. The rhetorical utopians convinced themselves that they had found the recipe for perfection. When their fellow men failed to share their enthusiasm, they embarked on a crusade to eliminate whatever was blinding them to their superior insight— Jews, capitalists, sinners. But when their crusade succeeded and men still failed to conform to their true faith, they found themselves forced to resort to coercion. Like all utopians, they were convinced they were coercing men for their own good, and that in time the coercion would become unnecessary. But as Masaryk pointed out about Marx in *The Foundations of Marxism* in 1898, the utopians are shoddy psychologists. Coercion produces not enthusiasm and agreement, but alienation and apathy, which in turn can be dislodged only by greater coercion, leading to still greater apathy. The escalating spiral of apathy and terror is the real *mors immortalis* of social messianism. The Czechoslovak experiment proved that the temptation to prod progress with a bayonet, so attractive to powerless radical rhetoricians, leads not to progress but to apathy and terror, regardless of the ideology in whose name it is exercised.

IV

What is it like, living in Utopia? Perhaps the most eloquent testimony is the recent Czech film, *The Fifth Horseman Is Fear.* Western reviewers interpreted it as just another wartime melodrama with bad Germans pitted against good Czechs and/or suffering Jews. That story is there, and the film does include some rather obvious period pieces. The resistance worker, his acts, even his clothes and his apartment, clearly belong to the war years. So does the surrealistic brothel scene, with its gas-chamber showers and Wehrmacht uniforms. But Czech audiences could not fail to recognize another dimension—Prague landmarks erected long after the war, late-model cars in the streets, contemporary clothes, all-Czech posters pasted over wartime bilingual ones.

This second dimension stands out most clearly in the official notices which appear in prominent close-ups throughout the film. Their format (though not their color—German notices were dark red) is that of the wartime bilingual notices, a German eagle in the center, with parallel German and Czech columns below. In the film, the parallel columns are retained, *but both sides are set in Czech.* The point of the film is clear: for the man who must live in Utopia, there is no difference between Right and Left Hegelians. The forties and the fifties, Hitler years and Stalin years merge. The only difference is that this time both the oppressors and the victims are Czech.

The Fifth Horseman is only one of the countless testimonies, produced both in the last months of gunpoint "socialism" and in the seven months of freedom, that the basic common fact of life in *any* Utopia is alienation. The word has become so fashionable that to restore it as a tool of social analysis we need to give it a more precise meaning. By alienation we shall mean a dissociation of an individual's public identity from his private one. Under ideal conditions, the two would be integrally related. Public life would serve to act out

private identity; private identity would in turn be enriched, reinforced, and challenged by the demands of praxis. When this
relation breaks down, for whatever reason, we can speak of
alienation—public life becomes formal, empty, lifeless, while private identity becomes involuted, explosive, and distorted.

That much is commonplace. The reason why alienation can today
serve as a revolutionary slogan, and not simply as a tool in the
perennial attempt to rescue Karl Marx from irrelevance, is that it can
be used as a bridge between private problems and public issues,
mobilizing the energy of individual failure and frustration for the
purposes of social action. But it is an ambiguous tool because it blurs
two phenomena which, though never altogether dissociated, are
still basically distinct and require different strategies: pathological
alienation and social alienation.

Pathological alienation is the dissociation of public acts and
private identity brought about by a defect in the latter. The subject is
unable to relate his private identity to (any) sustained public role,
regardless of social conditions, because his definition of personal
identity is in principle solipsistic, incompatible with the strains and
stresses of social existence. This is a phenomenon characteristic, for
instance, of both the extreme "left" and the extreme "right," and one
reason why the far "left" rejects all concrete social progress as
capitulation to "the system." If the cause of alienation is a pathological inability of the subject to function in *any* social system, only the
fairytale land of revolutionary apocalypse will do—and even that
only as long as it does not become reality—witness the regular
disenchantment of the far "left" with its successive Robin Hood
heroes whenever they actually succeed in bringing their experiment
into practice. Pathological alienation is only symptomatically relevant to social theory.

The alienation which the utopian experiment produced in
Czechoslovakia is an entirely different phenomenon. It is *social
alienation*, brought about by the structure of society rather than by
that of private identity. It is more closely analogous to the alienation
of American blacks, to whom the structure of society denies opportunity for participation, than to the alienation of disaffected students. The Czech protesters were generally adults; workers, students, writers, men from every social stratum, ready and able to

sustain the responsibility of being adults in a society. It was the utopian ideology of the regime which made successful integration of (any) private identity with social existence effectively impossible.

Social alienation is as characteristic of utopian societies as pathological alienation is of affluent, permissive ones. Utopian regimes invariably pay lip service to freedom and participation, but the logic of Utopia forces them to deny their subjects the materials from which a satisfactory private identity is built—privacy, personal security, and especially freedom. Freedom inevitably includes the possibility of error, and Utopia in principle demands perfection. The Czechoslovak regime was utopian, committed to remolding men in its image, and so, quite independently of the content of its ideology, it was also committed to paternalistic authoritarianism and its practical enforcement. Quite logically, the basic reality of life in Utopia was apathy—and terror.

V

Czechoslovak reform under Alexander Dubcek signified essentially a rejection of the Utopia that sacrifices men to the demands of a prescription. First of all democratic, it was determined to safeguard personal freedom and personal security, because twenty years of gunpoint "socialism" had taught the Czechs and Slovaks, Communists included, that the logic of terror is self-defeating. In Czechoslovakia there could be no question of whether personal freedom and security can be violated for the sake of a social ideal. Czechs and Slovaks have learned that once freedom and security are violated, any ideology becomes simply a rationale for self-perpetuating terror. The reform was democratic—and it was also fundamentally and emphatically socialist. Czechoslovakia is an advanced industrial country, in which democracy necessarily means economic democracy as well. In all its aspects, the heady Czechoslovak spring of 1968 was an experiment moving toward postmillennial socialism or, in traditional terms, toward social democracy.

Not that Dubcek and his colleagues were in any sense social democrats when they came to power. They weren't; they were Communists who still shared the aristocratic assumption of all utopians that a monopoly of power must remain in the hands of the enlightened elect, the Party. But they were determined to be humane authoritarians, respecting the rights of their subjects. In their seven months in power they discovered that the idea of a humane authoritarianism, the standard illusion of well-intentioned rhetorical revolutionists, is an illusion, a *contradictio in adjecto*. A humane authoritarianism would respect the rights and freedom of its subjects, and so inevitably create the possibility of dissent and opposition. Faced with opposition, the humane authoritarian faces the choice of ceasing to be authoritarian—or ceasing to be humane. Repression, whatever its overt aim, can be humane only in rhetoric—in practice it necessarily means breaking men. Czechs and Slovaks, including Dubcek, were too familiar with the logic of terror to opt for the latter alternative. After seven months, the program which started out as a program of humane communism became a program of social democracy.

To be sure, Czechoslovakia did not and could not become a social democracy overnight. The reformers worked in detail, steadily, on a hundred concrete programs, from rehabilitation of political prisoners to economic reform and social restructuring. They built consciously on Czechoslovakia's tradition of freedom and social progress. But the change was too radical to be spectacular. By August only the first steps had been taken. Still, the direction of change was clear, and received the full support of the whole nation. The experiment in democratic socialism was succeeding beyond the fondest hopes of its leaders and supporters.

VI

The end came on August 21, when the Hegelian Left repeated the pattern set by the Hegelian Right thirty years earlier. The workers of the Skoda Works, who painted swastikas on Russian tanks, made it clear that they failed to appreciate the difference.

But why did the Russians move in? The occupation of Czechoslovakia cost them much and won them little. The usual explanations about the threat posed by Czech liberalism side-step the crucial question—why should liberalism be a threat? It was no threat to Russian national interest. Czechoslovak security on the crossroads of superpowers is necessarily tied to a Soviet alliance, and the Czechs proved themselves fully aware, in both word and deed, of this fact. Nor was Czech liberalism a threat to socialism. Czechoslovakia is an industrial country in which socialism is a necessary consequence of democracy, and again the Czechs and Slovaks were obviously aware of this. Neither the Soviet alliance nor socialism were ever issues in the Czechoslovak reform—both were taken entirely for granted by the whole spectrum of national opinion.

Liberalism was a threat precisely because it *supported* socialism and the Soviet alliance, and so brought into question the very legitimacy of the utopian claim to power. This is no abstract consideration. Not only the Soviet regime, but any government in the world can exercise power effectively only as long as the governed recognize, tacitly at least, its *right to rule*—as long as they recognize it as a legitimate government. They might, and usually do, consider it a very bad government indeed. They might criticize it at every turn and resolve to replace its personnel or policies at the earliest opportunity. They might look forward to its fall and feel unhappy and alienated under its rule. Yet as long as they consider it a *legitimate* bad government, society will continue to function. The recognition of the legitimacy of power in the making and enforcing of social decisions is the constituting factor in society, and failure to acquire legitimacy in the eyes of the governed reduces even the most benign attempt at government to arbitrary tyranny.

Since the last echoes of "divine right" or "right of conquest" died out in the nineteenth century, legitimation in Europe has invariably meant legitimation by public interest. The democratic model interpreted acts in the public interest as acts receiving popular support: the legitimacy of a democratic government derives at least theoretically from the ability of the governed to confirm or reject their rulers. The model has achieved such prestige that even totalitarian regimes have felt the need to stage plebiscites and elections to give themselves an aura of legitimacy. Soviet elections in the past have invariably been elaborate, ostentatious affairs. They have also been invariably uncontested—a utopian revolutionary regime, finally, cannot equate public interest with public support. The governed, being unregenerate, cannot be expected to realize that the particular Utopia, whether nationalist or socialist, is in their true interest. They are too accustomed to their old self and the old order.

Soviet Communism, both at home and abroad, has always claimed the legitimacy of superior insight. The basic proposition of Soviet political philosophy, so basic that it is taken for granted in most rhetoric, is that the Soviet regime—or any regime—is legitimate because it is "socialist," orthodox, and so in the *true* interest of the people, *whether* they realize it or not. Anyone who dissents must be either a knave or a fool. It was this logic which led to the startling conclusion that a Tukhachevsky or a Beria, a Slansky or a Clementis, since they obviously were not fools, must have been imperialist agents. This is the logic which led to the condemnation of Dubcek as a traitor, and which makes the Russians insist that the Czechs produce acceptable scapegoats to explain their recent dissent. The grotesque insistence on Byzantine adulation of all things Russian, paralleled by men as disparate as Hitler, Franco, Trujillo, or Mao, is not simply a psychological quirk—it is a necessary corollary of the claim that utopian revolutionism legitimizes its own acts.

The Czechoslovak reform did not threaten the Soviet Union or socialism, but by supporting them challenged the basic premise of their rule. Soviet rule is predicated on the premise that it is legitimate because it is "socialist"—while Czechoslovak democracy admitted that socialism itself requires legitimation by popular consent.

VII

As a Czech, I find little consolation in the fact that tanks can exercise power but cannot make it legitimate or restore the shattered Hegelian illusions of utopian revolutionism. Czechs and Slovaks might be able to mitigate the impact of Russian rule through passive resistance, but the Russians are in effective control of the country, and able to impose absolute limits on its development. There will in all likelihood be periods of relative relaxation. This is to be expected—coercion produces apathy, and has to be relaxed periodically to allow for some life and spontaneity. But such relaxation creates the possibility of dissent, and the harsher the earlier coercion, the more radical the dissent will be. Unless the Soviet leadership is prepared to abdicate its authoritarian position, it must follow each period of relaxation with another freeze, as the purges of the thirties, postwar Stalinism, or the present hardening of internal and external policy. But the cycles are not progressive or cumulative—today's neo-Stalinism is no more benign than Lenin's war communism half a century ago, and it would be naïve to pin one's hopes on a gradual mellowing of Communism. The internal dynamics of utopianism make such mellowing most unlikely.

The ideals of human freedom and social justice remain valid. Democracy—democracy for blacks as well as whites, in economics as well as politics, at home as well as in remote reaches of Latin America or Eastern Europe, remains valid. Socialism, the ideal of social justice and social responsibility in industrial society, remains valid. Human and civil rights, the right of every man to personal identity and social participation, all remain valid. But the utopian myths of self-proclaimed rhetorical radicals do not advance these ideals. The detour on which too many socialists embarked in 1917 is over, finished, discredited, revealed as an exhilarating, aristocratic and ultimately reactionary social sport, not the radical social progress it claimed to be. The task that remains is the work of social progress—not the aristocratic sport of revolution, but the solid work of radical, deep-rooted transformation of society. Men may still demand their daily dose of illusion, the exhilaration of revolution or "confrontation" rather than the down-to-earth facts and figures of a Freedom Budget; but those who cater to this demand can no longer do so in the name of social progress—or in the name of socialism.

Utopia is dead. Czechoslovakia has been a graveyard of illusions. As a Czech social democrat, I can only hope that it will also prove the cradle of a new social progress.

MICHAEL WALZER
In Defense
of Equality
(1973)

At the very center of conservative thought lies this idea: that the present division of wealth and power corresponds to some deeper reality of human life. Conservatives don't want to say merely that the present division is what it ought to be, for that would invite a search for some distributive principle—as if it were possible to *make* a distribution. They want to say that whatever the division of wealth and power is, it naturally is, and that all efforts to change it, temporarily successful in proportion to their bloodiness, must be futile in the end. We are then invited, as in Irving Kristol's recent *Commentary* article, to reflect upon the perversity of those who would make the attempt.[1] Like a certain sort of leftist thought, conservative argument seems quickly to shape itself around a rhetoric of motives rather than one of reasons. Kristol is especially adept at that rhetoric and strangely unconcerned about the reductionism it involves. He aims to expose egalitarianism as the ideology of envious and resentful intellectuals. No one else cares about it, he says, except the "new class" of college-educated, professional, most importantly, professorial men and women, who hate their bourgeois past (and present) and long for a world of their own making.

I suppose I should have felt, after reading Kristol's piece, that the decent drapery of my socialist convictions has been stripped away, that I was left naked and shivering, small-minded and self-concerned. Perhaps I did feel a little like that, for my first impulse

297

was to respond in kind, exposing anti-egalitarianism as the ideology of those other intellectuals—"they are mostly professors, of course"—whose spiritual course was sketched some years ago by the editor of *Commentary*. But that would be at best a degrading business, and I doubt that my analysis would be any more accurate than Kristol's. It is better to ignore the motives of these "new men" and focus instead on what they say: that the inequalities we are all familiar with are inherent in our condition, are accepted by ordinary people (like themselves), and are criticized only by the perverse. I think all these assertions are false; I shall try to respond to them in a serious way.

Kristol doesn't argue that we can't possibly have greater equality or greater inequality than we presently have. Both communist and aristocratic societies are possible, he writes, under conditions of political repression or economic underdevelopment and stagnation. But insofar as men are set free from the coerciveness of the state and from material necessity, they will distribute themselves in a more natural way, more or less as contemporary Americans have done. The American way is exemplary because it derives from or reflects the real inequalities of mankind. Men don't naturally fall into two classes (patricians and plebeians) as conservatives once thought; nor can they plausibly be grouped into a single class (citizens or comrades) as leftists still believe. Instead, "human talents and abilities . . . distribute themselves along a bell-shaped curve, with most people clustered around the middle, and with much smaller percentages at the lower and higher ends." The marvels of social science!—this distribution is a demonstrable fact. And it is another "demonstrable fact that in all modern bourgeois societies, the distribution of income is also along a bell-shaped curve . . ." The second bell echoes the first. Moreover, once this harmony is established, "the political structure—the distribution of political power— follows along the same way . . ." At this point, Kristol must add, "however slowly and reluctantly," since he believes that the Soviet economy is moving closer every year to its natural shape, and it is admittedly hard to find evidence that nature is winning out in the political realm. But in the United States, nature is triumphant: we are perfectly bell-shaped.

The first bell is obviously the crucial one. The defense of inequality reduces to these two propositions: that talent is distributed unequally and that talent will out. Clearly, we all want men and women to develop and express their talents, but whenever they are able to do that, Kristol suggests, the bell-shaped curve will appear or reappear, first in the economy, then in the political system. It is a neat argument but also a peculiar one, for there is no reason to think that "human talents and abilities" in fact distribute themselves along a *single* curve, although income necessarily does. Consider the range and variety of human capacities: intelligence, physical strength, agility and grace, artistic creativity, mechanical skill, leadership, endurance, memory, psychological insight, the capacity for hard work—even moral strength, sensitivity, the ability to express compassion. Let's assume that with respect to all these, most people (but different people in each case) cluster around the middle of whatever scale we can construct, with smaller numbers at the lower and higher ends. Which of these curves is actually echoed by the income bell? Which, if any, ought to be?

There is another talent that we need to consider: the ability to make money, the green thumb of bourgeois society—a secondary talent, no doubt, combining many of the others in ways specified by the immediate environment, but probably also a talent which distributes, if we could graph it, along a bell-shaped curve. Even this curve would not correlate exactly with the income bell because of the intervention of luck, that eternal friend of the untalented, whose most important social expression is the inheritance of property. But the correlation would be close enough, and it might also be morally plausible and satisfying. People who are able to make money ought to make money, in the same way that people who are able to write books ought to write books. Every human talent should be developed and expressed.

The difficulty here is that making money is only rarely a form of self-expression, and the money we make is rarely enjoyed for its intrinsic qualities (at least, economists frown upon that sort of enjoyment). In a capitalist world, money is the universal medium of exchange; it enables the men and women who possess it to purchase virtually every other sort of social good; we collect it for its exchange value. Political power, celebrity, admiration, leisure, works of art, baseball teams, legal advice, sexual pleasure, travel, education, medical care, rare books, sailboats—all these (and much more) are up for sale. The list is as endless as human desire and social invention. Now isn't it odd, and morally implausible and unsatisfying, that all these things should be distributed to people with a talent for making money? And even odder and more unsatisfying that they should be distributed (as they are) to people who have money, whether or not they made it, whether or not they possess any talent at all?

Rich people, of course, always look talented—just as princesses always look beautiful—to the deferential observer. But it is the first task of social science, one would think, to look beyond these appearances. "The properties of money," Marx wrote, "are my own (the possessor's) properties and faculties. What I *am* and *can do* is, therefore, not at all determined by my individuality. I *am* ugly, but I can buy the most beautiful woman for myself. Consequently, I am not ugly, for the effect of ugliness, its power to repel, is annulled by money. . . . I am a detestable, dishonorable, unscrupulous, and stupid man, but money is honored and so also is its possessor."[2]

It would not be any better if we gave men money in direct proportion to their intelligence, their strength, or their moral rectitude. The resulting distributions would each, no doubt, reflect what Kristol calls "the tyranny of the bell-shaped curve," though it is worth noticing again that the populations in the lower, middle, and upper regions of each graph would be radically different. But whether it was the smart, the strong, or the righteous who enjoyed all the things that money can buy, the oddity would remain: why them? Why anybody? In fact, there is no single talent or combination of talents which plausibly entitles a man to every available social good—and there is no single talent or combination of talents that necessarily must win the available goods of a free society. Kristol's bell-shaped curve is tyrannical only in a purely formal sense. Any particular distribution may indeed be bell-shaped, but there are a large number of possible distributions. Nor need there be a single distribution of all social goods, for different goods might well be distributed differently. Nor again need all these distributions follow this or that talent curve, for in the sharing of some social goods, talent does not seem a relevant consideration at all.

Consider the case of medical care: surely it should not be distrib-

uted to individuals because they are wealthy, intelligent, or righteous, but only because they are sick. Now, over any given period of
time, it may be true that some men and women won't require any
medical treatment, a very large number will need some moderate
degree of attention, and a few will have to have intensive care. If that
is so, then we must hope for the appearance of another bell-shaped
curve. Not just any bell will do. It must be the right one, echoing
what might be called the susceptibility-to-sickness curve. But in
America today, the distribution of medical care actually follows
closely the lines of the income graph. It's not how a man feels, but
how much money he has that determines how often he visits a
doctor. Another demonstrable fact! Does it require envious intellectuals to see that something is wrong?

There are two possible ways of setting things right. We might
distribute income in proportion to susceptibility-to-sickness, or we
might make sure that medical care is not for sale at all, but is
available to those who need it. The second of these is obviously the
simpler. Indeed, it is a modest proposal and already has wide support, even among those ordinary men and women who are said to be
indifferent to equality. And yet, the distribution of medical care
solely for medical reasons would point the way toward an egalitarian
society, for it would call the dominance of the income curve dramatically into question.

II

What egalitarianism requires is that many bells should ring.
Different goods should be distributed to different people for different reasons. Equality is not a simple notion, and it cannot be
satisfied by a single distributive scheme—not even, I hasten to add,
by a scheme which emphasizes need. "From each according to his
abilities, to each according to his needs" is a fine slogan with regard
to medical care. Tax money collected from all of us in proportion to
our resources (these will never correlate exactly with our abilities,
but that problem I shall leave aside for now) must pay the doctors
who care for those of us who are sick. Other people who deliver
similar sorts of social goods should probably be paid in the same
way—teachers and lawyers, for example. But Marx's slogan doesn't

help at all with regard to the distribution of political power, honor and fame, leisure time, rare books, and sailboats. None of these things can be distributed to individuals in proportion to their needs, for they are not things that anyone (strictly speaking) needs. They can't be distributed in equal amounts or given to whoever wants them, for some of them are necessarily scarce, and some of them can't be possessed unless other people agree on the proper name of the possessor. There is no criterion, I think, that will fit them all. In the past they have indeed been distributed on a single principle: men and women have possessed them or their historical equivalents because they were strong or well-born or wealthy. But this only suggests that a society in which any single distributive principle is dominant cannot be an egalitarian society. Equality requires a diversity of principles, which mirrors the diversity both of mankind and of social goods.

Whenever equality in this sense does not prevail, we have a kind of tyranny, for it is tyrannical of the well-born or the strong or the rich to gather to themselves social goods that have nothing to do with their personal qualities. This is an idea beautifully expressed in a passage from Pascal's *Pensées*, which I am going to quote at some length, since it is the source of my own argument.[3]

The nature of tyranny is to desire power over the whole world and outside its own sphere.

There are different companies—the strong, the handsome, the intelligent, the devout—and each man reigns in his own, not elsewhere. But sometimes they meet, and the strong and the handsome fight for mastery—foolishly, for their mastery is of different kinds. They misunderstand one another, and make the mistake of each aiming at universal dominion. Nothing can win this, not even strength, for it is powerless in the kingdom of the wise. . . .

Tyranny. The following statements, therefore, are false and tyrannical: "Because I am handsome, so I should command respect." "I am strong, therefore men should love me . . ." "I am . . . etc."

Tyranny is the wish to obtain by one means what can only be had by another. We owe different duties to different qualities:

love is the proper response to charm, fear to strength, and belief to learning.

Marx makes a very similar argument in one of the early manuscripts; perhaps he has this *pensée* in mind.

> Let us assume man to be man, and his relation to the world to be a human one. Then love can only be exchanged for love, trust for trust, etc. If you wish to enjoy art you must be an artistically cultivated person; if you wish to influence other people, you must be a person who really has a stimulating and encouraging effect upon others. . . . If you love without evoking love in return, i.e., if you are not able, by the manifestation of yourself as a loving person, to make yourself a beloved person, then your love is impotent and a misfortune.[4]

The doctrine suggested by these passages is not an easy one, and I can expound it only in a tentative way. It isn't that every man should get what he deserves—as in the old definition of justice—for desert is relevant only to some of the exchanges that Pascal and Marx have in mind. Charming men and women don't deserve to be loved: I may love this one or that one, but it can't be the case that I ought to do so. Similarly, learned men don't deserve to be believed: they are believed or not depending on the arguments they make. What Pascal and Marx are saying is that love and belief can't rightly be had in any other way—can't be purchased or coerced, for example. It is wrong to seek them in any way that is alien to their intrinsic character. In its extended form, their argument is that for all our personal and collective resources, there are distributive reasons that are somehow *right*, that are naturally part of our ideas about the things themselves. So nature is reestablished as a critical standard, and we are invited to wonder at the strangeness of the existing order.

This new standard is egalitarian, even though it obviously does not require an equal distribution of love and belief. The doctrine of right reasons suggests that we pay equal attention to the "different qualities," and to the "individuality" of every man and woman, that we find ways of sharing our resources that match the variety of their needs, interests, and capacities. The clues that we must follow lie in the conceptions we already have, in the things we already know about love and belief, and also about respect, obedience, education, medical care, legal aid, all the necessities of life—for this is no esoteric doctrine, whatever difficulties it involves. Nor is it a panacea for human misfortune, as Marx's last sentence makes clear: it is only meant to suggest a humane form of social accommodation. There is little we can do, in the best of societies, for the man who isn't loved. But there may be ways to avoid the triumph of the man who doesn't love—who buys love or forces it—or at least of his parallels in the larger social and political world: the leaders, for example, who are obeyed because of their coercive might or their enormous wealth. Our goal should be an end to tyranny, a society in which no man is master outside his sphere. That is the only society of equals worth having.

But it isn't readily had, for there is no necessity implied by the doctrine of right reasons. Pascal is wrong to say that "strength is powerless in the kingdom of the wise"—or rather, he is talking of an ideal realm and not of the intellectual world as we know it. In fact, wise men (at any rate, smart men) have often in the past defended the tyranny of the strong, as they still defend the tyranny of the rich. Sometimes, of course, they do this because they are persuaded of the necessity or the utility of tyrannical rule; sometimes for other reasons. Kristol suggests that whenever intellectuals are not persuaded, they are secretly aspiring to a tyranny of their own: they too would like to rule outside their sphere. Again, that's certainly true of some of them, and we all have our own lists. But it's not necessarily true. Surely it is possible, though no doubt difficult, for an intellectual to pay proper respect to the different companies of men. I want to argue that in our society the only way to do that, or to begin to do it, is to worry about the tyranny of money.

III

Let's start with some things that money cannot buy. It can't buy the American League pennant: star players can be hired, but victories presumably are not up for sale. It can't buy the National Book Award: writers can be subsidized, but the judges presumably can't be bribed. Nor, it should be added, can the pennant or the award be won by being strong, charming, or ideologically correct—at least we all hope not. In these sorts of cases, the right reasons for winning are built into the very structure of the competition. I am inclined to think that they are similarly built into a large number of social practices and institutions. It's worth focusing again, for example, on the practice of medicine. From ancient times, doctors were required to take an oath to help the sick, not the powerful or the wealthy. That requirement reflects a common understanding about the very nature of medical care. Many professionals don't share that understanding, but the opinion of ordinary men and women, in this case at least, is profoundly egalitarian.

The same understanding is reflected in our legal system. A man accused of a crime is entitled to a fair trial simply by virtue of being an accused man; nothing else about him is a relevant consideration. That is why defendants who cannot afford a lawyer are provided with legal counsel by the state: otherwise justice would be up for sale. And that is why defense counsel can challenge particular jurors thought to be prejudiced: the fate of the accused must hang on his guilt or innocence, not on his political opinions, his social class, or his race. We want different defendants to be treated differently, but only for the right reasons.

The case is the same in the political system, whenever the state is a democracy. Each citizen is entitled to one vote simply because he is a citizen. Men and women who are ambitious to exercise greater power must collect votes, but they can't do that by purchasing them; we don't want votes to be traded in the marketplace, though virtually everything else is traded there, and so we have made it a criminal offense to offer bribes to voters. The only right way to collect votes is to campaign for them, that is, to be persuasive, stimulating, encouraging, and so on. Great inequalities in political power are acceptable only if they result from a political process of a certain kind, open to argument, closed to bribery and coercion. The freely given support of one's fellow citizens is the appropriate criterion for exercising political power and, once again, it is not enough, or it shouldn't be, to be physically powerful, or well-born, or even ideologically correct.

It is often enough, however, to be rich. No one can doubt the mastery of the wealthy in the spheres of medicine, justice, and political power, even though these are not their own spheres. I don't want to say, their unchallenged mastery, for in democratic states we have at least made a start toward restricting the tyranny of money. But we have only made a start: think how different America would have to be before these three companies of men—the sick, the accused, the politically ambitious—could be treated in strict accordance with their individual qualities. It would be immediately necessary to have a national health service, national legal assistance, the strictest possible control over campaign contributions. Modest proposals, again, but they represent so many moves toward the realization of that old socialist slogan about the abolition of money. I have always been puzzled by that slogan, for socialists have never, to my knowledge, advocated a return to a barter economy. But it makes a great deal of sense if it is interpreted to mean *the abolition of the power of money outside its sphere*. What socialists want is a society in which wealth is no longer convertible into social goods with which it has no intrinsic connection.

But it is in the very nature of money to be convertible (that's all it is), and I find it hard to imagine the sorts of laws and law enforcement that would be necessary to prevent monied men and women from buying medical care and legal aid over and above whatever social minimum is provided for everyone. In the United States today, people can even buy police protection beyond what the state provides, though one would think that it is the primary purpose of the state to guarantee equal security to all its citizens, and it is by no means the rich, despite the temptations they offer, who stand in greatest need of protection. But this sort of thing could be prevented only by a very considerable restriction of individual liberty—of the freedom to offer services and to purchase them. The case is even harder with respect to politics itself. One can stop overt bribery, limit the size of campaign contributions, require publicity, and so on. But none of these things will be enough to prevent the wealthy from exercising power in all sorts of ways to which their fellow citizens have never consented. Indeed, the ability to hold or spend vast sums of money is itself a form of power, permitting what might be called preemptive strikes against the political system. And this, it seems to me, is the strongest possible argument for a radical redistribution of wealth. So long as money is convertible outside its sphere, it must be widely and more or less equally held so as to

minimize its distorting effects upon legitimate distributive processes.

IV

What is the proper sphere of wealth? What sorts of things are
rightly had in exchange for money? The obvious answer is also the
right one: all those economic goods and services, beyond what is
necessary to life itself, which men find useful or pleasing. There is
nothing degraded about wanting these things; there is nothing
unattractive, boring, debased, or philistine about a society organized to provide them for its members. Kristol insists that a snobbish
dislike for the sheer productivity of bourgeois society is a feature of
egalitarian argument. I would have thought that a deep appreciation
of that productivity has more often marked the work of socialist
writers. The question is, how are the products to be distributed?
Now, the right way to possess useful and pleasing things is by making
them, or growing them, or somehow providing them for others. The
medium of exchange is money, and this is the proper function of
money and, ideally, its only function.

There should be no way of acquiring rare books and sailboats
except by working for them. But this is not to say that men deserve
whatever money they can get for the goods and services they
provide. In capitalist society, the actual exchange value of the work
they do is largely a function of market conditions over which they
exercise no control. It has little to do with the intrinsic value of the
work or with the individual qualities of the worker. There is no
reason for socialists to respect it, unless it turns out to be socially
useful to do so. There are other values, however, which they must
respect, for money isn't the only or necessarily the most important
thing for which work can be exchanged. A lawyer is surely entitled to
the respect he wins from his colleagues and to the gratitude and
praise he wins from his clients. The work he has done may also
constitute a good reason for making him director of the local legal aid
society; it may even be a good reason for making him a judge. It isn't,
on the face of it, a good reason for allowing him an enormous income.
Nor is the willingness of his clients to pay his fees a sufficient reason,
for most of them almost certainly think they should be paying less.

The money they pay is different from the praise they give, in that the first is extrinsically determined, the second freely offered.

In a long and thoughtful discussion of egalitarianism in *Public Interest*, Daniel Bell worries that socialists today are aiming at an "equality of results" instead of the "just meritocracy" (the career open to talents) that he believes was once the goal of leftist and even of revolutionary politics.[5] I confess that I am tempted by "equality of results" in the sphere of money, precisely because it is so hard to see how a man can merit the things that money can buy. On the other hand, it is easy to list cases where merit (of one sort or another) is clearly the right distributive criterion, and where socialism would not require the introduction of any other principle.

- Six people speak at a meeting, advocating different policies, seeking to influence the decision of the assembled group.
- Six doctors are known to aspire to a hospital directorship.
- Six writers publish novels and anxiously await the reviews of the critics.
- Six men seek the company and love of the same woman.

Now, we all know the right reasons for the sorts of decisions, choices, judgments that are in question here. I have never heard anyone seriously argue that the woman must let herself be shared, or the hospital establish a six-man directorate, or the critics distribute their praise evenly, or the people at the meeting adopt all six proposals. In all these cases, the personal qualities of the individuals involved (as these appear to the others) should carry the day.

But what sorts of personal qualities are relevant to owning a $20,000 sailboat? A love for sailing, perhaps, and a willingness to build the boat or to do an equivalent amount of work. In America today, it would take a steelworker about two years to earn that money (assuming that he didn't buy anything else during all that time) and it would take a corporation executive a month or two. How can that be right, when the executive also has a rug on the floor, air conditioning, a deferential secretary, and enormous personal power? He's being paid as he goes, while the steelworker is piling up a kind of moral merit (so we have always been taught) by deferring pleasure. Surely there is no meritocratic defense for this sort of difference. It would seem much better to pay the worker and the

executive more or less the same weekly wage and let the sailboat be
bought by the man who is willing to forgo other goods and services,
that is, by the man who really wants it. Is this "equality of result"? In
fact, the results will be different, if the men are, and it seems to me
that they will be different for the right reasons.

Against this view, there is a conventional but also very strong
argument that can be made on behalf of enterprise and inventive-
ness. If there is a popular defense of inequality, it is this one, but I
don't think it can carry us very far toward the inequalities that Kristol
wants to defend. Consider the case of the man who builds a better
mousetrap, or opens a restaurant and sells delicious blintzes, or does
a little teaching on the side. He has no air conditioning, no secretary,
no power; probably his reward has to be monetary. He has to have a
chance, at least, to earn a little more money than his less enterprising neighbors. The market doesn't guarantee that he will in fact earn
more, but it does make it possible, and until some other way can be
found to do that, market relations are probably defensible under the
doctrine of right reasons. Here in the world of the petty bourgeoisie,
it seems appropriate that people able to provide goods or services
that are novel, timely, or particularly excellent should reap the
rewards they presumably had in mind when they went to work. And
which they were right to have in mind: no one would want to feed
blintzes to strangers, day after day, merely to win their gratitude.

But one might well want to be a corporation executive, day after
day, merely to make all those decisions. It is precisely the people
who are paid or who pay themselves vast sums of money who reap all
sorts of other rewards too. We need to sort out these different forms
of payment. First of all, there are rewards, like the pleasure of
exercising power, which are intrinsic to certain jobs. An executive
must make decisions—that's what he is there for—and even decisions seriously affecting other people. It is right that he should do
that, however, only if he has been persuasive, stimulating,
encouraging, and so on, and won the support of a majority of those
same people. That he owns the corporation or has been chosen by
the owners isn't enough. Indeed, given the nature of corporate
power in contemporary society, the following statement (to para-
phrase Pascal) is false and tyrannical: because I am rich, so I should
make decisions and command obedience. Even in corporations

organized democratically, of course, the personal exercise of power
will persist. It is more likely to be seen, however, as it is normally
seen in political life, as the chief attraction of executive positions.
And this will cast a new light on the other rewards of leadership.

The second of these consists in all the side effects of power:
prestige, status, deference, and so on. Democracy tends to reduce
these, or should tend that way when it is working well, without
significantly reducing the attractions of decision-making. The same
is true of the third form of reward, money itself, which is owed to
work, but not necessarily to place and power. We pay political
leaders much less than corporation executives, precisely because we
understand so well the excitement and appeal of political office.
Insofar as we recognize the political character of corporations, then,
we can pay their executives less too. I doubt that there would be a
lack of candidates even if we paid them no more than was paid to any
other corporation employee. Perhaps there are reasons for paying
them more—but not meritocratic reasons, for we give all the attention that is due to their merit when we make them our leaders.

We don't give all due attention to the restaurant owner, however,
merely by eating his blintzes. Him we have to pay, and he can ask, I
suppose, whatever the market will bear. That's fair enough, and no
real threat to equality so long as he can't amass so much money that
he becomes a threat to the integrity of the political system and so
long as he does not exercise power, tyrannically, over other men and
women. Within his proper sphere, he is as good a citizen as any
other. His activities recall Dr. Johnson's remark: "There are few
ways in which man can be more innocently employed than in getting
money."

V

The most immediate occasion of the conservative attack on
equality is the reappearance of the quota system—newly designed,
or so it is said, to move us closer to egalitarianism rather than to
maintain old patterns of religious and racial discrimination. Kristol
does not discuss quotas, perhaps because they are not widely supported by professional people (or by professors): the disputes of the
last several years do not fit the brazen simplicity of his argument.

But almost everyone else talks about them, and Bell worries at some length, and rightly, about the challenge quotas represent to the "just meritocracy" he favors. Indeed, quotas in any form, new or old, establish "wrong reasons" as the basis of important social decisions, perhaps the most important social decisions: who shall be a doctor, who shall be a lawyer, and who shall be a bureaucrat. It is obvious that being black or a woman or having a Spanish surname (any more than being white, male, and Protestant) is no qualification for entering a university or a medical school or joining the civil service. In a sense, then, the critique of quotas consists almost entirely of a series of restatements and reiterations of the argument I have been urging in this essay. One only wishes that the critics would apply it more generally than they seem ready to do. There is more to be said, however, if they consistently refuse to do that.

The positions for which quotas are being urged are, in America today, key entry points to the good life. They open the way, that is, to a life marked above all by a profusion of goods, material and moral: possessions, conveniences, prestige, and deference. Many of these goods are not in any plausible sense appropriate rewards for the work that is being done. They are merely the rewards that upper classes throughout history have been able to seize and hold for their members. Quotas, as they are currently being used, are a way of redistributing these rewards by redistributing the social places to which they conventionally pertain. It is a bad way, because one really wants doctors and (even) civil servants to have certain sorts of qualifications. To the people on the receiving end of medical and bureaucratic services, race and class are a great deal less important than knowledge, competence, courtesy, and so on. I don't want to say that race and class are entirely unimportant: it would be wrong to underestimate the distortions introduced by an inegalitarian society into these sorts of human relations. But if the right reason for receiving medical care is being sick, then the right reason for giving medical care is being able to help the sick. And so medical schools should pay attention, first of all and almost exclusively, to the potential helpfulness of their applicants.

But they may be able to do that only if the usual connections between place and reward are decisively broken. Here is another example of the doctrine of right reasons. If men and women wanted to be doctors primarily because they wanted to be helpful, they would have no reason to object when judgments were made about their potential helpfulness. But so long as there are extrinsic reasons for wanting to be a doctor, there will be pressure to choose doctors (that is, to make medical school places available) for reasons that are similarly extrinsic. So long as the goods that medical schools distribute include more than certificates of competence, include, to be precise, certificates of earning power, quotas are not entirely implausible. I don't see that being black is a worse reason for owning a sailboat than being a doctor. They are equally bad reasons.

Quotas today are a means of lower-class aggrandizement, and they are likely to be resolutely opposed, opposed without guilt and worry, only by people who are entirely content with the class structure as it is and with the present distribution of goods and services. For those of us who are not content, anxiety can't be avoided. We know that quotas are wrong, but we also know that the present distribution of wealth makes no moral sense, that the dominance of the income curve plays havoc with legitimate distributive principles, and that quotas are a form of redress no more irrational than the world within which and because of which they are demanded. In an egalitarian society, however, quotas would be unnecessary and inexcusable.

VI

I have put forward a difficult argument in very brief form, in order to answer Kristol's even briefer argument—for he is chiefly concerned with the motives of those who advocate equality and not with the case they make or try to make. He is also concerned, he says, with the fact that equality has suddenly been discovered and is now for the first time being advocated as the *chief* virtue of social institutions: as if societies were not complex and values ambiguous. I don't know what discoverers and advocates he has in mind.[6] But it is worth stressing that equality as I have described it does not stand alone, but is closely related to the idea of liberty. The relation is complex, and I cannot say very much about it here. It is a feature of the argument I have made, however, that the right reason for distributing love, belief, and, most important for my immediate purposes, political power is the freely given consent of lovers, believers, and citizens. In these sorts of cases, of course, we all have standards to urge upon our fellows: we say that so and so should not be believed unless he offers evidence or that so and so should not be elected to political office unless he commits himself to civil rights. But clearly credence and power are not and ought not be distributed according to my standards or yours. What is necessary is that everyone else be able to say yes or no. Without liberty, then, there could be no rightful distribution at all. On the other hand, men are not free, not politically free at least, if *his* yes, because of his birth or place or fortune, count seventeen times more heavily than *my* no. Here the case is exactly as socialists have always claimed it to be: liberty and equality are the two chief virtues of social institutions and they stand best when they stand together.

Footnotes

1. "About Equality," *Commentary*, November 1972.

2. *Early Writings*, trans. T. B. Bottomore (London: Watts, 1963), p. 191.

3. I am also greatly indebted to Bernard Williams, in whose essay "The Idea of Equality," first published in Laslett and Runciman, *Philosophy, Politics and Society*, second series (Oxford: Blackwell, 1962), a similar argument is worked out. The example of medical care, to which I recur, is suggested by him. The Pascal quote is from J. M. Cohen's translation of *The Pensées* (London and Baltimore: Penguin Classics, 1961), no. 244.

4. *Early Writings*, pp. 193–94.

5. "On Meritocracy and Equality," *Public Interest*, Fall 1972.

6. The only writer he mentions is John Rawls, whose *Theory of Justice* Kristol seems entirely to misunderstand. For Rawls explicitly accords priority to the "liberty principle" over those other maxims that point toward greater equality.

OCTAVIO PAZ
Twilight of
Revolution
(1974)

The idea of revolution was the great invention of the West in its
second phase. Societies of the past did not have real revolutions;
they had changes of mandate and dynasty. Apart from these changes,
they experienced profound transformations: births, deaths, and res-
urrections of religions. In this respect, too, our era is unique: no
other society has ever made revolution its central idea. If this second
phase of Western civilization comes to an end, as many people
believe and as the reality that we all live tells us, the clearest sign
that the end is approaching will be what Ortega y Gasset propheti-
cally called "the twilight of revolutions." It is true that we have never
had so many; it is also true that none of them fits the Western
conception of what a revolution is. Like the first Christians waiting
for the Apocalypse, modern society has been waiting for the arrival
of the revolution since 1840. And revolution is coming: not the one
that we have been waiting for, but another one, each time another
one. Faced with this unexpected reality which cheats us, theologians speculate and try to prove, like Confucian mandarins, that the
mandate of heaven (the idea of revolution) is the same; what is
happening is that the prince (concrete revolution) is unworthy of the
mandate. But there comes a time when people cease believing in the
speculations of theologians. This is what has begun to happen in the
second half of our century. We are witnessing the denouement
today: revolution against revolution. It is not a reactionary move-

314

ment, nor is it inspired by Washington: it is the revolt of the underdeveloped peoples and the rebellion of the young in the developed countries. In both cases the idea of revolution has been attacked in its very center, as much as or more than the conservative idea of order.

I have written elsewhere of what must be called "the end of the revolutionary period in the West." I shall merely repeat here that the idea of revolution—in the strict sense of that word, such as it has been defined by modern thought—is undergoing a crisis because its very root, its foundation, the linear conception of time and history, is also undergoing a crisis. Modern thought secularized Christian time and from among the temporal triad—past, present, and future—it crowned the latter the ruling power of our lives and of history. The future has reigned in the West since the eighteenth century. Today this idea of time is coming to an end: we are living the decadence of the future. It is therefore an error to consider contemporary social upheavals as expressions of the (supposed) revolutionary process which history has been said to consist of. Although these disturbances have been unusually violent and will probably be even more violent in the future, they in no way correspond to the ideas concerning what a revolution is or should be that Tyrians and Trojans, from Chateaubriand to Trotsky, had worked out. On the contrary, all these changes, beginning with that in Russia and not excluding the ones that have taken place in China and Cuba, have failed to confirm the theoretician's predictions: none of them has occurred where it should have and none of the classes and social forces in the forefront of these changes have been what they should have been. Reality is perverse and stubborn: these changes have occurred in different places, among different classes, and with different results. Whatever their ultimate meaning may be, these events give the lie to the linear idea of history, the notion of the human course of time as a process possessed of a logic, in other words, a genuine *discourse*.

The idea of process implies that things happen one after the other, either in the form of sudden leaps and bounds (revolution) or in the form of gradual changes (evolution). Progress is a synonym of process because it is thought that every change results sooner or later in an advance. Both modes of succession, the revolutionary and the evolutionary, correspond to a vision of history as a march toward something—we are not exactly certain where this something is, except that this *where* is better than the situation today, and that it lies in the future. History is envisioned as a continuous, neverending colonization of the future. There is something infernal about this optimistic vision of history; the philosophy of progress is really a theory of the condemnation of man, who is doomed perpetually to move forward, knowing that he will never arrive at his final destination. This way of thinking is rooted in the Judeo-Christian tradition, and its mythical counterpart is the expulsion from Eden. In the garden of paradise, a present without a single flaw shone brightly; in the deserts of history, the only sun that guides us is the fleeting future. The subject of this continual pilgrimage is not a nation, a class, or a civilization, but an abstract entity: humanity. As the subject of history, "humanity" lacks substance; it is never present in person: it acts by means of its representatives, this people or that, this class or that. Persepolis, Rome, or New York, the monarchy or the proletariat, any one *represents* humanity at one moment or another of history as a member of the legislature represents his electors, and as an actor represents the character he is playing.

History is a theater in which a single person, humanity, becomes many: servants, masters, bourgeois, mandarins, clergymen, peasants, workers. The incoherent shouting of all these voices turns into a rational dialogue and this dialogue into a philosophical monologue. History is a discourse. But the rebellions of the twentieth century have violated both the rules of dramatic action and those of representation. We have unforeseen irruptions that disturb the linear nature of history: what should have happened has not occurred and what should have happened later happens now. If Chinese peasants or Latin-American revolutionaries are today the representatives of the subject "humanity," who or what do American and European workers, not to mention the Russian proletariat, represent? Both the events and the actors betray the text of the play. They write another text, or rather invent one. History becomes improvisation. This is the end of discourse and rational legibility.

What might be called *the inversion of historic causality* has its counterpart in the breaks in the linear order. I shall cite an example. It used to be supposed that revolution would be the consequence of the contradiction between the forces of production created by capitalism and the system of capitalist ownership. The fundamental opposition was: industrial production/private capitalist ownership. This real, material opposition could be expressed in terms of a logical dichotomy between reason (industrial production) and unreason (private capitalist ownership). Socialism would be the result of economic development; at the same time it would be the triumph of reason over the irrationality of the capitalist system. Necessity (history) possessed the rigor of logic; it was reason incarnate. Both history and reason were identified with morality: socialism was justice. And, finally: history, reason, and morality became one with progress. But modern revolts, including the Russian one, have not been the consequence of economic development, but of the absence of development. None of these revolts broke out because there was an irreconcilable contradiction between the system of industrial production and the system of capitalist ownership. On the contrary: in these countries the contradiction went through an initial phase and was therefore socially and historically productive. The results of these movements were also paradoxical. In Russia there was a leap from an incipient industrial capitalism to the system of state ownership. By doing away with the stage of free competition, unemployment, monopolies, and other disasters of capitalism were avoided. At the same time, the political and social counterpart of capitalism —free labor unions and democracy—was literally ignored. No longer a consequence of development, socialism has been a method of fostering it. Therefore it has had to accept the iron law of development: the storing up, the accumulation of capital (modestly called "the accumulation of Socialist capital"). Any accumulation brings on the expropriation of plus-value and an exploitation of the workers; the difference between capitalist and "Socialist" accumulation has been that in the first case the workers could group together and defend their interests, and in the second, because of the absence of democratic institutions, they were (and are) exploited by their "representatives." Socialism, which had ceased being synonymous with historical reason, has also ceased being synonymous with justice. It has lost its philosophical dignity and its moral halo. The so-called "historical laws" have disappeared completely. The rationality inherent in the historical process has proven to be merely one more myth. Or, better: a variation of the myth of linear time.

The linear conception of history makes three things necessary. First of all, there must be only one time: a present continually impelled toward the future. Second, there must be only one leading thread: universal history must be considered to be the manifestation of the Absolute in time, the expression of the class struggle, or some other similar hypothesis. The third requirement is the continuous action of a protagonist who is also unique: humanity and its successive transitory masks. The revolts and rebellions of the 20th century have demonstrated that the subject of history is multiple and that it is irreducible to the notion of class struggle as well as to the progressive and linear succession of civilizations (the Egyptians, the Greeks, the Romans, etc.). The plurality of protagonists has also demonstrated that the leading thread of history is also multiple: it is not a single strand but many, and not all of them are straight ones. There is a plurality of personages and a plurality of times on the march toward many *wheres*, not all of them situated in a future that vanishes the instant we touch it.

The decline of the future is a phenomenon that manifests itself, naturally, in the very place where it shone like a real sun: modern Western society. I will give two examples of its decline: the crisis of the notion of an avant-garde in the realm of art, and the violent irruption of sexuality. The extreme form of modernity in art is the destruction of the object; this tendency, which began as a criticism of the notion of the "work of art," has now culminated in a negation of the very notion of art. Things have come around full circle: art ceases to be "modern"; it is an instantaneous present. As for sexuality and time: the body has never believed in progress; its religion is not the future but the present.

The emergence of the present as the central value is visible in many areas of contemporary sensibility: it is a ubiquitous phenomenon. Nonetheless, it is most clearly seen in the youth movement. If the rebellion of the underdeveloped countries denies the predictions of revolutionary thought about the logic of history and the universal historical subject of our time (the proletariat), the rebellion of youth dethrones the primacy of the future and discredits the suppositions of revolutionary messianism and of liberal evolutionism: what excites young people is not the progress of the entelechy called humanity but the realization of each concrete human vocation, here and now. The universality of the rebellion of youth is the real sign of the times: *the signal of a change of time.* This universality must not cause us to forget that the movement of youth has a different meaning in each country: negation of the society of abundance and opposition to imperialism, to racial discrimination and war, in the United States and in Western Europe; the struggle for a democratic society against the oppression of Communist bureaucracies and against Soviet interference in the "Socialist" countries of Eastern Europe; the opposition to Yankee imperialism and local oppressors in Latin America. But these differences do not blur the most decisive fact: the style of the rebellion of youth rejecting the institutions and the moral and social systems that hold sway in the West. All these institutions and systems go to make up what is called *modernity,* in contrast to the medieval world. All of them are the offspring of linear time and all of them are being rejected today. Their rejection does not come from the past but from the present. The double crisis of Marxism and the ideology of liberal and democratic capitalism has the same meaning as the rebellion of the underdeveloped world and the rebellion of youth: they are the expressions of the end of linear time.

The twilight of the idea of revolution corresponds to the rapidity with which revolutionary movements are being transformed into rigid systems. The best definition I know of this process came from a guerrilla in Michoacán: "All revolutions degenerate into governments." The situation of the other heir of Christianity, art, is no better. But its prostration is not a consequence of the intolerant rigidity of a system but of the promiscuity of its various tendencies and manners. There is no art that does not create a style and there is no style that does not eventually kill art. By injecting the idea of revolution into art, our era has created a plurality of styles and pseudostyles. This abundance turns into another abundance: that of styles that die aborning. Schools proliferate and propagate like mushrooms until their very abundance finally erases the differences between one tendency and another; movements live about as long as insects do, a few short hours; the aesthetic of novelty, surprise, and change turns into imitation, tedium, and repetition. What is left for us? First, the weapon of dying mortals: humor. As the Irish poet Patrick Kavanagh said to the doctor paying him a visit: "I'm afraid

I'm not going to die. . . ." We can sneer at death and thus exorcise it. We can still begin over again.

What excites me about the rebellion of youth even more than their generous but nebulous politics is the reappearance of passion as a magnetic reality. We are not just witnessing another rebellion of the senses: we are confronting an explosion of emotions and feelings. This is a search for the sign *body*, not as a cipher of pleasure (although we must not be afraid of the word *pleasure:* it is beautiful in every language), but as a magnet that attracts all the contradictory forces that haunt us. It is a point of reconciliation of man with others and with himself; it is also a point of departure leading, beyond the body, to the Other. Young people are discovering values that excited figures as different as Blake and Rousseau, Novalis and Breton— spontaneity, the negation of artificial society and its hierarchies, fraternity not only with men but with nature, the ability to be enthusiastic and also to be indignant, and the amazing ability to be amazed. In brief: they are discovering the heart. In this sense the rebellion of youth is different from those that preceded it in this century, with the exception of that of the Surrealists. The tradition of these young people is more poetic and religious than philosophical and political; like Romanticism, with which it has more than one similarity, their rebellion is not so much intellectual dissidence as a passionate, vital, libertarian heresy. The ideology of the young is often a simplification and an acritical reduction of the revolutionary tradition of the West, which itself was scholastic and intolerant. The systematic spirit has infected many groups that arrogantly advocate authoritarian and obscurantist programs, such as Maoism and other theological fanaticisms. Embracing "Chinese Marxism" as a political philosophy and attempting to apply it to industrial societies of the West is at once grotesque and disheartening. It is not the ideology of youth but their attitude, their sensibility more than their thought, that is really new. I believe that in them and through them another possibility for the West is opening up, if only obscurely and con- fusedly as yet, something that has not been foreseen by ideologists and that only a handful of poets has glimpsed. Something still without form, like a world dawning. Or is this only an illusion of ours and are these disturbances the last sparks of a dying hope?

Hearing any participant or eyewitness of the rebellion of young people in Paris in May 1968 is an experience that puts our ability to judge things objectively to the test. In all the accounts I have heard there is one surprising note: the tone of the revolt, at once passionate and disinterested, as if action had been confused with representation, it was like a mutiny that turned into a Festival and a political discussion that turned into a ceremony; epic theater and at the same time public confession. The secret of the fascination that this movement exercised on all those (including the spectators) who were present at its demonstrations lay in its attempt to unite politics, art, and eroticism. There was a fusion of private and collective passion, a continuous ebb and flow between the marvelous and the everyday, the lived act as an aesthetic representation, a conjunction of action and its celebration. There was a reuniting of man with his image: mirror reflections focused in another luminous body. It was a true conversion: not only a change of ideas but of sensibility; more than a change of being, it was a *return to being*, a social and psychic revelation that for a few days broadened the limits of reality and extended the realm of the possible. It was a return to the source, to the principle of principles: being oneself by being with everyone. It was a discovery of the power of language: my words are yours; speaking with you is speaking with myself. It was a reappearance of everything (communion, transfiguration, the transformation of water into wine and of words into a body) that religions claim as their own though it is anterior to them and constitutes the other dimension of man, his other half and his lost kingdom—man perpetually expelled and torn away from time, in search of *another* time, a prohibited, inaccessible time: the present moment. Not the eternity of religions but the incandescence of the instant: a consummation and an abolition of dates. What is the way to enter such a present? André Breton once spoke of the possibility of incorporating an extrareligious sense of the sacred, made up of the triangle of love, poetry, and rebellion, in modern life. This *sacred* cannot emerge from anything but the depths of a collective experience. Society must manifest it, incarnate it, live it, and thus live and consume itself. Revolt as the path to Illumination. Here and now: a leap to the other shore.

And a nostalgia for Festival. But Festival is a manifestation of the

cyclical time of myth; it is a present that returns, whereas we live in
the linear and profane time of progress and history. Perhaps the
revolt of youth is an empty festival, the summons, the invocation of
an event that will always be a future event and never a present one,
that never will simply *be*. Or perhaps it is a commemoration: the
revolution no longer appears to be the elusive imminence of the
future but rather something like a past to which we cannot
return—yet which we cannot abandon either. In either case, it is not
here, but there, always beyond our reach. Possessed by the memory
of its future or of its past, by what it was or what it could have
been—no, not possessed but rather deserted, empty, the orphan of
its origin and its future—society mimics them. And by mimicking
them it exorcises them: for a few weeks it denies itself through the
blasphemies and the sacrilege of its young people and then affirms
itself more completely and more perfectly in the ensuing repression.
A mimetic magic. A victim anointed by the ambiguous fascination of
profanation, youth is the sacrificial lamb of the ceremony: after
having profaned itself through it, society punishes itself. It is a
symbolic profanation and castigation and at the same time a representation. The events on October 2, 1968, in the Plaza de Tlatelolco
in Mexico City evoked (repeated) the Aztec rites: several hundred
boys and girls sacrificed, on the ruins of a pyramid, by the army and
the police. The literalness of the rite—the reality of the sacrifice—
emphasized in a hideous way the unreal and expiatory nature of the
repression: the Mexican powers-that-be punished their own revolutionary past by punishing these young people.

In every case and in every country workers have participated in
the movement only as unwilling and temporary allies. This indifference is difficult to explain unless we accept one of the two following hypotheses: either the working class is not a revolutionary class
or the revolt of youth does not fit within the classical framework of
the class struggle. These two explanations are really one and the
same: if the working class is no longer revolutionary, and if social
conflicts and struggles become more acute instead of dying out; if the
recrudescence of these struggles does not coincide with an economic
crisis but rather with a period of abundance; and if a new world class
of the exploited has not appeared to take the place of the proletariat

in its revolutionary mission, then it is obvious that the theory of class struggle cannot account for contemporary phenomena. It is not that it is entirely false: it is inadequate, and we must seek another principle, another explanation. There are those who will tell me that the underdeveloped countries are the new proletariat. I need hardly point out in reply that the phenomenon of colonial dependence is not new (Marx was familiar with it); moreover, these countries do not constitute a class because of their social, economic, and historical heterogeneity. For this reason they do not have and cannot set up programs and universal plans as an international class, a party, or a church can.

The idea that intellectuals and technicians constitute the new class is more interesting, but unfortunately it has the defect that those groups are neither homogeneous nor can they be considered as a real proletariat—they are not a universal, exploited class. As for young people: no dialectical skill and no trick of the imagination can transform them into a social class. From the viewpoint of revolutionary doctrines, what is really almost beyond explanation is the attitude of young people: they have nothing to gain, no philosophy has named them agents of history and they embody no universal historical principle. This appears to be a strange situation: they are outside the real drama of history in the same way that the biblical lamb was outside of the dialogue between Jehovah and Abraham. But it no longer seems strange if we observe that, like the rite as a whole, the victim is a representation, or, more precisely, a hypostasis of the revolutionary classes of the past.

The modern world was born with the democratic revolution of the bourgeoisie which, so to speak, nationalized and collectivized politics. By opening to the collectivity a sphere that up until that time had been the closed preserve of a few, it was thought that general politicization (democracy) would immediately result in the distribution of power among everyone. Although democracy—because of the bureaucratic nature of political parties, economic monopolies, and the manipulation of the means of information—has become a method of a few to control and garner power, we are haunted by the phantoms of the principles, beliefs, ideas, and forms of living and feeling that gave rise to our world. Nostalgia and remorse—this is probably why society indulges in costly and sometimes bloody revolutionary rituals. The ceremony commemorates an absence, or more precisely, it at once convokes, exorcises, and punishes an Absent Guest. The Absent Guest has a public name and another secret name: the first is Revolution and refers to the linear time of history; the other is Festival and evokes the circular time of myth. They are one and the same: the return of Revolution is Festival, the recurring principle of principles. But they do not really return: it is all pantomime, and on another day fasting and penitence. It is the Festival of the goddess Reason—with Robespierre and without the guillotine but with tear gas and television. It is the Return as a verbal orgy, a saturnalia of commonplaces, the nausea that Festival brings.

Or is the rebellion of youth yet another sign that we are living *an end of time?* I have already expressed my belief: modern time—linear time, the homologue of the ideas of progress and history, ever propelled into the future, the time of the sign *non-body*, of the fierce will to dominate nature and tame instincts, the time of sublimation, aggression, and self-mutilation—is coming to an end. I believe that we are entering another time, a time that has not yet revealed its form and about which we can say nothing except that it will be neither linear time nor cyclical time. Neither history nor myth. The time that is coming, if we really are living a change at times, a general revolt and not linear revolution, will be neither a future nor a past, but a present. At least this is what contemporary rebellions are confusedly demanding. Nor do art and poetry seek anything different, although artists and poets sometimes do not know this. The return of the present: the time that is coming is defined by a *here* and a *now*. It is a negation of the sign *non-body* in all its Western versions: religious or atheist, philosophical or political, materialist or idealist. The present does not project us into any place beyond, any motley, otherworldly eternities or abstract paradises at the end of history. It projects us into the medulla, the invisible center of time: the here and now. A carnal time, a mortal time: the present is not unreachable, the present is not forbidden territory. How can we touch it, how can we penetrate its transparent heart? I do not know, and I do not believe anybody knows. . . . Perhaps the alliance of poetry and rebellion will give us a vision of it. I see in their conjunction the possibility of the return of the sign *body*: the incarnation of images, the return of the human figure, radiant and radiating symbols. If contemporary rebellion (and I am not thinking only of that of young people) is not dissipated in a succession of raucous cries and does not degenerate into closed, authoritarian systems, if it articulates its passion through poetic imagination, in the widest and freest sense of the word poetry, our incredulous eyes may behold the awakening and the return to our abject world of that corporeal and spiritual reality that we call *the presence of the beloved*. Then love will cease to be the isolated experience of an individual or a couple, an exception or a scandal. The word *presence* and the word *love* have appeared in these reflections for the first and the last time. They were the seed of the West, the origin of our art and of our poetry. In them is the secret of our resurrection.

Translated by HELEN R. LANE

ROY MEDVEDEV
Solzhenitsyn's
Gulag Archipelago:
Part Two
(1976)

The second volume of Solzhenitsyn's *Gulag Archipelago* has now appeared. Where the first volume consisted in a detailed investigation of everything that preceded the arrival of millions of Soviet people in Stalin's concentration camps—the system of arrests, the various forms of confinement, interrogation with torture, judicial and extrajudicial persecution, prisoner transports and transit prisons—the second volume gets down to the study of the primary and fundamental part of the Gulag empire, the corrective or, as Solzhenitsyn rightly calls them, the "destructive" labor camps. Here nothing escapes the author's attention: the origin and history of the camps, the economics of forced labor, the administrative structure, the categories of prisoners and everyday life of the inmates, the position of women and juveniles, the relations between ordinary *zeks*[1] and the trusties, between criminals and politicals, the camp guards, the convoy guards, the "information" service and the recruiting of stool pigeons, the system of punishments and "incentives," the functioning of the hospitals and medical stations, the way prisoners died and were killed, and the unceremonious way they were buried—all these things find their place in Solzhenitsyn's book. The author describes the various types of hard labor and the starvation diet imposed on the zeks; he studies not only the world of the camps but also the world immediately surrounding them, the world of "campside"; and he surveys the peculiarities of psychology

326

and behavior found among the prisoners and their jail keepers (or "camp keepers," in Solzhenitsyn's terminology).

Like the first volume, which came out in December 1973, this volume deserves the highest estimation, especially because it is a conscientious investigation, artistically presented and based on authentic fact. True, the second volume did not have the moral shock effect of the first, did not stun and shake the reader so. Perhaps because it was the second volume; or perhaps, for me, this impression has to do with the fact that I have read dozens and dozens of memoirs by former camp inmates (most of them, of course, never published) and have recorded hundreds of accounts and pieces of testimony about camp life. It is also significant that, while the basic facts are reliable (and there are noticeably fewer petty factual inaccuracies in the second volume of *Gulag Archipelago* than in the first), many of the author's judgments and opinions are too one-sided and categorical and his general observations are by no means always well grounded. This is particularly true of the way he obviously lays his colors on too thickly in depicting the world of "the free" in his chapter "Our Muzzled Freedom."

But, of course, none of the shortcomings of the second volume overshadow the artistic and social significance of this book, which has no equal in all our literature on the camps.

Several years ago I heard of a certain occurrence from a former "son of Gulag" who had gone to visit Vorkuta as a free citizen (many such veterans of the camps feel the urge to visit the places where their years had been spent working behind barbed wire; Solzhenitsyn too writes about this). It was an occurrence common in those parts. A foundation pit for a new school in Vorkuta had been started.[2] No sooner had the thin topmost layer of soil been removed than the teeth of the excavating machines revealed a huge deposit of human bones. This was not of course the site of a primitive human settlement, and no archeologists came there. It was one of those giant mass graves that grew near the northern camps—great pits, already dug in the autumn, into which thousands of corpses were thrown during the winter—prisoners who died or were shot—to be covered over later on, with the arrival of the brief northern summer. Construction of the school was temporarily halted, not for the purpose, naturally, of setting up a monument to the unknown convicts; the freshly bared bones of these zeks were carted off by night and buried somewhere outside the city limits, and this new cemetery was not marked in any noticeable way. At the original site of the mass grave, school construction was resumed and completed.

Alas, we can have little hope that memorials will be erected even where the largest concentration camps stood, or that the camp barracks, compounds, towers, and mines will be restored in museum form, or that some sort of markings will be placed at the countless camp cemeteries, where there are probably more Soviet people buried than fell in the war against Nazi Germany. There is little hope that an eternal flame will burn here or that the names of those who died and were killed will be chiseled in marble. It is quite possible that books will remain the only monuments to these people. One such book, *The Gulag Archipelago*, will easily outlive those who wish to suppress it and will stand as an unforgettable tribute for those to whom its author dedicated it, all those who perished in the camps, "all those who did not live to tell it."

CAMP MYTHS

In our country, where there is no freedom of the press or freedom of information, where most information circulates by certain secret channels, a multitude of rumors inevitably arise and dozens of different myths have public currency and are accepted by many as unquestionable truths. Under the conditions existing in the camps such legends, rumors, and myths—often far removed from reality —were all the more likely to find fertile ground. Natalya Reshetovskaya has recently contended that Solzhenitsyn's book is essentially based on this camp folklore.[3] That is certainly not so. Of course Solzhenitsyn, through no fault of his own, had no chance to check documentary evidence in order to verify much of the information he obtained from fellow inmates and from subsequent correspondents and informants. However, both his own camp experience and his intuition as an investigator and an artist enable him in most cases to distinguish sharply enough between truth and invention in the accounts he has recorded. If some legends do crop up in the pages of *Gulag Archipelago*, rare as they may be, this happens for the most part when the topic is the distant past or the lives and "affairs" of those high up in the "organs," for example, Minister of State Security Abakumov.[4]

I think that among such myths we must include Solzhenitsyn's story of the fourteen-year-old boy who on June 20, 1929, during Gorky's visit to the Solovetsky Special Purpose Camp asked to speak with Gorky in private and then spent an hour and a half telling the famous writer about all the illegalities committed in that camp.[5] According to Solzhenitsyn's account, Gorky, after talking with the boy, left the room in tears. But not only did he do nothing for the prisoners at Solovki; he even praised the Solovetsky Cheka agents many times thereafter—while the truth-loving lad was shot the same night by those Chekists.[6] Now Solzhenitsyn himself writes that the first juveniles came to Solovki only in mid-March 1929. How could the newly arrived inhabitants of the children's colony, isolated from the adult prisoners, find out everything that had gone on at Solovki for years before? But if this particular anecdote related by Solzhenitsyn seems dubious, no such doubts arise over his own story of the many illegal and arbitrary actions committed at Solovki, a narrative that can be confirmed by other accounts and other witnesses.

WHERE THE CAMPS CAME FROM

Solzhenitsyn dates the existence of concentration camps for political opponents in our country from 1918. This is not slander, as some of his detractors contend. Solzhenitsyn quotes Lenin's telegram to Yevgeniya Bosh, president of the Penza Province Executive Committee, advising, "Lock up all the doubtful ones in a concentration camp outside the city" (Lenin, *Polynoye Sobraniye Sochineniy* [Collected works], 5th Russian ed., vol. 50, pp. 143–44). Other official documents may be cited to the same effect. Thus, a special resolution of the Council of People's Commissars of the Russian Soviet Federated Socialist Republic (RSFSR) of September 5, 1918, says in part, "It is necessary to secure the Soviet Republic against its class enemies by isolating them in concentration camps" (*Yezhenedelnik ChK* [Weekly Bulletin of the Cheka], no. 1, September 22, 1918, p. 11). In February 1919 Grigory Sokolnikov, a member of the Central Committee of the Russian Communist party (Bolsheviks) and of the Military Revolutionary Council of the Southern Front, objecting to Central Committee directives on "de-Cossackization," the mass shooting of Cossacks who gave aid to Krasnov or served in the White army,[7] proposed that instead of being shot they be employed in socially useful labor in the coal-mining districts, for building railroads and digging shale and peat. For this purpose Sokolnikov requested by telegram that "work begin immediately on the construction of facilities for concentration camps" (Central Party Archives, collection 17, shelf 4, file 53, sheet 54). The concentration camps of civil war times were quite primitive structures, and the regimen enforced in them bore very little resemblance to that of the camps of the 1930s. Sometimes the people in them were put to work. In other cases, in districts near the battle fronts, an area outside a city would simply be fenced off, the "socially dangerous elements" would be detained there but would not work, and their relatives and friends would bring them food and hand it to them through the fences. Toward the end of 1920 most of those confined in concentration camps were peasants arrested for "speculation," as can be seen from documents of the Cheka. With the end of the civil war many of these camps were dismantled and their inmates sent home. At the beginning of NEP,[8] the camps for political prisoners were apparently abolished nearly everywhere, with the exception of the Solovetsky Special Purpose Camp and several "political isolators"[9]—of which Solzhenitsyn writes.

Space does not allow us to explore here the question of which elements in the early history of these political camps were dictated by the stern necessities of those years and which constituted plainly excessive and unnecessary cruelty. But it would be wrong to place the camps of the civil war period and those of Stalin's time on the same plane and ignore the fact that in 1918–20 the Soviet Republic was fighting a war on several fronts against foreign-backed White governments and that the numerous concentration camps set up on territory held by the White armies and foreign interventionist forces were usually far more savage than those in the RSFSR. In Stalin's time, on the other hand, the terror of the camps was directed against people who were unarmed and defenseless, and were not hostile toward the sole existing, and firmly established, power in the land. For Solzhenitsyn this distinction seems not to exist.

THE 1937 WAVE

Solzhenitsyn does not hide his distaste for the government, party, and economic leaders, top commanders of the Red Army, leading cadres of the Young Communist League and the trade unions, and especially the high-ranking personnel of the NKVD and the Prosecutor General's Office,[10] who themselves became the object of brutal repression in 1937 and '38. Even in the first volume of *Gulag Archipelago* Solzhenitsyn wrote:

> If you study in detail the whole history of the arrests and trials of 1936 to 1938, the principal revulsion you feel is not against Stalin and his accomplices, but against the humiliatingly repulsive defendants—nausea at their spiritual baseness after their former pride and implacability.

All these people, during the civil war or during collectivization and industrialization, so Solzhenitsyn asserts, were pitiless toward their political opponents and therefore deserved no pity when their own "system" turned against them.

In the second volume, we find the same attitude on the author's part toward the "1937 wave." With obvious satisfaction Solzhenitsyn cites the names of dozens of major Communist party figures shot on Stalin's orders in 1937–38. These people deserved their fate, he suggests; they got what they had made ready for, or given to, others.

> And though [he writes], when the young Tukhachevsky returned victoriously from suppressing the devastated Tambov peasants, there was no Mariya Spiridonova waiting at the station to put a bullet through his head, it was done sixteen years later by the Georgian priest who never graduated.[11]

But we can in no way share these sentiments and opinions of Solzhenitsyn's.

First, one cannot ignore the fact that the leaders who perished in the 1930s were not all the same kind of people, either in their personal characters or in the degree of responsibility they had for the crimes of the preceding years. There were people who had already degenerated greatly, who had been so caught up in Stalin's system that they carried out the most savage and inhuman orders without thinking of the country or the people, but only of themselves and their power. These people not only carried out orders but "demonstrated initiative" on their own, helping Stalin and the NKVD organs to "expose" and annihilate "enemies of the people." But there were quite a few who acted in error, who were simultaneously victims and instruments of another cult—the cult of party discipline. Among them were many honest, self-sacrificing, and courageous people who, too late, came to understand a great deal. There were quite a few who thought about what was happening in the country and were tormented by it, but who believed in the party and the party's propaganda. It would seem, from today's vantage point, that we could speak of the historical and political guilt of the entire active party membership for the events of the 1920s and 1930s. But we cannot simply lump all these people together indiscriminately as criminals who got what they deserved. The fate of the majority of the revolutionary Bolsheviks remains one of the most awesome tragedies in the history of our country, and we cannot in any way condone Solzhenitsyn in his mocking suggestion that in the obituaries published in our country the words "perished tragically during the period of the cult" should be replaced by the words "perished comically." The best Russian writers never indulged in mockery of the dead. Let us recall Pushkin, who wrote these lines:

> Riego did transgress against Spain's king.
> There I agree. But for that he was hanged.
> Is it seemly, tell me now, for us
> To hotly curse the hangman's fallen victim?[12]

Earlier, in reading the first volume of *Gulag Archipelago*, I was unpleasantly surprised by Solzhenitsyn's words that he had somehow been "consoled"—when describing the trials at which People's Commissar of Justice Krylenko appeared as the accuser— "consoled" by the thought of the degradation to which Krylenko was reduced in Butyrka prison before he was shot, the same Krylenko who had condemned others to similar degradation.[13] It seems to me that the author's attitude here is quite far removed from the simple standard of human decency, not to mention the Christian virtues of "understanding mildness" and "uncategorical judgments," which Solzhenitsyn proclaims at the end of the second volume.

Solzhenitsyn's position seems wrong to us not only because the government and party leaders destroyed were most often replaced by people who, it is common knowledge, were even worse. Thus, in Yezhov's and Beria's times one could with reason regret the passing of such Chekists as Latsis and Peters. The brutality of Latsis and Peters,[14] sometimes justified and sometimes not, was at any rate never self-seeking, sadistic, or aimed at currying favor. Those men apparently could not have gone down the road of crime as far as Yezhov, Beria, Zakovsky,[15] and their kind.

It must be said, simply, that no one deserved the dreadful fate that befell the leaders arrested in 1937–1938. It is impossible to take satisfaction in the thought of their degradation and torment, even knowing that many of them deserved death.

One of Shalamov's *Kolyma Stories* tells the fate of a deputy head of the Leningrad NKVD, Nikonov, an accomplice of Yezhov and Zakovsky, who during "interrogation" had his testicles crushed.[16] Solzhenitsyn himself in the first volume wrote about this method of torture as the worst kind, one that cannot be endured. In reading Shalamov's story I did not feel any gratification. It is quite likely that this Nikonov fully deserved to be tried and shot for his crimes. But even he did not deserve such cruel torture and abuse. It is a profoundly mistaken notion of morality to think that Stalin's reprisals against the main cadres of the Communist party and Soviet government represented, even in an extremely distorted form, the triumph of some sort of historical justice. No, the death of these people was the prologue to a reign of injustice still more terrible, affecting not only the party but our entire people.

Solzhenitsyn is prepared, oddly enough, to regard the entire Soviet people, Russians and non-Russians alike, as having deserved the unhappy fate they suffered in the 1920s, 1930s, and 1940s. Even in the first volume, having in mind not just the party but the most ordinary people of our land, he exclaimed: "We spent ourselves in one unrestrained outburst in 1917, and then we *hurried* to submit. We submitted *with pleasure!* . . . We purely and simply *deserved* everything that happened afterward" (Solzhenitsyn's emphasis). Many similar pronouncements can be found in the second volume as well. The error and injustice of this view seems too obvious to spend any time refuting it.

THE COMMUNIST CAPTIVES OF GULAG

Apparently the majority of those shot in 1937–1938 were Communists. In addition, however, hundreds of thousands of rank-and-file members and middle-level cadres of the party and youth organizations were arrested and sent to the camps along with other prisoners. Solzhenitsyn devotes one of the chapters of his second volume to their fate and discusses the Communists at some length in other chapters of this volume. Touching very briefly on those for whom "Communist convictions were inward and not constantly on the tips of their tongues," who did not make a great show of their "party attitude" and did not separate themselves from the other prisoners, Solzhenitsyn directs his attention mainly to those "orthodox Communists" and "loyalists" (the chapter on the Communists is entitled "The Loyalists") who sought to justify Stalin and his terror while they were in the camps, who would sing the [party song] lines "I know no other country/ Where a person breathes so freely" while en route in prisoner transports, and who considered virtually every other zek to have been justly condemned and only themselves to be suffering by accident. Solzhenitsyn finds a number of occasions for making fun of such "loyalists" and "orthodox Communists." Sometimes his irony is fully deserved. It is true that among the Communists arrested in 1937–1938 there were quite a few who continued to believe not only in Stalin but even in Yezhov, and who held themselves aloof from, or were even hostile toward, the other prisoners. But insight came rather quickly, although for understandable reasons it was not always complete, and after several months of "interrogation" the number of the "loyalists" and "orthodox" among arrested party members fell off rapidly. And there were very few of them in the camps. For the majority of Communists, however, condemnation of Stalin and the NKVD organs did not mean the repudiation of socialist and communist convictions.

Solzhenitsyn plainly sins against the truth when, in describing the fate of the Communists in the camps, he declares that they never objected to "the dominance of the thieves in the kitchens and among the trusties" and that "all the orthodox Communists . . . soon [got] themselves well fixed up." The author of *Gulag Archipelago* even raises the following hypothesis: "Yes, and were there not perhaps some written or at least oral directives: to make things easier for the Communists?"

No, Aleksandr Isayevich, no such directives ever existed, and you knew it well when, in your novel *One Day in the Life of Ivan Denisovich*, you told of the fate of the Communist Buinovsky, thrown into the cold punishment block for no reason.[17] From the fate enjoyed in the camps by Boris Dyakov and Galina Serebryakova,[18] you cannot draw conclusions about the position and conduct of the bulk of the Communists who found themselves in Stalin's camps. In many respects their circumstances were even worse than those of prisoners in other categories and quite a few of them died in the camps—in fact it is likely they died in greater numbers than other prisoners. On this point there are of course no reliable statistics. However, we know from the materials of party conferences, held after the 22nd Soviet Communist Party Congress,[19] that of the party members arrested in Moscow in 1936–39 only about 6 percent returned there in 1955–57. The remaining 94 percent were rehabilitated *posthumously.* And throughout the U.S.S.R., out of a million party members arrested in the latter half of the 1930s, not more than 60–80,000 returned after fifteen to eighteen years' imprisonment. The suffering they endured left a deep mark on these people, and very few were left among them who in any way resembled those Solzhenitsyn now writes of with such sarcasm.

SOCIALISM, REVOLUTION, OR RELIGION?

In part four of this book, on "The Soul and Barbed Wire," Solzhenitsyn specifically discusses his spiritual rebirth in the camps, his return to the belief in God instilled in him as an adolescent but abandoned by him as a young man in favor of Marxism. Although with reservations, the author, surprisingly enough, even expresses gratitude for the experience of the camps, for it was precisely the suffering he underwent in them that helped him return to the fold of

Christianity. *"Bless you, prison!"* the author writes in emphatic type at the close of his chapter "The Ascent."

In this part of his book Solzhenitsyn expresses some profound though very bitter thoughts. But much of what is written here strikes a false note (at least to my ears). All these extremely impassioned outcries against Marxism, "the infallible and intolerant doctrine," which demands only results, only matter and not *spirit*, all these arguments about how only faith in God saved and elevated the human spirit in the camps, while faith in the future triumph of social justice, in a better way of organizing society, failed to prevent spiritual corruption and virtually led one straight into the ranks of stool pigeons—all this has an unproved and arbitrary sound. A regrettable state of embitterment leads the author to that very "intolerance and infallibility" of judgment of which he accuses Marxism.

Solzhenitsyn does not even consider it possible for nonreligious people to distinguish between good and bad.

Equating socialism with Stalinism, he naturally cannot understand that there are people for whom the tragedy they or their countrymen experienced can only become a further incentive to struggle for social justice and for a better life for humanity on this earth, for the elimination of all forms of oppression of one person by another, including pseudosocialist forms of such oppression. Solzhenitsyn does not understand that socialist convictions can be the basis for a genuinely humanist set of values and a profoundly humane morality. And if up to now the problems of ethics and morals have not yet found satisfactory treatment in Marxist-Leninist theory, this by no means implies that scientific socialism is incapable by its very nature of establishing moral values.

Summing up the thinking he did in camp, Solzhenitsyn writes:

> Since then I have come to understand the truth of all the religions of the world: They struggle with the *evil inside a human being* (inside every human being). It is impossible to expel evil from the world in its entirety, but it is possible to constrict it within each person.
>
> And since that time I have come to understand the falsehood of all the revolutions in history: They destroy only *those carriers*

of evil contemporary with them (and also fail, out of haste, to discriminate the carriers of good as well). And they then take to themselves as their heritage the actual evil itself, magnified still more.

This juxtaposition seems to me neither accurate nor just. For it is necessary to fight against evil not only within each person, but also against the carriers of evil contemporary with us, and against unjust social institutions. This struggle goes on in various forms. Well and good if it takes the form of peaceful competition between ideologies and is realized through reforms and gradual changes for the better. But there still will be times when revolutionary forms of struggle must be resorted to, and although these may be accompanied by many sacrifices and disappointments, they by no means necessarily lead to the magnification of evil in the world. It is not socialist doctrine alone that can be distorted and turned against individuals and against all of humanity; so can the tenets of any religion. History offers more than a few examples of this, including the history of the Russian Orthodox Church, which has its own peculiar traditions of obscurantism. It is well known that in the sixteenth century the Russian Church was still burning heretics alive. Incidentally, one may find in Stalin's behavior and criminal actions not only the pragmatic attitude held by many revolutionaries toward violence and the use of extreme measures but also the dogmatism, casuistry, intolerance, and other qualities that are undoubtedly, to some extent, the result of his five years in an Orthodox school and three in an Orthodox seminary.

Terrible are the crimes Solzhenitsyn so vividly depicts in his book, and we are all as one with him in the condemnation of those crimes. But I continue to believe that only the victory of a genuinely socialist society, of genuinely socialist human and moral relations, can provide humanity with a firm guarantee that such crimes will never be repeated.

Translated by GEORGE SAUNDERS

Footnotes

1. *Zek:* In camp slang, abbreviation of the Russian word for "prisoner," *zaklyuchenny*.

2. Vorkuta: One of the largest labor camp complexes of the Stalin era, mainly set up for mining the coal of the Pechora River basin in the arctic northeast of European Russia. The town of the same name, center of the region, was built by prison labor in 1931–32 and is now a city of nearly 100,000. The Vorkuta camps were apparently dismantled after major strikes by prisoners in 1953.

3. Natalya Reshetovskaya (born 1920): Solzhenitsyn's first wife; they married in 1940, were separated by the war, then by his imprisonment in 1945; she divorced him in 1950 while he was in the camps. After his release and rehabilitation (1956–57), they remarried in the late 1950s before he won fame with *Ivan Denisovich*. In the late 1960s they separated again, and he established a relationship with his present wife, Natalya Svetlova. The authorities, to harass him further, long supported Reshetovskaya in her refusal to agree to a divorce. They were finally divorced by the time he was expelled from the U.S.S.R. Reshetovskaya's memoirs were published outside the Soviet Union (English edition, *Sanya: My Life with Solzhenitsyn*, New York, Bobbs-Merrill, 1975).

4. Viktor Semyonovich Abakumov (1894–1954): Minister of state security under Stalin and Beria, 1946–1952, tried and executed after Stalin's death.

5. Maxim Gorky (1868–1936): Prominent Russian writer who had close ties with Lenin and other Bolsheviks before the 1917 revolution. Critical of Soviet regime in its early years; often interceded with Lenin in behalf of threatened cultural and intellectual figures. After living in Western Europe, 1921–28, he returned to the U.S.S.R. and was highly favored by the Stalin regime. Died under mysterious circumstances, allegedly poisoned, on the eve of the first great Moscow show trial.

6. *Solovki, Solovetsky; Cheka, Chekist:* "Solovki" is slang for the Solovetsky camp, on the Solovetsky Islands; see the description of the camp in *Gulag Archipelago*, vol. II, chap. 2.

The Cheka was the first Soviet state-security organization (1917–22). The acronym derives from the Russian initials Ch and K, the official name being Chrezvychaynaya Kommissiya, or Extraordinary Commission. The state-security organs (secret police) were frequently renamed, and at various times known by such initials as GPU, OGPU, NKVD, MVD, MGB, and now KGB. But over the years *Chekist*, originally meaning member of the Cheka, has stayed on as an informal term for any Soviet secret police agent, regardless of the official initials at the time.

7. Pyotr Nikolayevich Krasnov (1869–1947): General of the czarist army; tried to suppress the October 1917 revolution in Petrograd; led rebellion against Soviet rule in Don Cossack region in 1918–1919; resigned and went into exile in Germany, many of his forces joining Gen. A. I. Denikin's White army.

8. NEP: The New Economic Policy, introduced in 1921, under which peasants were allowed to trade on the market and were taxed a certain amount of grain or other produce instead of having it requisitioned by the state. Grain requisitioning had been the policy under "war communism" during the 1918–20 civil war. The NEP ended with the beginning of forced collectivization and industrialization in 1929–30.

9. "Political isolators": Separate Soviet prisons for holding political oppositionists of the non-Communist left or dissident Communists.

10. NKVD: Narodnyi Kommissariat Vnutrennikh Del, or People's Commissariat of Internal Affairs, official name of the Soviet state-security organization (1934–46), made especially notorious by its role in the Great Purge of 1936–38.

11. Tukhachevsky, Tambov, Spiridonova: Mikhail Nikolayevich Tukhachevsky (1893–1937), one of the group of top Red Army leaders shot on Stalin's orders in the 1937 purge. Came to prominence as a Red general in the civil war. Active in the suppression of an anti-Bolshevik peasant rebellion in Tambov province in 1921–1922, which was led by members of the Socialist Revolutionary Party (SRs): Tambov province, in the Volga region of European Russia, was the center of SR influence from before the 1905–06 revolution. During that revolution the SR terrorist Mariya Aleksandrovna Spiridonova (1884–1941) shot the czarist official in charge of suppressing a Tambov peasant rebellion. Spiridonova was sent to hard labor for many years. In 1917 she emerged as a leader of the Left SR party, which joined the Bolsheviks in the first Soviet government but began to oppose them in 1918, led a number of revolts and assassinated Bolshevik leaders. Spiridonova was arrested in late 1918, imprisoned for a time, and after being amnestied, quit politics. Arrested by the NKVD in 1937, she died in the camps.

12. Pushkin; Riego: Aleksandr S. Pushkin (1799–1837), Russia's foremost classical poet. These four lines are from his 1825 poem "Na Vorontsova," written in response to a remark made by Count Vorontsov, a courtier of the czar.

Colonel Rafael del Riego y Nuñez (1785–1823) was the leader of a constitutionalist rebellion in 1820 against Ferdinand VI, king of Spain. Czar Alexander I urged the Holy Alliance to intervene in Ferdinand's behalf, and in November 1823 troops of the Holy Alliance defeated Riego's forces, and Riego was captured and executed. When word of this reached Czar Alexander's court, Count Vorontsov was heard to remark, "What happy news, Your Majesty; one scoundrel less in the world."

13. Krylenko; Butyrka: Nikolai Vasilyevich Krylenko (1885–1938), active Bolshevik from 1904. First people's commissar of war in 1917–1918; chief state prosecutor for important political trials, 1918–1931. Made commissar of justice of the Russian Republic in 1931, and of the U.S.S.R. in 1936. Arrested in 1937 and shot without trial. Butyrka—an old prison in Moscow that held political prisoners under the czars (built under Catherine the Great in the eighteenth century). Under Stalin it was one of three main prisons where "politicals" were held for interrogation and sentencing.

14. Latsis and Peters: Prominent Cheka officials of the civil war period, both Latvians. Martyn Ivanovich Latsis (1888–1938 or 1941, real name Yan Fridrikhovich Sudrabs), transferred to economic work in 1921; arrested in the Great Purge. Yakov Khristoforovich Peters (1886–1938), deputy chief of GPU, 1925–30.

15. Yezhov, Beria, Zakovsky: Nikolai Ivanovich Yezhov (1895–1939 or 1940), minor party official promoted by Stalin in early 1930s; made people's commissar of internal affairs in September 1936, to preside over the Great Purge of 1936–38, which is often called the Yezhovshchina ("the time of Yezhov") because of his role. Replaced by Beria in December 1938; arrested and shot.

Lavrenty Pavlovich Beria (1899–1953); chief of state security in Transcaucasia, 1921–31; head of Transcaucasian party organization after that. Replaced Yezhov as commissar of internal affairs; remained chief of Soviet security until his execution shortly after Stalin's death.

Leonid M. Zakovsky: A deputy commissar of the NKVD, 1934–38; supervised Leningrad and Moscow purges in 1937–38; liquidated soon after Beria replaced Yezhov as head of NKVD.

16. Varlam Tikhonovich Shalamov (born 1907): Soviet writer, survivor of seventeen years in the Kolyma camp complex in the Soviet Far East. His Kolyma Stories circulate in manuscript in the U.S.S.R.; published in a French edition: Récits de Kolyma (Paris, 1969). One of these stories, "Lend-Lease Comes to a Soviet Camp," appeared in DISSENT (Summer 1974).

17. Buinovsky: In Solzhenitsyn's story, the idealistic and defiant ex-naval commander, sent to the camps as a "spy" because an Allied officer he had met during wartime service had mailed him a gift. (Modeled after Boris Burkovsky, a fellow inmate of the author's.)

18. Boris Dyakov (born 1902) and Galina Serebryakova (born 1905): Both are Soviet writers and former camp inmates (Solzhenitsyn dismisses them as trusties). In the post-Stalin era both became prominent on the conservative side in Soviet literary disputes. Dyakov, author of standard socialist-realist production novels, wrote memoirs of the camps that were published in a Soviet magazine in early 1963 and reissued as a book in 1966. These *Memoirs of Survival* (*Povest o perezhitom*) were praised by conservatives, who counterposed them to Solzhenitsyn's *Ivan Denisovich* because Dyakov stressed faith in the party despite the cruelties in the camps. Serebryakova's memoirs, entitled *Sandstorm*, were published in a Soviet newspaper in 1964, but did not come out in book form in the U.S.S.R.

19. The 22d Congress of the Communist party of the U.S.S.R., held Oct. 17–31, 1961, publicly revived and extended the de-Stalinization campaign that had subsided a year or so after Khrushchev's secret speech at the 1956 20th Congress. The 22d Congress set off a new series of official investigations and revelations about the Stalin era that were only brought to a halt in the latter half of the 1960s, under Brezhnev and Kosygin. A notable event during the 22d Congress was the removal of Stalin's remains from the Lenin mausoleum.

MARSHALL BERMAN
"All That Is Solid Melts into Air"
Marx, Modernism, and
Modernization
(1978)

Several years ago I began a study of modernity. I meant to explore both the history of ideas—such ideas as "modern times," "modern society," "the modern predicament," and so on—and the human realities that these ideas were meant to grasp. I found that two large bodies of thought and discussion about modernity have appeared in the last twenty years, organized around two separate and distinct ideas: Modernization and Modernism.

"Modernization" has come to signify a complex of social, economic, and political processes: sustained economic development, industrial expansion, urban growth, bureaucratic regulation and rationality, mass media, mass participation in politics—including at least the pretense of democracy—large-scale social planning, shattering of traditional cultures and forms of life, continuous pressure to raise productivity and make progress. "Modernism" has come to denote a family of artistic and intellectual movements that have been radically experimental, spiritually turbulent and militant, iconoclastic to the point of nihilism, apocalyptic in their hopes and fantasies, savagely destructive to one another—and often to themselves as well—yet capable of recurrent self-renewal. Writers on modernization project us into a world of power plants, steel mills, mass rallies and media events, growth rates, five-year plans. When we read about modernism, we find ourselves in the midst of an endless series of spiritual upheavals and cultural

341

revolutions—the death of God, the theater of cruelty, Dada, jazz, the twelve-tone scale, Existentialism, abstract art, and on and on. I was surprised to find that writers in each group were, with very few exceptions, wholly unaware of the existence of the other.[1] It seemed bizarre that there should be no connection between them: after all, weren't they all thrown into the same modern world? I wanted to make these two worlds connect by discovering the underlying unity of life and experience that sustains them both.

As I explored the literature on modernization, I found, not surprisingly, that the figure of Marx bulks large. Even those writers who claim to refute and surpass him generally recognize his work as a primary source and point of reference for their own. On the other hand, in the literature on modernism, Marx is not recognized in any way at all. Modernist consciousness and culture are often traced back to his generation, the generation that came of age in the 1840s —to Baudelaire, Flaubert, Wagner, Kierkegaard, Dostoevsky—but Marx himself does not even rate a small branch on the genealogical tree: if he is even mentioned in this company, it is as a foil, or sometimes as a survival of an earlier and serener age—the Enlightenment, say—whose clear vistas and solid values modernism supposedly destroys. Some writers see Marxism as a dead weight that stifles the modernist spirit; others (Georg Lukacs is the most prominent) see Marx's outlook as far saner, healthier, and more "real" than those of the modernists; but everybody seems to agree that he and they are worlds apart.[2]

And yet, the closer I got to Marx, the less this dualism made sense. Take an image like this: "All that is solid melts into air. . . ." The cosmic scope and visionary grandeur of this image, its highly compressed dramatic power, its vaguely apocalyptic undertones, the ambiguity of its point of view—the heat that destroys is also superabundant energy, an overflow of life—all these qualities are supposed to be hallmarks of the modernist imagination. They are just the sort of thing we are prepared to find in Rimbaud or Nietzsche, Rilke or Yeats—"Things fall apart, the center does not hold." In fact, my image comes from Marx—not from any esoteric, long hidden Marx, but from the heart of the *Communist Manifesto*. It comes as the climax of Marx's description of "modern bourgeois society."

The affinities between Marx and the modernists are even clearer if we look at the whole of the sentence from which our image is drawn: "All that is solid melts into air, all that is holy is profaned, and men at last are forced to face the real conditions of their lives and their relations with their fellow men."[3] Marx's second clause, which proclaims the destruction of everything holy, is more complex and more interesting than the standard nineteenth-century materialist assertion that God does not exist. Marx is moving in the dimension of time, working to evoke an ongoing historical drama and trauma. He is saying that the aura of holiness is suddenly missing, and that we can't understand ourselves in the present until we confront what is absent. The final clause, "and men at last are forced to face. . .," not only describes a confrontation with a perplexing reality, but acts it out, forces it on the reader—and, indeed, on the writer too, for "*die Menschen*" are all in it together, at once subjects and objects of the pervasive process that melts everything solid into air.

As I followed this modernist "melting" vision, I found it throughout Marx's works. Everywhere it pulls like an undertow against the more "solid" Marxian visions we know so well. It is especially vivid and striking in the *Communist Manifesto*. Indeed, it opens up a whole new perspective on the *Manifesto*, as the archetype of a century of modernist manifestos and movements to come. This is the perspective I will develop here. I will take the *Manifesto* as my text and explicate several of its images and ideas, to show how it expresses some of modernist culture's deepest insights and, at the same time dramatizes some of its deepest inner contradictions.

At this point it wouldn't be unreasonable to ask: Aren't there already more than enough interpretations of Marx? do we really need a modernist Marx, a kindred spirit of Eliot and Kafka and Gertrude Stein and Artaud, on top of all the rest? I think we do, not only because he's there, but because he has something distinctive and important to say. Marx, in fact, can tell us as much about modernism as it can tell us about him. Modernist thought, so brilliant in illuminating the dark side of everyone and everything, turns out to have some repressed dark corners of its own, and Marx can shine new light on these. Specifically, he can clarify the relationship between modernist culture and the bourgeois economy and society—the world of "modernization"—from which it has sprung.

We will see that they have far more in common than either modernists or bourgeoisie would like to think. We will see Marxism, modernism, and the bourgeoisie caught up in a strange dialectical dance, and if we follow their movements we may learn some important things about the modern world we all share.

THE MELTING VISION AND ITS DIALECTIC

The central drama for which the *Manifesto* is famous is the development of the bourgeoisie and the proletariat, and the struggle between them. But we can also find a plan going on within this play, a struggle inside the author's consciousness over what is really going on, what the larger struggle means. We might describe this conflict as a tension between Marx's "solid" and his "melting" visions of modern life.

The *Manifesto*'s first section, "Bourgeois and Proletarians," sets out to present an account of what is now called the process of modernization and sets the stage for what Marx believes will be its revolutionary climax. Here Marx describes the solid institutional core of modernity. First of all, there is the emergence of a world market. As it spreads, it absorbs and destroys whatever local and regional markets it touches. Production and consumption—and human needs—become increasingly international and cosmopolitan. The scope of human needs and demands is enlarged far beyond the capacities of local industries, which consequently collapse. The scale of communications becomes worldwide, and mass media emerge. Capital is concentrated in a few hands. Independent peasants and artisans cannot compete with big capital and are forced to leave the land. Production is increasingly centralized and rationalized in factories or vast agricultural estates run like factories. The poor and uprooted pour into cities, which grow almost magically— and catastrophically—overnight. In order for all these changes to go on smoothly, administrative, legal, fiscal and political centralization must take place, and they do. National states arise and accumulate vast power, although that power is continually undermined by the international scope of capital. Meanwhile, the industrial workers, terribly exploited, gradually begin to organize. In all this we are on familiar ground.

As we read all this, however, strange things begin to happen. Marx's prose suddenly becomes luminous, incandescent; brilliant images succeed and blend into one another; we are hurtled along with a reckless momentum, a breathless intensity; he is not only describing, but evoking and enacting the desperate pace and frantic rhythm that capitalism imparts to every facet of modern life. He makes us feel that we are part of the action, drawn into the stream, hurtled along, out of control, at once dazzled and menaced by the onward rush. After a few pages of this, we are exhilarated but perplexed; we find that the solid social formations around us have, indeed, melted away. By the time Marx's proletarians finally appear, the world stage on which they were supposed to play their part has disintegrated and metamorphosed into something unrecognizable, surreal, a mobile construction that shifts and changes shape under the players' feet. It is as if the innate dynamism of the melting vision has run away with Marx, and carried him—and the workers, and us—far beyond the range of his intended plot, to a point where his revolutionary script will have to be radically reworked.

The paradoxes at the heart of the *Manifesto* are manifest almost at its very start: specifically, from the moment Marx starts to describe the modern bourgeoisie. "The bourgeoisie," he begins, "has played a most revolutionary role in history." What is startling about Marx's next few pages—and his original readers, in 1848, must have been even more startled than we are today—is that he seems to have come not to bury the bourgeoisie but to praise it. He writes an impassioned, enthusiastic, often lyrical celebration of bourgeois works, ideas, and achievements. Indeed, in these pages he manages to praise the bourgeoisie more powerfully and profoundly than its members have ever known how to praise themselves.

What have the bourgeois done to deserve Marx's praise? For one thing, they have "been the first to show what man's activity can bring about." Marx does not mean that they have been the first to celebrate the ideal of *vita activa*, an activistic stance toward the world. This has been a central theme of Western culture since the Renaissance; it has taken on new depths and resonances in Marx's own century, in the age of Romanticism and Revolution, of Napoleon and Byron and Goethe's *Faust;* Marx himself will develop it in new directions, and it will go on evolving into our own era. Marx's point is that what modern poets, artists, and intellectuals have only dreamed of, the modern bourgeoisie has actually done. Thus it has "accomplished wonders that far surpass Egyptian pyramids, Roman aqueducts, and Gothic cathedrals"; it has "conducted expeditions that put all former migrations of nations and crusades in the shade." Its genius for activity expresses itself, first of all, in great works of physical construction—mills and factories, granaries, bridges, canals—these are the cathedrals of modernity; next, in immense movements of people—to cities, to frontiers, to new lands—which the bourgeoisie has sometimes subsidized, sometimes brutally enforced, sometimes inspired. Marx, in a stirring, evocative paragraph, transmits the rhythm and drama of bourgeois activism:

> The bourgeoisie, in its reign of barely a hundred years, has created more massive and more colossal productive power than have all previous generations put together. Subjection of nature's forces to man, machinery, application of chemistry to agriculture and industry, steam navigation, railways, electric telegraphs, clearing of whole continents for cultivation, canalization of rivers, whole populations conjured out of the ground— what earlier century had even an intimation that such productive power slept in the womb of social labor?

Marx is neither the first nor the last writer to celebrate the triumphs of bourgeois technology and social organization. But his paean is distinctive both in what it emphasizes and in what it leaves out. Although Marx is supposedly a materialist (he has identified himself as such since 1844), he does not seem especially interested in the things, the material structures that the bourgeoisie creates. What matters here is the processes, the powers, the expressions of life and energy: men working, moving, cultivating, communicating, organizing and reorganizing nature and themselves; the new and endlessly renewed modes of activity that the bourgeoisie brings into being. Marx does not dwell much on particular inventions and innovations in their own right (in the tradition that runs from Saint-Simon through McLuhan); what stirs him is the active and generative process through which one thing leads to another, dreams metamorphose into blueprints and fantasies into accounts, the wildest and most extravagant ideas get acted on and acted out ("whole populations conjured out of the ground"), and ignite and nourish new forms of life and action.

The irony of bourgeois activism, as Marx sees it, is that the bourgeoisie is forced to close itself off from its richest possibilities, possibilities that can be realized only by those who break its power. For all the marvelous modes of activity the bourgeoisie has opened up, the only activity that really means anything to its members is making money, accumulating capital, piling up surplus value; all their enterprises are merely means to this end, in themselves of no more than transient and intermediary interest. The active power and processes that mean so much to Marx appear as mere incidental by-products in the minds of their producers. Nevertheless, the bourgeois have established themselves as the first ruling class whose authority is based not on who their ancestors were but on what they themselves actually do. They have produced vivid new images and paradigms of the good life as a life of action. They have proved that it is possible, through organized and concerted action, to really change the world.

Alas, to the bourgeois' embarrassment, they cannot afford to look down the roads they have opened up: the great wide vistas may turn into abysses. They can go on playing their revolutionary role only by denying its full extent and depth. But radical thinkers and workers are free to see where the roads lead, and to take them. If the good life is a life of action, why should the range of human activities be limited to those that are profitable? And why should modern men, who have seen what man's activity can bring about, passively accept the structure of their society as it is given? Since organized and con-certed action can change the world in so many ways, why not organize and work together and fight to change it still more? It is only a matter of time before this dialectic is thought through and worked out. The "revolutionary activity, practical-critical activity" (as Marx put it in 1845) that overthrows bourgeois rule will be an expression of the active and activistic energies that the bourgeoisie itself has set free. Marx began by praising the bourgeoisie, not by burying it; but if his dialectic works out, it will be the virtues for which he praised the bourgeoisie that will bury it in the end.

The second great bourgeois achievement has been to liberate the human capacity and drive for development: for permanent change, for perpetual upheaval and renewal in every form of personal and social life. This drive, Marx shows, is embedded in the everyday workings and needs of the bourgeois economy. Everybody within reach of this economy finds himself under pressure of relentless competition, whether from across the street or across the world. Under pressure, every bourgeois, from the pettiest to the most powerful, is forced to innovate, simply in order to keep his business and himself afloat; anyone who does not actively change, on his own, will become a passive victim of changes draconically imposed by his rivals. This means that the bourgeoisie, taken as a whole, "cannot exist without constantly revolutionizing the means of production."

But the forces that shape and drive the economy cannot be compartmentalized and cut off from the totality of life. The intense and relentless pressure to revolutionize production is bound to spill over and to transform what Marx calls "conditions of production" (or, alternately, "productive relationships") as well, "and, with them, all social conditions" and relationships.[4]

At this point Marx is ready to soar into one of his great set pieces, propelled by the desperate dynamism that he is striving to grasp:

> Constant revolutionizing of production, uninterrupted disturbance of all social relations, everlasting uncertainty and agitation distinguish the bourgeois epoch from all earlier times. All fixed, fast-frozen relationships with their train of venerable ideas and opinions are swept away, all new-formed ones become obsolete before they can ossify. All that is solid melts into air, all that is holy is profaned, and men at last are forced to face the real conditions of their lives and their relations with their fellow men.

Where does all this leave us, the members of modern bourgeois society? It leaves us in strange and paradoxical positions. Our lives are controlled by a ruling class with vested interests, not merely in change, but in crisis and chaos. "Uninterrupted disturbance, everlasting uncertainty and agitation," instead of subverting this society, actually serve to strengthen it. Catastrophes are transformed into lucrative opportunities for redevelopment and renewal; disintegration works as a mobilizing and hence an integrating force. The one specter that really haunts the modern ruling class, and that really endangers the world it has created in its image, is one thing that traditional elites—and, for that matter, traditional masses—have always yearned for: solid stability. In this world stability can only mean entropy, slow death, while our sense of progress and growth is our only way of knowing for sure that we are still alive. To say that our society is falling apart is only to say that it is alive and well.

What kinds of people do these permanent revolutions produce? In order for anyone, whatever their class, to survive in modern bourgeois society, their personality must take on an open form. Modern men and women must learn to yearn for change: not merely to be open to changes in their personal and social lives, but positively to demand them, actively to seek them out and carry them through. They must learn not to yearn nostalgically for the "fixed, fast-frozen relationships" of the real or fantasized past, but to delight in mobility, to thrive on renewal, to look forward to future developments in their conditions of life and their relations with their fellow men.

Marx absorbs this developmental ideal from the German humanist culture of his youth, from the thought of Goethe and Schiller and their Romantic successors. (This theme and its development, still very much alive in our own day, may be Germany's deepest and most lasting contribution to world culture.) Marx is perfectly clear about his links to these writers, to whom he is constantly alluding (to Goethe most of all), and to their intellectual tradition. But he understands better than any of his predecessors that the humanistic ideal of self-development grows out of the emerging reality of bourgeois economic development. Thus, for all his criticism and loathing of the bourgeois economy, he embraces enthusiastically the modern personality structure that this economy has produced. The trouble with capitalism is that, here as elsewhere, it destroys the human possibilities it creates. It fosters, indeed forces, self-development for everybody, but we can only develop in warped, distorted ways. Those traits, impulses, talents that the market can use are rushed (often prematurely) into development, and squeezed desperately till there is nothing left; everything else within us, everything nonmarketable, gets draconically repressed, or withers away for lack of use, or never has a chance to come to life at all. The outcome of Marx's dialectic is that "the development of modern industry cuts from under its feet the very foundation on which the bourgeoisie produces and appropriates products." The inner life and energy of bourgeois development will sweep away the class that first brought it to life. We see this dialectical movement as much in the sphere of personal as in economic development: in a system where all situations and ideas, human values and relationships are volatile, how can capitalist forms of life—private property, wage-labor, exchange-value, the insatiable pursuit of profit—alone hold still?

Where the desires and sensibilities of people in every class have become open-ended and insatiable, attuned to permanent upheavals in every sphere of life, what can possibly keep them fixed and frozen in their bourgeois social roles? The more furiously bourgeois society agitates its members to grow or die, the more likely they will be to outgrow it, the more furiously they will eventually turn on it as a drag on their growth, the more implacably they will fight it in the name of the new life it has forced them to seek. Thus capitalism will be melted by the heat of its own incandescent energies. After the Revolution, "in the course of development," after wealth is redistributed, class privileges are wiped away, education is free and universal, then—so Marx prophesies at the *Manifesto*'s climactic moment —then, at last,

> In place of the old bourgeois society, with its classes and class antagonisms, we will have an association in which the free development of each will be the condition for the free development of all.

Then the experience of self-development, released from the demands and distortions of the market, can go on freely and spontaneously; instead of the nightmare that it so often is in bourgeois society, it can be a source of beauty and joy for all.

This vision of communism is unmistakably modern, first of all in its individualism, but even more in its ideal of development as the form of the good life. Here Marx is closer to some of his bourgeois and liberal enemies than he is to traditional exponents of communism, who, since Plato and the Church Fathers, have sanctified self-sacrifice, distrusted or loathed individuality, and yearned for a still point at which all strife, and all striving, reach an end. Once again we find Marx more responsive to what is going on in bourgeois society than are the members and proponents of the bourgeoisie themselves. He sees in the dynamics of capitalist development—both the development of each individual and of society as a whole—a new image of the good life: not a life of definitive perfection, not the embodiment of prescribed static essences, but a process of continual, restless, open-ended, unbounded growth. Thus he hopes to heal the wounds of modernity through a fuller and deeper modernity.

We can see, then, why Marx gets so excited and enthusiastic about the bourgeoisie and the world it has made. Now we must confront something even more perplexing: next to the *Communist Manifesto*, the whole body of literature in praise of capitalism, from Adam Ferguson to Milton Friedman, is remarkably lame, pale, empty of life. The celebrants of capitalism tell us surprisingly little of its infinite horizons, its revolutionary energy and audacity, its dynamic creativity, its adventurousness and romance, its capacity to make men not merely more comfortable but more alive.

For all this we must go to its most notorious enemy, to Marx. The members of the bourgeoisie (and their ideologists), never known for humility or modesty, seem strangely determined to hide much of their light under a bushel. The reason, I think, is that there is a dark side to this light that they cannot blot out. They are dimly aware of this, and deeply embarrassed and frightened by it, so that they will ignore or deny their own strength and creativity rather than look their virtues in the face and live with them. What is it that the members of the bourgeoisie are afraid to recognize in themselves? Not their drive to exploit people, to treat them purely as means or (in economic rather than moralistic language) as commodities. Marx's bourgeoisie doesn't lose much sleep over this. After all, its members do it to themselves—it is the way they define themselves—so why shouldn't they do the same to everybody else? The source of the trouble is the bourgeois claim to be "the Party of Order" in modern civilization. The immense amounts of money and energy put into building, and the self-consciously monumental quality of so much of this building—indeed, throughout Marx's century, every piece of furniture built for a bourgeois interior was itself a monument—

testify to the sincerity and seriousness of this claim. And yet, the truth of the matter, as Marx understands, is that everything that bourgeois society builds is built to be torn down. "All that is solid"—from the clothes on our backs to the looms and mills that weave them, to the men who work the machines, the houses and neighborhoods the workers live in, the firms and corporations that support and exploit them, the towns and cities and whole regions and even nations that embrace them all—all are made to be broken tomorrow, smashed or shredded or pulverized or biodegraded, so they can be recycled or replaced next week, and the whole process can go on again and again, hopefully forever, in ever more profitable forms.

The pathos of all bourgeois monuments is that their material strength and solidity actually count for nothing and carry no weight at all, that they are blown away like frail reeds by the very forces of capitalist development that they celebrate. Even the most beautiful and impressive bourgeois buildings and public works are disposable, capitalized for fast depreciation and planned to be obsolete, closer in their functions and their fate to tents and camps than to the "Egyptian pyramids, Roman aqueducts, and Gothic cathedrals."[5]

If we look behind the sober scenes the members of our bourgeoisie create and see the way they really work and act, we realize that these solid citizens would tear down the world if it paid. Even as they frighten everyone with fantasies of proletarian rapacity and revenge they themselves, through their inexhaustible dealing and developing, hurtle masses of men, materials and money up and down the earth, and erode or explode the foundations of everybody's lives as they go. Their secret—a secret they have managed to keep even from themselves—is that, behind their staid façades, they are the most violently destructive ruling class in history. All the anarchic, measureless, explosive drives that a later generation of intellectuals will baptize with the name of Nihilism—drives that Nietzsche and his followers will ascribe to such cosmic traumas as "the death of God"—are located by Marx in the seemingly banal everyday working of the market economy. He unveils the modern bourgeois as consummate nihilists in action on a scale far vaster than modern intellectuals can ever dream.

The members of the bourgeoisie have alienated themselves from their own creativity because they cannot bear to look into the moral, social, and psychic abyss that their creativity opens up. Some of Marx's most vivid and striking images are meant to force us all to confront that abyss. Thus, "modern bourgeois society, a society that has conjured up such mighty means of production and exchange, is like the sorcerer who can no longer control the powers of the underworld that he has called up by his spells." This image evokes all the spirits of that dark medieval past our modern bourgeoisie is supposed to have buried. Its members present themselves as matter-of-fact and rational, not magical; as children of the Enlightenment, not of darkness. When Marx depicts the bourgeois as sorcerers—remember, too, their enterprise has "conjured whole populations out of the ground," not to mention "the specter of communism"—he is pointing to depths they deny. Marx's imagery projects, here as ever, a sense of wonder over the modern world: its vital powers are dazzling, overwhelming, beyond anything the bourgeoisie could have imagined, let alone calculated or planned. But Marx's images also express what must accompany any genuine sense of wonder: a sense of dread. For this miraculous and magical world is also demonic and terrifying, swinging wildly out of control, menacing and devastating blindly as it moves. The members of the bourgeoisie repress both wonder and dread at what they have made: these possessors don't want to know how deeply they are possessed. They learn only at moments of personal and general ruin—only, that is, when it is too late.

Marx's bourgeois sorcerer in fact descends directly from two literary figures who haunted the imagination of his whole generation: Frankenstein (Mary Shelley, 1819) and Faust (Goethe's *Faust*, completed in 1831). These mythical figures, striving to expand human powers through reason and science, unleash demonic energies that erupt beyond all human control, with horrifying results. Marx's bourgeoisie moves within this tragic orbit. But he places its underworld in a worldly context, he shows its dark powers working in broad daylight, propelling a million factories, exchanges, mills, and banks: his vision brings this abyss close to home.

Thus Marx lays out the polarities that will shape and animate the culture of modernism in the century to come: the theme of permanent revolution, infinite development, perpetual creation and renewal in every sphere of life; and its radical antithesis, the theme of nihilism, insatiable destruction, shattering and swallowing up the heart of darkness, the horror. Marx shows how both these human possibilities are infused into the life of every modern man by the drives and pressures of the bourgeois economy. Later on, modernists will produce a great array of cosmic and apocalyptic visions, visions of the most radiant joy and the bleakest despair. Many of the most creative modernist artists and thinkers will be simultaneously possessed by both, and driven endlessly from pole to pole; their inner dynamism will reproduce and express the inward rhythms by which modern capitalism moves and lives. Marx plunges us into the depths of this life process, so that we feel ourselves charged with a vital energy that magnifies our whole being—and are simultaneously seized by shocks and convulsions that threaten at every instant to destroy us.

Then by the power of his language and ideas, he tries to entice us to trust his vision, to let ourselves be swept along with him toward a climax that lies just ahead. The sorcerer's apprentices, the members of the revolutionary proletariat, are bound to wrest control of our modern productive forces from the grasp of the Faustian-Frankensteinian bourgeoisie. When this is done, they will transform these volatile, explosive social forces into sources of joy and beauty for all, and bring the tragic history of modernity to a happy end. Whether or not this ending should ever really come to pass, the *Manifesto* is remarkable for its imaginative power, its expression and grasp of the luminous and dreadful possibilities that pervade modern life. Along with everything else it is, it's the first great modernist work of art.

But even as we honor the *Manifesto* as an archetype of modernism, we must remember that archetypal models serve to typify not only truths and strengths but also inner tensions and strains. Thus, both in the *Manifesto* and in its illustrious successors, we will find that against the creator's intentions and probably without his awareness, the vision of revolution and resolution generates its own immanent critique, and new contradictions thrust themselves through the veil that this vision weaves. Even as we let ourselves be carried along by Marx's dialectical flow, we feel ourselves being carried away by uncharted currents of uncertainty and unease. We are caught up in a series of radical tensions between Marx's intentions and his insights, between what he wants and what he sees.

Take, for instance, Marx's vision of the revolutionary community. Its foundations will be laid, ironically, by the bourgeoisie itself: "The progress of industry, whose inadvertent promoter is the bourgeoisie, replaces the isolation of the workers through competition with their union [*Vereinigung*] through association." The immense productive units inherent in modern industry will throw large numbers of workers together, will force them to depend on each other and to cooperate in their work—the modern division of labor requires intricate cooperation from moment to moment on a vast scale—and so will teach them to think and act collectively. The workers' communal bonds, generated by capitalist production, will generate militant political organizations, unions that will oppose and finally overthrow the private, atomistic framework of capitalist social relations. So Marx believes. And yet, if his overall vision of modernity is true, why should the forms of community produced by capitalist industry be any more solid than any other capitalist product? Might not these collectivities turn out to be, like everything else here, only temporary, provisional, built to obsolesce? Marx, in 1856, will speak of the workers, as "newfangled men, . . . as much an invention of modern times as machinery itself." But if this is so, then their solidarity, too, however impressive at any given moment, may prove to be as transient as the machines they operate or the products they turn out. The workers may sustain each other today, on the assembly line or the picket line, only to find themselves scattered tomorrow among different collectivities with different conditions, different processes and products, different needs and interests. It appears that only the abstract forms of capitalism subsist—capital, wage labor, exploitation, surplus value—while their human contents are in perpetual flux. How can any lasting human bonds grow in such loose shifting soil?

Even if these workers do build a successful revolutionary *movement*, how, amid the flood tides of modern life, will they ever manage to build a solid communist *society*? What is to prevent the social forces that melt capitalism from melting communism as well? If all new relationships become obsolete before they can ossify, how can solidarity, fraternity, mutual aid be kept alive? A socialist government might try to dam the flood by imposing radical restrictions on personal, economic, cultural development. All "socialist" governments in our century have in fact done this, with different degrees of success.

To the extent that such a policy is effective, doesn't it, however, betray the Marxian aim of free development for each and all? Marx looks forward to communism as the consummation of modernity; but how can it entrench itself in the modern world without suppressing those very modern energies it promises to set free? On the other hand, if it gives those energies free rein mightn't the spontaneous flow of popular energy sweep away the new social formation itself?

Thus, simply by reading the *Manifesto* closely, and taking its vision of modernity seriously, we arrive at serious questions about Marx's answers. We can see that the fulfillment Marx sees as just around the bend may be a long time coming, if it comes at all; and we can see that, even if it does come, it may well be only a fleeting, transitory historical episode, gone in a moment, obsolete before it can ossify, swept away by the same tide of perpetual change and progress that brought it briefly within our reach, leaving us endlessly, helplessly floating on. We can see, too, how communism, in order to hold itself together, might stifle the active, dynamic, and developmental forces that have brought it into being, might betray many of the hopes that have made it worth fighting for, might reproduce the inequities and contradictions of bourgeois society under a new name. Ironically, then, we can see Marx's dialectic of modernity reenacting the fate of the society it describes, generating energies and ideas that melt it down into its own air.

NAKEDNESS: THE UNACCOMMODATED MEN

Now that we have seen Marx's "melting" vision in action, I want to use it to explicate several of the *Manifesto*'s most powerful images of modern life. In the passage below, Marx is trying to show how capitalism has transformed people's relationships both with each other and with themselves. Although, in Marx's syntax, "the bourgeoisie" is the subject—it is its economic activities that bring the big changes about—modern men and women of every class are objects, for all are changed:

> The bourgeoisie has torn apart the many feudal ties that bound men to their "natural superiors," and left no other bond between man and man than naked interest, than callous cash payment. It has drowned the heavenly ecstasies of pious fanaticism, of chivalrous enthusiasm, of philistine sentimentalism, in the icy water of egoistical calculation. . . . The bourgeoisie has stripped of its halo every occupation hitherto honored and looked up to with reverent awe. . . . The bourgeoisie has torn away from the family its sentimental veil, and turned the family relation into a pure money relation. . . . In place of exploitation veiled by religious and political illusions, it has put open, shameless, direct, bare exploitations.

Marx's basic opposition here is between what is open or naked and what is hidden, veiled, or clothed. This polarity, perennial in Eastern as well as Western thought, symbolizes everywhere a distinction between a "real" world and an illusory one. In most ancient and medieval speculative thought, the whole world of sensuous experience appears illusory—the Hindu "veil of Maya"—and the true world is thought to be accessible only through transcendence of bodies, space, and time. In some traditions, reality is accessible through religious or philosophical meditation; in others, it will be available to us only in a future existence after death—the Pauline "for now we see through a glass darkly, but then face to face."

The modern variation, beginning in the age of the Renaissance and Reformation, places both these worlds on earth, in space and time, filled with human beings. Now the false world is seen as a historical past, a world we have lost (or are in the process of losing), while the true world is the physical and social world that exists for us here and now (or is in the process of coming into being). At this point a new symbolism emerges: clothes become an emblem of the old, illusory mode of life, nakedness comes to signify the newly discovered and experienced truth, and the act of taking off one's clothes becomes a symbol of spiritual liberation, of becoming real. Modern erotic poetry elaborates this theme with playful irony; modern tragedy penetrates its awesome and fearsome depths. Marx thinks and works in the tragic tradition: for him, the clothes are ripped off, the veils are torn away, the stripping process is violent and brutal;

and yet, somehow, the tragic movement of modern history is supposed to culminate in a happy end.

The dialectic of nakedness that culminates in Marx is defined at the very start of the modern age, in Shakespeare's *King Lear.* For Lear, the naked truth is what a man is forced to face when he has lost everything that other men can take away except life itself. We see his voracious family, aided by his blind vanity, tear away its own sentimental veil. Stripped not only of political power, but of even the barest traces of human respect and dignity, he is thrown out of doors in the middle of the night at the height of a torrential and terrifying storm. This, he says, is what human life comes down to in the end: the solitary and poor abandoned in the cold, while the nasty and brutish enjoy all the warmth that power can provide. Such knowledge seems to be too much for us: "man's nature cannot carry/ Th'affliction, nor the fear." But Lear is not broken by the storm's icy blasts, neither does he flee them; instead, he exposes himself to the storm's full fury, looks it in the face and affirms himself against it even as it tosses and tears him. As he wanders with his royal fool, they meet a crazy beggar, stark naked, apparently even more wretched than he. "Is man no more than this?" Lear demands. "Thou art the thing itself; unaccommodated man. . . ." Now, at the climactic moment of the play, he tears off his royal robes—"Off, off you lendings"—and joins Poor Tom in naked authenticity. This act, which Lear believes has placed him at the very nadir of existence— "a poor, bare, forked animal"—turns out, ironically, to be his first step toward a full humanity, because, for the first time, he recognizes a connection between himself and another human being. This recognition enables him to grow in sensitivity and insight, and to move beyond the bounds of his self-absorbed bitterness and misery. As he stands and shivers, it dawns on him that his kingdom is full of people whose whole lives are consumed by the abandoned, defenseless suffering that he is going through right now. When he was in power he never noticed, but now he stretches his vision to take them in:

> Poor naked wretches, wheresoe'er you are,
> That bide the pelting of this pitiless storm,
> How shall your houseless heads, and unfed sides,
> Your loopt and window'd raggedness, defend you

From seasons such as these? O, I have ta'en
Too little care of this! Take physic, pomp;
Expose thyself to feel what wretches feel,
That thou may shake the superflux to them,
And show the heavens more just.

—*King Lear*, III, iv

It is only now that Lear is fit to be what he claims to be, "every inch a king." His tragedy is that the catastrophe that redeems him humanly destroys him politically; the experience that makes him genuinely qualified to be a king makes it impossible for him to be one. His triumph lies in becoming something he never dreamed of being, a human being. Here a hopeful dialectic lights up the tragic bleakness and blight. Alone in the cold and the wind and the rain, Lear develops the vision and courage to break out of his loneliness, to reach out to his fellow men for mutual warmth. Shakespeare is telling us that the dreadful naked reality of the "unaccommodated man" is the point from which accommodation must be made, the only ground on which real community can grow.

In the eighteenth century, the metaphors of nakedness as truth and stripping as self-discovery take on a new political resonance. In Montesquieu's *Persian Letters*, the veils that Persian women are forced to wear symbolize all the repressions that traditional social hierarchies inflict on people. By contrast, the absence of veils in the streets of Paris symbolizes a new kind of society where "liberty and equality reign," and where, as a consequence, "everything speaks out, everything is visible, everything is audible. The heart shows itself as clearly as the face." Rousseau, in his *Discourse on the Arts and Sciences*, denounces "the uniform and deceptive veil of politeness" that covers his age, and says that "the good man is an athlete who loves to wrestle stark naked; he despises all those vile ornaments that cramp the use of his powers . . ." Thus the naked man will be not only a freer and happier man but a better man. The liberal revolutionary movements that bring the eighteenth century to a climax act out this faith: if hereditary privileges and social roles are stripped away, so that all men can enjoy an unfettered freedom to use their powers, they will use them for the good of all mankind. We must note here a striking absence of worry as to what the naked

human being will do or be. The dialectical complexity and wholeness that we found in Shakespeare have faded away, and narrow
polarizations have taken their place. We find this same narrowing of
perspective in the counterrevolutionary *Reflections* of Edmund
Burke:

> But now all is to be changed. All the pleasing illusions that made
> power gentle, and obedience liberal, which harmonized the
> different shades of life, . . . are to be dissolved by this new
> conquering empire of light and reason. All the decent drapery of
> life is to be rudely torn off. All the super-added ideas, which the
> heart owns, and the understanding ratifies, as necessary to cover
> the defects of our weak and shivering nature, and to raise it to a
> dignity in our own estimation, are to be exploded as a ridiculous,
> absurd and antiquated fashion.

The *philosophes* imagined nakedness as idyllic, opening up new
vistas, beauty and virtue and happiness for all; for Burke it is
counteridyllic, an unmitigated disaster, a fall into nothingness from
which nothing can come. Burke's people lack King Lear's capacity to
learn something from their mutual vulnerability in the cold. Their
only hope lies in lies: in their capacity to construct mythic draperies
heavy enough to stifle their dreadful knowledge of who they are.

For Marx, writing in the aftermath of bourgeois revolutions and
reactions, and looking forward to a new wave, the symbols of nakedness and unveiling regain the dialectical depth that Shakespeare
gave them 250 years before. The bourgeois revolutions, in tearing
away veils of "religious and political illusion," have left naked power
and exploitation, cruelty and misery, exposed like open wounds; at
the same time, they have uncovered and exposed new options and
hopes. Unlike the common people of all ages, who have been
endlessly betrayed and broken by their devotion to their "natural
superiors," modern men, washed in "the icy water of egotistical
calculations," are free from deference to masters who destroy them,
animated rather than numbed by the cold. Because they know how
to think of, by, and for themselves, they will demand a clear account
of what their superiors are doing for them—and doing to them—and
they will be ready to resist and rebel where they are getting nothing
real in return.

Marx's hope is that once the unaccommodated men of the working class are "forced to face . . . the real conditions of their lives and their relations with their fellow men," they will come together to overcome the cold that cuts through them all. Their union will generate the collective energy that can fuel a new communal life. One of the *Manifesto*'s primary aims is to point the way out of the cold, to nourish and focus the common yearning for communal warmth. Because the workers can come through the affliction and the fear only by making contact with the self's deepest resources, they will be prepared to fight for collective recognition of the self's beauty and value. Their communism, when it comes, will appear as a kind of transparent garment, at once keeping its wearers warm and setting off their naked beauty, so that they can recognize themselves and each other in all their radiance.

Here, as so often with Marx, the vision is dazzling but the light flickers if we look hard. It isn't hard to imagine alternate endings to the dialectic of nakedness, endings less beautiful than Marx's but no less plausible. Modern men and women might well prefer the solitary pathos and grandeur of the Rousseauean unconditioned self, or the collective costumed comforts of the Burkean masque, rather than the Marxian attempt to fuse the best of both. Indeed, the sort of individualism that scorns and fears connections with other people as threats to the self's integrity, and the sort of collectivism that seeks to submerge the self in a social role, are probably a lot more appealing than the Marxian synthesis, because they are intellectually and emotionally so much easier.

There is a further problem that might keep Marx's dialectic from even getting under way. Marx believes that the shocks and upheavals and catastrophes of life in bourgeois society enable moderns, by going through them, as Lear does, to discover who they "really are." But if bourgeois society is as volatile as Marx thinks it is, how can people ever settle on any real selves? With all the possibilities and necessities that bombard the self and all the desperate drives that propel it, how can anyone definitively define which ones are essential, and which merely incidental? Where is there a clear point of reference for the self's ultimate identity? The nature of the newly naked moderns may turn out to be just as elusive and mysterious as that of the old, clothed one—maybe even more elusive, because there is no longer any illusion of a real self underneath the masks. Thus, along with community and society, individuality itself may be melting into the modern air.

THE METAMORPHOSIS OF VALUES

The problem of nihilism emerges again in Marx's next line: "The bourgeoisie has resolved all personal honor and dignity into exchange-value; and in place of all the freedoms that men have fought for, it has put one unprincipled freedom—free trade." The first point is the immense power of the market in modern men's inner lives: they look to the price list for answers to questions not merely economic but metaphysical—questions of what is worthwhile, what is honorable, even what is real. When Marx says that other values are "resolved into" exchange-value, his point is that bourgeois society does not efface old structures of value but subsumes them: old modes of honor and dignity do not die; instead, they get incorporated into the market, take on price tags, gain a new life as commodities. Thus, any imaginable mode of human conduct becomes morally permissible the moment it becomes economically possible—becomes "valuable"; anything goes if it pays. This is what modern nihilism is all about. Dostoevsky, Nietzsche, and their twentieth-century successors will ascribe this phenomenon to science, rationalism, the Death of God. Marx would say that its basis is far more concrete and mundane: it is built into the banal everyday workings of the bourgeois economic order—an order that equates our human value with our market price, no more, no less, and that forces us to expend ourselves in pushing our price up as far as we can make it go.

Marx is appalled by the destructive brutalities that bourgeois nihilism brings to life, but he believes that it contains a hidden tendency to transcend itself. The source of this drive is the paradoxically "unprincipled" principle of free trade. Marx believes that the bourgeoisie really believe in this principle—that is, in an incessant, unrestricted flow of commodities in circulation, a continuous metamorphosis of market values. If, as he believes, the members of the bourgeoisie really do want a free market, they will have to enforce the freedom of new products to enter the market. This in turn means that any full-fledged bourgeois society must be a genuinely open society, not only economically but politically and culturally as well, so that people will be free to shop around and seek the best deals, in ideas, associations, laws, and social policies as well as in things. The unprincipled principle of free trade will force the bourgeoisie to grant even communists the basic right that all businessmen enjoy, the right to offer and promote and sell their goods to as many customers as they can get. Thus, by virtue of "free competition in the realm of knowledge," even the most subversive works and ideas—like the *Manifesto* itself—must be allowed to appear, on the grounds that they may sell. Marx is confident that, once the ideas of revolution and communism become accessible to the masses, they *will* sell, and a "self-conscious, independent movement of the immense majority" will come into its own. Thus he can live with bourgeois nihilism in the long run because he sees it as active and dynamic, a nihilism of plenitude. Propelled by its nihilistic drives and energies, the bourgeoisie will open the political and cultural floodgates through which its revolutionary nemesis will flow.

This dialectic presents several problems. The first concerns the bourgeoisie's commitment to the unprincipled principle of free trade, whether in economics, politics, or culture. In fact, this principle has generally been more honored in the breach than in the observance. The members of the bourgeoisie, especially the most powerful, have always fought to restrict, manipulate, and control their markets; indeed, much of their creative energy has gone into arrangements for doing this—chartered monopolies, trusts, holding companies, cartels and conglomerates, price-fixing, open or hidden subsidies from the state—all accompanied by paeans in praise of the free market. Moreover, even among the few who really do believe in free exchange, there are fewer still who would extend freedom of trade to ideas as well as things. (Humboldt, J. S. Mill, Justices Holmes and Brandeis and Douglas and Black have been still, small voices in bourgeois society, embattled and marginal at best.)

A more typical bourgeois pattern is to praise freedom when in opposition, and to repress it when in power. Here Marx may be in danger—surprisingly, for him—of getting carried away by what ideologues say, and of losing touch with what the men with money and power actually do. This is a problem because, if the members of the bourgeoisie really don't give a damn about freedom, then they will do all they can to keep the societies they control closed against new ideas, and it will be harder than ever for communism to take root. Marx would say that their need for progress and innovation will force them to open up their societies even to ideas and movements they dread. Yet their ingenuity might avoid this through a truly insidious innovation: a consensus of mutually enforced mediocrity, designed to protect each individual bourgeois from the risks of competition, and bourgeois society as a whole from the risks of change.[6]

Another problem in Marx's dialectic of the free market is that it entails a strange collusion between bourgeois society and its most radical opponents. This society is driven by its unprincipled principle of free exchange to open itself to movements for radical change. The enemies of capitalism may enjoy a great deal of freedom to do their work—to meet, speak, write, organize, demonstrate, strike, elect. But their freedom to move transforms their movement into an enterprise, and they find themselves cast in the paradoxical role of merchants and promoters of revolution, which necessarily becomes a commodity like everything else. Marx does not seem to be disturbed by the ambiguities of this social role—maybe because he is sure that it will become obsolete before it can ossify, that the revolutionary enterprise will be put out of business by its fast success. A century later, we can see how the business of promoting revolution is open to the same abuses and temptations, manipulative frauds and wishful self-deceptions, as any other promotional line.

Finally, our skeptical doubts about promoters' promises must lead us to question one of the primary promises in Marx's work: the promise that communism, while upholding and actually deepening the freedoms that capitalism has brought us, will free us from the horrors of bourgeois nihilism. If bourgeois society is really the maelstrom Marx thinks it is, how can he expect all its currents to flow only one way, toward peaceful harmony and integration? Even if a triumphant communism should someday flow through the floodgates that free trade opens up, who knows what dreadful impulses might flow in along with it, or in its wake, or are even impacted inside? It is easy to imagine how a communist society committed to the free development of each and all might develop its own distinctive varieties of nihilism. Indeed, a communist nihilism might turn out to be far more explosive and disintegrative than its bourgeois precursor—though also more daring and original—because, while capitalism cuts the infinite possibilities of modern life with the limits of the bottom line, Marx's communism could launch the liberated self into immense, unknown human spaces with no limits at all.

THE LOSS OF A HALO

All the ambiguities in Marx's thought are crystallized in one of his most luminous images, the last one we will explore here: "The bourgeoisie has stripped of its halo every activity hitherto honored and looked up to with reverent awe. It has transformed the doctor, the lawyer, the priest, the poet, the man of science [*Mann der Wissenschaft*],[7] into its paid wage-laborers." The halo, for Marx, is a primary symbol of religious experience, the experience of something holy. For Marx, as for his contemporary Kierkegaard, experience, rather than belief or dogma or theology, forms the core of religious life. The halo splits life into sacred and profane: it creates an aura of holy dread and radiance around the figure who wears it; the sanctified figure is torn from the matrix of the human condition, split off inexorably from the needs and pressures that animate the men and women who surround it.

Marx believes that capitalism destroys this mode of experience for everybody: "all that is holy is profaned"; nothing is sacred, no one is untouchable, life beomes thoroughly desanctified. In some ways, Marx knows, this is frightful: modern men and women may well stop at nothing, with no dread to hold them back; free from fear and trembling, they are free to trample down everyone in their way, if self-interest drives them to it. But Marx also sees the virtue of a life without holy auras: it brings about a condition of spiritual equality. Thus the modern bourgeoisie holds vast material powers over the workers and everybody else, but it will never achieve the spiritual ascendancy that earlier ruling classes could take for granted. For the first time in history, all confront themselves and each other on a single plane of being.

We must remember that Marx is writing at a historical moment when, especially in England and France (the *Manifesto* really has more to do with them than with the Germany of Marx's time), disenchantment with capitalism is pervasive, overt and intense, and almost ready to flare up in revolutionary forms. In the next twenty years or so, the bourgeoisie will prove remarkably inventive in constructing halos of its own. Marx will try to strip these away in the first volume of *Capital*, in his brilliant analysis of "The Fetishism of Commodities"—a mystique that disguises the intersubjective relations between men in a market society as purely physical, "objective," unalterable relations between things. In the climate of 1848, this bourgeois pseudoreligiosity has not yet established itself. Marx's targets here are, both for him and us, a lot closer to home: those professionals and intellectuals—"the doctor, the lawyer, the priest, the poet, the man of science"—who think they have the power to live on a higher plane than ordinary humanity, to transcend capitalism in life and work.

Why does Marx place that halo on the heads of modern professionals and intellectuals in the first place? To bring out one of the paradoxes of their historical role: even though they tend to pride themselves on their emancipated and thoroughly secular minds, they turn out to be just about the only moderns who really believe that they are called to their vocations and that their work is holy. It is obvious to any reader of Marx that, in his commitment to his work, he shares this faith. And yet, he is suggesting here, in some sense it is a bad faith, a self-deception. This passage is so arresting because, as we see Marx identifying himself with the critical force and insight of the bourgeoisie, and reaching out to tear the halo from modern intellectuals' heads, we realize that, in some sense, it is his own head that he is laying bare.

The basic fact of life for these intellectuals, as Marx sees them, is that they are "paid wage-laborers" of the bourgeoisie, members of "the modern working class, the proletariat." They may deny this identity—for, after all, who wants to belong to the proletariat—but they are thrown into the working class by the historically defined conditions under which they are forced to work. When Marx describes intellectuals as wage-workers, he is trying to make us see that modern culture is part of modern industry. Art, science, social theory like Marx's own, all are modes of production; the bourgeoisie controls the means of production in culture, as in everything else, and anyone who wants to create must work within the orbit of its power.

As members of the proletariat, modern professionals, intellectuals, and artists

> live only so long as they find work, and . . . find work only so long as their labor increases capital. These workers, who must sell themselves piecemeal, are a commodity like every other article of commerce, and are consequently exposed to all the vicissitudes of competition, to all the fluctuations of the market.

Thus they can write books, paint pictures, discover physical or historical laws, save lives, only if someone with capital will pay them. But the pressures of bourgeois society are such that no one will pay them unless it pays to pay them—that is, unless their works somehow help to "increase capital." They must "sell themselves piecemeal" to an employer willing to exploit their brains for profit. They must scheme and hustle to present themselves in a maximally profitable light; they must compete against others (often brutally and unscrupulously) for the privilege of being bought, simply in order to go on with their work. Once the work is done they are, like all other workers, separated from the products of their labor. Their goods and services go on sale, and it is "the vicissitudes of competition, the fluctuations of the market" rather than any intrinsic truth or beauty or value—or, for that matter, any lack of truth or beauty or value—that will determine their fate. Marx does not expect that great ideas and works will fall stillborn for want of a market: the modern bourgeoisie is remarkably resourceful in wringing profit out of thought. What will happen instead is that creative processes and products will be used and transformed in ways that will dumbfound or horrify their creators. But the creators will be powerless to resist, because they must sell their labor power in order to live.

Intellectuals occupy a peculiar position in the working class, one that generates special privileges, but also special ironies. They are beneficiaries of the bourgeois demand for perpetual innovation, which vastly expands the market for their products and skills, often stimulates their creative audacity and imagination, and—if they are shrewd enough and lucky enough to exploit the perennial shortage of brains—enables them to escape the poverty of most workers. On the other hand, because they are personally involved in their work—unlike most wage laborers, who are alienated and indifferent—the fluctuations of the market strike them in a far deeper way. In "selling themselves piecemeal," they are selling not merely their physical energy but their minds, their deepest feelings, their visionary and imaginative powers, perhaps the whole of themselves. Moreover, they are driven not only by a need to live, which they share with all men, but by a desire to communicate, to engage in dialogue with their fellow men. But the cultural commodity market offers the only medium in which dialogue on a public scale can take place: no idea can reach or change moderns unless it can be marketed and sold to them. Hence they turn out to be dependent on the market not for bread alone, but for spiritual sustenance—a sustenance they know the market cannot be counted on to provide.

It is easy to see why modern intellectuals, trapped in these ambiguities, would imagine radical ways out: in their situation, revolutionary ideas would spring from the most direct and intense personal needs. But the social conditions that inspire their radicalism also serve to frustrate it. We saw that even the most subversive ideas must manifest themselves through the medium of the market. Insofar as these ideas attract and arouse people, they will expand and enrich the market, and so "increase capital." Now, if Marx's vision of bourgeois society is accurate, there is every reason to think that it will generate a market for radical ideas. This system requires constant revolutionizing, disturbance, agitation; it needs to be perpetually pushed and pressed in order to maintain its elasticity and resilience, to appropriate and assimilate new energies, to drive itself to new heights of activity and growth. This means, however, that men and movements that proclaim their enmity to capitalism may turn out to be just the sort of stimulants capitalism needs. Bourgeois society, through its insatiable drive for destruction and development, and its need to satisfy the insatiable needs it creates, inevitably produces radical ideas and movements that aim to destroy it. But its very capacity for development enables it to negate its own inner negations: to nourish itself and thrive on opposition, to become stronger amid pressure and crisis than it could ever be in peace, to transform enmity into intimacy and attackers into inadvertent allies.

In this climate, then, radical intellectuals encounter radical obstacles: their ideas and movements are in danger of melting into the same modern air that decomposes the bourgeois order they are working to overcome. To surround oneself with a halo in this climate is to try to destroy the danger by denying it. The intellectuals of Marx's time were particularly susceptible to this sort of bad faith. Even as Marx was discovering socialism, in the Paris of the 1840s, Gautier and Flaubert were developing their mystique of "art for art's sake," while the circle around Auguste Comte was constructing its own parallel mystique of "pure science." Both these groups— sometimes in conflict with one another, sometimes interfused— sanctified themselves as avant-gardes: they were at once perceptive and trenchant in their criticisms of capitalism, and, at the same time, absurdly complacent in their faith that they had the power to transcend it, that they could live and work freely beyond its norms and demands.

Marx's point, in tearing the halos from their heads, is that nobody in bourgeois society can be so pure or safe or free. The networks and ambiguities of the market are such that everybody is caught up and entangled in them. Intellectuals must recognize the depths of their own dependence—spiritual as well as economic dependence—on the bourgeois world they despise. It will never be possible to overcome these contradictions unless we confront them directly and openly. That is what stripping away the halo means.

This image, like all the great images in the history of literature and thought, contains depths that its creator could not have foreseen. First of all, Marx's indictment of the nineteenth-century artistic and scientific avant-gardes cuts just as deeply against the twentieth-century Leninist "vanguards," who possess an identical (and, of course, equally groundless and self-deceptive) faith in their own powers of transcendence. Next, it raises questions about Marx's own romantic image of the working class. If being a "paid wage-laborer" is the antithesis of having a halo, how can Marx speak of the proletariat as a class of "new men," uniquely equipped to transcend the contradictions of modern life? Indeed, we can carry this line of questioning a step further: if we have followed Marx's unfolding vision of modernity and have confronted all its endemic ironies and ambiguities, how can we expect *anybody* to transcend all this?

Once again we encounter a problem we have met before: the tension between Marx's critical insights and his radical hopes. My emphases in this essay, and maybe my sympathies as well, have leaned toward the skeptical and self-critical undercurrents in Marx's thought; and a sympathetic reader might well be tempted to take only the criticism and self-criticism to heart, and throw out the hopes as utopian and naive. To do this, however, would be to miss what Marx saw as the essential point of critical thinking. Criticism, as he understood and practiced it, was part of an ongoing dialectical process. It was meant to be dynamic, to drive (and inspire) the person criticized to overcome not only his critics but himself, to propel both parties toward a new synthesis. Thus, to unmask phony claims to transcendence. To give up the quest for transcendence is to erect a halo around one's own resignation, and to betray not only Marx but ourselves.

AFTER THE CONVERGENCE

I have been trying in this essay to define a space in which Marx's thought and the modernist tradition converge. First of all, both are attempts to evoke and to grasp a distinctively modern realm of experience. Both regard modernity with mixed emotions, awe and elation mixed with a sense of horror. Both see modern life as shot through with contradictory impulses and potentialities, and both try to resolve or dissolve the contradictions. Beyond these formal resemblances, I have tried to read Marx as a modernist writer, to bring out the vividness and richness of his language, the depth and complexity of his imagery—clothes and nakedness, veils, halos, heat, cold, etc.—and to show how brilliantly he develops the themes by which modernism will later define itself: the glory of modern energy and dynamism, the ravages of modern distintegra-tion and nihilism, the strange intimacy between them; the sense of being caught in a vortex in which all facts and values are whirled, exploded, decomposed, recombined; a basic uncertainty about what is basic, what is valuable, what is meaningful, even what is real; a flaring up of the most radical hopes, in the midst of their radical negations.

At the same time, I have tried to read modernism in a Marxist way, to suggest how its characteristic energies, insights, and anxieties spring from the drives and strains of "modernized" economic life: from its insatiable pressure for growth and progress, its demands on everybody to exploit not only one's fellow men but also oneself, its absorption of all values as commodities, the volatility and endless metamorphoses of all its market values, its pitiless destruction of everything and everyone it cannot use—so much of all the "premodern" worlds, but so much of itself and its own modern world as well—and its capacity to exploit crisis and chaos as a springboard for still more development, to feed itself on its own self-destruction.

It may seem that I have overplayed this theme of convergence. If I have, it's been to compensate for the fact that it has always been so badly underplayed.[8] Marxists have generally ignored modernism, or done their best to repress it—out of fear, I suspect, that (in Nietzsche's phrase) if they look into the abyss, the abyss will start looking back into them. For them, I've tried to close off an exit, by showing how this abyss opens up within Marxism itself. I should say, too, that Marxism's strength has always lain in its willingness to start from frightful social realities, to confront them, work through them and work them through; it would be sad—and self-destructive—to stop now. We will never ride the wave of the future if we don't learn to steer our way through the maelstrom we all live in now; if we try to act as if it isn't there, we may be the first to be swept away. Meanwhile, modernists have similarly avoided or shunned Marxism, largely out of fear that it will strip them of a halo they hold dear: their conviction of the artist's creative autonomy. To them I would say that although, indeed, a Marxist understanding would take this halo away, it could give them back something better in exchange: a heightened capacity to imagine and express the endlessly rich, complex, and ironic relationships between them and the "modern bourgeois society" they deny or defy. A fusion of Marx and modernism would melt the too-solid body of Marxism—or at least thaw it out—but it would give modernist art and thought a new solidity and invest its creations with an unsuspected resonance and depth: it would reveal modernism as the realism of our time.

The bourgeois' responses to both Marxism and modernism over the last century have fluctuated with the market. At first they recoiled in shock and horror from both, because both forced them to

face the world they had created and the people they had become.
But as time went by they learned, as usual, to adapt. In times of
expansion and prosperity, like the 1920s and the 1960s, they managed to live with, and even enjoy, the most subversive Marxist and
modernist ideas—as the bejeweled Berlin audience of 1928 cheered
Brecht's *"Erst kommt das Fressen, dann kommt die Moral"*—
comfortable in their nihilism, confident that they could exploit any
challenge or change and make it pay. In periods of retrenchment and
depression, like the 1930s and the 1970s, they donned their Party of
Order robes, waxed righteous, accused political, racial, or cultural
Outside Agitators, and passed the buck in every direction to deny
their own complicity in collapse. Thus modernism in the '70s, like
"degenerate art" and "cultural Bolshevism" in the '30s, has played a
prominent scapegoat's role. What has been disguised, both then and
now, is the fact that these cultural movements, for all their eruptive
power, have been no more than bubbles on the surface of a social
cauldron that has been teeming and boiling for more than a hundred
years. It is modern capitalism, not modern art and culture, that sets
and keeps the pot boiling—reluctant as capitalism may be to face the
heat today.

There are many people in the modern world—mostly in capitalist countries, but many in "socialist" ones too—who are honestly
searching for integration and integrity that they cannot seem to find
in the life options that confront them. Such people often become
very bitter toward modern culture and feel that if they could only
assimilate and internalize another—Oriental, classical, medieval, or
primitive—they could bring their lives together. The point of this
essay is that so long as the modern economy remains intact—an
economy that reduces all values to market values, that runs on
compulsory or compulsive acquisition, requires endless, mindless
growth, and measures growth in quantity alone—people's lives are
going to keep falling apart. Only the most radical economic and
social changes could begin to lift modern men and women out of the
maelstrom. Until these changes take place—which could be a
while—they are going to need a modernist culture to show them
what they are doing and who they are. Even after such a revolution,
they will still need it to show them what they were, could be, and
might yet become.

Meanwhile, those of us who are most critical of modern life need modernism most, to show us where we are and where we can begin to change our circumstances and ourselves. In search of a place to begin, I have gone back to one of the first and greatest of modernists, Karl Marx. I have gone to him not so much for his answers—since his dialectical genius often generated questions that dissolved his own answers—as for his questions. The great gift he can give us today, it seems to me, is not a way out of the contradictions of modern life, but rather a surer and deeper way into these contradictions. He knew that the way beyond the contradictions would have to lead through modernity, not out of it. He knew we must start where we are: psychically naked, stripped of all religious, aesthetic, moral halos and sentimental veils, thrown back on our individual will and energy, forced to exploit each other and ourselves in order to survive; and yet, in spite of all, thrown together by the same social forces that pull us apart, dimly aware of all we might be together, ready to stretch ourselves to grasp new human possibilities, to develop identities and mutual bonds that can help us hold together as the fierce modern air blows hot and cold through us all.

Note

The literature on both modernization and modernism is immense, though the former has dropped off somewhat in the past decade, while the latter is still in the process of developing. Here is a brief sampling:

On modernization: Daniel Lerner, *The Passing of Traditional Society: Modernizing the Middle East* (1958); W. W. Rostow, *The Stages of Economic Growth: a Non-Communist Manifesto* (1960); S. M. Lipset, *The First New Nation* (1963); Michael Walzer, "The Only Revolution: Notes on the Theory of Modernization" (*Dissent*, Fall 1964); David Apter, *The Politics of Modernization* (1965); C. E. Black, *The Dynamics of Modernization* (1966); S. N. Eisenstadt, *Modernization: Protest and Change* (1966); Dankwart Rustow, *A World of Nations: Problems of Political Modernization* (1967); Lloyd and Suzanne Rudolph, *The Modernity of Tradition* (1967); Daniel Lerner, James Coleman and Ronald Dore, articles on modernization in the *International Encyclopedia of Social Sciences* (1968), vol. 10; Alex Inkeles, *The Modernization of Man* (1975).

On modernism: Harold Rosenberg, *The Tradition of the New* (1959); Jacques Barzun, *Classic Romantic & Modern* (1961, 1975); Lionel Trilling, "The Modern Element in Modern Literature" (1961), reprinted with additional discussion in *Beyond Culture* (1965); Stephen Spender, *The Struggle of the Modern* (1963); *The Modern Tradition*, an anthology edited and introduced by Richard Ellman and Charles Feidelson (1965); Paul de Man, "What Is Modern?" (*New York Review of Books*, August 1965); Caesar Grana, *Modernity and its Discontents* (1964, 1967); Clement Greenberg, "Modernist Painting," in *Art and Culture*

(1966); Irving Howe, "The Culture of Modernism" (*Commentary,* January 1967), reprinted as Introduction to Howe's anthology, *Literary Modernism* (1967); Renato Poggioli, *The Theory of the Avant-Garde* (1962; English version, 1968); Louis Kampf, *On Modernism* (1970); Daniel Bell, "The Cultural Contradictions of Capitalism" (*Public Interest,* Fall 1970; reprinted with further discussion in the book, same title, 1975); various discussions by Hilton Kramer, in *The Age of the Avant-Garde* (1972); Harold Rosenberg, "What's New" (*New Yorker,* February 1973; reprinted with further discussion in his book, *Art on the Edge,* 1976).

Footnotes

1. Among the few exceptions are Henri Lefebvre, *Introduction à la Modernité* (1965); Peter Berger, Brigitte Berger, and Hansfried Keller, *The Homeless Mind: Modernization and Consciousness* (1973).

2. The one really striking exception here is Harold Rosenberg. I owe a great deal to his brilliant essays of 1949, "The Resurrected Romans" (reprinted in *The Tradition of the New*) and "The Pathos of the Proletariat" (in Howe, ed., *The Essential Works of Socialism*); and a later piece, "Marxism: Criticism and/or Action (in *Voices of Dissent,* 1958); the last two essays can also be found in Rosenberg's collection, *Act and Actor: Making the Self* (1970).

3. Most of my citations from the *Manifesto* are drawn from Samuel Moore's classic translation (London: 1888), authorized and edited by Engels, and universally reprinted. I have sometimes deviated from Moore, generally in the direction of more literalism and concreteness, or for the sake of a diction that is less Victorian and more vivid. These changes are frequently but not always indicated by bracketed citations from the German.

4. The German word here is *Verhältnisse,* which can be translated as "conditions," "relations," "relationships," "circumstances," "affairs," and so on. At different points in this essay it will be translated in different ways, whichever seems most apt in its context.

5. Engels, just a few years earlier, in *The Condition of the Working Class in England* (1844), was appalled to find that workers' housing, built by speculators for fast profits, was built to last only forty years. He little suspected that this would become the archetypal pattern of construction in bourgeois society. Ironically, even the most splendid mansions of the richest capitalists would be gone in less than forty years—not only in Manchester but in nearly all cities dominated by capital (New York's Fifth Avenue is a vivid example)—leased or sold off to developers, pulled down by the same insatiable drives that had built them up. Considering the rapidity and brutality of capitalist development, the real surprise is not that so much of our architectural and constructive heritage has been destroyed, but that there is anything still left to preserve.

6. In *Capital,* in the climactic chapter on "The Historical Tendency of Capitalist Accumulation" (Volume I, Chapter 32), Marx says that when a system of social relations acts as a fetter on "the free development of productive forces," that social system has simply got to go: "It must be annihilated; it is annihilated." But what would happen if, somehow, it didn't get annihilated? "To perpetuate it" would be, Marx says, "to decree universal mediocrity." This seems to be one thing—perhaps the only thing—that Marx is utterly incapable of imagining.

7. The word *Wissenschaft* may be translated in many ways, narrowly as "science," or more broadly as "knowledge," "learning," "scholarship," or any sustained and serious intellectual

pursuit. Whatever word we use, it is crucial to remember that Marx is talking here about the predicament of his own group, and hence about himself.

I have intermittently used the word "intellectuals" as shorthand for the diverse occupational groups Marx brings together here. I realize the word is anachronistic—it stems from the turn of the twentieth century—but it has the advantage of bringing together, as Marx seeks to do, people in diverse occupations who, despite their differences, all work with their minds.

8. There are two kinds of exceptions, which I plan to discuss in detail in the future. First, those who have tried to act out an outright fusion of the two, to make revolutions simultaneously in art and in politics: e.g., the Expressionists, Futurists, Dadaists and Constructivists of 1914–1921. Next, those who experience modernism as a maelstrom, Marxism as *ein' feste Burg* of solid rock, and who expend great energy and anguish plunging back and forth between them: e.g., Mayakovski, Brecht, Benjamin, Adorno, Sartre.

PART FOUR
Short
Subjects

IGNAZIO SILONE
Prosperity— and Then What?
(1964)

It may seem strange to some people that a writer who is chiefly
known for stories set in depressed or backward regions should now
turn to the problems of prosperity. It may well be asked: is this
perchance due to the fact that for some time now these problems
have become fashionable? Nonsense. First of all, with regard to
myself, I can say that I have never liked those judgments of my
literary work which were limited by some sociological or party
concept. The only thing which really interests me is the condition of
man caught in the gear wheels of the present-day world. And,
naturally, I take my stand on the side of man and not the gear wheels.
If my characters are most often poor peasants, disquieted intellectuals and priests, bureaucrats of opposing apparatuses who move
against an arid landscape, this does not occur because of my pre-
dilection for a certain local color. It is simply the reality which I know
best, I bear it, so to speak, inside of me, and in it the human
condition manifests itself in a starker, almost naked form.

On the other hand, are not poverty and wealth correlative
terms? They are in fact like heat and cold, and it is impossible to have
a clear idea of one except as it stands in relation to the other. I can,
however, add some more personal details on my far from recent
interest in the problems of prosperity, since this may help to clarify
my point of view and its gradual formation amidst the conflicting
diatribes of the specialists.

379

Although I was born and grew up in a region which if rather poor was not backward but on the contrary overburdened, even wearied and exhausted by a surplus of ancient and medieval history, my first reflections on, and experience of, the situation of man in a rich and technically advanced country go back to the very beginning of my life as a writer and proceed hand in hand with it. I am speaking of the time when I began to write *Fontamara*, about 1930, at the start of my long exile in Switzerland, indeed, in the German-speaking cantons.

It would be hard to imagine a more flagrant contrast than that between the theme of my first novel (the poverty, exploitation and rebellion, or rather the first awakening of consciousness, of peasants in a southern Italian village) and the social conditions of the region in which I had found refuge: a region, as everyone knows, which is among the most advanced in Europe, and where poverty, if not totally abolished, has long become a matter of exceptional instances.

The sense of that contrast was sharpened for me by my social contacts with some Swiss friends, with whom I enjoyed discussing the opposed situations in our two countries. They belonged to different social classes (architects, doctors, Protestant ministers, artisans) and also espoused different ideologies; but they had in common a number of typically Swiss characteristics which ordinarily escape foreign tourists—above all, a dislike for rhetoric and loose talk in general, which are so dear to us Latins. With some of them, especially, I shared a sense of mourning for "the God who had failed," that is, the disappointment of the hopes for freedom placed in the Russian revolution; with others, despite our different religious backgrounds, a rather unconventional way of applying Christian ethics to the events of the day and the mores of the ruling class, to states and churches. It should also be said that the feeling of solidarity with the exiles was, for these Swiss, a consequence of their natural aversion to dictatorial governments; but this did not at all attenuate the frankness with which they criticized the defects of their own fellow citizens and their own institutions.

So while I, goaded by nostalgia and political passion, which I could not express in any other manner, found myself at grips with that story about poor southern Italian peasants and was trying to narrate the vicissitudes of the often tragic, sometimes grotesque clash between their still semifeudal mentality and the new forms of exploitation and tyranny, I kept hearing from my Swiss friends no less merciless criticisms of the spiritual decadence of their country. Alluding in particular to the Swiss in the richer cantons, my friends would berate their vulgar hedonism, their mental obtuseness, their technological infatuation and the boredom it inevitably entailed. In support of their jeremiads, they cited the most recent statistics on the increase in divorce, suicide, deafness, the growing vogue of psychoanalysis in all social classes and the mediocrity of artistic and literary production, despite a generous patronage both public and private. This criticism did not spare the working-class movement, especially the cooperatives and the trade unions in the most important branches of industry, against which the charge was brought of following a completely clannish policy of the defense of high salaries and indifference to problems of general import. Therefore in our discussions it was impossible to avoid the question as to whether the decadence or spiritual stagnation of which my friends complained should not really be considered the result of the growing collective prosperity. And was it legitimate to predict that this would be the fate of any other country which might achieve prosperity?

This was not, nor could it be, even for me, an abstract or negligible problem. Certainly this problem did not prevent me from pursuing my duty as an exiled and therefore free Italian writer. Problems must be faced as they arise, I repeated to myself, and it will be quite a long time before the *cafoni* of Fontamara would have to contend with the drawbacks and difficulties of opulence. But I could not expect from action more than it can give. And how could I delude myself? For each revolutionary action unfolds in relation to a perspective. So, in my subsequent novels, after *Fontamara*, the problems of the future began to cast their gray shadows on the narrative present. Some character would ask: When we will no longer be persecuted, will we in our turn become persecutors? And if we will be able to eat every day so as to wholly satisfy our appetites, will nothing else remain for us but to digest? The insidious problem of the relationship between collective prosperity and moral life remained with me, like a flea in my ear. It was only one aspect of my reflections on the reconstructive capacities of Marxism and the varying experiences with it which were being had in Russia and the Scandinavian countries. It had already been established that, in this

Janus of socialism, the cruel and enraged face shown in the East was frankly repulsive; but how should we interpret the benevolent and optimistic smile on the other face? Was it not a bit too smug, too satisfied with itself? The urgency of making a strict distinction between what should be regarded as essential to socialism and what was only a contingent accessory, was forced on us by the horrible aping of some of its aspects on the part of fascism and Nazism (for example, their organizations for the entertainment of workers during their free time).

An attempt to define the new situation had already been made a few years before by the Spanish philosopher Ortega y Gasset in his book, already then a classic, *The Revolt of the Masses*. But what rendered his interpretation unacceptable to many of us was the obvious fear, mingled with aristocratic contempt, which filled him when confronted by the popular masses' participation in public life. It was not so much the mass man that Ortega denounced—about whom in fact he knew very little—as it was the uncultivated man, "the mediocre spirit who knows he is mediocre and has the audacity to proclaim the rights of the mediocre and to impose them whenever he wishes." Furthermore, the new phenomenon which had to be studied was not the so-called "mass," a reality and concept in all ages, but rather the fact of "massification," and one could no longer study it from outside since all of social life was saturated by it, and we ourselves were inside of it. The same hatred of novelty, though based on a more radical historical vision, was expressed by the Italian Guglielmo Ferrero, who also lived in Switzerland at that time, an isolated and haughty political exile, almost an exile among the exiles. To Ferrero undoubtedly goes the credit of having criticized modern mass civilization as early as the first decade of this century, during an era of general optimism. Fundamental to his conception was the distinction between a qualitative civilization and a quantitative civilization. In his book, *Between The Two Worlds*, which appeared in 1913, that idea had been expounded through the conversations among some passengers on a luxury liner, who were returning from America to Europe. They were in fact discussing the future of industrial civilization, of which America was the model for the rest of the world, and in this civilization they discovered the elements of a dangerous instability. America was, in Ferrero's judgment, a quantitative civilization, due to the fact that its dynamism was based on the uncontrolled and uncontrollable development of productive techniques. In spite of the greater prosperity put within the reach of the many, it was therefore a civilization without stable values and without inner checks, and thus was preparing its own catastrophe.

What irked us most in Ferrero's gloomy vision was its blank uniformity and, consequently, the absence in it of a slight crack or flaw that might permit one not merely to affirm a different principle but also to act in accordance with it. In fact, at the point we had reached, many principles we had believed in before this—and first among them the myth of Progress—seemed to us to have gone up in smoke and without any great regret on our part. Yet there survived in us an instinctive repulsion to any idea which excluded the possibility of fighting back.

Since those days, with the industrialization of new regions and the spread of the expressive means of the so-called mass civilization, the proportions of the conditioning have extended and become much more burdensome. And, keeping pace with it, those which in the past seemed to us the shrill voices of lone Cassandras have been replaced by a vast chorus of professors and students of sociology armed with statistics, and against these people we can only oppose an act of faith in man. Indeed, it seems to me that this is the major issue confronting us at the present time.

Until a short time ago, the idea that prosperity, indeed wealth and the superfluous, would cease to be the privilege of a few and would be guaranteed, with a minimum of effort, to an increasing number of men through the use of prodigious sources of energy, such as nuclear energy, was still a science-fiction dream. Even now, unfortunately, many peoples are far from that goal and live in conditions of poverty and neglect. Yet we know that prosperity for all has entered the sphere of possibility and that already it is part of our historical perspective (together with its opposite, the general catastrophe of a third world war, in which everyone now refuses to believe). The very leaders of the Communist world, at least those leaders converted to peaceful coexistence, never pass up an opportunity to announce to their peoples the achievement of a general state of prosperity within the next ten years. I do not think that there is anyone who does not sincerely hope for the complete fulfillment of their promises. A decade passes quickly, and real prosperity for those immense populations, so long afflicted by privations of every kind, would be an excellent thing.

And what then? We know that prosperity solves many problems, and that it creates many new ones. This is certain; but what are these problems? This is the real problem.

Translated from the Italian by RAYMOND ROSENTHAL

DAVID BROMWICH
Blood Orange, or Violence in the Movies
(1972)

Hollywood movies used to make the gangster "understandable" by allowing him a human weakness, and the same trick of complication was played on cops. The unstated principle seemed to be: cops and robbers have more in common with each other than either can ever have with the organization man. They work by their own peculiar skills, and organizations are alien to them because they are individuals. This was the situation more than thirty years ago that gave us everything from *Scarface* down to *Angels with Dirty Faces* and *The Maltese Falcon*. Recently, however, on television and in the movies, there has been a shifting of the current. Corporate evil, which used to be the enemy of independent cop and robber alike, has been transformed into an angel of light. The evidence remains the same—what was evil and is now good has been steadily cold-blooded—but we are asked to draw a different conclusion. John Dillinger and Sam Spade would feel equally out of place in this world. Tamburlaine, a hot-blooded type, could never have worked for the intelligence squad of "Mission: Impossible," but then neither could Bogart or Cagney or Edward G. Robinson. Their good and evil, and their energy, belonged to themselves alone—and the age has set new demands.

The signs of what was coming go a long way back. In *White Heat*, for example, a 1949 Cagney vehicle with Edmund O'Brien as the cop, the endearingly psychotic criminal is pursued and finally caught by radar, and thousands of blue Los Angeles policemen watch like furies as he commits suicide. Cagney is not killed; he is eliminated. As early as that, however, technological good guys were impossible without the element of individual pluck and wit. O'Brien provided just the right touch of native intelligence when he got isolated from the police network but still rebuilt his own radar set, illustrating the point that if we were to respect organizational cops at all they had to break with the organization at some stage and go it on their own. All this changed beyond recognition by the time of a film like *Experiment in Terror*, made in the early 1960s and heavily influenced by television. The law-enforcement agents are mannequins with not even a flicker of human warmth, and they quarry the criminal—a homicidal pervert played by Ross Martin—by pretty nearly landing a helicopter on him in Candlestick Park. The pervert, at least, is as human as his perversion, but the cops have turned into a Big Brother who is good precisely because he is terrifying. "Mission: Impossible" takes the next and final logical step: quite commonly, the agents of that program choose not to kill their enemies outright, preferring to drive off in limousines after having tricked the hunted man into the snares of another criminal. Ordinary sympathy, in other words, has departed altogether, and so has irony.

To this state of affairs Stanley Kubrick bears an intriguing relation. On the one hand he is a good and pious liberal: *Paths of Glory* is solidly built on his faith, as is *Dr. Strangelove*, beneath all its veneer of iconoclasm. Kubrick is also something of an idolator of technology, that most pervasive manifestation of corporate evil: this fact lies behind the characteristic imagery of *2001* and was, I think, an aspect of *Dr. Strangelove* that many of us were apt to ignore at the time. (Remember CRM-114?) The game has always worked both ways with Kubrick. In *Dr. Strangelove* he couldn't satirize the obsession with gadgetry without first taking it seriously, explaining the gadgets; in *2001*, where computers are meant to be taken very seriously indeed, he couldn't help making the whole business rather winningly foolish. If, then, *2001* is its own best parody, *Dr. Strangelove* may contain less of satire than we had imagined. The confusion is owing to divided feelings in Kubrick himself, a friend of individualism who seems nevertheless to be an ally of Big Brother. (Remember the monolith?) Such are the circumstances relevant to his new and ambitious contribution to the gangster film genre, *A Clockwork Orange*, which is his worst work to date.

Certainly it is his most confused. The film leaves no doubt that the object of its attack is, indeed, corporate evil—a welfare state that has reached advanced decadence—while what it seeks to propagate, the moral of the story, is the need for a free instinctual life among men. But what happens when that insistent moralism gets loaded into the conventions of a gangster film? Well, for one thing, it spoils all the fun, makes it a terribly dull movie to watch. *Public Enemy* thought of preaching to its audience, too, but it was never this slow and solemn; and though the comparison may be lowering, I would much rather see *Public Enemy* again than *A Clockwork Orange*. Let us take the comparison one step further and see where it leads. James Cagney and Malcolm McDowell both do the type of the hometown boy gone wrong: their environment has become intolerable, they turn to a life of crime, and we follow their exploits. Cagney ends badly and McDowell ends well—and why? Because Kubrick is throwing a sop to his audience; he is preaching a different sermon, and the physical resemblance between the two actors serves to heighten the contrast. Murderous violence has, in *A Clockwork Orange*, become the test case for all human instincts, so that Kubrick means something rather unusual when he speaks of solving the crime problem. Crime is life. Instinctual repression—dressed, naturally, in a police uniform—is death.

The didactic scheme of *A Clockwork Orange* could scarcely be sillier: I do not think my summary has done it any injustice. However, the simple-mindedness of the film seems to me inseparable from what has gone sour in it at a far deeper level. The plot itself fits nicely with Kubrick's intentions. Alex, a streamlined Hell's Angel with plenty of experience in chainfighting, takes particular pleasure in rape ("the old in-out in-out") and the music of Beethoven ("Ludwig Van"). The film is done in an urban futuristic setting, and he is the hero; no one else is allowed to act the least bit human. Alex has a charming smile, and reminds one a little of Holden Caulfield, and when he gets carted off to jail it is a great tragedy; but he earns his freedom before too long by submitting to the Lodovico treatment, which looks something like a polite lobotomy. The treatment has made him hate sex and Beethoven, and when he stumbles into the house of a famous writer—who turns out to have been married to his last rape victim—this old hypocrite, who leads the left-wing opposition to the Lodovico treatment, actually makes an attempt (if I may borrow the language of the movie) to ninthsymphony Alex to death. The poor boy jumps out the window, but recovers; the shock of hitting cement has apparently sufficed to restore him to his old self; he indulges in an altogether pleasant sexual fantasy, and that finishes the story. "I'm cured!" he says. But the plot is utterly subverted, or at any rate muddied, by a frigid stylization that deadens every action in the film. This is literally true in the slowed-down fight sequences that have been set against Beethoven plus other-worldly electronic flourishes. And there is, consequently, no sense of humor in the entire film, though there is a great deal of portentous frivolity (doorbells ringing the first notes of the Fifth Symphony, and the like).

Kubrick has made his visual style surrealistic on a grand scale, using the kind of sets that give every parking lot the appearance of a crater on the moon. Also, and I think this accounts for the film's attraction for otherwise intelligent people, he has understood the possibilities of pop art as a form of violence. That discovery may be the most original thing in *A Clockwork Orange:* in the Korova Milk-bar episodes, for instance, with their molded enamel interiors, chill decor; and in the Cat Lady sequence, where green leotards become a pop invitation to murder. But alas, Kubrick gazes too long into the eyes of the dragon. He becomes what he contemplates. And his film moves quite naturally in the ambiance of Big Brother, so that its steady portrayal of Alex's enemies seems more like a complicity. How odd, in a tract about liberating the human spirit, that every image should feel predigested. For *A Clockwork Orange* is—like the propaganda movies that were a part of the Lodovico treatment, and despite its ostensible message—a terribly oppressive film to have to see. I say this without reference to the controversy that grew up around the film and for a time seemed about to bury us all.

A Clockwork Orange, Straw Dogs, and *The Godfather* can all be seen as reactions against the notion of corporate good, really a vicious notion, which lately has become fixed in our popular culture: the attempt to win sympathy, that is, for the insulated group in its war against the isolated individual. The first two of these movies follow out their reaction to the point of folly, and substitute for corporate violence an old-fashioned respect for private *virtu*, personal violence. Their folly consists in mistaking *virtu* for virtue, when their heroes are in fact redundantly vicious. To stay on the "humane" bandwagon, Kubrick ends by apologizing for Alex's worst moments with the sentiments of all-purpose mitigation, "he was a born loser"; Sam Peckinpah, the director of *Straw Dogs*, being a more rigorous artist, assumes that one needn't stay on that bandwagon at all—which is certainly a more interesting line to take. You may not like my idea of virtue, but that's just too bad—pow! *The Godfather*, which seems to me one of the best American films ever made, puts paid to corporate violence with the emphasis on both words. But I shall return to this. Meanwhile, let us unravel some more confusions.

Those who objected to the depiction of violence in Kubrick's film were importantly wrong, because the gross physical violence in *A Clockwork Orange*, quite apart from its ideological content, was of a much lower order of magnitude than anything in a film like *The French Connection*. The "X" rating of *A Clockwork Orange* had more to do, as these things will, with pubic hair than with blood. Why, then, was the debate over that movie conducted so fiercely? Probably the answer is that a good many people sensed the complicity to which I have alluded: complicity in every kind of violence, even the technological. This comes out not in the overt message but in the style. It is not that Kubrick likes violence. Rather, he likes the *idea* of violence, put to Beethoven music and processed and sterilized. We can find traces of a deeper resonance: Alex winning entrance to his victims' houses by complaining, "My friend is lying in the street, Ma'am, he's bleeding." But nothing is made of it. Again, the confusion—or is it bad faith?—shows through when Hitler appears in the films that are to deprive Alex of his rightful human inheritance, his instinct for blood. Surely, Hitler represents precisely the impersonal violence that had better not be assimilated to Alex's revolt. It is an unfortunate movie and, unfortunately for Kubrick's reputation among intellectuals, a feeble-minded one. The only moments of relief come when McDowell steps out of his role, hopping or skipping or overacting, and making us laugh a little, thank God.

There is no such relief in *Straw Dogs*. Peckinpah is a director of westerns—the best of them is *Ride the High Country*, though better than any of his films was a television adaptation of *Noon Wine*—and *Straw Dogs* is, so far as I can tell, a plague that he has sent down personally on the human race. He is a great misanthrope, and this is his *magnum opus* of hate. His story makes simple enough retelling, hate being among the simplest of emotions. Well then: a weak American academic is setting up residence in Britain (gentle insinuations of a flight from student turmoil: his wife bothers him vaguely about "commitment"); his wife is a bit of a kitten, a flirt (question never to be resolved: how did they get together?); the local rowdies rape his wife, and then try to break into the house to capture a mentally retarded criminal, whom the academic is protecting until justice can be brought. The academic, up to now a pretty tame fellow, finds that he must kill all the rowdies to protect his home, and that is just what he does, and in the most exotic ways, too. (A bear trap over the head takes care of one.) The violence in this film, rated "R," is atrocious. And the message of it all is: he killed a lot of men, and he saw that he was good. Presumably, though this is to move past the end of the film, sex with the kitten will now be better than ever.

Is this such a very hard movie to render judgment on? We are being asked, it seems to me, not whether or not we assent to Peckinpah's view of human nature, but whether or not we can value his work in its particularities of expression. Yet the director has tricked his audience into a curious quandary. If one likes the film, he and his admirers suggest, that must be because it communicates a right vision of human nature through high art. If on the other hand one cannot abide the film, that must be because one is not sufficiently tough-minded, not sufficiently even-handed, about the pathological violence it so surely (indeed moralistically) commends, and one is thereby disqualified from judging the thing dispassionately on artistic grounds. Hence the phrase offered by a cautious admirer but an admirer all the same, "a fascist work of art."

My complaint against *Straw Dogs* is that it is a bad film. The dialogue, and I don't see how anyone can have missed this, has been stiffened absolutely beyond belief, as if the director stood trembling with anticipation of his climactic scene, where words will not matter. Dustin Hoffman as the academic manages to look surprisingly like a turtle, but characterization here never reaches far beyond caricature: this is a western director's picture of an intellectual, the

Hemingway picture. It was not respectable in Hemingway and it is not respectable here. Of course, Peckinpah like Kubrick has a didactic purpose. Like Kubrick, he is fond of citing a hack screen-writer and anthropologist named Robert Ardrey, who may fairly be described as a two-penny Hobbes. Peckinpah believes that we are aggressive beings after all, and that in this film he has finally got down to the root of the matter. Why do misanthropes want to convert everybody? But no matter: in a didactic way—as in any other—the film simply does not convince. During the most violent parts of *Straw Dogs*, when I saw it, the audience was driven to protect itself with laughter; it was just too much. And that, I suggest, is not the way we respond to art.

What, in any case, can be meant by "a fascist work of art"? Works that are systematically antihuman cannot be called art, because a necessary point in any definition of art is that it humanizes. *Gulliver's Travels* is not apposite as a counterexample; its great lesson is not misanthropy but humility, and its effect is to chasten. Among directors, Clouzot strikes me as a fascist who made works of art: but somehow the two remain separate with him. *Wages of Fear* may be the supreme adventure movie, but the director's inhumanity stays always in the background—at worst, irritatingly in the background. And that film offers an ideal of heroism in which we want to believe, as does Peckinpah's *Ride the High Country*. It is, to be sure, one sign of critical maturity to be able to say: I do not like this work but I must allow it is art. However, I submit that to make this response to *Straw Dogs* would be wrong, and propose the following explanation instead.

Frank Kermode speaks somewhere of political myths as "degenerate fictions," and refers to fascism as one such myth. We have to use this label loosely with respect to Peckinpah, of course—anyhow the label is not of my own devising—but never mind that for the moment. The fiction, I think, in Peckinpah's case, was a rather narrow conception of heroism borrowed from Hemingway; and yet that conception plainly had a certain power and nobility, as anyone who saw *Ride the High Country* will recall. What we have been getting in place of the fiction, lightly disguised in *The Wild Bunch* and now, in *Straw Dogs*, emerging in all its repellent bareness, is a degenerate fiction. In short, a myth of violence. Having lost his belief in human decency, Peckinpah can no longer give us living

characters—only lurid glimpses of the eternal principle of vicious-
ness, with slight variations from one person to the next. Bleak
landscape can work nicely to objectify this kind of nihilism: when
Hoffman gazes out at the unfertile expanse of ground beyond his
front yard—sparse brown grass, rubble, a few unconsoling trees—
we know it is the best moment in the film. But when Hoffman
exclaims over his feat of killing off the better part of the supporting
cast "I did it! I did it!" we want to ask him, as we might care to ask the
director: what is it you have done?

The first line in *The Godfather* is "I believe in America." Don
Vito Corleone, played remarkably by Brando in his most solid role
since Terry Malloy, is being petitioned to murder a few young men
who have raped a young Italian woman. The hoodlums have got no
respect, her father says. He is a small-time undertaker and he
believes in America, and America, for him, has begun to mean the
Mafia. The Family. The shades of the room are drawn and the only
color we see is a faded brown. Justice, the man goes on, demands
that the rapists be killed. Ah, but that would not be justice, Don
Corleone replies, because your daughter is still alive. And why have
you waited till this moment to seek the kinship of the Family? Why
have you waited till now, when you seek us only for protection? But
never mind, we will find these hoodlums. And we may, someday, ask
you to return the favor. Later in the movie, Don Corleone will ask
the undertaker to clean up his son's corpse, which is riddled with
bullets, to make it fit for a mother's eyes to see.
    This is corporate violence with a vengeance, so to speak; it is
Family life experienced simply as a part of family life. The family,
small f, supplies warmth and comfort and, yes, love. The Family,
large f, supplies cool business sense—takes care of finances. Here,
we notice, is the characteristic separation of powers in American life.
"I don't like violence," says a character. "I'm a businessman. Blood is
a big expense." No garish light plays over the faces of these
gangsters: to comtemplate a tactical murder is not to blackmail
someone on penalty of "rubbing him out," in the melodramatic
flourish of the old days, but to "make him an offer he cannot refuse."
The director of *The Godfather*, Francis Ford Coppola, has not been
able to present his slice of life without a certain sacrifice. Because the
story lacks a hero, it lacks also—I hesitate to say moral involvement,

but no other words seem right. However, a story in the naturalistic vein about a subject like the Mafia looks forward to that weakness, and affords other satisfactions besides. It has, for example, the satisfaction of inevitability. Al Pacino as Don Corleone's intelligent son, Michael, at first regards his family from a distance, estranged from it by a university education and war experience, adopting as far as he can the Ivy League man's opinion of bloody murder. He is brought into the family circle again by the attempted murder of his father, decides to do a murder himself, and thereafter becomes all but nominal head of the family. His gradual absorption of Brando's physical mannerisms, quirks of speech, executive logic, turns into an entire show in itself. There is nothing quite like it in the American cinema.

Coppola, one hopes, will now get the recognition he has long deserved. Even a glance at his first film, *You're a Big Boy Now*, will show where he parts company with another young director like Mike Nichols. In Coppola's film, for all the straight Salingerisms, we know right away that the director has thrown himself into life—take him where it will. He did not descend to the manner of a nightclub routine for a laugh, just as, in *The Godfather*, he does not descend to melodrama for a shudder. The writing and acting have a fullness, here, that one rarely finds in ambitious American films: Coppola has imported the great European middle style of Renoir and Ophuls— deep focus, fluid movement, minimal editing—and he has done it right. For anyone who cares about movies in this country, it is above all an encouraging film to watch. But it is also, and here I shall have to recur to my original point, something of an event. For it changes once and for all the image of corporate violence in America, in the same way—if with small things we may compare great—that *Madame Bovary* forever altered the image of the bourgeoisie in France. When a man gets strangled in *The Godfather*, we strangle with him. We do not see it covered over, made acceptable, by our driving off in a limousine. Coppola has put the rigor back into death; he has dissected the Family and made its warmth insidious; he has made room again, I think, for the free-lance detective and the free-lance hero. From now on, perhaps, "Mission: Impossible" really will not be possible.

STANLEY PLASTRIK
The Russian
Revolution Revisited
(1977)

Those of us who were raised on that version of the Russian Revolution symbolized in the storming of the Petrograd Winter Palace and the dramatic gesture of Antonov-Ovseenko, he of the broad-brimmed, black felt hat, as he bursts into the room where Kerensky's ministers are seated and, with a gesture of his arm, sweeps them all into the "dustbin of history"— we will never forget the impact this conception of the revolution had upon us. It is therefore a little disconcerting to read in Alexander Rabinowitch's revisionist account of Petrograd 1917[1] that the Winter Palace was never really "stormed," but that the collapse of resistance led, rather, to a gradual "infiltration."

Many elements had joined together to form an essentially romantic notion of the revolution, not the least Trotsky's classic *History*, John Reed's passionate *Ten Days That Shook the World*, Eisenstein's great film *October* (the original version, not the shamefully truncated one with Trotsky excised that now circulates on public television).

But then, with time, under the impact of the horrors of Stalinism—and with a new view of Lenin, single-handedly and by the force of his magnetic personality and powerful mind forcing through the revolution against his own party's backsliders—a new view emerged, presenting the revolution as a Blanquist *coup d'état* engineered by a conspiratorial handful at whose head stood Lenin, master of the "hardline" strategy. The revolution was the achievement of a determined group, with the Petrograd masses forming a confused and pliable backdrop to the events.

Alexander Rabinowitch has reexamined these contradictory views and produced the most serious study of the October revolution to appear in many years. His political study of revolutionary events in Petrograd and Russia from the summer of 1917 to the Bolshevik seizure of power in October is based on impressive original research using the Russian sources, including minutes, protocols, and accounts of meetings of the Petrograd district soviets and other institutions whose activities were hitherto unknown, at least to a non-Russian audience. The author gives us the full range of Bolshevik political opinion, including major disagreements within the party—disagreements he analyzes dispassionately and in remarkably nonpolemical fashion.

Rabinowitch rejects the views of Masaryk ("The October Revolution was anything but a popular movement; the revolution was the act of leaders working from above and behind the scenes.")—and he gives us a new context for the viewpoint implicit in Trotsky's scornful response to Masaryk that, "as a matter of fact, it was the most popular mass-insurrection in all history." While stressing the deep link between the party's revolutionary tactics and the Petrograd masses, Rabinowitch attacks the notion that, thanks to Bolshevik unity, discipline, and, above all, to Lenin's revolutionary leadership, the revolution was "inevitable." That Lenin's tight, highly disciplined and monolithic party was ready to seize power when the opportunity arose, according to this author, is sheer myth—and he proceeds to demonstrate that the Bolshevik party grew in 1917 precisely because it was relatively open, relatively democratic in practice, and far more sensitive to the wishes of the Petrograd masses than its rivals. This is a fundamentally fresh view of Lenin, his role, and his party.

In 1917 the influx of tens of thousands of new members necessarily led to a considerable weakening of Lenin's prior concept of the party as a closed movement of professional revolutionaries. The Petrograd workers who poured into the party were not interested in that kind of existence. Hence the Bolshevik organization in 1917 was one of "lively debate and spirited give-and-take." Hence "my research," writes Rabinowitch, "suggests that the relative flexibility of the party, as well as its responsiveness to the prevailing mass mood, had at least as much to do with the ultimate Bolshevik victory as did revolutionary discipline, organizational unity, or obedience to Lenin." It was this "lively debate" and "spirited give-and-take" that often aroused Lenin's rage. He saw in it indeed signs of wavering, if not a downright betrayal of the revolutionary cause itself, as his denunciations of Zinoviev, Kamenev, and other leading proponents of "moderate Bolshevik" views testify.

If we take the Kronstadt soviet as typical of the political evolution of the thousands of workers', peasants', soldiers' and sailors' district soviets throughout the land, in late August and early September 1917 the demands of this vanguard soviet were still strikingly moderate and democratic: "a decisive rupture with the capitalists; the transfer of power into the hands of revolutionary workers, peasants, and soldiers; and the creation of a democratic republic." In this projected soviet democratic government, all socialist groups would work together (the Kronstadt soviet was noted for the harmony of its internal political relationships). The political resolutions adopted from time to time were not the property of any single party but the work of Bolsheviks, left SRs (Social Revolutionaries), and left- or Internationalist-Mensheviks. "Some called for the creation of a government representing workers, soldiers, and peasants; others . . . insisted on transfer of power to the soviets or creation of a revolutionary government responsible to the soviet, often coupling such demands with a call for another national Congress of Soviets." There was no hint of any single party's monopoly or seizure of power.

Basic tasks set forth for the new government included confiscation of manorial lands without compensation, and their transfer to peasant committees was put into effect in advance of any scheduling of a first session of the already convoked Constituent Assembly (all parties and tendencies agreed on this measure). Also immediately, all repressive measures against working-class organizations were revoked. So was capital punishment at the front, and from now on there was to be full freedom for political activity within the army. By now the army's General Staff had been purged.

Among the proposals that were to be brought before the Assembly was workers' control over industrial production, nationalization of key industries, and a special proposal for a universal democratic peace. Above all, the Constituent Assembly now was to decide democratically on Russia's future form of governance. The "moderate" Bolshevik Kamenev expressed these views in a general statement stressing the role of the soviets as "the mortar binding all fundamentally democratic forces. . . . no one can say that there exists at the present time any organization more powerful than the soviets."

One must realize that not until August 31 did the Bolshevik faction in the Petrograd soviet (which, of course, now had become the most powerful soviet) receive the vote of a clear majority of deputies present—and it was a majority based upon the deputies' response to the moderate Bolshevik proposals presented by Kamenev. The party's tactical course in those days centered around the forthcoming Congress of Soviets. "Prepare for the Congress of Soviets on October 20!" "Convene Regional Congresses Immediately!" "In our view the all-powerful authority over the Russian land is the Congress of Soviets. . . . All Power to the Soviets!" So wrote Zinoviev in the Bolshevik press. "Let's concentrate all our energies on preparations for the Congress of Soviets," the Central Committee of the Bolsheviks declared; "it alone will assure that the Constituent Assembly will be convened and carry forth its revolutionary work . . ." There is no question that this echoed the views of the Petrograd masses, just as there is no visible intent here of staging an insurrection before the Congress of Soviets and the Constituent Assembly were scheduled to meet.

As it became clear that the Bolsheviks, despite the opposition of a substantial minority among their leaders, were intent upon mobilizing their forces, not simply to defend the Congress of Soviets but rather to seize power in advance through an uprising, the ranks of the Left were thrown into turmoil and confusion.

Things were to turn out quite differently than the Petrograd masses were sure they would. Soon the Bolsheviks under Lenin's whiplike leadership and with the backing of Trotsky, chairman of the Petrograd Soviet, will emerge as the dominant force; walkouts by the opposition Menshevik and SR factions will leave the Bolsheviks in control and, in essence, power will fall exclusively into their hands. The Left-SR's and the Left- or Internationalist-Mensheviks (whose spokesman was the much underrated Martov), though exhibiting great prescience, will find their warnings unheeded: "A coming-out by the workers and soldiers would be a monstrous crime . . . an attack, not on the Provisional Government, but on the soviets." The Left SR Boris Kamkov declared at an SR gathering:

> . . . it became clear to those of us working in factories and barracks that the Bolsheviks were mobilizing their forces not simply to defend the government established by the congress [of Soviets], but rather to seize power in advance of the congress. . . . Their course seemed to us both dangerous and senseless . . . it seemed to us that it would be possible to rid ourselves painlessly of this skeleton [the Kerensky coalition] by action of the All-Russian Congress of Soviets. At the same time we believed that if this were done in another way, say by means of the seizure of power in Petrograd before the congress, this might appear to be adventurist—as the seizure of power, not by the soviets, but by one political party. It seemed to us that this would immediately complicate the situation and make it *impossible to avoid civil war* [emphasis added—S. P.].

The Bolshevik moderates had, of course, long sounded a warning note against a unilateral seizure of power by their party. In a written summary of their arguments against Lenin's strategy, Zinoviev and Kamenev underlined the importance of the "petty bourgeoisie" (middle class). The Russian working class, they stated, could not by itself complete the revolution.

> We simply cannot lose sight of the fact that between us and the bourgeoisie there is an enormous third camp, that of the petty bourgeoisie. The camp joined with us during the Kornilov affair [an attempted monarchist coup] and brought us victory. It will ally with us again more than once . . . , but for the time being it is closer to the bourgeoisie than to [the Bolsheviks].

Denying Lenin's contention that a majority of the Russian people backed the Bolsheviks, they expressed the view that perhaps a majority of the workers and a "significant percentage" of the soldiers were with the Bolsheviks, "but everything else is questionable." Future elections to the Constituent Assembly, they accurately predicted, would find the Bolsheviks in a minority, behind the peasant-backed SR party.[2]

Before examining Rabinowitch's version of the seizure of power, the much-argued question of Lenin's precise relation to the October revolution must be considered. We must realize that there was an extensive evolution in Lenin's own position. The Lenin of October, fiercely demanding the party's immediate seizure of power, differed considerably from the Lenin of September who, as Rabinowitch points out, had tried to reassure the moderate socialists that an end of the coalition with the bourgeois parties (Kadets, etc.) would not necessarily lead to civil war: "Only the immediate transfer of all power to the soviets would make civil war in Russia impossible." "A civil war begun by the bourgeoisie against an alliance of the Bolsheviks with the Socialist Revolutionaries and Mensheviks, against the soviets of workers', soldiers', and peasants' deputies, is inconceivable. . . ." Astonishing though it may seem, some of the more radical leaders of the Petrograd Bolshevik committee objected strongly to the views of the "moderate" Lenin. But this moderation, which Lenin's opponents said was a mere ruse, quickly ended, to be replaced by the final, abrupt demand that power be seized immediately in the name of the soviets.

Rabinowitch recounts the story of how Lenin, raging at the party's hesitation and in defiance of the party's instructions to remain in hiding, donned a disguise and emerged from hiding to go to the Smolny Institute in order to spur on the party leadershp. On his way to Smolny, Lenin, with his traveling companion, boarded an empty trolley car run by a conductress. He conversed with her about the political situation, found her dissatisfied with the lack of action and proceeded to explain to her his belief in the need to take power at once!

Rabinowitch sums up Lenin's effect upon the evolution of events:

Looking back over the period between the Kornilov affair and the decision of October 10 [to seize power] one can say that, as in April, chief responsibility for this drastic transformation in the outlook of the party's top hierarchy belongs to Lenin. It was Lenin who, over a period of several weeks, alternately cajoled, pressured, and threatened his colleagues, and who, by force of argument and personal authority, ultimately succeeded in turning a majority of the Central Committee toward an insurrectionary course. . . . Few modern historical episodes better illustrate the sometimes decisive role of an individual in historical events.

As the author convincingly demonstrates, from the February revolution onward, the danger of dissension within the Bolshevik party was quite strong. Hence, whether the party would have the will to follow Lenin's increasingly urgent drive to take power remained "very much an open question." The party was in a fluid state. In the end, Lenin's insistence, supported by very few of the top Bolsheviks, that the risks of such a course were outweighed by the need to create at once an exclusively Bolshevik regime would carry the day.

The armed forces of the Bolsheviks, centering their attack upon the Winter Palace, will take possession of the city. The armed conflict, which Trotsky had just said "is not in our plans," will be unleashed and the Provisional Government will cease to exist. "The population slept peacefully," Trotsky will declare before the soviet, "and did not know that at this time one power was replaced by another." Lenin will make his dramatic appearance in the hall and announce "the construction of a proletarian socialist state." And the long midnight, now entering its sixtieth year, will have begun.

When an obsure delegate cries out, "You are anticipating the will of the Second Congress of Soviets," Trotsky retorts: "The will of the Second Congress of Soviets has already been predetermined by the fact of the workers' and soldiers' uprising." But had it? Previously, the moderate Mensheviks and SRs had pulled out of the Congress, later to be followed by the Menshevik-Internationalists (Martov) and the left SRs, which left the Bolshevik faction in full command. Rabinowitch feels that this action played directly into Lenin's hands, "paving the way for the creation of a government which had never been publicly broached before—that is, an exclusively Bolshevik regime."

Although he remained a Leninist to the end, Trotsky later regretted the sharp personal break that would take place at this point between himself and Martov, leader of the Left Mensheviks. "No, here no compromise is possible. To those who have left and to those who tell us to do this we must say: You are miserable bankrupts, your role is played out; go where you ought to go: into the dustbin of history." To which the weary Martov shouted his response: "Then we'll leave." This seems the most poignant moment of the October revolution.

Rabinowitch has written a brilliant, convincing, and exciting book. His first conclusion concerns the nature of the Bolshevik party and its evolution in the eight months between the February and October revolutions. Acknowledging the historic significance of Lenin's leadership, but rejecting as largely mythical the notion of the party's organizational unity and discipline, Rabinowitch proposes to emphasize the party's "internal relatively democratic, tolerant, and decentralized structure and method of operation, as well as its essentially open and mass character—in striking contrast to the traditional Leninist mode." More important is his conclusion that goes to the heart of the nature of the October revolution itself:

. . . the Petrograd masses, to the extent that they supported the Bolsheviks in the overthrow of the Provisional Government, did so not out of any sympathy for strictly Bolshevik rule but because they believed the revolution and the Congress to be in imminent danger. Only the creation of a broadly representative, exclusively socialist government by the Congress of Soviets, which is what they *believed* the Bolsheviks stood for [emphasis added— S. P.], appeared to offer the hope of insuring that there would not be a return to the hated ways of the old regime, of avoiding death at the front and achieving a better life, and of putting a quick end to Russia's participation in the war.

Footnotes

1. *The Bolsheviks Come to Power: The Revolution of 1917 in Petrograd*, Alexander Rabinowitch (New York: W. W. Norton), 1977.

2. Elections to the Constituent Assembly were held in November, as scheduled. The Bolsheviks, while winning in Petrograd, were a poor second in the Assembly, which met in Petrograd on January 5, 1918, refused to endorse the Bolshevik seizure of power, and was then forcibly dispersed by the Bolsheviks after one session.

JOSEPH CLARK
Dreams
and Nightmares[1]
(1978)

Now I know why I flunked the test given by Vivian Gornick at lunch
in a Chinese restaurant. It turned out that she was screening me for
an interview to be used in a book she was writing on the romance of
American Communism. But between the egg roll and the fortune
cookie she apparently concluded that I was not among those who
"walked the wire successfully and remained whole and strong."
Clearly, both her thesis and ideology were so neatly packaged in
advance that she did not want to add my experience to that of an old,
departed friend and comrade whom she had already interviewed.

My friend had been terribly disruptive of her *idée fixe* of Communism as creator of that "inner passion" and "intensity of illumination that tore at the soul," to cite a bit of her description. Gornick
wanted no more tampering with her dream of Communism, which
spoke "with such power and moral imagination." If only she had
shared with her readers what she meant by "moral imagination,"
there might have been far more than the singularly cluttered, but
uninformative contents of her account.

Whatever the Communist experience was, it is touching to see
how some—in what we once lovingly called the capitalist press—
have taken the Gornick description to heart. The *New York Times*
published a section of the Gornick "passion" in its *Book Review*,
followed by a laudatory review by a democratic socialist, whose
emphasis on the crucial requirement, that socialism must above all
be democratic, played a part in the departure of this reviewer from

402

the Communist movement. A number of "capitalist" journals now print reviews of books on the Communist experience, which twit former Communists for daring to entertain bitter recollections and give them good marks only if they remember that experience without regret or recrimination. This was the message of the review in *Newsday*, a paper of considerable circulation and solid capitalist paternity. Its reviewer, Jessica Mitford, was the author of that witty satire on the American funeral business, *The American Way of Death*. Now she had written a book on her experiences in the American Communist party, a more amusing and a better crafted book than Gornick's, but equally lacking in candid recollection and equally barren of political appraisal.

Still another book, by Peggy Dennis, widow of Eugene Dennis, the former general secretary of the American CP, turns out to be far more significant than Gornick's or Mitford's, but in a way that the author, alas, never intended it to be. Peggy Dennis never meant to depict the rejection of mind and reason, the acceptance of a discipline that prompted acquiescence in anything demanded from above, even to the point of leaving an only child with the Russians permanently, on orders from Communist International leaders Georgi Dimitrov and Dimitri Manuilsky. But that is what she has done, and it emerges in painful detail.

Leopold Trepper, a Polish Jewish Communist who worked for Soviet intelligence and indeed organized the Soviet espionage network in Western Europe when it was occupied by Hitler, performing incredible feats in behalf of the Red Army battling against the Nazis, has also written about the Communist experience. Some of it dovetails neatly with the Dennis book. He lived in the same Comintern Hotel Luxe in Moscow where Peggy and Gene Dennis lived. On his return to Moscow after his war service he "sat" ten interminable years in Soviet jails. After Stalin died he was exonerated of any kind of "guilt" and allowed to return to his family in Moscow. He tells how he is reunited with his sons, but they cannot recognize him. He says to his eldest son, "I am your father. Ten years ago I returned to Russia, and for ten years I have been in prison. I have just been released and brought here to you—do you have any questions to ask me?" His son replies: "Only one. Why were you sentenced? In this country, innocent people don't spend ten years in prison."

II

The subject matter of all these books has acquired an insistent timeliness, whatever the shortcomings of the books themselves. Commentators and statesmen debate Eurocommunism. The discussion goes on and on about Communists in America after World War II, when they became the excuse for the blight of McCarthyism. Some value may be wrung from the Gornick and Mitford books because there are Americans who will discover that Communists were real live people, fed with the same food, hurt with the same weapons, subject to the same diseases. From all four books there comes a realization that the 1956 revelations by Nikita Khrushchev about the horrors of Stalinism inaugurated a deep and endless crisis of Communism.

Of the four authors, only Trepper confronts the issue. He writes: "We wanted to change man, and we have failed. This century has brought forth two monsters, fascism and Stalinism, and our ideal has been engulfed in this apocalypse."

If an insoluble crisis developed among Communists in the middle 1950s, we still must face up to a great paradox: there is every reason to believe that Communist power, in the Soviet Union, China, and Communist satellite nations will be with us for a long time. And Communist movements will flourish in certain West European countries.

Much of the current discussion of Eurocommunism leaves more questions than it answers, because it pays too little attention to the central factor that emerged in 1956: a *Communist* rebellion against Communist tyranny. That is the origin and essence of Eurocommunism. True, there were precursors of Eurocommunism that go back to the founding days of Italian Communism. But to understand the quality and direction of Italian Communism under Berlinguer is to know, above all, the crisis that swept over Communist movements in 1956. The early signs of that crisis first appeared when the tyrant died in 1953. But it flared up everywhere in the Communist world after Khrushchev's speech in February 1956.

If the Spanish Communists under Santiago Carrillo have moved further than any other CP toward revising the tenets of *both* Leninist and Stalinist tyranny, it is because the Spanish Communists have carried even further than the Italians the evaluation of Stalinism, and to an extent of Leninism, begun by Togliatti in Italy in 1956. This was the same analysis conducted in the middle '50s by the John Gates faction of the American CP. In 1956 Togliatti criticized the circular reasoning that the Soviet Communists applied to the Stalin phenomenon. Stalinism was the fault of the "cult of the individual"; Stalinism and Stalin were the fault of Joseph Stalin. Togliatti suggested that this was a mockery of Marxism, let alone of common sense, the latter being far more powerful a force for reason and logic than the former. The revisionism of Togliatti in Italy was applied rigorously by Gates in America and then extended into the experience of the Spanish Communists under Carrillo.

This revisionism was deepest in Spain, but more massive and meaningful in Italy, and no more than a façade in France. The French Communists under George Marchais adopted "Eurocommunism" and unanimously "rejected" the dictatorship of the proletariat in the same way that they had accepted Stalinism and the dictatorship of the proletariat before.

III

From the storms that blew over the Communist countries and through the Communist movements in 1956 came a reaffirmation of a basic fact of contemporary political experience—there's a "Kronstadt" in every Communist movement. There was a rebellion against the Soviet regime by the workers and sailors of the Kronstadt naval base in 1921. It was not an antisocialist rebellion, as the Communists said at the time. It was a defense of the *promises* of the 1917 revolution in Russia. It was a protest against the betrayal of those promises that were made immediately after the Bolsheviks seized power. It was a rebellion against Lenin and Trotsky. This, too, bears emphasis because many who come to the study of Communism in a scholarly manner and with high ideals come with illusions about the purity of Leninism as compared with the absolute tyranny of Stalinism.

Some 15,000 Kronstadt sailors and workers demonstrated on March 1, 1921, in solidarity with some of the demands of the workers of Petrograd who were striking not only for economic demands but for free elections to factory committees and soviets. The demands of the Kronstadt demonstration were also for new elections to the soviets by secret ballot and with unrestricted political freedom. They demanded freedom of assembly and liberation of political prisoners, because by this time there were more dissident socialist prisoners in Soviet jails than supporters of the bourgeoisie. They demanded the right of peasants to own their own land and the right of all workers and peasants to assemble, to organize, to agitate—to receive the freedom that was promised to them.

True, there is an enormous gulf between the theory and practice of Lenin and of Stalin. But it did not prove to be an unbridgeable gulf. Lenin and Trotsky ordered the machine-gunning of the Kronstadt rebels. Suppression feeds on itself. Only days after the Bolshevik seizure of power the opposition press was banned as "poisoners of the mind of the people." A rereading of John Reed's *Ten Days That Shook the World* might cause some wonder among those who were enthusiastic about Reed and about Trotsky's explanation that "the closing of the newspapers is a legitimate measure of defense." How scornful the Leninists were of such Bolsheviks as Karelin who protested the suppression of newspapers with the prophetic words: "Three weeks ago the Bolsheviki were the most ardent defenders of the freedom of the press. . . . The arguments in this resolution suggest singularly the point of view of the old Black Hundreds and the censors of the Czarist regime—for they also talked of 'poisoners of the mind of the people.'"

So it was that the early but burgeoning tyranny of Lenin and Trotsky (*only* a few concentration camps, *only* hundreds and then several thousand killed in reprisals) became the monstrous tyranny of Stalin.

The 1950s saw many "Kronstadts," notably in East Germany, in Poland, above all in Hungary. On October 23, 1956, student demonstrations in Budapest led to the placarding of the city with demands for evacuation of Soviet troops from Hungarian soil, elections by secret ballot in the Hungarian Workers' party, and a long list of requirements adding up to a free and democratic socialism for Hungary. The uprising that followed was as spontaneous and broad-based as the revolution that overthrew the Czarist regime in Russia in March, 1917. Nevertheless, both Jessica Mitford and Peggy Dennis view the Hungarian uprising as a dark manipulation of "fascist" forces. The extraordinary thing about the 1956 events was the extent of support from workers in the most farflung parts of Hungary. But in the Mitford version of "a fine old conflict," she prettifies the regime against which the entire Hungarian people arose in 1956.

More than two decades after the Hungarian Communists themselves had admitted that their pre-1956 regime was a police state in which first Rakosi and then Gero ruled with an iron fist and with the secret police as the major instrument of political repression, Mitford writes of her 1955 visit to Hungary and reaffirms "everything we saw of socialist accomplishment." She rereads her dispatches to the *People's World* and finds them—not misleading, not refuted by events that horrified democrats and socialists—merely "rather tedious." Mitford is still enthusiastic about the "exhilarating experience" of discovering the sumptuous food enjoyed by the collective farmers. Her husband, Bob, born in Hungary, "was particularly struck by the evident prosperity and sense of progress we found everywhere." No less than "everywhere. Shortly after they left, the people rebelled—*everywhere*. True, Mitford attempts an explanation, the Hungarian people were "manipulated by the CIA from without and counterrevolution from within."

On a Potemkin tour Mitford might not have been able to see everything as it was then in Hungary. But here it is, twenty-one years later when she should have been able to go back and review Hungary's tragic history, and all she sees is confirmation that the Hungarian Freedom Fighters were "grasping, neo-fascist types." "Fascist" types, such as Anna Kethly, the Hungarian socialist leader who declared in November when Russian tanks were ranging everywhere to put down the rebellion: "The Hungary of tomorrow will be a socialist state. . . . We must be watchful so that the results of the Revolution do not disappear, as was the case in 1919."

Though she admits that terrible revelations were made by Khrushchev, Mitford stands by the "socialist" achievements of pre-1956 Hungary despite everything that even the current rulers of Hungary have admitted. As to the prosperity that she and Bob saw in 1955, she could have used some of the twenty-two years since that visit to research what both the Russian and Hungarian Communists divulged about the declining economic standards brought about by the Stalinist pre-1956 regime. Rakosi and other Hungarian leaders had been summoned to Moscow after Stalin died in 1953. The Hun-

garians could say little when the Russians accused them of bringing
the Hungarian economy to the verge of collapse.

Peggy Dennis takes strong exception to the denunciation of the
Soviet invasion of Hungary in 1956 by the *Daily Worker* under the
editorship of John Gates. She admits that the struggle of the Hungarian people had started as a "people's rebellion" but then adds that
"the fascist elements grouped around Cardinal Mindszenty had
turned the people's rebellion into a blood bath." Dennis complains
that the *Daily Worker* at the time did not provide a "factual analysis"
of what was happening in Budapest. This brings us to a fascinating
failure of both Mitford and Dennis to review some of the factual
information the *Daily Worker* and the *People's World* were getting
from Budapest in that fall of 1956. First of all, the London *Daily
Worker* correspondent in Budapest at the end of October, Peter
Freyer, had refuted the reports of a fascist counterrevolution. He
did note that many of the secret police who were universally hated
had been killed during the uprising, but that this had in no way
deprived the uprising of its popular character; it only pointed up the
universal feeling about a secret police that had even pulled out the
fingernails of Janos Kadar, later installed as the head of the Hungarian government by the Russians.

But even more intriguing is the correspondence that came to the
Daily Worker and *People's World* from Freyer's successor, Sam Russell, who covered the events in Budapest after the second Soviet
tank invasion starting on November 4. Russell was chosen because of
his political reliability and indeed he remained in the British CP
long after these events. But he was a reporter, and he was with the
Hungarian workers at the huge Csepel and Dunapentele steel and
machine works. He sent dispatches describing the Budapest workers' councils as the real and unanimous representatives of *all* the
workers. He wrote about a strike without a single scab as an example
of worker solidarity such as he had rarely seen anywhere else in the
world. He tried to put the best face possible on the Russians, and in
one dispatch he described a worker delegation that had gone to the
Russians to negotiate and, though the Hungarians remained unper-
suaded, they suggested that possibly "the devil was not as black as he
was painted." This was a loyal British Communist writing about the
Soviet fatherland as a devil, if perhaps not quite as terrible as

pictured. What a pleasure it was for the *Daily Worker* editor, Gates, and for his foreign editor, myself, to spread the dispatches from the Csepel factories across five columns above the masthead. Here was class struggle and a national liberation struggle in all its glory. But drowned in blood.

It is instructive to see how Vivian Gornick manages to cast those who supported the Hungarian rebellion and sought to eradicate Stalinism from the American CP as the ugly Communists who did not manage to maintain the "wholeness," the "passion" and the "moral imagination" of the clear-cut hero of her interviews. The hero of her "romance" is called Lanzetti. His "Marxism," she writes, "is, indeed, not so much a political doctrine as it is a philosophical perspective, a piece of truth that lives inside him with such sure knowledge it is not necessary for him to sacrifice reality to theory." Truth? Reality? On the page before, Gornick writes about Lanzetti:

> For, if you meet him today and in his presence you attack the Party or Stalin or the Soviet Union, he flies into a passion and cries: "Don't talk to me about the atrocities of Stalin! He only killed Russians! We kill *everyone*. Don't talk to me about Vietnam, the energy crisis and Watergate, and then dare to tell me what is wrong with the people and the Party and the movement that I represent and will belong to with honor as long as I live.

Quite apart from the incongruity of comparing Stalin's killing of millions with America killing "everyone" there is the "technical" matter of Stalin killing only Russians. In the Luxe Hotel where Trepper lived and where Gene and Peggy Dennis lived, Stalin killed Finns and Poles, Italians and French, Germans and Spaniards, and the list could go on until we exhausted all the "national" parties affiliated with the Comintern. It has been accurately noted that Stalin killed far more Communist leaders and far more rank-and-file Communists than Hitler did. Trepper describes how Stalin ordered the murder of every member of the Central Committee of the Polish Communist party! He tells how Togliatti sat on the Comintern tribunal that condemmed Béla Kun, the leader of the Hungarian Communist revolution of 1919, to die as an imperalist spy.

IV

What then can be gleaned from these books about the Communist experience? From the Gornick book, precious little. You wouldn't even learn the name of the organization when it was transformed under Browder; she got that wrong. Her chronology is all wrong. The reader of the Mitford book would learn as little about CP history and politics, but a little bit more of what an experience it was to fight for Negro rights and to go to the Deep South in the fight to save the life of Willie McGee.

What then was the Communist experience? Obviously, it had to be many different things. It included high idealism and passion, self-sacrifice, and often a great brotherhood among its adherents.

But when examining the Communist experience, far more emphasis should be devoted, I think, to the rebellion of the Communist when confronted with the betrayal of his ideal, more accurately, when the Communist perceives that betrayal. Call it revisionism, a Kronstadt, Titoism, nationalism, workers' control, democratic centralism, the Workers' Opposition, self-determination. Call it the Hungarian rebellion of 1956, the Czechoslovak struggle in 1968, the German workers battling Soviet tanks in 1953, the children of Moscow fighting Beria's police troops in the streets on the day of Stalin's funeral. Call it revolt of the damned at Kolyma, call it Trotskyism, Bukharinism, a right-wing, a left-wing, a left-cum-right deviation. Call them Djilas, Mikhailov, Solzhenitsyn, Sakharov, Scharansky; call them the bearers of wreaths to Chou En-lai's memorial; liquidators, economists, even God Seekers. Call it whatever you will, there is this built-in spark of rebellion against Communist tyranny and betrayal in almost every Communist heart.

What are the great moments in the experience of this former Communist? One such moment is half-described in Peggy Dennis's book. She tells about an article her husband had written for the *Daily Worker* in 1956; more important, it was written for and appeared in Moscow's *Pravda*. It was a careful, oh so restrained criticism of Stalin. But Peggy Dennis censors the account of that article as it appeared in *Pravda*. The Communist world had learned a few days after Stalin died that one of his crimes had been the murder of the entire top ranks of the Soviet Union's Yiddish writers.

The very first foreign Communist article critical of Stalin ever to appear in the Soviet press was written by Eugene Dennis. Making every effort not to offend the then Soviet leaders, who themselves were up to their ears in Stalin's terror, Dennis wrote of "the shocking crimes and crass violations of socialist law and ethics." He condemned "the use of tortures, rigged trials . . . and snuffing out of lives of more than a score of Jewish cultural figures." But even at that time, after Stalin, the word "Jewish" was an alarming sign of impending heresy to those who had survived in Soviet leadership. So, in printing the Dennis article, *Pravda* cut out the reference to the murder of all the leading Jewish literary figures!

But Dennis never complained about this censorship. Nor does Peggy Dennis, twenty-one years later, summon up the candor or courage to relate how *Pravda* mutilated her husband's article. She gets around that episode by omitting the fact that *Pravda* reprinted it.

What pleasure it was for me, then foreign editor of a *Daily Worker* edited by John Gates, to write about the phrase that *Pravda* eliminated from the article. "If the charge was untrue, all *Pravda* had to do was to deny it. . . . Deleting the phrase from Dennis's article solved no problems for *Pravda* or for anyone else. It only compounds the wrong that was done in the first place. Candor, not suppression, is called for."

Which illuminates an aspect of "Kronstadt" that makes it such a stunning part of the Communist experience. When Vivian Gornick presents her scurrilous portrayal of her arch villain, the man she calls Bitterman, the man who wanted to deprive her of the "romance of Communism," she quotes him as saying, "The things we did, the lies we told . . ." Gornick also quotes Richard Crossman as an early culprit in this regard, for he had written: "Once the renunciation has been made, the mind, instead of operating freely, becomes the servant of a higher and unquestioned purpose. To deny the truth is an act of service . . ." What is one to make of such sentences, Gornick asks? What one should make of them is, indeed, that those sentences quite accurately describe the minds of *Pravda*'s editors, of Dennis and, sadly, of Peggy Dennis even now. If there were truly ecstatic moments in the Communist experience they came when the mind was suddenly freed from the obligation to conform to a "higher" verity. That was why 1956 was such a singular year for many of us.

For thousands of others it had come earlier. What a wonderful time it was for some who spoke their minds when the Moscow trials took place in the '30s! If nothing else, freeing one's mind at that time spared many Communists the necessity of accepting the proposition that Bukharin had tried to assassinate Lenin.

What could have been a better time than the year when Molotov told the Communist world that fascism was "a matter of taste," when Stalin leered at the world standing by the side of Herr von Ribbentrop? What better moment for mind and conscience than the time when the Nazi-Soviet pact unleashed World War II? And what is one to make of a book such as Gornick's, which cannot fathom the gulf between a free and sovereign mind and one that is the servant of a "higher and unquestioned" purpose?

How suitable the phrase, "renunciation of the mind" in the light of Peggy Dennis's Moscow experiences. She arrived there with Gene, who was to work in the Comintern, in 1931. She quickly discovered that an iron curtain separated foreign Communists from Soviet citizens, except those at the Luxe. "No one could give me a plausible reason why this was so," she writes. She and Gene developed warm friendships with others at the Luxe. These included "Boris," a China expert; "Bob," whose specialty was India; Boris's wife, "Musa," on the faculty of the Soviet Institute of Red Professors; and Bob's wife, "Valerie," who was studying at a Party school.

Gene and Peggy finally left Moscow, but they were back for more in 1937. This time they could find no trace of Boris or Musa, Bob or Valerie. Only on her third visit to Moscow in 1941 did she see Valerie walking in her direction on Gorky Street. "I started to greet her warmly, but she passed me with a slight flicker of recognition," Peggy writes. She then implored her comrades to tell her what had happened, and she learned that Bob had been executed. Boris and Musa disappeared, never to be seen among the living, and Valerie must not be approached. "I was told for her sake to leave her alone." Why was all this happening? Peggy Dennis discovered that, "In the purges of the Comintern in 1937 and 1938, the very international activity and foreign travel demanded by the Comintern became the basis of charges of 'foreign agent' that sent hundreds of Soviet and European Comintern workers to labor camps and firing squads."

Peggy Dennis's friends were murdered in the '30s, twenty years before the Khruschchev speech. Peggy learned about that in Moscow at the time; but she had made that renunciation of mind, that relinquishing of conscience, and there was always Gene to explain it to her. If there are mysteries that Gornick must probe it is not the Crossman quote, but how people accepted such renunciation of mind.

Trepper rejects the notion that his was a wasted life. He feels pride and satisfaction for the part he played in the war against the Nazis. But his book and his experience are sharply distinguished from those of Gornick, Mitford, and Dennis. Trepper heaps scorn on those Communist leaders who feigned astonishment after the Twentieth Congress in 1956. He calls to account all who did not rise up against the Stalinist machine; all, he says, are collectively responsible. And he writes, "I am no exception to this verdict."

Within the Soviet Union in the '30s, Trepper says, only the Trotskyists can lay claim to the honor of having resisted. "By the time of the great purges, they could only shout their rebellion in the freezing wastelands where they had been dragged in order to be exterminated. In the camps, their conduct was admirable. But their voices were lost in the tundra."

Though an ever advancing socialization of life imposes social responsibility and social action on the individual, it is the person who remains essential and sovereign. Brought to a violation of the human condition and of human rights the individual, even the Communist as individual, discovers that "the only part of the conduct of anyone, for which he is amenable to society, is that which concerns others." And Communists will harbor ever new "Kronstadts" because, "Over himself, over his body and mind, the individual is sovereign," whether or not he knows that the words are those of John Stuart Mill.

Footnotes

1. *The Romance of American Communism*, Vivian Gornick (New York: Basic Books), 1978; *A Fine Old Conflict*, Jessica Mitford (New York: Alfred A. Knopf), 1978; *The Autobiography of an American Communist: A Personal View of a Political Life*, Peggy Dennis (Westport, Conn.: Lawrence Hill & Co.), 1978; *The Great Game*, Leopold Trepper (New York: McGraw-Hill), 1978.

MURRAY HAUSKNECHT
Metaphors
of Life and Death
(1979)

Discussions of the death penalty have a lot in common with the traditional, tiresome arguments about race. In both instances there is a façade of rationality: some races are demonstrably inferior to others and executions deter homicidal crime. The available evidence on race and achievement clearly contradicts racist assumptions, but since the question of race and intelligence is recurrently raised by "respectable" sources, the ideology of race takes on a veneer of reason. While there is no proof of the deterrent effect of capital punishment, the evidence lends itself to argument. A recent attempt to apply the sophisticated tools of econometrics to the problem concluded that capital punishment does have a deterrent effect. That conclusion was immediately challenged. The mere existence of such solemn and arcane analyses, where the only passion is in defense of technique, lends an air of reason to the proponents of the death penalty.

It is particularly appropriate that the latest controversy appears in the scholarly journals of the economists, since the deterrence argument must ultimately rest on a conception of the murderer as a variant of *Homo economicus*. Capital punishment can only deter homicide when a potential murderer has calculated the pains of being caught and convicted against the pleasures of killing. But, as Albert Camus once remarked in a classic essay, the typical murderer rises from his bed in the morning not knowing that by day's end he

414

will have killed someone. The certainty of punishment is a critical influence only when the behavior is highly "professional"; that is, when it is highly rational. Calculation and foresight, though, are spectacularly absent in almost all cases of homicide. People die as a result of passions aroused by love, fear, and anger; as a result of panic, as in a bungled robbery; from the drunkard's loss of sense and inhibition; or from the irrational maliciousness of some kinds of mugging.

The point, of course, is that it is difficult to muster a reasonable argument for the instrumental functions of capital punishment in the prevention of crime. Camus underscores this by noting that if the death of a murderer is to be used to encourage others to virtue, then logic demands that the execution—the dread fate awaiting the murderer—be a public execution. To witness an actual hanging, electrocution, or gassing would have a more telling effect than merely reading that it took place. Yet even the most vociferous proponents of the death penalty do not call for the televising of executions as a way of deterring crime.

The reluctance to accept the logical implications of the deterrence argument is not as illogical as it seems. Public hangings in England drew enormous crowds (and attendant pickpockets who could themselves be hanged if caught) that treated the executions as public entertainments. When the death of a person is a source of entertainment, the value of individual life is reduced and the texture of public life immeasurably coarsened. Public execution, the ultimate abuse of body and person, is a form of sadistic pornography, and a society that hides its executions from its own sight recognizes, in effect, the questionable moral consequences of capital punishment.

Although one does not hear it frequently, there is another, stronger argument in which the death of the offender, whether public or hidden, is the critical issue. In this view the social control function of punishment is trivial or irrelevant. Punishment, to borrow Émile Durkheim's words, affirms the fundamental value that the criminal act has violated "by an authentic act which can consist only in suffering inflicted upon the agent." The position has its difficulties. First, execution for murder is appropriate only when "premeditation" is present, but how is one to define premeditation?

Does a drunken quarrel resulting in homicide involve premeditation? Is the panic response of a robber an act of premeditation? The other difficulty involves the question of whether the death of the murderer is the only "authentic act" that can affirm the value of the sacredness of human life. In any event, the interesting fact is that this moral justification for capital punishment is rarely heard; at best it is an afterthought to the utilitarian argument.

One reason why that argument is the prominent one is that the fundamental issue may not be a concern about crime as such. Here a recent report on the anti-abortion movement is instructive. Two Catholic women active in the movement polled other anti-abortion Catholics and found, according to the *New York Times*, "that many of those in the movement see abortion at the deepest psychological level, less as a taking of human life than as a practice threatening to existing social patterns and customs in families, marriages and sexual relations." That is to say, the abortion issue symbolizes the painful experience of social change within the private spheres of life. Some of those involved in the anti-abortion movement are less concerned with the morality of abortion as such, though this is certainly a central issue for many, than with the difficulties of coping with the problematic effects of changing sexual and family relationships. The ideology of the movement is a symbolic or metaphorical way of expressing fears and anxieties about the consequences of social change for private life.

Similarly, capital punishment is a way of talking about social change and its effects on the public life of the society. Just as the anti-abortionists are less concerned with "a taking of human life," so those calling for a return to capital punishment are not primarily concerned with, to quote Durkheim again, "repairing the evil [the murder] inflicted on society." Rather, talk of the death penalty is a means of expressing the fears and anxieties about the decline of public civility.

That concern centers on the high incidence of crime, particularly street crime. When the crime rate increases the urban stranger is transformed from an object of civil indifference to a menacing figure one cannot afford to ignore, and even one's own neighborhood loses its essential quality of predictability and security. Fear is accompanied by anger at being in a situation in which one is forced to be fearful. There is also a pervasive frustration over the sheer intractability of the problem of street crime; rape and muggings go on, seemingly impervious to human efforts to cope with them. Fear, anger, frustration, and the felt need constantly to attend to strangers heighten the tensions and strains of city life; the loss of civility is experienced as a loss of ease with and satisfactions from urban existence.

But how one talks about social change and its effects can determine political positions. Metaphors, by their very nature, are freighted with meanings that predispose us to one kind of orientation and action rather than to others.

Some metaphors are attractive because there is a good fit between them and a persistent psychological tendency that is especially salient in times of change. There is in all people, argues Peter Marris in *Loss and Change*, a "conservative impulse" that attempts to "preserve the continuity of past and present" in our understanding of the world. Social change is experienced as a disturbance of the familiar and the expected, a loss of orderliness and predictability. When the present is ambiguous, the past is seen as more stable than it ever could have been in reality. On the level of politics, this conservative psychological impulse can be translated into an attempt to return to a golden age or to impose its structure of meanings and actions on the present. The metaphors we use to talk about our present discontents and anxieties link past and present.

The idea of capital punishment is related to the biblical "an eye for an eye" with its resonance of a world that is part of a balanced, symmetrical, easily understood natural order. In this world crime is a result of sinful people, and the larger their number the higher the crime rate. Orderliness is restored to that world by ridding it of sinful people.

The attractiveness of the metaphor depends upon what it ignores. Most obviously, it overlooks the problem of the social conditions that produce sinful individuals. It also avoids confronting the messy and ambiguous relationships among "social conditions," individual behavior, and crime rates—relationships that, at best, are intricate, complex, and difficult to grasp. In other words, to talk of incivility in these terms merely underlines the instabilities that are at the root of the current discontent.

The metaphor of abortion, too, carries implications of a stable social world that is part of a cosmic natural order. Abortion is a violation or defiance of an inherent biological order in which sex and procreation are inextricably connected. In this order women are childbearers and, therefore, must accept their pregnancies and the resulting responsibilities of child rearing. In short, to be against abortion means to reject the present disorderly world in which there is no "natural" connection between sex and procreation and in which men and women have no fixed, predictable positions in the world. To be in favor of abortion is to embrace an ambiguous and unpredictable world of sex and family relationships, one that is radically discontinuous with the past.

These metaphors can play hell with the ambitions of liberal politicians. They are particularly vulnerable because liberals are identified with feminists and the underclasses, precisely those who seem to be creating the disorderliness by desiring to change their place in the natural order of things. On the other hand, politicians like New York's Mayor Ed Koch, a former congressman of liberal reputation, can use the metaphor to neutralize the liberal image by displaying his sympathy with those anxious about incivility. (Here, of course, the metaphor connects with racist impulses that run like a dark underground stream through most of the rhetoric about street crime.)

Curiously enough, under some conditions the metaphor may be less useful for conservative candidates. In the 1978 New York gubernatorial election the Republican, Perry Duryea, made it the centerpiece of his campaign against Hugh Carey who had vetoed a bill restoring capital punishment earlier in the year. When the issue, no matter how prominent its place, is part of a platform containing other issues, the latter can serve as countervailing forces to the attractiveness of the death penalty. In New York, Carey received the votes of both proponents and opponents of capital punishment. When, however, the issue can be segregated, as in the California referendum, the lure of returning to a golden age becomes very powerful indeed.

There is a noticeable paradox about the politics of abortion and capital punishment. Those who favor "the right to life" are usually those who also favor the death penalty. The paradox disappears once we realize that in neither instance is the morality of "a taking of life" the main concern; the fundamental problem is social change and the fears and anxieties it evokes in those caught up in it. Since change is a fact of life, we may expect the metaphors to be with us for some time, because they help translate fears into what appears to be a rational politics.